He Never Liked Cake

Janna Leyde

For my parents, with love. You have taught me to see the world through kindness, curiosity, and resilience.

Om Tat Sat

(all that is truth)

BALBOA.
PRESS

A DIVISION OF HAY HOUSE

Balboa Press books may be ordered through booksellers or by contacting:
Balboa Press
A Division of Hay House
1663 Liberty Drive
Bloomington, IN 47403
www.balboapress.com
1-(877) 407-4847

Because of the dynamic nature of the Internet, any web addresses or links contained in
this book may have changed since publication and may no longer be valid. The views
expressed in this work are solely those of the author and do not necessarily reflect the
views of the publisher, and the publisher hereby disclaims any responsibility for them.

The author of this book does not dispense medical advice or prescribe the use of any
technique as a form of treatment for physical, emotional, or medical problems without the
advice of a physician, either directly or indirectly. The intent of the author is only to offer
information of a general nature to help you in your quest for emotional and spiritual well-
being. In the event you use any of the information in this book for yourself, which is your
constitutional right, the author and the publisher assume no responsibility for your actions.

Cover Photo: Photographer, Meghan McNeer and Prop Stylist, Amy Taylor.
Author Photo: Photographer, Meghan McNeer

Printed in the United States of America

ISBN: 978-1-4525-6828-7 (hc)
ISBN: 978-1-4525-6826-3 (sc)
ISBN: 978-1-4525-6827-0 (e)

Library of Congress Control Number: 2013902347

Balboa Press rev. date: 03/13/2013

Table of Contents

Part One

Part Two

Part Three

the sky turns blue

"Look at those tits."

I was wearing my favorite outfit that summer, a cornflower-blue Ann Taylor dress made of soft jersey cotton. The dress was hardly formfitting, and nothing about it invited the usage of *tits*.

"Since when did you get those?" He whistled. "I mean, look at 'em. Look … at … them."

He was staring at them.

I felt a lump in my throat. I tried to swallow it, tried to swallow the overwhelming vulgarity of … *tits*. It felt like my esophagus was filling up with lead. I was choking, suffocating, until I allowed hot tears to pour down my cheeks. I wiped them away and gripped the handles of his wheelchair until my salty, wet knuckles turned white.

I was fourteen. He was my father.

That was the longest summer of my life. It may as well have been three summers. I can only recall sharp splinters of memory that cut consciousness into a blur of wearisome, muggy days that fell somewhere between the solstice and the equinox.

That summer, he spit orange juice at me, a deliberate attack from straw to face. That summer, he was okay with getting naked and jerking off in front of me. That summer, he taught me a poem so I would know every cuss word in the English language. That summer was catcalls, broken dishes, slammed doors, restraining belts, IVs, tantrums, pills, spills, license plate numbers, and lukewarm cans of vanilla Ensure. It was my adolescence too, but I don't remember much about it—except, of course, my tits.

I FEEL AS THOUGH I own a day. I feel I've earned the rights to it. It is a Tuesday that lies in the back of my mind in fragments, in a pile of objects—

the sketched lines of the flowers on the wallpaper, the stars flung across a black sky, the defogger lines on the rear window of my grandparents' Civic, the flecks in the linoleum floor, the sliding-glass doors, the yellow lines on the highway, the seatbelt in my mom's Accord, the leaves of the cherry trees that lined the driveway, the silver antenna of our late '90s cordless phone, the patch of stairway carpet where I spilled coffee and kept it a secret, my white bathing suit, a red dog collar patterned with white bones, empty flower crates, fat raindrops, the speed bump on Delaware Trail, the fringe on a checked blue-and-white tablecloth, a bag of Cool Ranch Doritos, a glass paperweight, the ceramic cup in our downstairs bathroom, an oversized T-shirt that read, "Art Crimes '96."

I've never asked my mother what she remembers of that day, or my father. I have an idea of what they would say. They would both tell me for different reasons that they don't remember.

I do.

I SHOT STRAIGHT UP IN bed. The digital clock in my room glared 5:14 a.m. A shadow loomed over me, swaying from the roof of my canopy bed. My heart was pounding, and I gasped to catch my breath. My eyes had not yet adjusted, but I could smell the summer air and a whiff of Old Spice mixed with something earthy and familiar.

"Hey, hey, Peanut, it's me," my dad whispered, groping the object swaying directly above me. "I didn't mean to wake you. I just bought you a T-shirt. Go back to sleep. It's still early."

I squinted at him and tugged my present from the rungs of the canopy bed. It was black and enormous. I grumbled, knowing that whatever he had bought me was an extra-large.

"Dad," I mumbled, disoriented, "what are you—wait. What time is it?"

"*Shhh*, it's early, Peanut," he whispered into my ear. He pulled the sheet up to my chin to get me to lie back down. "Don't wake your mom."

"No, Dad ..." I fumbled for sleepy words and sat up again. "You can't go to work today. I had this dream, and Mom was ... in this accident ... and ... she—"

"*Shhh*," he said. "It's early. Mom's fine. I'll get you some water."

He left my room. I sat in the dark, listening for the water to run in the bathroom.

"Take some of this," he said when he came back. He brought a ceramic cup up to my face.

I gulped the water. It was lukewarm, and I thought it tasted a little like clay, even though the cup was years old and couldn't possibly taste like anything except maybe soap or toothpaste. I handed it back, disgusted.

"Mom was in this accident … in my dream … and …" I protested, now with more consciousness. "Just please don't go to work today. Where do you have to go? Just stay home, please."

"Will you relax?" he asked. "I'm going to drop off a car at a dealership in Pittsburgh. I'll be home, and we'll go skiing. I'm picking up Jackie and Sarah on the way home. Go back to bed, ya ninny."

I grabbed the cup from him and took another swig. I handed it back and pulled the oversized shirt under the cool summer sheet with me, tucked my legs up to my chest, and closed my eyes. I felt him lean over me, and I could smell him. He pulled the sheet tight around my shoulders and kissed my cheekbone. His mustache tickled.

"I'll see ya later, Peanut," he whispered. "I love you."

"Love you," I yawned into my pillow.

I heard the creak of the floor under his silent footsteps, the exasperated pants of our golden retriever, and the slow whine of the screen door falling back into place. I was out before it clicked shut.

By 10:39 a.m., sun streaked through my room. I decided to stop fighting the light and get up. I swung my feet over the side of my bed, and Meagan rubbed her wet nose on my shins. Repulsed and groggy, I padded out to the hallway. I opened the door, tapped my thigh, and coaxed her outside. In the hallway, I found a yellow slip of paper tucked under a glass paperweight on my mom's desk. Her neat slices of angled letters were written on invisible lines.

Weed the back walk
Brush the dog
Wash towels
Sweep

I put it back under the weight and skipped to the kitchen.

Heels up and toes fully extended, I stretched on a stool to reach the top cupboard, where I scooted a big plastic jug of cat food to the edge. While up there, I snagged a bag of Cool Ranch Doritos from the basket on top of the fridge. When she heard the *clink-clank* of dried morsels being poured into her metal bowl, our mildly handicapped tortoiseshell cat bounded into the kitchen, and unable to control her wonky back legs, she slid on the hardwood floor. As Marble dug into her breakfast, I reached down to run my hand along her back to the tip of her tail, the place where I could feel how the bone had been cracked into an L-shape—the other reminder of the damage a horse hoof can do to a kitten.

I filled a bowl with a heaping mound of chips, knowing that it was a terrible choice of breakfast food and something that my parents would highly disapprove of unless it was after noon and accompanied by some form of lunchmeat between slices of wheat bread. No one was home.

I committed another disapproved-of act by heading downstairs to the basement with my bowl of Doritos, now topped with a wobbly stack of Oreos. After mindless hours of flipping between spring-break game shows on MTV and *Pop-Up Video* on VH1, I realized it was pouring outside. I raced upstairs and out onto the back porch.

"*Meeeeaaaagan!*" I screamed. "*Meeeeaaagan!* Come on, pup! Let's *goooooooooo!*"

I stood in the downpour and called her name. I tried to whistle for her like my dad did. I couldn't whistle. I couldn't make my lips work the air to produce that shrill sound like my father could. His whistle pierced through the trees and neighbors' yards. He used it to call his dog and his daughter home. I always heard it, but I didn't always listen. I assumed Meagan was no different.

I gave up. I went inside and pouted in my room, standing at my windowsill with my arms folded as I stared across the yard at our neighbors' house. It was well into the afternoon, and I sat down on my bed, still in my pajamas, fretting about the lost dog and all the trouble I'd be in and how the western Pennsylvania weather was going to ruin my afternoon of waterskiing. Thunder cracked. I stood up, yanked on a T-shirt and a pair of cut-off jean shorts, and slipped my feet into a pair of permanently laced K-Swiss.

"Hi, Pat," I said, standing on the Riegs' stoop with a sheepish look. I was drenched from the rain.

"Hiya, kid," she said. "Now what are you doing? It's raining, and you are sopping wet. Get in here, will ya?"

She sat me down at her kitchen table and brought over perfectly proportioned PB&Js made with her homemade elderberry jam. Between sticky mouthfuls, I whined about the stupid dog and the stupid weather.

While she cleaned our dishes, I slumped in my chair, moping and pulling at the fringe on the blue-and-white checked tablecloth. She brought over a stack of Thin Mints, went into the mudroom, and returned with her umbrella and the keys to her truck.

"Come on. Let's go. We'll go find her."

Fat, bulbous raindrops smeared into a thousand tiny specks as I watched the wipers snap spastically across the windshield. We headed down the driveway, and the truck rattled with the sound of gardening tools and empty flower crates. That day, with the rain, it smelled of fresh earth.

Pat had a wildflower garden. She spent hours in colorful garden gloves, crouched down in the foliage, pruning foxgloves, planting woodruff, digging up weeds, and adjusting the sculptures and bird feeders along the winding pathways. I could spend hours following her around the garden, planting my skinny little butt on stumps and rocks and talking about life and plants.

Don't walk on the rocks. That was the only garden rule that I broke constantly. I respected the plants and watched where I stepped. I didn't pull the leaves or blooms off anything. But walking on the rocks—the simple balancing act of putting one foot in front of the other, rock by rock, at the edge of the garden bed—now, that was tempting. It took skill not to fall. My mother said the same thing. *Don't walk on the rocks.* It wasn't about me falling. It was about the rocks. It loosened them.

Two summers ago, Pat helped me start my own herb garden. I was having problems with the sage taking over the dill that particular July. Today, I'd lost the dog, which was a bigger problem.

"I hate Meagan." I was crying. "I hate her, stupid dog, damn dog. Why?"

"Janna Marie, come on," Pat said, looking at me with a face that told me I should be embarrassed at this behavior, that fourteen is too old to be crying about something like this and that swearing is also rather inappropriate. "We are going to find her. Will you relax, kiddo? We haven't even started."

I rolled down the window and stuck my face into the rain, screaming her name over and over again through tears and thunder. The truck rolled over the lonely speed bump on Delaware Trail, our own tar-and-chip road. Pat tuned the radio to an oldies station. We headed down one block to Lake Latonka Drive, the paved road that ran the three-mile circumference of the lake.

Meagan loved the lake. She was a happy dog who made friends with every lakefront resident within half a mile of our house, always after easy access to water, geese, and anyone willing to throw a floatable object off a dock repeatedly. Her love of water was her biggest fault. Recently, my mother had decided the dog was no longer going to come on the boat with us, because every time we anchored, she jumped overboard. Minus the wet dog smell, it wouldn't have been a problem, except she never wanted to get back in the boat, and my dad would have to lean over and sweet talk her to the stern, where he'd drag all seventy wet, squirming pounds of her onboard. It was an ordeal.

A few weeks ago, we had gone out on the lake, just the three of us, and left Meagan at home on her chain, happily digging a hole where she was allowed to dig a hole. We had barely been on the water an hour. Just as I was about to jump in with my ski, a security boat putted over to us.

"John!" the uniformed captain yelled, motioning to the shaking, wet, whimpering dog on the floor of his boat. "I think she belongs ta yinz. Looks 'ike she missed yinz 'n gone for a swim."

I thought about that day, how we made a scene getting her from one boat to the other, how my mother had not been happy. We turned back onto Delaware Trail.

"I'm in so much trouble," I said, lamenting my fate to Pat. "She is such a stupid dog. This is the worst thing that could happen today."

I sat in the passenger seat, messing with the air vents and imagining my death, certain that my mother was going to kill me, because this was at least the fortieth time this summer that I'd have to tell her I lost the dog. The clock blinked to 4:27 p.m. I had been sure we'd find Meagan after driving around for more than an hour. Pat parked the truck under the basketball hoop, and I slid out the passenger side, defeated. The rain had let up, and the sun came out as the clouds rolled off the blue sky. I trudged through the mucky grass back to my house, fixating on the loud *squish* of my saturated sneakers.

"Janna Marie!" Pat yelled when I was halfway between houses. "Look who's on your porch."

Damn dog. There she was, sopping wet, reeking of lake water, lying on the top step, hanging her muddy paws over the edge with a big, panting grin.

I grabbed her by the collar—red, printed with white bones—that hung limp around her wet, matted neck. I had bought it for her for Christmas with my babysitting money.

"Dumb dog!" I said, yanking her into the garage. She held her head low as I shoved her into the darkness and slammed the door. I stomped into the house and let the screen door smack behind me. My mother would be home in an hour. I had done nothing on the list under the paperweight.

"I'm home!" my mom yelled into the hallway. "*Jannaaaaaaa?* Why is the dog in the garage?"

Meagan trotted in with her, carrying the stench of wet lake dog. My mother dropped her purse on the hall chair and went upstairs. She never wanted to do anything until she could change out of her work clothes and wash her face—not even have a conversation. I was a loquacious kid, like my father.

I followed her to edge of the steps and watched her go upstairs. I said nothing and sat on the bottom step.

Our log cabin, commercially crafted in 1978 by Log Cabin Homes, as advertised on the magnet on the side of our fridge, had only one room on the third floor. This was my parents' bedroom, and next to the kitchen, it was the best room in the house—a space that spread from one side of the house to other, narrowed by the angles of the roof. The closets were crawl spaces, and my mom's bathroom was a hazard to anyone who couldn't remember to duck. But they had a special window, a square cut in the wall, covered by a slab of wood that when precariously propped up with a large dowel rod afforded an aerial view of our living room. This neat little window was a favorite part of our house at the lake.

My mom yelled down from the window for me to turn on NPR. I went to the dry sink, the giant antique cabinet in our hallway, and opened the wide doors to its lower level where I fussed with the tuner and volume on a complicated arrangement of radios, tape decks, and the new CD player that my dad had stacked and wired to speakers throughout our house. My first attempt blared Jimmy Buffett in every downstairs room.

"The news!" my mom yelled, annoyed.

"I know!" I yelled back, annoyed.

I made a couple more failed attempts, and then Bob Edwards was recounting the day's events, which were centered on a potential war in a desert somewhere. I didn't listen. I went to my room and wriggled into my white bathing suit. I put in my own mixtape, which just sounded muted and scratchy compared to *All Things Considered* booming through the house.

I was irritated and impatient for my dad to get home. NPR reminded me of school mornings. NPR and the smell of coffee brewing was enough to make me want to sleep through breakfast. I turned up my boombox, sat on my bed with the cat, and opened my pink diary to write—complain—about my stupid day and my stupid dog. I finished the entry, thankful for the blue sky that was here in time for Dad to get home. He would have my friends with him, and he would be taking us skiing soon.

The phone rang. I waited two more rings and ran into the hallway to grab it.

"Hello," I answered. "No, this is her daughter. Yes, just a second please … *Mom!*"

I held the phone to my chest and raced up the stairs. Knowing the reception was scratchy in the loft, I bit the top of the long silver antenna and pulled it out with my teeth. Multitasking with teeth was something my father did. Perched at the top step, I yelled over the sound of running water in the bathroom.

"I think it's some salesperson!"

"Why?" my mom asked. I heard the water turn off and the floor creak as she walked toward the stairs.

"Cuz they can't pronounce our last name."

I slid the phone across the carpet so she wouldn't have to meet me at the top of the stairs. I listened for her to answer and sat down on the steps, out of sight. I stayed there, smoothing out a patch of very faintly discolored carpet where I had spilled a cup of coffee when I was eight. I had lied about it. Rather than cleaning it, I reasoned that if I rubbed the brown coffee into the carpet, it would look no different from the silver, gold, and tan tufts.

It worked, I think. I didn't tell my mother about it until I was twelve. She laughed. She never would have laughed on the day I spilled it.

I sat, quietly listening. I heard my mom's short answers to a series of closed questions. I heard her gasp and drop the phone. I heard a loud thud. Afraid she would catch me eavesdropping, I scooted down the rest of the stairs and turned the quick corner to my bedroom. Straining to listen, I stood beside my bed. I heard her yell—not a word, just a loud sound. I didn't move. I couldn't move. I heard her come halfway down the steps.

"Janna, you need to get changed." Her tone was urgent. "You need to change right now. We have to leave."

"Why?" I protested, trying to take the imminent whine out of my voice, because she hated whining. "Mom, why? I just put my suit on, and Dad's com—"

"Your father's been in an accident, and we have to go to the hospital."

THE AFTERNOON'S THUNDERSTORM HAD MELLOWED to a downpour, leaving the Pennsylvania Turnpike slick, covered in a thick sheet of rainwater. The big white body of the 1996 Chrysler Sebring rode the highway like a hovercraft. Its tires spun freely above the pavement, gliding through the water, never connecting with the surface of the road.

Somewhere outside of Pittsburgh, Herman Stillman had set the cruise control. The speedometer read 62 mph. It was an easy ride. The two car salesmen talked of makes and models and families and hobbies over the drone of the pelting raindrops.

The clock on the radio blinked to 4:30 p.m.

They were a few miles from the exit to the dealership where Herman would drop off John with the Sebring and return to Pittsburgh in a Honda. It was the second leg of the trade. Earlier that day, John had taken a used Honda to Herman's dealership.

Herman cruised along in the left lane, hands cradling the wheel, glancing over as John told stories of the beautiful women in his life—his wife and daughter. He noticed an accident blocking the right lane ahead. He thought to slow down so he could pass it safely. He tapped the brake pedal. Nothing happened. He pounded it to the floor—still nothing. No slowing down, no brakes. The car started to slide left toward the cement barrier that divided the highway.

Herman spun the wheel to the right to avoid the collision ahead. All the way clockwise. Nothing. No steering. No braking.

4:31 p.m. Somewhere in that minute, Herman had lost control.

Hours later, the police would say that "Mr. Stillman was driving too fast for weather conditions" and that "the car began to *hydroplane*, at certain points, riding on water an inch above the surface of the pavement."

John braced himself. He was wearing a seat belt. They both were buckled up for safety.

The tail end of the Sebring slammed into the cement barrier, leaving red and orange shards of taillight scattered over the wet pavement. The car careened into the right lane. The passenger-side door smashed into the bumper of a green Taurus with a blow that folded the three-thousand-pound Sebring in two. The windshield cracked into a thousand glass veins and burst.

Herman and John hit heads.

Both men were unconscious as the Sebring snapped back and forth, trapped between cement and aluminum for the next tenth of a mile. The car crashed back into the cement barrier, which crunched the hood, and then ricocheted across the highway, where the botched passenger side took a second beating from the green Taurus.

Then the tires found traction, allowing the safety mechanisms to kick in. Both airbags deployed, and the seat belts locked tight. The mangled car screeched to a halt sixty seconds after Herman first tapped the brakes.

At 4:32 p.m., five cars littered the highway. The Sebring was at rest, crushed between the green Taurus and a black Chevy Beretta.

Passengers and drivers crawled out of the tangle of metal. Witnesses rushed over from their safely parked cars to investigate. Arriving cars slowed and pulled over to the shoulder. The northbound highway started to clog. Someone called 911.

Herman had pulled himself out of mauled Sebring. He was confused. He walked down the highway in the rain, away from the wreckage. He had hit his head. He had a headache. What had he hit? What had he hit his head on? What happened?

Traffic backed up, and the interstate was eventually blocked off. A slew of police cruisers appeared, parking around the mess of aluminum and fiberglass. Some officers asked questions of the people standing around, and others made calls on their radios. One ran down the highway after Herman. Most began to sift through the debris, assess the damage, count the drivers and the passengers, and deduce the missing—the ones who were not walking around, confused.

Fire trucks arrived in a cacophony of blaring sirens and flashing lights. The Jaws of Life rolled up to the heap of cars to tear away twisted hunks of metal, battered doors, and broken sections of frames. Most of the metal being pried away from the pile was white. The task was becoming precarious.

An EMT called Life Flight. Reporters from the local paper and TV station showed up. It was chaos and sirens and rain and phone calls and shouting and maneuvering. A spot was cleared for the helicopter to land as close as possible to the ambulance, which was parked as close as possible to the Jaws of Life.

A single gurney had been prepared. It stood empty, soaking up the rain. Almost everyone was okay. Herman was okay.

The crews worked to delicately free a man from the heap. He was alive— alive and kicking, screaming, throwing his arms and legs in every direction, at every face. He was angry, senseless, and covered in blood.

His violent thrashing made it extremely difficult to pull him safely out of the wreckage and over to the gurney, where several EMTs strapped down his arms and legs and wrapped belts around his torso and head. They had to keep him from hurting himself. His clothes were stripped away, and he was hooked up to wires that fed information to machines that could more accurately measure his damage. His belongings were tossed to someone who zipped them up in a plastic bag while someone else searched for his license so he could be called to and questioned by name. Names draw attention, focus people in traumatic situations.

"John!" they said. "John, can you hear us? John. Stay calm. Look at me."

John was incoherent, foaming at the mouth, fighting and bellowing loud, freakish sounds. He made no attempt to understand what was being asked of him. He had no control. Simple things were failing. His head was swelling.

Within seconds, he was silent, his body limp, his nerves numb with the proper sedation for a helicopter ride. His condition was determined severely unstable, and calls were made to the nearest trauma unit with the capacity to handle an injury of this magnitude. Doctors and nurses would be curbside when the helicopter landed. It was now a race to keep him alive, to keep his brain from swelling to the point where it would lose the ability to instruct the vital organs. There was no wound. There was nothing to see. But inside his skull, his brain had been jarred and the gray matter bruised. The pressure building could be fatal. There was a chance he might die. Everyone involved found those odds to be quite likely.

On land, the mess was cleaned up. The cars were towed away, and the glass was swept off the pavement. People got rides from friends and family members happy to hear that no one—no one they knew—was hurt or being rushed to a hospital emergency room. Someone came for Herman. The news crews left, and traffic started to move again.

A man's dress shoe lay wedged between a steering wheel and a white doorframe. Its brown leather had been ruined by the rain. Abandoned in the bedlam, no one had bothered to pick it up and find its owner. It belonged to a left foot.

circling a star

"WHAT?" I ASKED AS I SLAMMED my bedroom door and tore off my suit. "Is he okay? An accident? What do you mean? Mom!"

My mom didn't answer. I could hear her going from room to room, locking doors and shutting windows. I scrambled for some kind of shorts and sleeveless shirt combo.

To this day, what I was wearing is one detail I cannot remember. I can't remember whether I wore shoes or sandals, whether I had on a tank top or some other summer shirt. I don't know whether I pulled my hair up in a scrunchie or left it down. Hell, I don't even remember what length my hair was. I only remember grabbing my purse—rather, the forest green nylon pouch with a long black strap and several detachable hooks that I bought in Denver that I called a purse. It was my very first. I felt like I should be an adult, with a purse, that day.

My mom wore khaki capris and a baggy T-shirt with a horse on it, wedge sandals, and her thin gold watch and thick gold wedding band. She had a beautiful, tan face. It had been scrubbed clean of makeup and was terrifyingly expressionless when I came out of my room. She rushed through her typical leaving-the-house routine—grabbing her keys from the hook in the hallway, locking the door, latching the screen door so Marble wouldn't get stuck between the two, and checking that Meagan was in the garage with food, water, and the garage door cracked an inch from the ground to let in fresh air.

She insisted I put on my seat belt, flung the clutch in reverse, and screeched through a three-point turn. As the car lurched down the driveway, I looked up to see the sun splinter through the leaves of the cherry trees. The branches looked black against the white light.

The back wheels of the Accord spit gooey gravel behind us as we peeled down the road. The speedometer crept up to 45 mph. The speed limit on

Latonka Drive was 30. My mom had not put on her seat belt. My mother did not break rules.

I was speechless as we sped through stop signs and then out the entrance of the lake, down the country road that led to the highway, and around the ramp to I-79, south to Pittsburgh. Once we were on the highway, the speedometer read 75 mph. My mother did not break rules.

"Mom," I said. "Mom! Watch your driving! Please slow down. Please. Please tell me what's wrong. Please slow down."

The car zigzagged from one lane to another. We were reaching 90 mph. She was not paying attention. She had started crying at some point, and now she was gasping, sobbing, wiping her face, and shaking her head. I looked down at the window control. I flipped the switches around and listened as the power control hummed my window down and then hers. I thought fresh air would help. Fresh air always helps when one of us gets carsick. I didn't know what would help, make her pay attention to her driving, or make her explain what was happening. I steadied the steering wheel with my left hand. I felt small, feeling the tug of the car swaying in and out of lanes, afraid it was going to fly off the shoulder and into the trees.

"Mom!" I yelled. "Please tell me what is wrong. What is happening? Please slow down. Please, at least, put your seat belt on."

She looked at me. As her gaze shifted right, the car followed. My legs stiffened, and I grabbed at the window frame to make up for an "oh shit" bar that wasn't actually there. She had been hitting the brakes so many times that my seat belt was choking me. She kept looking at me, ignoring the road and the cars and the fresh air billowing through our windows.

"He might be dead," she said, and she turned to face the road ahead.

My heart stopped—I think. The pulse was unfathomable, heavy, a gigantic beat suspended in my chest. I didn't think it could recover, but then it beat again. And then I had trouble finding air. It was plastering my face, but I couldn't breathe it in. Then my lungs filled—eventually. Next, my brain stopped—maybe. I didn't understand what words meant. My mom was speaking these words—the same words over and over. I couldn't make sense of any of them, couldn't find any meaning in four simple words. I stared at the yellow lines whirring underneath the car, first under the right wheel and then the left and then disappearing somewhere on the other side of the driver's-side window.

"What?" I whispered, realizing I was still in a body that could talk and breathe and pump blood. "What do you mean he could be dead? What are you talking about?"

"Janna," she said. Her voice was stern now. She had stopped gasping and swerving as we merged onto 279 South to Pittsburgh. Not even twenty minutes had passed. Driving at times over 100 mph significantly shortened the trip, normally a fifty-minute drive. The worst of it was over, the worst of her driving.

"Your father has been in a car accident, and he is in the hospital, and he may be dead. You have to prepare yourself, because he's probably dead. Okay?"

Blurry evergreens and neon green road signs whizzed by as we rounded the mountains and the city came into view. I listened to her repeat the same words over and over again.

"He's probably dead, Janna. You need to be ready for this when we get there. I just know he's dead. Your father could be dead."

Her words started to sound like an ugly, unbelievable mantra. I wanted out of the car. I was terrified but too afraid to let my mother know what I was feeling. So I argued with her for the next seven minutes it took us to get to Exit 8A toward the Veterans Bridge.

"Mom, please stop. You're wrong."

"He might be dead, Janna. You need to be ready for this when we get there."

"You don't know that! How do you know that? Did they say that? Why do you keep saying that? Tell me he's not dead. He's going to be alive. He'll be alive when we get there. Dad's alive. Right? He'll be talking, and everything will be fine."

All I wanted was to hear my mother say was that he was alive. He could be hurt or broken but not dead. He had to be alive. I asked her more times than necessary, hoping for a new answer.

"Why can't you tell me?" I begged her. The whole time, I was trying to not cry; so far, I was successful. "What's really happening?"

"Now," she said. "Listen to me, Janna."

I listened.

She told me to be prepared for the worst. She told me that she didn't know, either. She told me that no one had told her, so she couldn't tell me. She told me that we would know when we got there. She told me she was scared. She told me that she didn't think he was alive. She told me she loved me. She explained the phone call. It was a woman trying to get in touch with Mrs. Leyde, John Leyde's wife. Mr. Leyde had been in a car accident and had been life-flighted to Allegheny General Hospital. She was not aware of his condition but requested that his wife get to the hospital immediately. She was not able to release further information until Mr. Leyde's wife was present. The woman on the phone was not able to say if he was dead or alive.

So there we were, searching for a parking spot at AGH.

I pulled and tugged at my seat belt, too tight across my neck and chest, convincing myself that no matter what my mother told me or didn't tell me, we would get there, and he would most definitely be alive. I told myself I had to believe for both of us. I told myself that he would probably be talking, and everything would be okay.

We found a spot not fifty yards from a wide entrance with sliding glass doors. I sat in the passenger seat, clutching my only possession—my purse—that made me feel like I was on my way to becoming a responsible adult. My mother wiped her eyes and rolled up our windows. I didn't want to leave, to go in, to find the real answers to my questions. But I followed her, a few paces behind, over to the entrance and through the sliding glass doors.

A woman at a desk directed us down a wide hallway yellowed by dingy lighting. It led us toward the Trauma Unit, where we ran into my father's boss, who was there with his wife. Tom was a tall man who reminded me of most of my father's friends, jovial and a little schmooze-y, with a mustache. Standing in front of us, he looked sad, scared, and exhausted. He looked like he didn't know what to say.

His wife, Cheryl, spoke first. "He's … well—come with us."

Tom and Cheryl knew where to take us. This fact alone made me feel like things might not be so bad. As we rode in a tiny elevator up to the Trauma Unit, my mother asked them questions about his condition.

"He's suffered a head injury," Tom said. "We don't know how severe, pretty severe. They don't know the damage."

My stomach flipped with each floor. I looked at my mother, thinking about how her stomach must be doing the same thing. I could see how annoyed and scared she was becoming. Neither of us likes elevators. Nothing was getting any better.

When the elevator dinged and the doors creaked open, I saw a new hallway, white walls and white linoleum floors flecked with dirt and marked up from the soles of a thousand rubber shoes. The Trauma Unit stunk like sickness and antiseptic. It reminded me of a vet's office. We followed Tom and Cheryl into the waiting room, and my mother walked up to a desk buzzing with nurses holding clipboards. She was told to sit down and wait. She didn't. She told me to sit down and wait. I did.

The nurses at the desk told my mom over and over again that she could not see her husband. She asked around for other nurses, who said the same thing. She tried to catch them as they came out to the patient rooms to ask where he was. These nurses told her that he was not cleaned up; therefore, she was not able to see him. That was the only thing they told her—he wasn't clean yet.

I sat in a hard chair, wooden and upholstered in coarse blue fabric. I was surrounded by other people sitting in chairs, all of us having been told to wait by nurses, doctors, and family members. I didn't know any of these people, who they were here to see, how long they had been told to wait. I wanted someone other than Tom to tell my mother something. She was getting angry.

I sat alone with my green purse on my lap and watched the news, watched people, and watched the clock. It was a little past 7:00. I thought about being bored, but it didn't seem appropriate. But there was nothing to do and no one to talk to. Whatever was taking place was ruining my evening skiing plans. I wondered if anyone was going to tell Sarah and Jackie that my dad was not going to pick them up after work. I hoped they weren't waiting. I pulled out my purple nylon wallet with "Janna" written in white bubble letters on the outside flap. I went through it and took out the plastic sleeve that held all my friends' school pictures. I started to worry that this might affect our family vacation to North Carolina next week. I would have to tell Rebecca she couldn't come.

Cheryl eventually came around to check on me. I felt uncomfortable— Cheryl and Tom were the only other people I knew there. I hated that this man that my father worked for was the only person trying to console my mother. She didn't like that my father sold cars. She never did. And now she was stuck in the trauma unit on a Tuesday crying to his boss because of something terrible that happened when he was selling damn cars.

I felt like I'd been waiting for hours, but I'd been told that only one had actually passed. Finally, Gram and Pa came. I don't know who called my grandparents, but they must have driven fast, too. My mother still had not seen my father, even though she had been pleading with the three or four nurses who were taking care of him. When she came out to talk to Gram, I couldn't hear them, but I could see through all her composure that she had not stopped crying.

Pa came over and sat with me while Gram and my mother tried to gain more control over things. Pa, the man my father is the spitting image of, the man who is unable to find the bad in even the worst of things, did his best to keep me entertained. He brought over a blank notepad and two pencils. We sat in the waiting room and took turns drawing objects we could see—a lamp, the TV mounted on the wall, a stack of magazines with a Kleenex box on top. Pa and I did this in church. Drawing was a good cure for boredom. I didn't ask him any questions, because I knew he didn't know what was going on, either.

There was a small room next to the waiting room. When my mother was not arguing with the hospital staff, she sat in the small room with a cream-colored phone and a Kleenex box one of the nurses had brought her. It was the same one I had drawn. The glass door stayed closed, but I could watch her inside. She sat upright in the chair, digging for things in her purse and making phone calls. She made three that night.

The first call was to Fred, our close family friend. He was a psychologist who my mother worked for part-time. She had an appointment with a little girl scheduled for the next day, and Fred would need to cancel it for her.

The second call was to Brenda McBride. She was a woman I didn't know, one of my mom's friends, an attorney. The accident had happened on the job, and so far, my mother had not signed a single piece of paperwork. She had refused to every time she was asked or advised by someone in hospital administration. She needed Brenda to verify that she was handling things right. (She was.) She needed Brenda to get her another attorney immediately. (She did.)

The third call was to Pat. She asked Pat to call everyone else.

Not long after I watched my mother make the phone calls, the waiting room went silent. A Pittsburgh police officer walked in, grabbed my mother by the arm, and without saying a word, walked her straight into the trauma unit. He was young and handsome, and the nurses were not able to protest. He and his uniform had everyone's attention.

I hadn't seen Danny in a long time and never expected him to show up, but as soon as he walked into the room, I felt better. I was always happy to see him, and he looked sharp in his uniform. I hoped he would come out and tell me what he saw behind the doors. I wanted to go home, but not until I knew my dad was okay. I wondered how he had heard what happened.

His mother had called him. Pat and her husband, Bill, had three kids. Before I was around and everyone was younger, they were like my parents' kids, playing with our dog, borrowing my dad's go-cart, and eating sandwiches in our kitchen. Now Leah Ann taught biology, and Danny and Keith were cops like their dad.

Danny came out and sat next to me. He put his arm around me and asked how I was doing. *Okay.* Had I eaten anything? *No.* Did I want to? *No.* Was I sure I was okay? *Yes.*

I felt important. People were watching me talk to a Pittsburgh police officer. I liked the idea that people might have been intimidated by him. I bet others were curious, because the very handsome cop-on-duty came in just for me, just for my family, just to help my mother break a rule to see my father.

"Is he okay? Is he—"

"I don't know, kid, but he's not dead."

Danny couldn't stay long—he had to get back to work.

In a room to the left, behind swinging doors, my dad lay in a hospital bed, conked out in a mess of IVs, swollen, drugged, and black and blue. The blood was cleaned off, and he was dressed in a freshly starched hospital gown. His face was broken, his left eye socket cracked in half, and his nose crushed. I was told that he didn't look like himself. I was told I couldn't see him and that I wouldn't want to.

THAT NIGHT WAS MY FIRST lesson in brain injuries. My dad had a "subarachnoid hemorrhage and maxillary sinus fracture" with "multiple punctate left frontal and occipital region diffuse injury." Pa tried to explain to me what that meant and what they needed to do to make my dad better.

Earlier that day, the doctors had to drill a hole in my dad's head. They used an actual drill, spinning clean, right through the cranium. It seemed frighteningly similar to the drill in our garage that cut clean holes into two-by-fours under my dad's careful guise. It was—drill bits and all. Then they attached a drain to the hole to suck liquid from his brain.

The injury had caused diffuse bleeding, and if the doctors didn't relieve the pressure, his brain would swell, and he would die. I wanted to know more about diffuse bleeding and what it meant so that I could use it if anyone asked. Other people in the waiting room had asked me why I was there.

My dad was sedated and had a hole in his head with a drain for the diffuse bleeding.

I learned about ventilators, too. Watching hospital soaps with my grandmothers and hearing my aunts' tales of working in the ER, I had some understanding that people who could not breathe needed to use ventilators. My father had been sedated on the scene and since then had lapsed into a medicated coma. He was on a ventilator.

"His head is very, very swollen, Janna," my mother said. She had come out to tell me what I needed to do that night. "Very swollen on the left side. He is also very black and blue. He has a lot of bruises on his head and face. There is a drain in his head and lots of tubes."

"Oh," I said.

"It will be hard to see him," she said. "He doesn't look like your father right now."

"Do you think he'll open his eyes soon and talk to us?"

"I really don't know, Janna."

"Oh."

"Do you want to see him?"

"Not really."

"I think maybe you should. Just come in and say hi to him. Tell him you love him."

"I really don't want to—"

"Come with me."

I took my purse with me and we walked in through the swinging doors of the trauma unit. The vet's office smell was stronger, and the lights were brighter. I felt like I was somewhere I was not allowed to be. Nurses scurried around on autopilot, and the hallway hummed with activity. When we walked into my father's room, I expected to see doctors bustling over him. But there was just one nurse, Jan, standing by his bed, and only the beeping machines broke the silence.

The drain was there. I couldn't see the hole in his head, because his head was wrapped in white gauze, but I could see the drain winding down from behind his head like a misplaced tail. The drain tube was clear. Had it sucked everything out?

He was appalling to look at. I found myself looking away from his face, at my K-Swiss, at his hospital ID bracelet, or at the railing on the bed. Someone had blown up his head like a balloon from a helium tank. The skin around his forehead, cheeks, and neck stretched tight in pinks and purples. I thought about the times he'd sneak away with Danny and Keith at parties to suck helium from the tank and they'd come back talking in funny voices. He'd only recently let me try it with them.

The room smelled terrible— stale and medicinal. He didn't move. His hands and forearms were threaded with IVs. I didn't want to touch him or talk to him. His eyes were closed. His left eye looked like it would never open because someone had shoved a baseball under his eye socket, and now his eyelid was a bulbous red slit with no eyelashes.

The nurse had left, and it was just my mother and me, alone with him.

"Tell him you're here," my mother said from the other side of the bed. "Just tell him."

"Hi—"

The cluster of machines surrounding his bed chirped. I wanted to throw up. I wanted to run out of the room and never come back.

"Hi, Dad," I said, leaning closer to his puffed-up face. "I love you, and ..."

His thick, full mustache was the only thing I could recognize on him. He smelled like an old person.

"You're going to get better," I said. "You're not a wuss."

I looked at my mom, who was looking at him. I walked out to find Gram and Pa, leaving my mother with my father, who was motionless and mangled.

The nurses had been right. This was a look not suitable for even the strongest of loved ones to witness. It wasn't even permitted for children under sixteen, but someone had fought for me to see him.

My mother hated the nurses and doctors. Hate wasn't a strong enough word for what she felt. She felt lost and ignored. She thought their communication skills were deplorable. She felt like they didn't care whether he lived, died, or continued breathing. She thought her arguments should have yielded an explanation from them. She felt exhausted from hoping that her husband's condition might change or that she would have some time to prepare for what was coming.

The swelling in his face could go down, and his bruises could yellow and heal, but the doctors were vague about whether he might ever move, blink, or smile again. Chances were slim that he would regain those functions. He had hit his head hard. No one knew how hard.

When my mom could no longer fight for answers and was no longer allowed to see him, she wanted his possessions, familiar objects from a time before that night. Somewhere he had clothes and a wallet. He had wire-rimmed glasses and maybe Jimmy Buffett tickets, the tickets he was planning to buy that day. She wanted to make sure she could get the tickets and give them to someone else. They were expensive. The concert was in two days, and they wouldn't be going this year. He had the keys to a blue Civic sitting alone on a lot at New Honda and Nissan City and his house keys. She figured she could talk to the right person, and all those things would be found shoved in a bag somewhere. No one could help her find his belongings, so she pleaded with the nurses to see him again.

While my mother stayed on the other side of the trauma unit doors and Gram went into the room with the phone to call her two daughters and tell them they needed to drive over the next morning to see their brother, Pa stayed with me.

We had already drawn every object in the room, so we tried to chat with the nurses on duty. He kept it light and comedic and got them to smile every now and again with punny jokes and tricks with inanimate objects. I watched them soften ever so slightly. Did they really have to walk around with a scowl? I was a kid. I had a father we all cared about. Wasn't this their job? My aunts were nurses, and they were happy, smiley, and helpful women. I, like my mother, found the nurses deplorable.

"They're just tired, Toots," Pa said. "It's late. Let's go get a snack. How about we find a Snickers bar?"

We raided the vending machine, even though no one but me wanted to eat. It was now well after 10:00. Pat and Bill had shown up. I told them about

Danny and about how he helped my mother. Pat told me that my mother wanted me to go home with Gram and Pa and sold it to me as an impromptu sleepover. It didn't matter. I slept over all the time. I was more concerned with where my mother was going to sleep or when my father would wake up. I was too tired to voice my opinion, so when it was time to leave I left.

No one asked me if I wanted to say good-bye to my dad. I didn't.

On the way home, I sat in the backseat with my head craned around so I could see the stars through the rear window. It made me carsick, but I wanted to look at the stars. I thought about when my dad would explain the universe to me as we stood with the dog on the grassy hill behind our house, staring at the night sky. I spent the entire ride asking my grandparents questions, leaving no room for them to have their own conversation.

I asked about brains and comas. I asked about nerves and pain. I asked about swelling, car accidents, and driving in the rain. I asked about praying and God. I asked if we were good people. I asked if Dad was a good person, if Mom was. I asked what they thought would happen tomorrow and if they were scared or sad. I asked if I would be able to talk to my dad tomorrow. I pressed my finger pads against the defrost strips and searched for the North Star. I asked about wishes and stars. I asked if they thought he was going to die.

I knew he wasn't going to die, but I wished on a star anyway.

We pulled up to Gram and Pa's ranch-style house, which sat at the intersection of a busy main street with a traffic light and a quiet neighborhood road. It was dark, and I couldn't see the familiar yellow siding. We pulled into the garage, and I squeezed out of the narrow car door opening, blocked by a wall lined with protruding garden tools, and raced to the door. There were no happy animals to greet us. The house was dark and quiet inside.

That night, I had to sleep in Gram's pajamas. I loved an excuse to sleep in one of her long cotton nightgowns covered in a loud floral pattern. Gram and I washed our faces and brushed our teeth while Pa got a glass of milk for himself in the kitchen. I situated myself where I always slept, in the twin bed closest to the wall and the window, in the room where my aunts grew up. It was the one that was Aunt Jeannie's, the aunt that everyone agrees I most resemble. I didn't see it.

Pa came in with his milk, and the three of us talked for a long while. I sat crossed-legged on my bed with a glass of water, and my grandparents sat across from me on the other twin. First we talked about getting my clothes at my house for the next day at the hospital; making sure I fed the dog, the cat, and my dad's fish; and giving keys to our neighbors. Then we exhausted all the what-ifs. We prayed out loud together, counted our blessings, and thanked God and asked him to keep us safe.

I couldn't sleep that night. I sat up at the edge of my bed and looked out the open window. The summer night air was crisp. I stared at the sky and thought again about all the times I'd discussed the universe with my dad. What was really out there? I laid down in a corpse pose under the sheets. They were soft and smelled like the cabinet where Gram kept all the fluffy towels and excessive towers of toilet paper. I prayed again, and it felt silly. I stuck my leg out and traced the lines of stenciled flowers on the wallpaper with my big toe, straining to hear the conversation my grandparents were having down the hall. I wasn't sure what going to sleep would mean for tomorrow.

When I was little, my parents developed a tactic to trick me into going to sleep.

"What are we *keeping* forward to?" I would ask as a four-year-old.

I lived in constant forward motion with an incessant desire to know what we were going to do next. I refused to take naps for fear of missing something and detested going to bed earlier than other people. My parents told me the faster I got to sleep, the faster I would wake up and get to do whatever extraordinarily fun thing was planned for the next day. It worked. I had a lot of fun things going on.

That Tuesday night turned to Wednesday morning in July, and I was afraid to go to sleep. What the hell was coming next? What were we looking forward to?

the best map

THE NEXT MORNING, THE TRAUMA UNIT was quieter. It was almost empty. My two aunts had arrived from Columbus and taken my cousins to the hospital cafeteria for breakfast, but my mother stayed in the waiting room. No one had been allowed to see my father since the previous night. She didn't want to miss an opportunity.

The sound of high heels clicking on linoleum broke the quiet, and my mother looked up to see a woman in pumps and a cherry-red pantsuit walking around the waiting room. She carried a folder, and my mother knew she was the Workers' Compensation caseworker, looking for John's wife.

"Hi," she said, walking over to the woman, extending her hand.

"Hello," said the woman. "You must be Claudia Leyde."

"It's Li-dee. Yes, I'm Claudia."

"Li-deeee. Yes, sorry. How are you?"

The two sat down. The caseworker asked standard questions and reviewed the facts with my mom: John had sustained a head injury in a car accident, as a passenger, wearing a seat belt, while on the job. His injuries were severe, and treatment was going to be extremely expensive. There would be a lot of legal paperwork.

"Now, what else can I do to help you?"

"You can help me find his personal belongings."

An hour later, the woman in red returned with a plastic bag and a social worker. The social worker asked more questions. My mom knew the drill. She ran a social service agency that helped children and their families deal with difficult situations. Her marriage would be questioned.

"Claudia, are you going to use this opportunity to charge John's credit cards and run up his bills while he is indisposed?"

"No."

"Are you going take everything he has, using his IDs and the contents of his wallet?"

"No, I am not."

"Are you going to use this as an opportunity to get your hands on all of John's money?"

"No."

"Are you going to—"

"No. No, I—"

"Are you—"

"No. I am not trying to steal his money and take advantage of him. My husband and I are getting along."

The woman in red handed her the bag, a weathered Ziploc containing all the items he'd been carrying the day before—except his clothes. There would have been no use for them anyway. His short-sleeved cotton button-up and single-pleat Dockers would be unrecognizable, bloodstained, cut in shreds by the shards of glass and the paramedics.

Everything in the bag was waterlogged and dirty. My mom found his leather wallet, soft and worn, still intact, with his driver's license, cash, credit cards, a tattered Social Security card, faded receipts, and business cards all in their proper places. There were no Jimmy Buffett tickets.

She found a thin leather belt and one shoe, still laced. She found a set of keys that she didn't recognize and one that she did—a New Honda and Nissan City navy and gold clasp with a neon orange spongy float and keys identical to her own. She found his wedding band, thick, gold, and plain, like hers.

The social worker had left, but the workers' comp caseworker stayed while she carefully inspected the bag's contents.

"All six dollars?" my mother said. "That would get me real far."

The caseworker smiled and told my mother she had to go.

"Thank you," my mother said.

"Have a good morning," she said, leaving the waiting room. "We'll be in touch."

I WOKE UP STARING AT the stenciled flowers on the wallpaper. I couldn't remember falling asleep. In those first naked, unblemished moments of the day, I felt disoriented. Then I remembered with a rush of consciousness so acute that I had to sit up and straighten out my brain before I could think about what to do next.

I plodded down the hallway to Gram's bathroom, a tiny room with pink tiled walls and pink plush carpet. Gram and Pa were probably both dressed and ready to go. I hated being the last one dressed—it was embarrassing to be the only person still in pajamas. I washed my face with Gram's slimy hand soap, brushed my teeth, and ran back to my room to scramble into yesterday's clothes.

Downstairs, I found Gram and Pa dressed and sipping coffee at their kitchen table. I saw the Maxwell House tin on the counter. Unlike my parents, good coffee to them was hot water and scoops of flaky powder.

"Morning, Toots," said Pa. "What do you want to eat?"

"I don't really want anything," I said. "Have you talked to Mom?"

"Yes. We need to do a few things—check on the horses and get you clothes from home," he said. "Then we'll go back to the hospital."

"What do you think Mom's been doing this morning?" I asked, plopping myself down at the kitchen table.

"Janna Marie, you have to eat something," Gram said. "It's going to be a long day." She handed me an overripe banana.

"Really?" I asked.

I peeled it all the way down, its limp skin and banana strings draping over my hand. It was more brown than banana-colored.

"It's kinda gross," I said.

"Gross?" Pa asked.

"Yeah, one-forty-four," I said with a smile, referencing his old joke. "I should have said two-eighty-eight, because this is *tooooooo* gross."

"That's my girl," Pa said, grabbing my hand and squeezing.

"Eat," Gram said.

I made a face with each bite while Gram dumped their half-finished coffees down the sink.

Twenty minutes later, feeling lightheaded and nauseated, I decided the banana had made me carsick. I was thankful to hear the gravel crunch as we pulled into the driveway of my other grandmother's house.

Gram Mary's house sat close to the two-lane country highway in front of a barn, a pond, and forty acres of field. It was a brick house built in the early 1800s as the Boston Tavern, a bed-and-breakfast stop between Pittsburgh and Erie. Nights when I slept over, curled up next to Gram Mary in her huge bed, I willed myself to ignore the fact that the house was haunted so I could close my eyes and sleep. I'd spent most of my childhood days with Gram Mary, riding around in her Chrysler LeBaron to visit friends and get her hair done at the beauty shop on Fridays, baking apple pies from scratch, doing yard work in our bare feet, playing with the animals, and picking bouquets of wildflowers. She would always tell me that I was her favorite person in the whole world.

In the last few years, she'd gotten very sick. It had started when I was in grade school. I'd get off the bus at her place and discover that all the doors and windows had been locked. I would fight and cry to get inside, and she would peer out of the windows and swear at me. Some days, I would give up and go to the barn to play with the latest litter of kittens or talk to the horses. Other days, I'd persuade her to let me in only to find her still in her nightgown, hiding peanut butter sandwiches in the couch cushions. She'd chase me through the house with a broom or a wooden spoon, swearing and telling me how I was a bad kid and that she hated me. I would try to fight back, but my insults felt juvenile and mean, because I knew she had to be sick, so I'd retreat to a quiet corner and cry until I realized it was almost time for my mother to pick me up. Then I'd wipe away my tears and get back to playing outside or sitting cross-legged in front of the TV.

That year, my mother hired first Kelly and then Sally, live-in caregivers who were responsible for Gram Mary. Sally came outside to greet us. Sally was a heavy, kind woman who was always smiling. Dressed in her housedress and slippers, her frizzy hair a mess, she ran up to the car, sniffling and wiping her eyes with a blue tissue.

"How is John?" she asked, giving my grandparents no time to get out of the car. "Oh, good Lord, is he going to be all right? Kelly told me this morning. I'm just so upset. What can I do?"

I didn't say anything to Sally, just gave her a hug and raced to the barn to check on the horses and give them their morning grain. I unlatched the side door, and a hungry litter of kittens immediately gathered at my feet and began mewing. I tiptoed around them, opened the feed bins and stuck my hands into the first two, feeling the avalanche of smooth grain on my skin. Then I opened the third, scooped a heap of cat food, and dumped it into a cookie tray. I bent down to pat their soft heads while I rationed various grains into round tins.

First, I fed my mom's chestnut Arabian Jamal. After I kissed his velvety nose and told him to be good, I made the rounds, filling everyone else's feeder and giving them a pat or an ear rub. I saved Thunder, my father's stout, black Morgan, for last. I sat up on the ledge and rubbed his ears, whispering into them the story of what had happened the day before. He tossed his head around and nudged me down. He was hungry. I filled his feeder. Before embarking on the difficult and messy task of filling the water buckets, I climbed back up on the ledge of Thunder's stall to watch barn swallows dart in and out of the rafters and listen to the contented crunching, chewing, and snorting.

When I finished, I went into the house to say hello to Gram Mary. She was sitting at the kitchen table, staring into space. I didn't tell her anything, just gave her a quick kiss on the cheek and left.

"You're wet," Gram said as I hopped into the back seat.

"It's just on the front," I said, buckling up in the center.

"Why are you wet?"

"I had to water the horses," I said. "The buckets are hard to carry without splashing."

"Is it on the car seat?"

"No, just the front, Gram."

The next stop was Gabany's, a machine shop run by four brothers, all who had names that started with *R*, all friends of my father. Gram and Pa stayed in the car while I went inside and sat at the counter. I thought about getting a Snickers from the candy machine, but my dad wasn't with me, so I'd have to pay for it.

I'd spent countless hours with my dad at Gabany's. He'd come in to check on a car, a part for the boat or mower, or just to hang out with the brothers. I would have to entertain myself by drawing at the counter, examining cars' underbellies, or wandering the vast rooms lined with shelves holding car parts. I liked the smell of the shop.

"Kiddo, what are you doing in here?" Randy asked as he came out from the back room. "Your dad with ya?"

"No." I stood up from the stool as if to suggest the matter was less than casual.

"What's up?" Russ asked, walking in and wiping his hands with a stained blue cloth.

"Well, I have to tell you something," I said. "My dad ..."

The words caught in my throat. I'd never said any of it before. I thought maybe I should have rehearsed this on someone other than a horse.

"My dad was in a car accident yesterday—"

Randy cut me off: "Is he okay?"

"We don't know. He hasn't woken up."

"He's in a coma?" asked Ray.

I told them what little I knew. I told them Gram and Pa were waiting in the car and that I had to hurry. I asked Randy if he could mow the grass at Gram Mary's and take care of the animals today. I told him my mother asked me to ask him.

Randy and Russ told me that we were in their prayers. The phrase seemed so awkward. *Tell John he's in our prayers.* I didn't know how it would help anything.

When we got to my house, I jumped out as soon as Pa parked the car. I felt like I hadn't been home for days. I opened the garage door and let Meagan out.

"Hiya, pup," Pa said as she ran circles around him.

Inside, I checked the answering machine. There were five messages. The first two were from Sarah, calling about being stood up for waterskiing. The third was also from Sarah, saying my dad was in their prayers and to let her know if there was anything she and her mother could do to help. The fourth was from Vicky, our close friend and neighbor, who said we were in her prayers and that she and the kids had taken care of the animals. The fifth message was a man who was confused because my father had forgotten to deliver his new car on Wednesday morning. He said it was now 10:16, and he was supposed to have dropped off the car by 8:00.

I went to my room. I picked up my white bathing suit from the floor and put it away. I changed into fresh clothes, jean shorts, and a button-up sleeveless shirt. The raw linen of my shirt smelled like hay, and I liked that. I shoved more clothes and underwear into a bag along with a drawing pad and a few paperbacks. We were on the road again by eleven.

As soon as we got off the elevator near the trauma unit, my Aunt Biz greeted us.

"Hi, Aunt Biz," I said.

"Hiya, Sweets!" she said, picking me up to give me a long, strong bear hug. "I love you so much, Janna Marie."

"I love you, too."

She kissed me on the cheek. It was sloppy and wet, and her cheek smushed against mine, smearing her tears on my face.

"Where's my mom?"

"With us."

Aunt Biz squeezed my hand and led me over to everyone in the waiting room sitting in clusters. Our friends and family had taken over—my aunts from Columbus, my cousins, my mom's sister and her family, my grandparents' minister, Pat and Bill, Tom and Cheryl, and my mom's aunt and uncle. Morning papers and coffee cups were strewn across chairs along with a box of Dunkin Donuts.

My mother looked tired but smiled and hugged me and sat down beside me. I started to ask her how he was but Reverend Moon interrupted.

"We're all together this morning for John," he said. "Let us take some time to pray."

Gram and Pa were Methodists and very involved in their church. Gram had told me that praying to God helped her feel at peace. As Reverend Moon led his prayer, I sat straighter in my chair, looked down at my lap, and closed my eyes. I listened to his words, strings of sentences with hard intonations on words like "God," "Savior," "Lord," and "John."

Aunt Biz, the younger of my father's two sisters, started to cry. Then other people started to cry. I wanted the praying to end. I looked over at my mother. Her eyes were closed. I was afraid I'd get caught with mine open, get caught not caring about the prayer.

When it was over, I asked my mother if I could have a donut from the box.

"Sure," she said. "We found your dad's things. I don't think there are any Jimmy Buffett tickets."

It would have been my first Buffett concert. I had wanted to go since I was eight, and my parents had finally given in.

I ate a chocolate donut with blue sprinkles, and my mom showed me the plastic bag of things.

"Only one shoe?" I asked. "Where's the other?"

"I don't know," she said. "Maybe they couldn't find it."

"Why? Which one is this one?"

"I think it's his right."

"What about the left one?"

"I don't know. We'll see if we can find it later, okay? Are you okay out here for a while?"

I nodded. When my mom left, I took out my black and white composition book to write down what was happening.

"Hi, Janna."

I looked up.

"I'm Herman," the man said. "Can I sit next to you?"

"Sure."

Herman Stillman looked like a banged-up Santa Claus with a round, red face; a bristly white beard; and a bruise covering the right side of his forehead—black and blue and yellowing around the edges where it had begun to heal. I didn't like Santa Claus. As a kid, I cried every time someone put me on his lap.

"How are you doing?"

"I'm fine," I said. "How are you?"

"I'm so sorry—"

"I know. It's okay."

"Do you know that your dad was talking about you and your mother when it happened? He loves you both very, very much."

"I know he does. Do you remember what happened?"

"No, not really."

"Did you get hurt?"

"I hit my head, and I don't remember after that."

"Oh. Do you know where his other shoe is?"

My mother walked over. Given the circumstances, she did not particularly like Herman or want to talk to him, either.

"Hi," she said. "Thanks for coming. How are you?"

"Fine," he said. "How is John?"

"Pretty much the same. Could you do something for us? When you go to see the car, could you look for his other shoe? She's really upset about it."

"I just want him to have two," I said.

I want him to have all his things when he wakes up. I want nothing to be missing. I want to hand him a bag and say, "Look, Dad. It's all here, and here's what happened to you …"

Finally, I was left alone with my notebook. Well after lunchtime, I realized I was hungry. People in the waiting room had told us that the AGH cafeteria had delicious food, so I asked Pa if he wanted to go down.

"Good idea," he said. "But how about you visit your dad first?"

I looked at him, shaking my head.

"Come on, Toots. Just real quick."

I pushed open the double doors to the trauma unit and stood in the doorway to my dad's room. Swollen, puffy, intubated, and lying in a swarm of tubes, nothing about him looked different or better than the night before. I walked over to his bed. He smelled. I saw the tube from a catheter dangling out from under his sheets. I could see the urine in the tube. I felt sick.

My mother came in. We stood and looked at him, silent. Then she put her arm around me and led me to the side of his bed. She showed me that his right eye, under a closed lid, flickered every few seconds. This was a good sign, Aunt Biz had explained.

I asked my mother to come down to lunch with us, but she wanted to stay. I told her I'd bring her something, but she didn't want me to.

"I can bring you some better coffee."

"No."

"What about a piece of bread?"

"No."

"Nothing, Mom?"

"No, you go ahead and go eat with everyone. I'll be okay. Let me know how it is."

The cafeteria was huge, sleek, and sunny. There was so much to choose from—different soups, hot dishes, a salad bar, desserts, a separate ice cream bar with every topping imaginable, and a bagel bar. I chose chicken gumbo and a toasted bagel with a heaping scoop of salty, creamy chicken salad. It was perfection—mayo, chicken chunks, celery bits, and a sprinkling of salt and pepper.

When we got back, the Gallos were there: my parents' best friends, Fred and Carolyn. They'd brought me a puzzle from the Smithsonian. The rest of the day was quiet. Adults were having conversations I was not to be privy to, and I wasn't asked to visit my father again. I occupied my time trying to solve the puzzle. First I tried to put it together on my lap, and then I had to lay it out on the floor. It looked easy, but all the pieces were triangles, all the same.

I had solved the puzzle three times by 8:00. It was a picture of marine life, fish and crabs. By then, my Aunt Biz and my cousins had gone home with Gram and Pa. Everybody had left except Pat, Bill, and Aunt Jeannie. Pat and Bill were going to take me to Danny's. Aunt Jeannie would stay at the hospital with my mother.

Danny was on duty that whole night, so I watched the Olympics and ate pizza with his wife and kids. I hated the pizza. The cheese was rubbery and the sauce gross. I wished that Danny had been there.

THE NEXT SIX DAYS WERE all the same, and they would eventually blend into one memory. I solved the puzzle more times than I could count. I developed an unhealthy affection for chicken salad sandwiches and frozen candy bars, which Pa helped me indulge. I played countless rounds of Idiot's Delight with an old deck of cards I found at the nurses' station. Pa and I made friends with other families who were waiting for someone to wake up from a brain injury.

We talked mostly to Mr. and Mrs. Tokash. Their seventeen-year-old boy, Danny, had been in a motorcycle accident a week and a half ago, and he still hadn't woken up. They'd planned to take him to the Jimmy Buffett concert on Saturday. It would have been his first.

I saw little of my mother that first week, and I never saw her eat. I would bring her cups of coffee and frozen yogurt, but often the yogurt would go untouched. She sat in a chair beside my father's bed with the bed rail down so she could lean over him. She would lay her head on his chest and hold his hand. Sometimes she would clean off his face, chest, neck, and arms with a warm washcloth. She would always talk to him—about the people she'd met, the terrible nurses, the animals at home that missed him, their life together, me, Gram Mary, and all the people in the waiting room waiting for him. She would tell him over and over to wake up, to talk to her, to say something.

My father never stirred and only made scarce eye movements. People would go in to visit him and come out crying.

I never cried. That fact became a major concern to everyone. I was constantly interrupted from my daily activities or pulled away to sit with someone who would want to talk to me about how I was feeling. I watched everyone, and I could see that they were all constantly sad and scared. I didn't feel any different. I was sad, and I was scared, but I reassured myself that crying would mean I had given up, given in. Maybe if I started crying, I wouldn't be able to stop. And if I started crying, then I would be letting my parents down, both of them.

I didn't want my father to think I was a wuss. I didn't want my mother to worry about me. She had been worrying about everyone—my father, the animals at home, people ignoring their lives to be at the hospital, her own sick mother, and her job and the people she had left at work. I figured if I didn't cry, then I would be kept off that list.

Fred was the only person who seemed to understand me.

As a kid, I had three favorite people: Wayne, Bill, and Fred. These three men were always doing fun things with my dad, and they always included me. Wayne, who had been my dad's best friend for years, lived in Fort Lauderdale and always sent us Christmas cards with Santa in the pool, on the beach, or in a red and white bathing suit. Bill was Pat's husband. He was calm and kind and taught me things I needed to know, like how to build things with wood and how to shoot free throws. Fred and his wife, Carolyn, used to work with my parents, and now the four of them went out to dinner a lot. Sometimes I was allowed to join, sometimes not.

"Janna Marie, can I tell you something?" Fred asked the second night at the hospital. He sat down in the chair next to me. He looked sad. I'd never seen Fred look sad.

Fred was Italian, a small guy with silver hair, a mustache, and a boisterous personality. He was from New Castle, Pennsylvania, where his twin brother ran an Italian restaurant. I knew Fred as silly, but the serious side of him was extremely smart and on his way to becoming a world-renowned psychologist. He had just published his first book on energy psychology, and I was the subject of his photos on meridians. I wanted to be a psychologist like Fred.

"Yeah. What?"

"Well, you know what has happened to your dad, and I know you know what's going on."

"Yes."

"Do you feel scared?"

"Scared?"

"How do you feel, Janna?"

"Yeah, kind of scared, maybe. People are getting mad at me because I won't cry."

"Do you want to cry?"

"No, not really. Should I be crying?"

"Let me explain something. This accident has happened to your dad. It did not happen to you or your mom, but it may change your life forever, because when he wakes up, he might not be the same. We don't know."

"The same?"

"Well … he might not be the same John we know … the same dad …"

"Oh, okay."

"So here is what you are going to have to do. You have to be strong. No matter what happens, this is part of your story. You can always tell it that way—like a story. This will not be your entire life, just one piece. Your dad may not wake up, and if he does, he may be very different. You have to remember, always, how much he loves you and how great of a dad he is. Both your parents love you very much. No matter what happens, it's all a part of your life, but it's not your whole life."

"Do you know what's going to happen?" I asked.

"No, I don't know."

"I think he's going to live," I said. "I know he will. It just doesn't make sense if he doesn't."

"No, it doesn't."

ON THURSDAY, MY FATHER STARTED to flutter his eyes and at times open them for a few seconds. It was another promising sign, but we were told that it wasn't a medical indication of whether he would be able to eat, walk, talk, write, smile, or be himself ever again. It did, however, necessitate a new rule.

"No talking while touching," the nurses repeated to each of his visitors. "No touching while talking. You get one, not two."

Everyone who went to visit him wanted to hug and nuzzle his still body. They would whisper, cry, and beg him to wake up, giving him every reason they could, hoping those would be reason enough. Danny and Aunt Biz were almost banned from seeing him because of talking and touching at the same time. My mother followed the rule. She would take precise turns doing one and then the other.

He still hadn't woken up.

That afternoon, Aunt Jeannie took the kids—me, my cousins, Annie,

Carrie, and Stephen—to a playground she had discovered behind one of the hospital wings. A few hours earlier, Annie, who was six, had stuck a penny up her nose. Though she was fine and one of the nurses on duty had successfully removed it, my entire family overreacted. Someone needed to get the kids out of the waiting room.

The playground was simple, a no-frills jungle gym and swing set on a patch of gritty, dark brown sand sandwiched between a hospital wing and the back fence of a residential neighborhood. Annie and Stephen climbed around on the jungle gym while I held Carrie and watched them alongside my aunt. Carrie was too young for any of it, and I was too old. In a matter of minutes, everyone was bored.

"Come on over here," Aunt Jeannie said, motioning us all towards her.

She had found a stick lying on the ground and started to write something in the sand. She walked a few steps backward after she had finished. She didn't say anything.

WE LOVE YOU JOHN

I found two more sticks, one each for Annie and Stephen, and then found another for myself. The five of us stayed out there for two more hours, writing in the sand the names of everyone my father knew. The playground was littered with the names of friends, relatives, co-workers, neighbors, pets, and all of my friends. We had to leave when it got dark.

I spent the next few days worrying about other kids trampling on our ode to my father. No one ever did. I checked every day until eventually it rained, the message beaten away by tiny raindrops, and the patch of sand smooth again.

On Friday night, I went home with my mother. It was the first time she'd been home in three days, and we were back in the trauma unit by 9:00 the next morning, the first visiting hour allowed. The waiting room was frigid, and Tom and Cheryl were the only ones there. No one was allowed to visit for another hour, so we waited for the nurse.

Sarah was one of the friendliest nurses. She welcomed us in and told my mother that my father was in okay physical shape. He was no longer intubated and had breathed on his own through the night. The only tube

I could see was the brain drain. His bed was elevated to 30 degrees—high enough so he could observe things.

"Last night, John had two blueberry popsicles," Sarah said.

"Blue popsicles?" I repeated.

"Sure did," Sarah said. "Loved 'em."

"Wow," I said. "Yuck. He would hate those."

"John doesn't eat any kind of sweets," my mother said. "He doesn't like them. Never has."

"Jolly Ranchers and M&Ms," I said. "He eats those, but not popsicles."

"Yeah, he sure does," Tom said. "He loves those Jolly Ranchers."

"Why were they blueberry?" I asked.

"We needed him to eat something blue so we could trace it in his digestive tract to make sure everything was working okay and he could digest food," said Sarah. "He ate two for us—a very good thing—and now we can watch where that blue fluid goes in his system."

His eyes were open, and he was looking around. He was watching us. I looked at him, still trying to picture him sucking on blue popsicles. The swelling had gone down, but where there had been pinks and purples, there were now yellows and blacks, equally ugly. His left eye was still puffy but struggling to stay open and focus on us. His lips were tinged blue.

My mother leaned over the bed to say good morning to him. He turned his head slightly toward her, eyes following, tracking.

"Gimme a kiss," he said.

Sarah clapped.

My mother leaned over, kissed my father, and started to cry but stopped herself. "Oh, John," she said. "Hi."

He slowly turned his head to the other side. "Hi," he said, making eye contact with me.

"Hi, Dad," I said. I walked over, closer to my father. I felt like he was approachable again.

His next bits of speech were fast and hard to decipher. His voice was garbled and scratchy, like someone talking with too much spit and a sore throat. The words and thoughts were overtaking each other, competing. He started asking about Marble, then Danny's kids, then cars—all completely arbitrary.

"John, can you count to ten for us?" Sarah asked, cutting his ramble short.

"One, two, three, four, five, six, seven, eight, nine, ten, eleven, twelve, thirteen, fourteen, fifteen, sixteen, seventeen—"

"Dad, we get the picture!" I said, laughing. "You can count, too!"

"If wishes were horses," Cheryl said. "What's the rest, John?"

"Beggars would ride," he said, his speech clipped.

My mother hugged him. His arms lay at his sides.

"A kiss," he said, looking up at her before he closed his eyes.

Sarah shooed us all back out to the waiting room so he could rest, and we happily shared the news with the visitors of the day.

Later that morning, Herman showed up. He carried the missing shoe and my father's tie. He had found them when he went back to see the car, which had been reduced to a crumpled mess in a junkyard. "The passenger seat had been smashed into the steering wheel," he told us. "They were one and the same."

He didn't understand how it all happened, and he couldn't explain. My mother didn't particularly want to talk about it with him. That day, we all focused on progress.

Over the next few days, our presence in the waiting room dwindled. My father's sisters and families had to go back to Columbus—back to their jobs and lives. They left in tears, still not having been lucky enough to hear him speak. Other friends and family alternated days, nights, and mornings. My mother, Gram, Pa, and I came every day. I made friends with the cafeteria checkout ladies, who came to recognize me and my chicken salad sandwiches. They started giving Pa and me a discount.

It had been a week since the accident, and everyone who visited hoped to have a conversation with my father, just to exchange a few words or listen to him mutter. It was rare. Mostly, he slept. My mom talked to him like he heard her but couldn't talk back—almost like she was leaving him long messages that he'd respond to later.

Spending time with him was painfully boring. I had little to say to him. I couldn't entertain the idea that I might not ever talk with him like I used to. If I had to tell him something, I wanted to at least be honest.

"Dad, this is pretty boring. You would be bored, too. Mom really misses you. This has been hard on her. So, come on."

I would pull up my chair to the side of his bed, prop my feet on his bedrail, and flip through a magazine I'd found in the waiting room. We existed in silence. Finally, his breath would get heavier, more nasal, and he'd start snoring.

"All right, Dad. I'm leaving … I'll see you soon. I love you."

I didn't kiss him, though. He was too unfamiliar.

On Monday, after almost a week in the trauma unit, he was scheduled to move to the sixth floor—the Intensive Care Unit—where he could be closely monitored while my mother worked with doctors and caseworkers to choose a rehabilitation facility for his recovery.

The morning of his move, my mother was anxious and rushed me out the door. She wanted to beat my grandparents to the hospital so she'd be there first, so no one else could make decisions about his care. Near the exit, a woman in a red convertible cut us off. She'd been taking up several lanes with her erratic driving. She took all our turns in front of us, and each one put my mother more on edge. I sat quietly in the passenger seat, carsick from the hard braking. With each turn, I watched my mother's anger escalate. We parked on the seventh floor of the parking garage, and I watched the red convertible barrel up a few more levels. I liked her car, and I wondered who she was.

"Janna, I was really going to kill that woman," my mother said, holding open the door to the staircase that would take us the back way to trauma.

"I could see that," I said. "I wonder who she is."

"I don't care," my mom said.

We were the first ones there that morning. My father was sitting up in a trauma chair. The fact that it was a chair was a very big deal. While my mother made final arrangements for his move, I stayed with him. The chair wasn't that different from his hospital bed. It looked like a bed someone had bent in half and propped him up in. He sat blankly and looked at me, his neck craned awkwardly to one side with a sheet pulled up to his chin. His feet stuck out the bottom in awkward directions.

My mother had bought him a pair of moccasin slippers. They were fleecy and warm, and they looked like the boat shoes that sat by the door at home, the ones he wore on the boat, in the garage, and to take the dog out. The moccasins, with their fleece, would help him stay warm. It was August.

He was starting to look gaunt and weary—eventually, doctors would use the term *emaciated*.

"Why does he look depressed?" I asked the nurse on duty. "He doesn't smile. He looks so sad."

"He's fine," she said.

"Hey, Dad," I said.

Nothing. No acknowledgement.

"You get to move today. It should be better."

"He's tired," the nurse said. "He probably won't want to talk to you."

My dad pulled his sheet up.

I spent the next hour trying to coax one word or smile out of him. He fell asleep. Pa came in to get me, because we were told he needed to rest so he could handle the move.

I wanted to say good-bye to our friends, the Tokashes. I told them we were moving to the ICU. Danny still hadn't opened his eyes. Yesterday had been his eighteenth birthday. Pa gave them a carving of bearded sailor he had made, smiling and holding a fish.

My mother's aunt and uncle came that day. Pa and Uncle Jim were co-conspirators. They were both World War II veterans and always competing to get the most laughs. Pa told jokes and riddles and made plays on words. Uncle Jim made funny noises, spooked people, and barked like a dog. He sounded exactly like a dog.

While they moved my father, we all went down to lunch. Pa and Uncle Jim played tricks on the staff and hid my candy bar from me as we waited in the long cashier line. We sat outside at a concrete table.

"Will you two quit?" Gram told them. "This is enough."

Uncle Jim barked.

"Now stop it," said Aunt Shorty. "We've had enough of you two."

"Janna, couldn't you have ordered something else?" my mother said to me. "No one wants to smell another one of those."

"Mom, it doesn't smell," I said. "It tastes really good. I like it."

"I wish you would've gotten something else."

"Yes, you've got to be sick of that stuff," said Gram. "You eat it twice a day."

"I really like it," I told them. "Why does it matter?"

Pa slid my Snickers bar to me under the table and winked.

When we came back, my father had been moved. The ICU waiting room felt foreign, and the patients on that floor were much noisier. They were seizing and talking and crying and yelling. The atmosphere felt volatile, like something bad was always on the verge of happening.

The six of us crowded into my father's room. He was awake, alert, and able to answer basic questions about himself, his family, and his pets.

We watched him struggle to lift a cup of ice water to his mouth. Expressionless, he concentrated on wrapping his fingers and palm around the plastic cup and pawing it to the edge of his bedside tray. Everyone watched like it was a show. His grip was weak but effective enough to lift the cup. Next he stretched his neck and puckered his lips, reaching out for the straw, which was swinging in the cup as his hand shook.

I walked over to him.

"No," my mother said.

"Why can't I just help him?"

"He has to learn for himself," said the nurse on duty.

We watched him struggle to lift the cup closer and try desperately to wrap his lips around the straw. At last, he bit the straw, took two slurpy sucks, and set it back down on the tray.

Next he fingered a damp green washcloth my mother had been laying across his forehead. His stiff, claw-liked fingers tugged at it. He couldn't fold it and put it back on his forehead the way everyone else could. He held it out in front of him, never moving his eyes from it, and flipped it around on his lap, eventually depositing it in a crumpled heap on his forehead, half hanging over his left eye. He looked ridiculous.

"Have to be there at 3:20," he said when no one was paying attention. "Have to be there, have to be there at 3:20." He repeated this one sentence over and over again. He started to lose his breath. The washcloth had slid off. "Have to be there at 3:20."

We asked him why—what he was talking about. Then we told him it was okay and that he didn't have to go. Pa even tried telling him he'd go for him, and it would be taken care of.

My dad must have said the sentence fifty times before the nurse asked everyone but my mother to leave.

I spent the afternoon in the new waiting room with no one to talk to. Aunt Shorty and Uncle Jim left. Then Gram and Pa left. It was past dinnertime, and I was hungry. Finally, my mother decided it was time to go home, but we could first stop downstairs for something to eat.

"Will you be mad at me if I—"

"No, Janna; it's fine," she said. "Just get what you want."

We sat outside. She drank coffee and picked at half a sandwich. She never ate real meals anymore. She also never slept. The pockets of skin under her eyes were sagging, and I'd noticed she'd stopped wearing her contacts and started wearing her wire-rimmed glasses instead. Her clothes were baggy, and I could see where her beige nail polish was chipping. I'd never seen my mother with chipped nails before.

A woman walked over to say hello to us. There was no one else sitting outside. I looked at my mother to gauge her reaction. I wanted to see if she noticed that it was the woman from the red convertible. The three of chatted for a while. We didn't ask her why she was at the hospital.

"Did you know who that was?" I asked when she finally walked away.

"Yeah. Pretty weird, huh?"

"Yeah, very."

That night, on the way home, my mother told me that my father had eleven broken ribs. She'd discovered them when she rolled him over to wash him off with the washcloth after everyone had left.

"The whole right side of his body is black and purple. When I asked the nurse what had happened, she told me he had eleven broken ribs."

"How many ribs do people have?" I asked.

"I don't know—twelve or thirteen. That made me pretty mad. No one told us he had anything more than a head injury. We have to be really careful with him."

"Do you think it hurts him?"

"Yes, I'm sure it does."

"Am I going with you to help him move to Squirrel Hill tomorrow?"

"No, you can stay with Suhries. I talked to Vicky. You don't need to come."

I was relieved. I wanted to help my mother, but I didn't want to see any more nurses or doctors. I didn't want to meet my dad's new physical therapist and see him in another new room. Most of all, I didn't want to watch people I didn't know move my father around like a limp puppet and watch my mother give orders and subsist on coffee.

"Do you care if I go on the boat with them?"

"No, you can."

"Mom," I said. "I love you."

"I love you, too, very much."

"I'm sorry."

She put her hand on my thigh and turned on the radio to catch the end of *All Things Considered*.

take me back

MY PARENTS MET EACH OTHER WHEN they were eight years old, the day my father's Boys Scout troop took a field trip to the Eckman's famously haunted house. Gram Mary and my mother served the boys cookies in the kitchen. At least this is exactly how Gram Mary had told me the story, and old photos and facts match it up seamlessly.

Thirteen years later, my parents both married their high school sweethearts. The first time I heard about this, I freaked out. Divorce was supposed to be evil and sad, and I couldn't comprehend how my parents could have loved someone else. Even more frightening was the idea that I might have to meet my new half brothers and sisters.

I didn't have any—only my mom's nieces from her first marriage. By that time, I already worshipped the model-gorgeous, twenty-something Dee Dee and her hip little sister, Jenny. They both had platinum blonde hair, funky eighties style, boyfriends, and a mom, Jan, who was cool as shit. Jan was one of my mom's best friends—who was also her ex-sister in law, who was also divorced, and after that much deviation, I didn't really care about the Mattocks family tree anymore.

When I was invited to Dee Dee's bachelorette party, my very first, I felt cool as shit, too. I was fourteen, and the place was littered with penises—penis straws, penis cupcakes, penis pens, penis napkins, penis plates, all sprinkled with penis confetti. Being around my mother and all the penises at the same time made me feel embarrassed and out of place, but when Jan and I accidentally lit our entire penis tablecloth on fire with the penis candle, I felt like I fit in.

A few weeks later, at Dee Dee's wedding reception, a man came up to me when I was ordering a shirley temple at the open bar. He was tall, older, and objectively very handsome.

"Hello there," he said.

"Hi," I said. I was wearing heels as high as I was allowed and a short dress and felt very much like someone who fit in.

"Wow, you look just as beautiful as your mother. Just like her."

"Oh … thank you."

"That's how I knew it was you. I'm Mick."

This was Mick, the banker guy who my mother divorced because he liked to fish.

"We just didn't have enough things in common," she would say. "He really liked to fish, and you know how I feel about fishing."

He stuck out his hand, and I took it. Instantaneously nervous and caught extremely off guard, I shook with more force than a girl probably should have. But I didn't want to have a limp handshake, because my father taught me never to have a limp handshake.

Mick was there with his family, a wife and a boy my age. When I saw them sitting at their table, all I could think about was how much more beautiful my mother was than his wife, who was not nearly as slender, polished, or poised. I didn't like her outfit. And then, there was my father, at my table. I'd never be meeting his ex-wife. She supposedly lived in Mexico with a giant sum of cash from drugs left by her third or fourth late husband.

"I never loved her like I love your mother," my dad would say. "There is no one like your mother. I'd say you're pretty close." And then he would smile and wink.

MOST KIDS HAVE IDEALISTIC VIEWS of their parents. You can't yet see them as human beings, as people with the ability to make bad choices and good choices, so it is possible that I have warped these stories about my parents into the way I want to remember them. I may have embellished the stories to make them more entertaining. Or maybe that is exactly how they had been told to me in the first place by the people from that life. Either way, I can't take credit for crafting their narratives, because they are not from my life. These stories are from my parents' life, the one they had before I came along.

I was curious as a kid, always asking tons of questions about everything, including my parents. When I was old enough to care, they showed me the dozens of photo albums from before I was born and when I wasn't old enough to remember. I was entranced by these, hundreds of pictures of people I knew but who looked very different. Over the years, my parents, Gram and Pa, Gram Mary, my aunts, and my parents' friends have indulged my curiosity by telling me their stories. Some of them match the photos, and others are only memories.

Both of my parents were born in 1950, and they both grew up in Mercer County, Pennsylvania, the same place I grew up. My dad was the city boy in blue-collar Hermitage, the town just shy of the Ohio border. He played baseball in the streets, hung out in the park, and fixed cars with Pa. My mother grew up in Mercer, a farm town. She rode horses with her girlfriends, helped take care of dozens of animals, and spent hours at Westminster University, where her dad was a psychology professor.

My dad was born on March 10, 1950, to Jack and Margaret Leyde. He had two different colored eyes (green and brown) and ears that stuck out from his head. He did not utter a word until he was four. "Jack Jill up down fell down broke crown after all."

After that, he was loquacious, like me, and a voracious reader. Nana, his grandmother, taught him about proper manners, English poetry, and how to be polite, respectful, and nice to girls and his little sisters. He was bright, one point shy of what I knew to be gifted, according to the same IQ test I took in third grade, where I got the same exact score. But schoolwork was neither fun nor challenging, so he simply did exactly what he needed to get by. Adults liked him (the manners), and he had tons of friends (the talking).

On weekends, Gram and Pa taught my dad and aunts how to waterski out on the Shenango Reservoir, first on two skis, and as soon as they could, on one ski. My dad skied from May until it got too cold in September. He was devoted and became an excellent slalom skier, cutting sharp turns around all twenty-two buoys, dipping parallel to the water to skim his elbow over it. He skied the way I wish I could ski.

Gram and Pa threw parties on Saturday nights, either when my father and my aunts were in bed upstairs or when they were out with their friends. They'd pull out the folding card tables and chairs that Gram stored in the dining room under a trough of fake plants and set them up in the basement. Friends and neighbors came over to play cards, smoke cigarettes, and listen to music. Gram and Pa made cocktails, and the bar was littered with jiggers, tumblers, ice buckets, and swizzle sticks. As a kid, I loved the swizzle sticks that Gram kept in the ice bucket under the bar. I'd always ask her if I could get one to stir my chocolate milk. I'd go downstairs and make an ordeal of choosing between plastic sticks topped with monkeys, wedges of fruit, palm trees (which Gram hated), flamingos, stars, words, road signs, guitars, flags, Christmas trees... There were so many of them, I could make up games based on swizzle sticks.

On Sundays, the Leydes always went to church. My dad was an altar boy, and my aunts sang in the choir. Gram found her peace, and Pa socialized with all their friends.

When my dad was old enough, Pa brought him to Leyde Automotive, the family shop that they kept in business until I was about eight. He started to work there when he was fourteen, memorizing car parts, helping customers, and tinkering with transmissions, fan belts, brake pads, axels, pistons, and radios. He also started smoking pot, and he and his high school buddies discovered 3-2 beer—3.2% alcohol content and available to any eighteen-year-old willing to drive twelve miles to the Ohio border.

When my dad was in tenth grade, Gram was institutionalized at the psych ward at Warren State Hospital in Pennsylvania for severe depression. She was being treated with electroshock therapy. My father refused to visit her, perhaps because Warren State was a terrifying place.

I remember the first time I heard about this. It was significantly more shocking than any familial history that I had heard. I was well past my teens, and the fact that maybe Gram and Pa drank too much or that my dad was a sweetheart of a badass was palpable, but shock therapy (inducing seizures to numb emotions) was a bit too Hitchcock for my taste. Once my best friend and I visited an abandoned hospital in Athens, Ohio. She was in med school at Ohio University. We stood outside, peering in through ghostly windows at what used to be the psych ward, and I told her the story of Warren State.

It was 1965, so Pa promised to buy my dad a pony car—a first edition Ford Mustang—if he would visit. This was one of my dad's dream cars, so he went with the rest of his family to Warren State. Only once. A few weeks later, after his sixteenth birthday, he crashed the red Mustang. Around the same time, my mom was driving a burgundy red Fiat Spider. She got a speeding ticket.

"That was a nice car," my mom said. "It could fly, a little too fun to drive, so we traded it in, and the son of the dealership took it and totaled it two days later."

When Gram eventually returned home, no one talked about her therapy, and everything shifted back to normal. Pa worked at the shop. My aunts excelled in school, dated steady boyfriends, and traveled to Romania to sing in the church choir. Gram cooked dinners, played bridge, and hosted parties on the weekends.

My dad worked at the shop to earn enough money to buy himself an MG Midget. He was sixteen, five foot ten, lean and limber, and his curly brown hair was starting to thin at the crown. He compensated by growing a mustache like Lennon's. He kept this same mustache forever. In the nineties, it was hard for me to imagine a balding sixteen-year-old with a mustache having friends and girlfriend. Apparently, my dad was pretty cool. He was witty and popular, with good taste in music, the start of the records he raised me on—Beatles, Stones, Cream, Buffalo Springfield, The Doors, The Who, and Simon and Garfunkel. And by the time he was a senior, he had been dating Sherry, the tall, blonde Homecoming Queen who graduated Valedictorian. Aunt Biz calls her a "walking dictionary."

College, like high school, was not a challenge, but Youngstown State was not a challenging school. My understanding was that dodging the draft was my dad's main motivation, as he was liberal, against being in Vietnam, and did not want to fight in a war. Pa had fought in a war in a different time. Pa's stories are filled with U-boats, New York City subways, Navy parties, and making jokes with the nurses who took care of them. My father's friends were crippling and dying.

At YSU, my dad breezed through a poli-sci major, dating Sherry, smoking pot, drinking beer, reading novels and poetry, listening to records, and driving his car too fast with all his buddies. His newest was Wayne, who had a motorcycle, a golden retriever named Molly, and strict rules about dogs. Dogs must be goldens, must be girls, and must have a name that begins with *M*.

My dad and Sherry had two dogs—bassett hounds with ridiculous names. As a kid, I tried to memorize them as if they were difficult spelling words—Ignacious Melrose Smith (Natz) and Mona May Jones (Mona). I named one of my stuffed dogs, a beagle, Mona.

My dad worked with Pa at the shop, and Sherry taught German. They got married in 1971, and my father thought about going back to school to get his master's in social work. When the dogs died a few years later, they got two golden retrievers, two girls, both named with an *M* (Mava and Myra), both in accordance to the rule about dogs. Over the years, I've re-chosen the *M* name for my future golden, because other people have taken them one by one, and I've yet to get a golden of my own.

Three years later, my father was halfway through his master's, and he started working at Mercer Association for the Retarded (MCAR). He was a department supervisor. He liked his job and the people he worked with. He was good at it. Sherry wanted to move to California.

MY MOTHER WAS BORN ON January 3, 1950, to Claude and Marie Eckman. She was very blonde and blue-eyed, and her first word was, not surprisingly, *horse.*

When my mom was four, Gram Mary and Claude moved from faculty housing at Westminster to a brick house that sat on forty acres of land with a pond and a barn. They had two girls and a restoration project to fix up and fill with antiques. Gram Mary and my mother have always had a keen sense of interior decoration and design.

My mother was quiet and well-behaved, the result of a strict German upbringing, where kids could only speak when spoken to. Gram Mary did not give a lot of hugs, which never made any sense to me, because she hugged me all the time. But she made dresses for my mom and Aunt Pamela. There were chests of dresses, all kinds, like swizzle sticks. As a kid, I had my favorites, and I begged to wear them to school, because I loved dresses so much. Looking back, I am glad that I'd been told no, seeing as I would have looked outdated and overdressed.

My mother's favorite thing to do was to be outside with the animals, helping her dad. She loved them—horses, rabbits, stray dogs, barn cats—but she hated the chickens. The chicken stories, of collecting the eggs, sounded like nightmares. The chicken coop under the apple tree was full of poop and dirty feathers flying everywhere, and the nasty chickens squawked and pecked at her. My mother hates chickens, because they are mean. By the time she got her first horse, Gram Mary was storing garden tools in the chicken coop.

Star was my mom's first pony. He sounded just like anyone's first pony should be, cute with a white patch on the bridge of his nose. My first pony was more like a chicken. My mom rode Star every day. She fed him, brushed him, cleaned his stalls, and made sure he came in at night and ran around the pasture during the day. When my mom was ten, she got her first horse, Capers, a dapple-gray Arabian—another horse that sounded like he should be in a storybook, along with her chest in the barn full of as many blue ribbons (equitation and dressage) as there were dresses and swizzle sticks.

My mother was disciplined in ways I never could be. She got good grades and blue ribbons, and she still made time for trail rides with her girlfriends, watching basketball games, and dating. She went to the same high school as I did; we even had one or two of the same teachers. It is funny to think that we existed in the same space—Mercer Junior Senior High School—I, gregarious with curly brown hair and a tendancy for getting a little too bored in class, and my mother, with her pin-straight, platinum-blonde hair and blue eyes, who never got in trouble for talking. She dated Mick, a quiet, good-looking boy. He asked her to be official on New Year's Eve of 1964, three days before her fifteenth birthday. They went to basketball games to watch Mick's cousin and the other Mustangs win back-to-back state championships.

After graduation, my mom followed her aunts, uncles, and cousins to Wittenberg University, a private liberal arts school in the middle of Ohio, where she majored in Sociology. She kept riding horses, getting good grades, and dating Mick.

When my mother was a sophomore, Claude was diagnosed with a malignant melanoma—"too much being out in the sun on the farm when he was a kid," my mother would remind me if I whined about sunscreen.

My mom transferred from Wittenberg to Westminster, a similar school where she pledged Chi Omega and lived closer to home to help her family. Mick worked at a local bank, a job burning the unused money, to get himself through school. He helped the Eckmans as much as he could, and Claude paid for his last semester at Cleveland State. On Christmas Eve of 1970, Mick gave my mom a big, beautifully wrapped box, and she unwrapped it to find another wrapped box, and another. When she tells the story, I imagine this slightly annoying her. Five boxes and one diamond ring later, he proposed. They got married after college, before her father got too sick, and she wore Gram Mary's dress.

Mick and my mom moved into a small apartment in Mercer, looked for jobs that would help them pay off school debt, and helped her parents with projects, like gardening and refurnishing antiques for their aparment. Claude got very sick. The cancer took over, reducing him to a wheelchair, and he lost both of his legs. Hearing this story, about a man I never met was as unsettling as Gram's shock therapy. My mother always says that he would have loved me, but maybe that is what she is just supposed to say, because there really is no way to know. He died two years later. Mom had just turned twenty-four.

She and Mick bought a house in Mercer that needed a lot of work but would be fun to fix up. She started taking classes for a master's degree in social work and had a job working at MCAR as a department supervisor, while Mick was busy working at the bank and studying to take his CPA exam. Sometimes they went to visit Mick's family, who had a house on the Chesapeake Bay, but mostly they both worked a lot. My mom became best friends with Mick's brother's wife, Jan, and Jan's daughter from her previous marriage, Dee Dee, spent a lot of time with my mom. She loved Dee Dee and Jan, but life wasn't all that fun with Mick. It wasn't terrible or dramatic, just not that fun.

"I had a realization," my mother once told me, maybe because I was finally old enough for things not to be about fish anymore. "The reason I got divorced was because my life was boring, and Mick was very content with that. It was not fishing, Janna. It was boring. Nice guy, but boring. And your dad was not boring!"

The day I learned that my fear-of-being-bored gene was not only from my super-talkative and mildy hyper father, but also from my disciplined and rational mother, was like finding a piece of sanity. Coming from both sides, it made so much more sense. Nice guys, rich guys, accountants, builders, engineers, animal lovers, good-looking, smart, funny, talented—it didn't matter, because there was not a shot in hell if I was bored.

MY MOM AND DAD WERE department supervisors together at MCAR. They were in different departments but were involved in many of the same meetings and projects. My dad was more confident and fun than most people, which caught my mother's attention. And she was smarter than most. He likes smart women who are beautiful. They always told me that they had fun working together.

In 1977, my mother filed for divorce and moved in with Gram Mary. She rode her horse, managed things at MCAR, and finished her degree. My dad left Sherry, who fought him about it. He took Myra and moved in with Ed Yewell, a friend who had returned from flying fighter jets in Vietnam. Ed lived in an old farmhouse that had been vacant since his days at Grove City College and was flying ultra lights for kicks. Wayne came over a lot with Molly, and the three of them relished in reliving their youth—at least, that is how the stories tell it.

"The place was a dump," my mother said.

"A dirty old farmhouse with bad plumbing," Aunt Biz said.

"Ed's girlfriend and I used to come over and clean," my mother said.

My mom's divorce was final the following February, but Sherry was still fighting for my father. My aunts say that he was the first thing she ever lost, and Sherry didn't lose. In April, my dad told my mom to pack her bags, and he surprised her with a week in Aruba, where everything had been taken care of and planned out. I think it was the only surprise she has ever enjoyed, maybe even her favorite vacation.

That summer, my mom rented a house on Lake Latonka. It was very small but lakefront, along with all the other newly-built log cabins and doublewides that Pittsburghers called summer homes. My dad bought a boat and taught her to ski—on two. Everyone hung out at the lake—the boys from the farmhouse, the dogs, and his sisters. I'd like to think of these times as everyone being tan and eating grilled steaks and pasta salads, the women drinking Chardonnay and the men drinking Rolling Rocks and probably smoking pot while they grilled the steaks. That summer, when Sherry signed the papers and moved to California, my dad invited Gram and Pa to the lake for the first time.

My dad told me that he had wanted to marry my mom for months, almost as soon as he met her. He was lucky to have someone like her love him. But he had been too worried about respect—marrying my mom so quickly would be disrespectful to Sherry and their marriage. Sometimes I think strange things matter to my father, like Christmases in Columbus, making sure we have my mother's approval, fish, naming things, and memorizing poems.

My parents started looking at a house, because the lakefront house was too small for two. She loved him, and she wanted to spend time with him, so she gave him an ultimatum. This seemed to be what women in the '70s did if they really wanted to be with a guy, and it always seemed to work.

"I told your dad that I would not take out a mortage with someone that I wasn't married to," she told me. "I loved him, but I wasn't doing that."

My dad called Aunt Biz and Aunt Jeannie, both nurses in Columbus, to see when they could come home next. He asked my mom what kind of ring she wanted, and he bought two thick gold bands.

On October 14, 1978, my dad wore brown tweed and trimmed his curly hair and mustache. My mom parted her short, thick, strawberry-blonde hair to the side and wore an off-white suit.

"You wore a wedding suit?" I asked. "Why didn't you wear Gram Mary's dress? Why would you wear a suit to get married?"

"It was a small wedding, and it was a very nice suit," she said. "I'll show it to you."

The wedding suit lives right beside Gram Mary's dress. It is a sleeveless off-white chiffon dress with a knee-length skirt, billowy and pleated in thousands of narrow pleats. There is a blazer to match.

My parents got married in the Presbyterian church in Mercer, the one with the red door right across the street from the courthouse. All my aunts were there with Gram, Pa, and Gram Mary. Jan stood on my mom's side and Wayne on my dad's. Their new friends from MCAR, Fred and Carolyn Gallo, came. Gram Mary had all their close friends and family over for a small reception. In the pictures, my parents look like they are having a great time, a blast. They don't look like they are at a wedding. My dad's arm is around my mom's shoulder, and both of them are smiling a lot.

They spent a week in the Bahamas, because my dad had won a trip there. And in November, the week they were going to move in, Ed flew his ultra light too low over some trees, and it caught fire. I could never understand how trees catch a plane on fire, but that is apparently what happened. Gram and Pa, Gram Mary, and my aunts ended up moving my parents' stuff into the log cabin on Delaware Trail, two streets up from the lake on the dirt road, so that my parents could go to Ed's funeral. Whether it was the fire or the impact, no one knows what killed Ed. And everyone was so sad that no one will talk about it.

"That is when we saw how many shoes your mother had," Aunt Biz says. "Wow."

My mom did have a lot of shoes, lots and lots of heels. I played with them, lining them up in the same fashion I lined up my My Little Ponies—red ones, gray with bows, cream colored peep-toes, patent leather ones, browns, blues, navys.

My mom taught my dad how to ride, and they took care of the horses and helped Gram Mary with yard work and housework. They built an addition off the side of the house—a bigger kitchen with picture windows and cathedral ceilings—with the help of Pat and Bill Rieg, their new neighbors. Bill was a retired Pittsburgh police officer and knew how to build houses. They babysat Dee Dee, went out to eat with Fred and Carolyn a lot, and took trips to California to visit my mom's cousin, Jayne, and her husband, Paul, in San Francisco.

I remember once, they left without me. I was nine. My mom packed up an old, hard, blue suitcase for me and took me to Gram Mary's for the week. I was so angry that I couldn't see California with them that I sat on my suitcase in the middle of the hallway after they left for so long that Gram Mary convinced me if I didn't move, I'd freeze, and my butt would be stuck to a blue suitcase for the rest of my life. It was very unfair, because they had made flying into LA, driving up the Pacific Coast Highway, spending the night by the ocean (in places like Laguna and Carmel), and then waking up the next day to drive up to Jayne and Paul's sound so fun. They also left me out of all the fun they had at Jimmy Buffett concerts.

My dad bought a Nikon. He took it everywhere with him and took pictures of everything—vacations, holiday parties with their families, on the boat out on the water, on trail rides. He took pictures of Myra, the horses, his friends, stuff out in nature. Sometimes his friends even paid him to take pictures at weddings. He was pretty good with it. He took endless pictures of my mom, who is not a fan of having her picture taken. I, unfortunately, was never given a choice growing up with the Nikon in my face from day one.

My parents both got better jobs. My mom worked at Gateways for Better Living in Youngstown with retarded (because that was the PC term back then) adults and children. People she worked with still remember her in places like grocery stores to this day. My father sold insurance for Grey Rock, which will forever be known as his highest-paying job.

In the winter of 1980, Myra died from cancer, and my mom thought they should get another dog. My dad, so the story goes, thought they'd be good parents. Strange, seeing as neither my mother or father had ever wanted kids. He convinced my mother that they'd have fun with a daughter. And he didn't want her to have a nickname—no Katharine to Katie, no Anne to Annie. He never liked being called Johnny.

"I wanted to name you Jillian," my mother had told me one day on the way home from work after we'd stopped for milk and two Snickers bars. "But Jillian Leyde has too many *L*s."

"Yuck!" I said. "Why Jillian?"

"I like that name."

"Jillian is your favorite name?"

"Janna is my favorite name."

"Why did you name me Janna?"

I was named after my mom's friend in Florida, Jana, with one *N*. But too many people pronounced her name with a long *A* rather than the way that rhymed with banana or cabana. She told my mom to give me two *N*s so people would say it right.

So my parents started trying to have a kid, and two miscarriages later, they were anticipating a June 15 due date. My mother admittedly hated being pregnant. She was sick every day, uncomfortable, and everyone told her she was having a boy. She didn't want a boy. One day, in her ninth month, Danny, the Riegs' oldest kid, found her sitting down in the living room, sobbing by herself.

"Claudia—" he said.

"I hate this," she said. "This baby just won't—"

"Claudia, do you wa—"

"I can't be pregnant anymore!" She kept crying and yelling. "Why is this baby so late? I can't do this anymore! I can't move. I don't feel good. I hate this baby."

"Do you want me to go get my mom?"

"Yes, that would be a good idea."

"Okay. I will. Are you in labor?"

"Noooooo!"

Sixteen days later, my parents still had not picked out a name for a boy. They told me they would have defaulted to choosing John. On a Monday morning, in the summer of 1982, my dad drove my mom to the hospital in Greenville, twelve miles away, in his beat-up, tan Ford pickup. At the hospital, my father called everyone, because I was the first grandkid, niece, or nephew on all sides. Meanwhile, my mother spent the day trying not to have a baby in the hallway. That summer, the hospital was renovating the maternity ward, and because her baby was not planned to be born on June 28, she had to wait in line. I can only imagine how unhappy and furious she was—the heat, the lack of organization, and her late kid.

At 7:20 p.m., my mom had a healthy baby—seven pounds, fourteen ounces, and twenty-one inches.

"It's a little boy," the doctor said, holding me up. "A little boy without a penis!"

changin' channels

THE FOLDS OF THE PILLOWCASE PRESSED into my cheeks. I didn't want to get up. I wanted to lie there forever, listening to the whir of the mower outside and breathing in the smell of freshly chopped grass wet with morning dew clinging in soupy green chunks to the mower deck. I'd gotten in trouble before for running through damp grass in my bare feet and straight into the house—or worse, dragging the green flecks onto the boat. I lay there, replaying the memories of getting in trouble like I was watching a movie.

A tiny prick pierced the skin of my forearm and sunk in deeper, splicing a crevice into my flesh.

"Youch!"

I flipped over, swung my unscathed arm around, and grabbed Marble's fluffy belly. She hung limp in my hand for a second before squirming to be released from my grip.

"You," I said, looking her in the face and dangling her over the side of my bed, "are a little jerk."

Thud. She hit the floor without a bit of feline grace. I sat up to inspect my arm. I never understood what people meant—or if they were even serious—about cat-scratch fever. This must have been the eighty-nine millionth scratch I'd gotten. It stung, but I'd forget about it in minutes.

I closed my eyes and lay back down while she paced the foot of my bed. She made two failed attempts to jump up before creeping toward my face and settling above my head in a little ball. I reached above my head to scratch her ears. She had missed us. She had been pissed.

"Well, kitty, we've got to get up and face this day," I said, cradling her angry, wriggling body to my chest as I hopped down from my bed.

The house was empty. Marble ran off to the kitchen, and I went to the bathroom. I examined my face in the mirror. I looked tired. It was dented and scarred, with red welts across my cheeks. I took my time brushing my teeth, letting the toothbrush hang from my mouth and drip globs of white, pasty drool on the counter as I poked through my father's shaving kit. He kept all its little tools on the third shelf of the cherry cabinet hanging to the right of the mirror. I pulled them out and set them in a neat row on the counter. I ran his shaving brush over the sleep marks on my cheeks. He told me once it was made from the hair of a badger. It wasn't damp this morning. It was brittle and dry.

I put my toothbrush back in the drawer, put the kit back together, and wiped every corner of the counter and sink. I straightened the towels and rinsed the dried white toothpaste off the cup. It was my bathroom and my father's, but we kept it clean for guests and for my mother.

The answering machine in the hallway beeped. I played the one message left at 8:12 a.m.

"Good morning, Janna Marie," said Vicky's voice. "Come over when you wake up. We'll have breakfast, pack up, and go. It's supposed to be sunny today. Love you!"

It was a little after 9:00. I hadn't seen the water in more than a week. I hoped Vicky would have frozen chocolate chip cookies for us. She used extra flour and lots of chocolate chips, and we'd gnaw on them when they were hard as rocks. I wanted one for breakfast, but she would inevitably make me eat cereal and drink all the milk in the bowl. I hated milk that wasn't chocolate. I hated being forced to eat things I hated. She made me eat tomatoes, too, and take vitamins. I wished I could lie and say I'd already eaten, but she'd know.

I rummaged through the bottom drawer of my dresser for my white bathing suit. I had only worn it a few times that summer. My mother had bought it for me at Fashion Bug a few weeks ago.

"You know you do not need another suit, Janna," she said when I brought it over to her.

"Yeah, but Mom, but I like this one," I said. "It's all white—and look at this pattern. I don't have a white one, and that other one we bought from here is getting too tight. This one is *different*. I'll wear it when we go to Clarion on Saturday. I can ski in it."

"You really like it, huh?" she asked, adding it to the pile of junior's summer tops and shorts that was growing in the crook of her elbow. "And you'll wear it?"

"Yes."

"Well, it is a nice suit."

"Thanks, Mom! I need this one."

"I think you mean *want*, Janna."

It looked nice with my tan. The white straps crossed at my shoulder blades, and it dipped low in the back. To the touch, the raised pattern felt funny, like a quilt. I was happy my mom had bought it for me. It had been perfect for our day on the Clarion River.

"Janna Marie, that's a nice suit," my dad said the morning we were getting ready to leave.

I was balancing, my toes wrapped around the trailer hitch of our Explorer, trying not to fall as I stretched up to pound in the last two snaps to cover the boat.

"Thanks, Dad."

He hopped up on the wheel of the trailer to scale the side of the boat, and I watched him put them in place with one pound of his palm on each one.

"Why is that so easy for you?"

"I have the right angle. You're climbing all over the truck, ya ninny."

"I tried it your way, but I couldn't get them in."

"Snaps are tough. You got most of them. Are you ready to go? Let's go help your mom bring stuff out."

"Okay, but I didn't get them all."

My dad put his arm around me, and we walked to the house.

"White, huh? Did your mom get it for you? She has good taste."

"Yeah, she did. I do, too."

"I'm lucky to have such beautiful girls."

I put it on and sat down sat cross-legged in front of my dresser, piling up my bathing suits on the floor and replaying the last time I'd gone skiing with my dad like another old movie scene.

We'd packed up two boats—me, my mom and dad, the Suhries, my friend, Vanessa, and her sister—for a day on the Clarion River. In the early hours, the water was glass, so we hooked up two ropes to the Suhries' boat, and my dad and I slalomed side by side, him yelling over at me to "jump the wake!" We tubed, skied, kneeboarded, putted around, anchored, swam, and ate all day long. Vanessa and her sister had said my new suit was cool.

I wished I'd tried to jump the wake. I took off the white suit and shoved it back in the drawer, trading it for a blue and white two-piece. It was my first bikini, and it looked more like a plaid bra and underwear set from Laura Ashley. Staring at myself in the mirror, all I could see was the strawberry patch birthmark on my stomach, as big as a thumbprint. If I sucked in my stomach, the malformation disappeared under the shadow of my rib cage. My birthmark was ugly, and I'd only worn this once on vacation with my aunt and uncle when there were no boys around.

Today, there would be no boys on the lake. Zac and Ryan were at two-a-days, the beginnings of football season, so they wouldn't see me and my birthmark as they zoomed around on their WaveRunners. I tugged on a pair of Levi's Silver Tab cut-offs and put on the Steely Dan T-shirt. The T-shirt fit a like a dress, a good cover-up. My head could fit through the sleeve it was so big.

I filled a tiny cooler with five Faygos—two orange, one red, and two grape. They were all I could find in our empty kitchen. I locked all the doors and put Meagan in the garage. I hooked the house key around the belt loop of my shorts and sprinted down the driveway and across the street, slowing down when I got to Vicky's garden path, where I placed one foot in front of the other, rock upon rock, until I reached the front porch, where I took all four steps in one leap and scared their cat, Jack, from his perch on the railing.

"Hi, guys," I said as I shoved open the door.

"Jannnnaaaa!" three voices greeted me.

"We've missed you," said Nicole, the oldest of the Suhrie kids. Nicole, with brown eyes and brown hair like her mother, was born the same month I turned three. We were close. I wanted a sister. She wanted a best friend. Our relationship was a compromise between the two.

"How's John?" asked Lisa.

Lisa, with pin-straight, sandy blonde hair and sea-green eyes, was the youngest at eight years old. She still had a round face and chubbier cheeks than her brother and sister. I handed her the cooler, and she lifted it with both hands, as if it weighed too much.

"Is he still in the hospital?"

"No, Lis!" Steven said, interrupting her. "He's moving to rehab today with Claudia."

Steven, the boy, was the middle child. He grabbed the cooler from his sister with one hand and led me over the counter with the other, where I hopped on a bar chair and started eating grapes.

"Janna Marie!" Vicky said, swatting my hand away and pushing a bowl full of cereal toward me. "Those are for the boat. Eat some breakfast."

Nicole, Steven, and Lisa had already finished theirs, evidenced by the half-empty bowls and warm puddles of milk on the counter.

"Can—*may* I have more sugar on this, please?" The Cheerios tasted like bits of drowning cardboard.

"No," Vicky said. When she turned away to wash dishes, Steven dumped a scoop into my bowl.

By the time we got the skis, gear, food, towels, and everyone on the boat and then got the boat into the water, it was nearly eleven. Lake Latonka was crowded, and it was too choppy for good skiing. I regained some of my tan, made a sad attempt at the slalom course, ate an entire bag of Nacho Cheese Doritos, and forgot about my life until the sun went down.

When I got home, my mom was on the front porch, curled up on our wooden front porch chairs with the seats woven thick like baskets, wearing a pair of emerald green scrubs and drinking a cup of coffee.

"How is he?" I asked.

"He's very tired."

"But he's okay?"

"Yes, I think so."

I sat down in the chair next to hers. We said nothing and just watched fireflies in the front yard. Vicky came over, and I stayed up for awhile, sitting on the porch with them, listening to them talk. When I got too tired, I went to the bathroom, pulled off my suit from under the T-shirt, rinsed it in the sink, and hung it on the back porch. I brushed my teeth and crawled in my bed in just the T-shirt. My skin was hot, and my hair soaked the sheets in lake water.

"TIME TO GET UP," MY mom said. "Let's go."

She came into my room, rattling off morning instructions and smelling like Clinique Aromatics Elixir. That morning, I took an exceptionally long time to get ready—redoing my hot rollers twice and trying different kinds of bronzer, stalling.

"Janna!" she yelled. "What are you doing? Let's go! The bus is leaving."

The drive to the Rehabilitation Institute of Squirrel Hill felt twice as long as going to AGH. We had to wind around the city, passing the stadiums and the mirrored building that looked like a castle and riding over bridges and through the tunnels on the south end. She told me about the shopping, nice restaurants, and neat shops in Shadyside, which was very near Squirrel Hill.

"We can go walk around Shadyside on the way home today," she said once we were on the other side of the Squirrel Hill Tunnel.

"Okay," I said.

"Or get dinner there."

"Sure." I was carsick.

The rehab building was underwhelming, a brick complex that stretched from one end of the parking lot to the other. Vans took up most of the parking spaces near the entrance. All the vans were colored the same, as if they belonged here and nowhere else.

"Are you coming?" my mom asked, reaching a hand back, either to grab for mine or to motion me forward.

I trotted up behind her. Inside, it was stale, white walls and floors made of gray tile. There was no one there to greet us, but my mother managed to lead us down a few halls, past patients and medical-looking people, to my father's room, where he was sitting up in a chair—not a real chair. It was a chair similar to that of the hybrid bed-chair from AGH but with fewer apparatuses. Someone had dressed him in a forest green Champion T-shirt and tucked it into dark green sweatpants. The greens didn't match. I'd never seen him in such an outfit. His sweatpants were pushed up past his ankles, and I wondered if he had done that himself. It was summer and hot outside.

His head bobbled as he looked our way. His mustache was taking over his thinning face. I looked at him without saying anything. I didn't want to be there. I wanted the three of us to go back home. I stood, staring at my father, struggling for words, but I was empty. For the first time, the acute thought occurred to me: *I want this to be over.*

At the head of his bed, there was a mesh canopy of sorts gathered around a wire. I couldn't make sense of the need for it, and I assumed it was for some other ailment that my father didn't have. All these beds must be the same with their canopies and buttons and levers, all raised high off the floor on what looked like shocks. Perhaps if someone needed to move it rapidly, the bed was designed to keep its passenger from bumping around, from hurting his brain and spine more than he already had to get here in the first place. I locked myself in a daydream in which my dad was whizzing down a bumpy sidewalk in this bed. He slept like a baby while the shocks took all the bumps for him. *Genius.*

"Janna, what are you doing?" my mother asked, coming out of the bathroom. My dad had his own bathroom now, huge, bland, drab, and sterile like the rest of the 300 square feet attached to the nameplate near the door that had been written in sloppy Sharpie. He had a window, too, looking out onto nothing—just grass. It needed to be cut.

"Nothing," I said, staring outside, away from the room and my father.

"Come talk to him while I go see if he can go outside for a walk with us."

"Where?"

He was watching us talk, looking dumbfounded. His expression seemed to say, *Stop speaking in a foreign language.*

"Outside. I'm going to see if we can take him for a walk."

"Oh. Does he want to go?"

"It will be good for him. He needs some fresh air."

"Mom, may I have a ginger ale?"

"Sure. What do you want to eat, though?" my mom asked, putting down the menu.

"Pancakes, I guess. What are you getting?"

"I don't know."

Pamela's Diner was famous for pancakes, and I was starving. We'd spent the last two hours walking up and down Walnut Street in Shadyside, twenty-five minutes of which was spent in a little shop that sold cards.

"Isn't this place neat?" my mother had asked.

I busied myself reading books and quotes on magnets and checking out the stuffed animal collection while she picked out cards for birthdays and thanks-yous, and ones with horses on them, just because she liked the horses.

I loved Shadyside. On Walnut Street, the main drag, there was a Banana Republic, a Talbots, a Victoria's Secret, and a smattering of galleries and boutiques. I'd only been one time before that I could remember. It was a random day that my parents had decided it would be fun to drive around Pittsburgh, up to Mount Washington, and back down and through the tunnels for the sole purpose of looking at houses they would never buy. They did that a lot. It was boring. They drove around neighborhoods to look at the houses just to see their structures, how close to the water they were, or how nice their yards looked. We wound up in Shadyside, walked around, shopped, and ate steak salads with French fries at Walnut Grove for dinner.

"I hope they put the syrup on the side," I said.

"Oh, you'll live," she said. She was holding the coffee mug to her cheek, fresh coffee steaming up her right lens. We had not been permitted to take him for a walk. I was biting on the straw of my ginger ale. She looked at me and raised an eyebrow.

"Sorry." I moved my drink to the center of the table, away from the edge.

"For what?" she asked.

"Funny."

"Are you hungry?"

"Yeah, are you?"

"A little."

We ate our pancakes and didn't talk about my father. We talked about other things. We talked about Gram Mary. She was getting really sick, and things might need to change. We talked about volleyball, how I would be starting two-a-days, and how if I was going to play volleyball, I had to do speech, too. We talked about the stores we wanted to go into the next time we were here. She asked me more about my trip to New York with my father that had been a week before the accident. On the way home, it was too late for the news, so we listened to Jimmy Buffett.

"Mom, how come you won't sing?"

"I'm tired; you sing."

"It's not fun if you don't."

"Okay, what song?"

"What's your favorite?"

"I don't have one."

"Yes, you do."

"Janna, you have favorites. You pick one. I don't pick favorites."

I pawed through the CDs. Rebecca and her brother had bought me a Jimmy Buffett collection called *Beaches, Bars, Boats, and Ballads* for my birthday that year, and I'd brought it with us. Her brother was a lot older than us, lean and lanky, with round glasses that made him look like John Lennon. He smoked a lot of pot. When Rebecca had sleepovers, her brother would come in and tell us stories of adulthood and pick me up and spin me around because he said I weighed nothing. It was a really nice gift, expensive.

I put on "Tin Cup Chalice." "I—I wanna be there …" My mother sang along, and we rolled down the windows. It was one of her favorites, not mine.

MY FATHER HAD BEEN AT Squirrel Hill for almost two weeks, and he wasn't doing well. I didn't visit every day like my mother and Gram and Pa. I stayed at home, doing yard work and playing with the Suhries. While I dug holes in the dirt near the swing set, explored a creek in the woods (which we later we were told was sewage runoff), threw a Frisbee to Meagan, went out on the boat, and watched MTV shows like *Undressed*, my father got worse.

"Worse?" I asked my mother one evening.

I chose not to believe the word. It didn't make sense. The worst had to be over. He was in recovery time, right?

"Well, Janna, he's not doing very well," she said.

She seemed okay, or maybe I was too used to her new small, tired frame. Nothing seemed to shake her, and I could no longer read how the day at rehab had gone by her mood or expression. I had to ask her.

"I don't understand. What's the matter with him?"

"He's sick. He's very weak. They think he might have pneumonia."

"Will he be okay?" *People die from that,* I thought. *He can't have that. He never even gets a cold. Well, sometimes he got colds, and he acted like they were the flu. Maybe he might not be okay.*

"Well—"

"Is he still talking?"

"No, and he's lost a lot of weight."

The next day, an ambulance came to Squirrel Hill to take my dad back to AGH. I was at the Suhries when my mother called. I wanted to cry, but I couldn't. I was scared. There was nothing I could do. Apparently, pneumonia is just something that happened with brain injury sometimes.

It rained, so Vicky took us to Patcatan's to find some crafts. She wanted to make John something that reminded him of the lake. We found a lighthouse made out of logs. Vicky beamed as she walked down aisle after aisle, grabbing flowers, eucalyptus, baby's breath, and a miniature wooden street sign. We spent the afternoon sitting at the kitchen counter, gluing tiny twigs and dried flowers to the base of the lighthouse. It poured for hours. Steven and Lisa got bored, quit, and played Sega instead. Nicole and I got bored, quit, and watched Vicky continue to decorate it. She wrote "The Leyde Light House" on a little wooden sign that she glued in front of the small hole of a front door. She slowly rotated the finished product 360 degrees to inspect all sides. Nicole and I nodded in approval.

"You know, Janna Marie, I had a dream about your father," she said.

Nicole and I were now watching her roll greasy balls of chocolate chip cookie dough, placing them in neat rows on the baking trays. It was like someone had set her on autopilot.

"What about?"

"Well, you know the day that the accident happened, we saw it on the news."

"You did?" I asked. "Did you see my dad? Could you see the cars, or that Herman guy? What did it look like? Nicole, did you see it?"

"Nope, just Mom," she said.

"No, I didn't see John, but it was on the news, because the interstate was closed for a long time because of a four-car accident. It was an aerial view. They didn't say any names, and you couldn't see any people."

I felt disappointed, as if all of this would be more special if Vicky had seen him on the news.

"Then a few nights later, I had the dream. I saw your dad. He was walking around in your front yard with the dog, picking up sticks. He was fine."

I said nothing, and she stopped rolling dough and looked at me.

"It makes me feel like everything is going to be okay. After that dream, I knew he was going to live."

"Yeah, I knew my dad was going to live, too."

GOING BACK TO AGH WAS the first sign of regression. Regression— reversion, to go back—another word that would become part of the new summer vocabulary.

I stayed home, started volleyball summer two-a-days, and spent even more time with the Suhries. My mother drove back and forth to Squirrel Hill, fed her horses, and cared for her kid, husband, and aging mother, who'd just been diagnosed with Alzheimer's—the medical explanation for the locked doors, peanut butter sandwiches wedged between the couch cushions, and all of her swearing. My father laid in a bed, letting his muscle tone waste away, his immune system fade to the point of pneumonia, and his hippocampus fail. He was weak and getting weaker, and rehab had not worked the way the doctors, nurses, specialists, and my mother had anticipated. He'd stopped talking and stopped making sense of things. He'd stopped progressing.

All I could do from home was be concerned. I chose to concern myself with pneumonia. I was not there for his transfer back to the hospital, but I pictured him being wheeled around on a gurney, coughing up mucus from congested lungs and getting stuck with IVs full of fluids to save his life as doctors wheeled even faster through the parking lot and into the building to get to the ER.

His doctors were far more concerned with his hippocampus—the horseshoe-shaped patch of brain cells that wraps to the right and to the left of some other cells located just above the brain stem. My father's had just quit on him. Without a functioning hippocampus, one cannot form new memories, store new information, or stimulate the senses to evoke emotion. Smell, sound, sight, taste, and touch had no relevance to my father. There was nothing in his brain to explain (to fire synapses and connect things, the way that brains do) that a certain citrusy smell is emanating from that orange, which is in fact the color orange and feels sticky when you peel it. Nothing to remind him that oranges are to eat and that he thinks they are delicious. He had no interest in oranges, or in eating, or knowing what color a yellow cube was.

My father's second stay in the hospital was short—short enough that I don't remember hours of anxious boredom in the waiting room, chicken salad sandwiches, or seeing the Tokashes. He was in the ICU, doped up on clear liquids to reboot his body and give his brain a rest. If there were any moments of touch and go, no one ever told me. The medicines and the rest worked, and he was back to his new home in Squirrel Hill, and I had a month until school started.

The first couple visits to rehab felt like watching life in rewind. I'd already seen him struggle to form sentences, to recognize faces. I'd already made faces at the goopy food he was given each day and watched him push it around on a tray like a monkey. I felt frustrated. He was alive. Vicky had the dream, but he looked crippled, smelled terrible, and couldn't speak without exerting a great amount of effort, turning red, and losing his breath. His expression didn't change. He looked like a basset hound, everything sagging and sad. His eyes were like holes in his drooping face, so dark and lifeless that it was hard to tell which one was green or which one was brown.

Then one afternoon, something peculiar happened. My mom and I came to visit and found him sitting up in a chair, spindly and propped up with pillows and shouting.

"Eight seven six G two Y," he said, looking at my mother, who was looking at his therapy aide. He kept repeating it, getting increasingly aggravated.

"He's been doing this since yesterday," said the aide.

"Eight seven six G two Y," he said for the sixth time.

"Do you know why?" my mother asked.

"No clue." The aide, in blue scrubs and orthopedic shoes, was chubby with facial hair that needed to be groomed. He was young and looked like he belonged on some college campus and was forcing my father to fit into his educational curriculum.

"You don't know," said my mother.

"I've never seen or heard of anything like this," he said.

"G two Y. G two Y. One-eight-eight-five-six-five-three-oh-oh-oh-B-nine. B-two-nine!"

The three of us took turns staring at each other. Clearly, he wanted something.

"B-two-nine! B-two-nine! One-eight-eight-five-six-five-three-oh-oh-oh-B-nine. One-eight-eight-five-six-five-three-oh-oh-oh-B-nine!"

He was yelling, his face strained and crimson, his jugular swelling in anger. Stringing the letters and numbers together as if he was forming sentences, enunciating some and dropping his voice or changing his tone to add inflection to others.

"Does he say the same numbers?" my mother asked.

"No, all kinds," the aide said. "No clue what he's doing. No clue what it means."

"I think he wants something," I said. I couldn't understand why no one had tried harder to interpret his nonsense. "Dad!" I said, cutting him off.

He looked at me, let out an exasperated breath, and stopped.

"Dad? What do you want?"

"B-two-nine," he said, looking at me. "B-two-nine," he said, looking at the TV.

I turned off Fox News. He smiled and closed his eyes. No one said anything. My mother and I left his room to go wait for Gram and Pa.

The next few days were hell. He would speak louder and faster at us, but only in these fragmented sequences. This was my father—my dad. He hadn't said a word in days, and maybe this is all he would ever say. He liked numbers and math, so maybe his brain had just given up on the rest. I hated numbers. I hated math. I pondered the idea of having a father who lived through a giant accident only to come out speaking in number tongues. I was embarrassed. No one understood him, and he didn't even have enough strength to lift his arms and point at things he wanted.

"They're license plate numbers," Pa said, having just returned from wheeling my dad around the parking lot. "John's reciting the license plate numbers in the parking lot—an old Dodge, a Cavalier, and a Mustang."

"You're kidding me," my mother said.

For the last week, we'd been trying to take him on walks, do something other than sit around and figure out what he was trying to tell us. Walks were a challenge. At first, I tried to do it by myself. I wanted to wheel him around the parking lot, up and down rows of cars, and tell him all about my life. I wanted John and Janna time.

My mother let me try it by myself. It was like wheeling around an oversized Slinky. He had zero muscle mass. His feet would get stuck underneath, or his arms would dangle near the spokes. When we rolled over a pebble or the slightest crack in sidewalk, he did one of two things: lost his balance and toppled forward or slid out of his seat, dragging his lower limbs on the pavement. He was a dead weight, too heavy for me to pick up. The whole thing was too scary, and he was too unruly and fragile. I couldn't do it, and he didn't care anyway. Half an hour later, I wheeled him back in and told everyone that it was too hard by myself.

The adults had to wheel him around while he stared blankly into space as they told him about the weather, the animals, and all the things he was going to do again someday if he kept trying to get better. Sometimes I would walk alongside him and contribute to the conversation. He would just tilt his head and drool as the gooey spit dried crusty in his mustache.

"I think some of them might be car-part numbers, now that I think about it," said Pa.

"He can remember that?" asked my mother, wiping down his bed rails and food tray with a warm washcloth.

"Sure can," Pa said. "And those license plate numbers from the lot."

"He can *remember* something?" my mother asked.

"I suppose he can," Pa said, smiling.

My dad quit with the number sentences a few days later and went back to saying nothing. It was mid-August and I missed talking to my father. I even missed the stupid arguments we used to have, the most recent being about my friend Vanessa, who was one of two vegetarians I knew. The boys always laid out pieces of ham on her cafeteria chair on ham and cheese sandwich day.

"You know we're at the top of the food chain, right?" my dad had said. He was watching the Pirates beating the Reds. I was reading *YM*.

"So," I said. "We should be nicer to the animals." I was protesting, mostly in Vanessa's defense. I loved well-done steaks on the grill and ham and cheese sandwich day.

"So we shouldn't be nice to the plants?" he asked. "If we have to be *nice* to the animals, it would only be fair to treat the plants the same."

"Dad!"

"So what are we going to eat?"

"Dad, that is not what I mean."

"Well then, what do you mean?"

"I mean we should be nice to animals, because they are beings, like us. It's mean to eat them."

"Oh, ya ninny, they don't have feelings."

"Yes they do! The dog and cats and horses do!"

"They are the same as plants. Humans have a higher consciousness—*we* think about stuff. Plants and animals can't think. They don't care."

"Well, eating them is mean, I think."

"No, it's the food chain. We are omnivores. Check out your teeth—designed to eat animals and plants. We're not doing anything mean."

"Dad!"

"Peanut!"

"I wish Andy Van Slyke stilled played for the Bucs," I said, changing the topic of conversation half purposefully and half due to my inability to form a smooth segue.

"If wishes were—" he started to say.

"He's kinda old now, huh?"

"Just for baseball, Peanut."

"He was cute."

"Cute, huh?"

I went back to reading about nail polish.

the tears were falling

THE PAIN WAS KILLING ME, a thousand tiny pins pricking into my right foot. I unwound my legs, revealing a mess of photos. I picked up my right thigh with both hands and then let the leg fall with a thud. Nothing. I started beating my heel on the floor.

"Janna. Please."

"It's asleep!" I said, continuing to pound my heel into the floor. "I have to."

My mother does not like things in her face or banging noises. I figured she'd argue with me to stop. Instead, she took off her glasses to rub her eyes. I wondered when I'd see her in contacts again.

"Mom, what's the matter?"

"We don't have any pictures of Thunder." She swept our neatly sorted picture piles into one heap.

"Mom! Why did you do that?"

It was almost midnight. We had spent hours staring at, discussing, and choosing photos from our picture albums. I had been enjoying myself. Looking at our photo albums was one of my favorite things to do. We had so many pictures, more than I thought any of my friends had. They were all chronologically arranged, sitting spine by spine in the jelly cupboard—a fat little library of faux leather-bound books in all colors, some with gold details. I would waste afternoons taking out all the albums (remembering not to lose any photos, tear any pages, or put them back in the wrong spot) and page through, examining each picture. Some felt so alive that it was hard to believe the memory had been captured and was now history.

"This is just stupid," my mother said, putting her glasses back on. "We don't have any good pictures of the horses or Gram Mary. What the hell am I supposed to do? He hasn't taken enough pictures. We have no good pictures for this!"

I felt like I was helping my mother with her homework. An assignment from Squirrel Hill: Make a bulletin board of pictures for my father—family, pets, friends, and places—and tag each one to trigger his memory. We stopped at the new Walmart on the way home to buy a corkboard and other accessories for the assignment. I wanted to buy an orange but thought better of asking my mother for a dollar, because I didn't want to answer her when she'd ask what for.

When the Walmart opened on a random weekday at 8:00 a.m. earlier that year, my dad was the first customer—his crisp dollar bill in exchange for an orange. I had expected to see the dollar bill framed and scribbled with "JTL" hanging on a wall of plaques at the Walmart, like the one at Gabany's. I never did.

Our endeavor had morphed into something of map, a suggested route back to normal John. We laid out all the familiar guide posts: the blue and white boat out on the lake; Gram Mary's haunted brick house surrounded by ferns, pines, and miles of grass; all the horses; Gram Mary in her coiffed charcoal curls, gigantic glasses, and red nails; Meagan holding a Frisbee; Christmastime; Gram, Pa, and all his sisters at Easter; vacations to North Carolina; my birthdays; he and my mother at her cousin's wedding; he and my mother at Applebutter; the Suhries; the Riegs; the Gallos; barn cats; golden retrievers; our Explorer and Mom's Honda; my cousins; his cousins; work colleagues; school pictures with my friends; my eighth-grade school photo with splash color; the two of us waterskiing at the same time; the view of our house from the front and from the back. Endless memories, all neatly tucked and arranged, were held in place with straight pins and surrounded by arrows and captions that were written in my mother's sliced cursive capital letters.

"Here he is!" I said. I handed her a picture of my father and me on a stalky black horse standing in front of Gram Mary's pond, me hugging the horn of the saddle and him stretching to pat the neck, both of us wearing goofy grins.

"That's Dodger!"

"Oh."

"Dodger's dead, Janna! Come on now."

"Oh."

She started to put certain pictures back into piles. I wondered if I should help. Instead, I sat and watched. She hated this, people watching when they could be helping. I didn't know how to help her, so I sat there, refolding my legs, holding a picture of my dad and me on a dead horse.

On the bad days, he called my mother Sherry. On the bad days, he thought I was Aunt Biz. There were no good days. With no short-term memory, we became strangers to him, just people he was constantly agitated or enraged with. He didn't speak; he only yelled or grunted when he wanted something or didn't want something. We were strangers to him. He was a stranger to me. A new man, a man who was always mad.

"People don't get mad," he would always say, carrying on the cloying verbal traditions of his English grandmother. "Dogs get *mad*, people get …" He'd wait for me to finish.

"People get *angry*, Dad."

Mad, he would explain, defines someone who is positively psycho, rabid. This man was that kind of mad—seething, red-faced, as close as you get to foaming at the mouth, raging, yelling, mad. Rabies-like mad, contagious. I didn't want to be around him. I didn't want to be this man's daughter.

Yet his face was the same. Despite the sagging cheeks and exhausted expression, it was the same face in the frame that still sits on his dresser, the cover shot from *The Edge*, a local business magazine. He's looking down, reading something, head tilted a bit, and wearing a pair of wire-rimmed glasses. The editors chose him because he looked intelligent and kind, because he knew about selling things, and because he sold the guy from *The Edge* a Honda. A couple years after that cover shot, and the face was the same. Nothing else.

My dad hated us. Why wouldn't he? We made the pain, and we clogged his thinking. We made his brain fuzzy. We gave him bruises and cracked his ribs. We squeezed his lungs and turned his muscles to putty. We bored him to death, and we wore him out. We took away his appetite and the control of his bowels and bladder. We made his tongue dry as sandpaper. We wiped clear his memories, and we stole his balance. We even stole his legs, his job, and his freedom. We did all of this to him. I would battle us, too. John versus us. My dad, in faded green sweats, versus the world.

My dad's life in rehab was a tedious schedule—brain injury curriculum: bed times, meal times, nap times, bath times, bathroom times, walks, therapy sessions, tests, workouts and pills to take. Pills after pills after pills, to be taken on the hour, with meals, at bedtime, three times a day. Pills you could see through and pills that left a powdery residue. Pills you could write on a chalkboard with and pills you could pop like a Gusher.

The grueling itinerary and his buffet of pills were elemental in getting him on track with his recovery, something that would give him shot at his old life. The accident had left us starting out from scratch, building him back into a real man, from medicines and mealtimes, rules and activities.

When people would ask how he was doing, I felt like I was spouting off rudimentary action verbs—simple action verbs, the kind you learn when you are first learning a language. He'd failed Spanish twice in high school.

Well, my dad has to relearn how to ... walk ...

A smiley man, what a human being would be like if he was crafted from a Care Bear, was helping him put one foot in front of the other. Down a path of parallel steel bars they went, as painful as watching paint dry, every day.

"'At's it, John!"

I watched them, driven by the pure curiosity of how you teach a grown man to walk paired with the hope that he would do it on his own in my presence. The smiley man stood at one end, coaxing him forward, applauding his strength and stamina as he panted and sputtered, dragging his feet as if they were tied to cement blocks. As he made millimeters of progress, the cheery man clapped him on.

"You da man!"

Learning to walk, again, at forty-six. Funny how you can't start out crawling.

Oh, he has to learn how to talk all over again ...

"Gimme a kiss." His first words, said to my mother, were spoken in a scratchy, coarse whisper the day he woke up from his coma. Now all he did was swear, grunt, bellow, holler, and hiss between spurts of breath, with poor diction on the few words he did choose to use. Never a complete sentence.

"John, you have to tell us what you want," my mother would say to him. "We'll get it for you, but you need to tell us what it is."

"*No!*"

I suppose No! is a sentence, complete with punctuation the way he said it.

They have him learning to write ...

At first, he scribbled all over the notepad we gave him. He was more impressed by the marks a pen could make than anything else. Then he started to write letters, out of sequence, but in his familiar, barely legible penmanship—choppy caps from an awkward lefty.

Janna

He wrote my name first, his first word. The pride felt backwards.

We have to help him learn to eat again …

Vanilla Ensure, cleverly designed to open with the same enjoyment of a pop can, was a recipe tailored to people older than my grandparents who had bodies that rejected nutrients and supplements. I popped the tab down and stuck a straw into the frothy, cement-gray liquid posing as a milkshake. I wanted to know if it was as chalky and awful-tasting as it appeared. I took a sip. Worse! How could he stomach them? He hated sweets, and I hated vanilla. The nurse told me he fought harder against the chocolate than the vanilla. Vanilla Ensures—two cans a day.

We're hoping he'll learn to read again …

He stared blankly at Dick-and-Jane style paragraphs and pushed flash cards off his tray. Books, magazines, and newspapers piled up in stacks around him. I thought about reading to him. How do you read to your father? What do you read to your father? What would he read to you? English poetry? American? How about Frost? "Whose woods these are I think I know/His house is in the village though/He will not see me stopping here/To watch his woods fill up with snow." He promptly fell asleep. A poem about snow in summer is stupid.

To use the bathroom …

My father was wetting the bed, wetting his pants. Was *I* supposed to potty train him? I was fourteen and had never pissed anything before—myself, my pants, the bed, nothing. And he was shitting the bed at forty-six.

When my father had to go to the bathroom, his body was not able to keep up with the pace that he wanted to move. He'd lean his torso over the side of his bed and forget to swing his legs out from under the sheets to properly plant his feet on the ground.

"Dad, hey … hey …"

As he teetered, I came closer, my arms stretched out. I wanted him to reach for my help, but he just swatted at me, flirting with his imbalance.

"Hang on!"

If he fell, the weight he might put into my arms would be a bridge to cross if I ever got to it.

"Get!" he said, still leaning forward, still forgetting about his legs.

He leaned, pulling pillows, cords and sheets with him. He didn't want help from his kid. But I was petrified of him falling. That fear has never gone away.

I would watch him struggle and dodge his swats, and my mind would roll horror footage. His head cracking open on the floor, or the doorframe, or the pavement, or the porcelain sink. Me, sitting in a pile of blood, holding together the two sides of his skull. I've always been well aware that all this damage was a closed head injury, but my mind wanted more gore. Me, hopeless, his blood dripping down my wrists, to my elbows, staining everything. He would die. And I would just cry. Years later, when *Dexter* became a hit, something felt too familiar. I'm aware how fucked up these notions are, so messed up they keep me apart from the actual reality.

And then in reality, his legs always caught up, he'd charge towards the door, looking like some kind of primate rather than a father, sights set on the door handle, which would always catch him. Once he was inside the bathroom, I could breathe again. The design was built for his reckless behavior, and with the door shut, my opportunity to help was over. What he did in there was out of my league and into my mother's. Knowing what she did for him made me queasy.

She did everything. She cleaned him up and dressed him the same way you would a baby. A giant, cranky, helpless baby man. She would get a washcloth and run it under hot water in the bathroom—the sign for me to leave the two of them in the room and shut the door on my way out. She would lift his gangling appendages one by one, turning and rotating each of them at the joints, bending his elbows and knees. With the warm washcloth, she would wipe down the limp, pale skin that clung to nothing more than his skeleton. Then she'd turn him over, put medicine on his bedsores, and rub his back with lotion, checking for bruises. Sometimes she would have to change his diaper. He wore a diaper, because he frequently did not make it to the bathroom in time. I could not dream of having such love for someone.

That August, my father quit loving me.

"Hey, Dad, can you just try some for me?" I asked, picking up a plastic container that looked like it should hold pudding rather than six ounces of watered-down orange juice.

"No!"

"This will help you get stronger, so you can walk and do things like—"

"I don't want it!"

"Dad, you've got to eat *something* today."

"No!"

I took a deep breath. I closed my eyes and conjured up the caretaker Janna, a patient and firm woman, like my mother.

"Please. Stop yelling at me."

"No!"

I jabbed a hole in the foil cover with the straw and set it down in front of him on his tray, which hinged around him in bed like a school desk. He stared at me. He shoved the tray away, swinging it wildly. The orange juice cup slid like a beer mug on a bar. I cupped it, catching it midair before it fell to floor.

"I. Said. Yes."

I set it down in front of him, again. He picked it up with a quivering grip, took a huge breath, puckered his lips around the straw, and sucked. One long suck until the pudding container was empty. He set it back down and removed the straw.

"Thanks, Dad." I smiled at him.

He put the straw back in his mouth, sat up straighter, and leaned towards me. I walked closer. What was he doing with the straw? He had always chewed on things: toothpicks, wads of paper, swizzle sticks, grass blades, straws. Still holding the straw to his lips, he looked at me. He pulled the accordion end straight with his free hand and took an audible breath through his nose. I leaned towards him.

A stream of orange juice hit me in the forehead. It trickled down my face. I stood, mouth agape, in complete stillness, taking in the sticky droplets clinging to my eyelashes and the warm streams running down my neck, soaking into my shirt.

He chuckled and threw the straw at me. It glided through the air, just like the paper airplanes he taught me how to make as a kid. We'd fly them through the rafters of the living room and kitchen. Mine were often duds.

His ascended effortlessly, picking up air currents I never knew existed in our house.

I walked into the bathroom, braced my arms on the sink, and looked in the mirror. My hipbones pressed against the porcelain. It hurt. I hated him; I wanted to. I hated being sticky. I hated that he was always throwing things, at people, at walls—food, forks, books, pens, spoons, pillows, insults, fits, tantrums—all the time.

The doctors increased his medications. Now the mesh net at the head of his bed had a purpose.

"Mom, what is that for?"

My father lay silent, sleeping in his mosquito net.

"Well, he gets very angry, and he needs restrained."

"By a net?"

I now felt stupid for the first day I saw the net and for secretly wishing to see destruction in action. It was the same thrill I felt when the local programing was interrupted by the "severe weather warning for Mercer County," tornadoes spinning frighteningly close, touching down and maybe tearing some barn, stretch of woods, or house to shreds. The imminent sense that something powerful and dangerous was about to happen. Hurricanes hitting the coast, thrashing through beach towns. Crazy men confined in mosquito netting—exhilarating.

"If you let him be, he'll try to escape, and he'll hurt himself."

"Oh, so it's kinda like a net cage?"

The netting looked like something that belonged on a ski boat, white and waterproof, something made to withstand the elements—thick, shiny cotton thread and chunky metal zippers. Inside, his feet and hands were bound in white nylon straps, thick as seat belts, which kept him from moving.

"He can get pretty nasty, Janna," said my mother, trying to explain the reason for what I was seeing. "It's one of the stages that they say he might go through during recovery."

Combative.

I thought about the summer Fourth of July picnic at the Riegs' when Nicole, Steven, Lisa, and I had found a rabid raccoon trapped in the drainpipe that ran under the street. We spent hours entertained by fear and a gripping curiosity, shining a flashlight in the pipe to watch it flinch and hiss, trying to fight and climb its way out. It darted from one end to other, flailing and screeching. Trapped. Combative. Eventually, someone shot it.

"So it's kind of a good thing?" I asked, fingering the zipper.

"What do you mean?"

"Well, if he is going through the stages."

"Janna, he's pretty nasty."

There was nothing I could say. There was nothing nice my mother was saying about my father lately, so maybe there was nothing I wanted to hear. I didn't see him that much. With school around the corner, I was busy dealing with ninth grade, finding adolescent worries that I challenged to be as important.

The net confinement only lasted a week or so. After the net cage was rolled back up, his anger lessened. He was calming down and starting to talk to us in full sentences—all good things, nothing major. Maybe he was moving through the stages.

In the first days of the accident, when death was the biggest thing to fear, a nurse gave me a book. Simply because I was the fourteen-year-old whose dad had just come out of a coma and now had a brain injury, and according the Glasgow Coma Scale, at 5, he was just two points shy of being in a vegetative state. The book was supposed to help me navigate what could happen if (and when) he woke up. *When a Parent Has a Brain Injury: Sons and Daughters Speak Out.*

It was a poor excuse for a book—a pamphlet, really. In the hospital, I paged through it, but the writing was boring. I was not able to relate to people talking about dating their boyfriends and bringing their father home and getting into drugs, so I put the book in my desk drawer, thinking I might have a need for it someday.

I pulled it out that week and flipped to the chapter titled "Impulsiveness," a behavior I was recognizing. I wanted to know what else to expect and how I could detect progress in all his weird behaviors, to know if there was anything I could do, because my mother's energy ran on his progress.

I watched her, firm with him, forceful when necessary, calm and calculated, organized and goal-oriented with all his treatments. She's tough and resilient. I believed these qualities she had would directly benefit his recovery. If he threw his food, she forced him to eat more. If he thrashed about, swearing and yelling, she would refuse to take him outside. He was expected to bathe every day, to go to the bathroom a few times a day, and to sleep when it was suggested. There was no room for excuses. Absolutely no getting away with things. She simply didn't take his shit.

My mom and Gram started to argue about his care, about how to handle his constant misbehaving and how far to push him. His mother babied him. All his misbehavior was okay, because he had a head injury. He threw his food, his shoes, and his tantrums, and Gram and Pa practically cooed at him.

I took my mother's side, constantly venting to my diary. One entry is peppered with words like *hate* and *real love* and lots of *stupids,* big letters made from harsh strokes that cut through two pages of paper. It remains the angriest entry I'd ever written; it was searing. I wanted to disown my grandparents. I wanted to ban them from rehab. I wanted them to shut up, because my mother is always right. Everyone should listen to her. She's mean to him, because that is what he needs. Her jobs have prepared her for this—delinquent kids, mentally retarded people, broken families. She always makes people better. She always knows what she's doing. Why couldn't Gram and Pa do it her way?

If he didn't want to drink Ensure, they got him ice cream. If he didn't want to stay awake, he could doze off. If he didn't want to try harder, he didn't have to. If he didn't want to sit up straight, they got him a pillow or two or three—however many he wanted.

"Hi, Dad." I picked up the orange juice container and set it deliberately in the far right corner of his tray. It had been only a few weeks, but I still had a grudge against orange juice. "Hungry?"

Nothing. He never talked anymore. I opened packets and made piles of their contents on his plate. I daydreamed about starting the school year off with the cuffed shorts, button-ups, preppy crewneck tees, and these tortoiseshell hair clips I'd seen in the J. Crew catalogue. If only I could magically wake up as one of those sun-kissed women in the catalogue.

"Ready for lunch?" I walked the tray over, making a mental list of things to look for when my mom took me school shopping later. Ross Park Mall had a J. Crew.

He said nothing, didn't look at me. He was covered by a sheet, propped up on a mountain of pillows, and clutching another one to his stomach. He was smiling, grinning—stupidly happy, looking up at the ceiling and then down at the pillow. The bed was moving, or something under the sheets was, making the pillow on his stomach bounce.

"I brought you some lunch."

He turned to look at me. The pillow fell, and he whipped the sheet up off of him and threw it over the side of the bed. His pajama pants, which he'd taken off, fell to the floor. He continued looking at me, bouncing, happy like an overexcited kid, the bed squeaking. His hands were cupped around his penis.

I was frozen, stuck to the floor while his pelvis was moving up and down in rhythm with bed squeaks and happy bouncing.

"Dad!" I was stuck. He was smiling at me and bouncing and breathing hard. "I'm … gonna—"

He stroked and moaned and grunted. I closed my eyes and willed my feet to move. Eyes still closed, I walked over to his dresser and set the tray down. I heard the squeaks and grunts and moans. I tiptoed out of his room and shut his door. I walked down the hallway, as casually as possible, trying not to move in a way that would cause someone to ask what was wrong.

I shoved open the outside doors with so much force it hurt my wrists and sprinted to the end of the parking lot. I looked up. The sky was azure blue. *Azul*—Spanish for *blue*. Perfectly blue, with not one single cloud to mar all the blue. I was sweating, beads coming from every pore. I dug my fingers into my immaculate ponytail and yanked clumps of hair out of place. Then came tears. Tears and an acute choking sensation. I squeezed my temples as hard as I possibly could, trying not to cry.

Masturbation—that word from health class. It made teenage boys shrink down in their seats or mumble crude remarks about dicks and wangs. I suppose I knew what it entailed. I'd heard stories from my friends about boys and hand jobs. I never gave anyone one. And I had no plans to be touching anyone's penis anytime soon.

I found the soft spot of my temples and pressed harder, thinking about boys giving themselves hand jobs. Hands all over their penises, gripping them like joysticks. But this was *my father*, allowing me to watch, bouncing up and down, while I stood there like a dumbass, holding his lunch tray.

"I'm his daughter!" I yelled out loud. I squeezed harder and walked in circles. My biceps hurt now, not my head. "How can I be normal? My father's penis. My father's hard penis. That was hard, right? No. No. No. No. No. No, I did not see that! I don't care. It doesn't matter."

I squeezed, trying to muscle the vision out of brain. I jumped up and down. I ran in place, pounding my K-Swiss into the pavement, squeezing and squeezing and squeezing. Nothing. I was stuck with that. Forever.

I took a deep breath, walked back, and sat down on a bench near the entrance of the building. I spent the next five minutes going through round after round of ponytails until I had the perfect one. No bumps, super tight. My arms hurt even more.

"Hi, Mom," I said, as I ran into her in the hallway.

"How's your dad?"

"He's fine; he's sleeping."

I lied. I lied to my mother, but you have to lie to your mother when you see your dad jerking off. You have to lie, right? You have to, because your dad has a brain injury. He's not retarded. He's not a child. He's not sick. He's not twisted. He does love you. He'll get better. He's not himself. He's not a pervert. He didn't mean to. He has a brain injury. I hoped I didn't have mascara all over my face.

The next week, she caught him with his hands under the sheets, starting to do the same thing while I was sitting in the chair beside his bed, reading a magazine. She asked me to leave. I left. He did this a lot for a while.

Maybe this was in that damn book under "Sexual Behaviors," which I had noticed followed "Impulsiveness." But no, this was not in *When a Parent Has a Brain Injury: Sons and Daughters Speak Out.* "Damage to specific parts of the brain can result in lowered control over sexual thoughts and impulses … The importance of privacy for intimacy or nudity may be overlooked. Strangers or friends may be asked personal questions. Embarrassing comments may be made." That was followed by a story about a girl being picked up for date. Her dad asked her boyfriend if they were going to have sex. That girl had it easy.

My mom had bought me a new dress. It was from Ann Taylor, one of her favorite stores. It was blue and comfy, like wearing a T-shirt, but it looked nicer, cuter. Mom and I were going out to eat after visiting Dad. He had been talking more, still swearing but conversing on the good days. And I was slowly getting over my encounter. He did have a brain injury, after all.

It was nice out, a beautiful August day, one of the sneaky ones that feels more like the warmest day in October, not the coolest day in August. I liked my dress. My hair was pulled back in a sleek, pretty ponytail. It was a good day. Today I thought I would take him for a walk, because I could do that now that he had more strength and awareness than a Slinky.

"I thought I could take you outside for a bit," I said as I strapped him into the wheelchair. "Just you and me on a walk?"

"Sure," he said.

We had just rounded the first row of cars when he pulled the brakes on the left wheel, causing the chair to screech to a stop on one side and to fly forward on the other.

"Dad! Come on!"

"Come on?" he asked innocently.

He played the game with the brakes a lot. Other times, he ran over my toes or bumped into me. Maybe he just wanted to use his arms. They were useful. Not much else was.

"Yeah. Why do you do that?"

"Do what?" Still innocent.

"With the brakes!"

I came around to the front of the wheelchair and leaned down to unlatch the lever. It was no use asking him to do it himself. That was part of the game.

"Jesus, Dad!"

"Jesus?"

"Yeah, this gets old."

I stood in front of him, hands on my hips. I could feel the day going to shit. I still liked my outfit, and I felt pretty, in the awkward way that you do at fourteen—like a girl who a boy would talk to and a girl that looked a little bit like my mom. But here I was, fighting with my father about wheelchair brakes.

He whistled. He hadn't whistled since before the accident.

"What was—"

"Look at those tits," he said, looking up at me, beaming.

Tits, I thought. *What is he talking about?* I shivered. I was supposed to be flat, like flat in the way that all my friends made fun of me. Just this summer, Rebecca had finally quit calling me "Sweet Valley Girl."

"You're so flat that they indent," she'd explained the day she honored me with the nickname at recess in sixth grade. "They indent, just like valleys! You're just so cute, Janna Marie. Janna Marie, our Sweet Valley Girl."

Sixth grade, and everyone had boobs. Everyone could do back handsprings at recess. Everyone had a boy on "National Hug and Kiss" day. Everyone was in the "who's got the better bubble butt" walk-across-the-kickball-field competition. Everyone was shaving their legs. Everyone who had braces had the cool color bands. Sixth grade, and I was a shrimp, short with curly hair, braces, and skin that was about to go from bad to worse. I was not everyone.

"Look at 'em!" he said. "So nice—"

I thought about them. I guess they had been growing, but they were not tits. They were miles away from boobs. Two lumps tucked into a barely B-cup bra with one of those pink flowers with green leaves where the cups met. Definitely no need for underwire. What was he looking at? I didn't have tits. I had little baby breasts. Nothing about my outfit invited the usage of *tits.*

"Dad, please stop. Please."

"Since when did you get those?"

My throat closed. My esophagus filled with lead. Heavy. I might die. Just lie down, curl into a ball, and melt through the pavement.

"I mean, look at 'em. Look … at … those tits." He kept talking about them. He wouldn't stop staring at them. "Those tits!"

"Stop it!"

Hot tears poured down my cheeks. I walked behind him and wiped my face. With nothing else to do, I gripped the handles of his wheelchair until my salty, wet knuckles turned white. I pushed him forward to continue our walk.

The next day, I stayed home. Nicole found me sitting in the ditch of my front yard, exactly where I'd hoped she'd find me. I planned to tell her everything, but when she sat down next to me, I had no words. I opened my mouth to talk, but a surge of tears flooded my eyes, and I could only cry. Tears and words I hadn't planned poured out.

"Cole, It's so unfair. Why did this happen to my dad?"

She sat closer and shook her head. "I really don't know, Janna."

"I don't understand. Why did this happen to us? Why my dad? It's so unfair. Why him?" I didn't know how to stop crying or breathe like a normal person. She didn't know what to say. I wanted words, but this was so far past words now. "What am I supposed to do? This is so unfair. Why *my* dad? Why? Why, Nicole? Why him?"

"I don't know."

"What had happened to my life? My dad was supposed to help me with math and skiing and, like, teach me how to be cool and …" I felt silly and stupid for crying. I wanted the ground to swallow me, but it wouldn't. "I don't know how to do this, Cole. I don't know what's happening."

She scooted closer and put her arm around me. I was fourteen. He was my father. I couldn't stop crying. My heart was breaking. I was on my own. This man could teach me nothing.

Shit piss suck fuck gobble nibble chew ovum scrotum nipple tit rag cunt screw dirty-assin' rag-fuckin' cock-suckin' goddamn mother-fuckin' son of a bitch.

Oh, yeah. He had just taught me that.

get on back to school

A FEW DAYS BEFORE SCHOOL STARTED, VICKY took us to Walmart, where Nicole, Steven, Lisa, and I stocked up on pens, pencils, erasers, folders, and Five Star notebooks. Vicky bought me a Nike Trapper Keeper that was black, turquoise, and purple. It was chic and sporty, something a ninth-grader could be caught dead with.

My mother took me back-to-school shopping for clothes. As I was standing in dressing rooms, arguing with her about fit and style and the appropriateness of outfits, I reveled in how deliciously normal it felt. We tackled two malls in one Saturday afternoon—an early start at one, an early dinner in between, and on to the second. We got home late, weary in the way that only comes from a good day of shopping. I lugged armfuls of bags from the trunk and piled them onto my bed. My mom went upstairs, washed her face, and went to sleep. I stayed up for hours.

First, I laid out each item, draping them over my chair, stretching them out on my bed, and neatly arranging the accessories on my desk. Then I collapsed the bags, folding them on their neat creases, and put them in the copper bin in the hallway so they could be reused. Last, I tried on all my clothes again before putting them away. My mother bought me a lot that year, more than she ever had. I had grown out of my old clothes, and those that still fit were not cool enough to wear anymore. Some purchases she approved of (a short khaki skirt, an orange V-neck sweater from L. L. Bean, a plum-colored, wool blend dress from The Limited). Others she simply hated (the flannel button-up shirts, baggy Silver Tab Levi's, forest green Converse All Stars). She bought me new bras and gave in to a pair of Nikes that were crisp white with orange and blue details—real volleyball shoes. She thought they were ugly. They were. I thought the bras were ugly.

I was excited for school to start, excited to show off my new look: a little preppy and as grunge as my mother would allow. I couldn't wait to see my friends, sit at a desk, doodle on my book covers, and listen to teachers drone on about photosynthesis, the Pythagorean Theorem, predicates and subjects, how Bandar Seri Begawan is the capital of Brunei, and whatever else they planned to stuff into our freshman brains. I daydreamed about talking to boys and planning my life around Friday night football games. I was looking forward to focusing on something—anything—but the summer.

"BUT, MOM, I FEEL BAD," I said.

It was the night before the first day of ninth grade. My mom was ironing downstairs in the laundry room, and I was perched on the washer, showing off my Trapper Keeper and talking persistently about how exactly I was supposed to go back to school and be normal. The impending freedom felt amiss. With school starting, I got to walk away from everything when I should be there with her to take care of my dad. I felt guilty. I felt even worse that I was excited about it. There was no one to tell me whether it was okay to feel what I was feeling. I didn't know who to ask, and the stupid brain injury book didn't tell me anything.

"This is not your job, Janna. Going to school and being with your friends and doing all your activities is what you need to do. He will understand."

"But what about you?"

"Me?"

"Yeah, Mom. What about you?"

"This is what I have to do, not you. I just want you to go school. You have to do all the things you have planned. That is how you can help me."

But I didn't have anything planned. My father had monopolized our schedule since the hour he didn't take my friends and me skiing on July 30. The day after he didn't wake up, I called a long list of them, one after the other, to cancel vacations, sleepovers, birthday parties, babysitting jobs, and summer practices. Even though all my friends now knew what happened, I hadn't seen most of them in months.

IT WAS 7:00 A.M. I was running late. The day had started wrong. My hot shower, an uncalled-for twenty minutes of steaming waterfall, was rudely interrupted.

"Janna!" my mother said, cracking the door. "Let's go! I have to get ready, too. What are you doing? You're wasting water! You've been in there too long. And you have to keep this door cracked. It gets too hot, and you'll warp the wood."

Waking up to her voice in the dark had been unsettling. That was my father's job—a nice back scratch with the reminder that he would be back in ten minutes, after he took the dog out. Ten minutes later, he would come back into my room, flip on my light, and depending on my state of consciousness, whip up the covers. In the winter, if I didn't respond, he'd put a snowball in my bed, which would melt and smell exactly like wet dog.

Some mornings, to be especially annoying, he'd whisper-sing "Gooooood morning … good morning … it's time to say this morning … good morning. Good morning, to you," with a tap dancing stroll back and forth by my bed, as if he himself were Gene Kelly in *Singin' in the Rain*.

"I'm almost done!" I yelled over the rush of the water.

I stood, scalding water beating between my shoulder blades, penning my day's three wishes into the steam on the white walls of the shower. If I smashed my face up against it at the right angle, I could see the traces of my finger tracks in the light.

have a good day
Amber and Rebecca will like my outfit
be in a class with Zac or Ryan

"Well, you need to hurry up! I'm gonna be late for work!"

"Okay!" I said, knowing I still needed to rinse conditioner out of my hair and shave my left leg.

I had to shave. I was wearing a skirt. A short jean skirt and a pale yellow summer sweater, silver rings on three of my fingers and one that used to be Gram Mary's for my thumb, white K-Swiss and my new Bass book bag made from buttery dark brown leather. I'd chosen the perfect outfit—one part hot, one part cute, and all parts Janna. I hoped my friends would agree.

I ran from the shower, wrapped in a towel, dripping puddles of water from the bathroom, through the hallway, and into my room. I plugged in my hot rollers and hair dryer to start the task that was doing my hair. It was thick and took a long time to dry, enough time that the hot rollers, perfect for creating big, soft curls, would be blazing when I was finished.

I pulled the front section of curls off my face a thousand times, until I got it right: half up, no bumps, in a silver barrette, which only showed off the welts and bumps on my face—the evidence that over the last year, my hormones had caught up, finally. I had my Clinique trio of liquid, powder, and bronzer. Real makeup, a step toward maturity. My friends could no longer make fun of me and my baby's-butt cheeks, soft and smooth, enviable. Just like them, I would have to blend makeup lines where my caked face met the tanned skin of my neck.

I looked in the mirror, my face smooth, flawless, a job well done. Too much like a ghost. I flicked black ink over my long eyelashes and dabbed gloss on my plump lips. They were my good features.

I tucked the sea-green compact and lip gloss in the front pocket of my book bag and ran to the kitchen. My mom handed me a purple Arctic Zone nylon lunch box. Its contents were coveted, craved—a bagel sandwich (very Panera-style), Doritos (Cool Ranch or Nacho Cheese), some sort of fruit (always nectarines when in season) or a vegetable (my favorite were cucumber slices drowning in lemon pepper dressing), dessert (Oreos, chocolate chip cookies, or bite-sized Snickers bars), and when she was being generous, a Jell-O or pudding cup.

I refused to eat cafeteria food. Never ate it in elementary school and certainly not in high school. Every morning, for as long I could remember, my mother would stand at the kitchen counter in her robe, packing my lunch, drinking black coffee, listening to NPR, and feeding lunchmeat scraps to Marble.

"Tell the Suhries to have a good first day of school," she said, giving me a kiss. "I love you."

"Love you, too," I said, shoving the purple box into my bag.

I arrived at the Suhries' ten minutes early, like every morning—extra time to snack on shaved ice in a Dixie cup and reexamine my entire ensemble in their bathroom mirror while Vicky put the finishing touches on the girls' hair. Sometimes I helped with Lisa's. She liked perfect ponytails, like me.

When everyone was ready, Vicky gathered us all on the deck steps, beside a dogwood, for our first day of school picture. Other moms and dads came down with their kids and their cameras, which made me miss my dad and his Nikon.

As I was shoving my book bag into my new locker (finally upstairs with the upperclassmen), I had to conquer my nausea. I swallowed and smiled through endless pre-first-period hugs and hellos. I couldn't talk. Fifteen minutes into my day, and I was still carsick. My spit tasted like the ugliness of the morning, all NPR and coffee and the kid-stink of Bus 12. On the way to first period, I waved at Amber and Rebecca going to their respective first period classes, which apparently were not Graphic Journalism.

"Look at you, Janna Marie," Rebecca said, throwing me a wink. "Ca-yute!"

I was a real high schooler now. I had to dress cool and be cool. I had quit band and packed away my alto sax—too dorky. Some of the boys quit chorus, but we girls stayed, because girls who could sing were cool. I made the volleyball team, and I was good, very scrappy in the back row. I stayed on the speech team, nerdy as it was. This was far less an option than an ultimatum. My mother told me if I quit speech, then I had to quit the rest—chorus, volleyball, musicals. It wasn't worth the fight, so I was paired up with a girl in my grade for Duo Interpretation, acting out acts of Neil Simon plays as different characters with invisible props.

I spent the morning rushing to new classes, where I secured desks by my friends, one of which had the famed jagged *TRENT REZNOR* hashed into it. That was cool. Our small town had one claim to fame: Nine Inch Nails.

On my way to lunch period, I took the steps into the cafeteria two at time. My irregular heartbeat refused to let me ignore how uncomfortable I was walking in by myself. I didn't know where my friends were or where I would sit. I had a lot of friends. I had grown up with them, shared sleepovers and family vacations with them, and now we were in high school. We shopped, rode horses, ice skated, played sports, did gymnastics, and talked about boys.

There was Sarah, who I'd known since we were four. She had a horse and lived in the country, and her mom had a job in social work. I had a pony, lived on a lake, and had a mom in social work. We bonded by throwing plush chairs at one another in the dark of the Mercer County library on Tuesday nights when we were locked up for an hour or two in the preschool room while our mothers were in a work meeting. And there was Amber, a quiet, beautiful girl who I'd befriended in third grade. We were opposites but inseparable ever since. And Rebecca, who was funny as hell, and always daring the rest us to do stuff a little beyond our limits. Vanessa, a girl whose dad knew my dad from the world of cars and parts. She was bubbly and fun, a preppy hippie in a house with three sisters. Jodie, who always kept me responsible. And there were Amelia, Leah, Jackie, and Rayshelle. And all the guys, too. I still couldn't figure out whether it was easier to have crushes on them or be their friend.

I found some of my girlfriends staking their claim at a long table right next to a table of all our guy friends—the cool tables, where a good number of the popular kids in the class of 2000 would be sitting. Someone had saved me an end seat, which was between Jackie and three feet of air space that separated me from Ryan, who sat at the end of the guys' table. I'd already made fun of him for his head-to-toe FUBU gear earlier in Algebra I.

"Did the The Claudmeister pack Doritos?" Amber asked as she plopped down across from me.

"Yup," I said, handing her the baggie. "I'm going to the snack line. Want anything?"

"Cheese crackers. Thanks, Janna Marie."

As I walked by the guys' table, I pointed toward the lady standing behind the snack cart. Five minutes into lunch, there was a line.

"Raspberry iced tea," yelled Zac. "Please!"

"I know," I said, taking two dollar bills from him.

My friends were more popular than I was. I was the *nice* one. I shared my lunch-box lunch and ran snack line errands. Way too damn nice. Sometimes when I got back from buying everyone's snacks, parts of my lunch had been rationed out, the sweet parts almost gone. I never told my mother about how much I "shared." She would have quit packing it for me if she'd known. She had already chastised me for how I let my friends treat me with their head pats and recess games.

"Janna, I can't believe you let them do that!" she had said. "That is how you treat a dog, patting you on the head like that. Now why do you allow that? You have no idea how mad this makes me."

"It's cuz I'm short."

"That is not an excuse. I'm very disappointed in you."

"In *me?* It's my friends that are doing it!"

"*You* are the one that allows it."

It was the same with elementary recess games, where my classmates literally tossed me around, like crowd surfing in a circle. I weighed less than a toothpick.

"Now, that is inappropriate behavior," she had said.

"But Mom, it's fun!" I said. "It's cuz I'm the smallest!"

"Why do you let people treat you like that? Who allows such behaviors? It's disappointing, Janna."

I would not tell her about lunch.

AT FIRST, MY SUMMER STORY was lost in the newness of ninth grade. No one really knew how severe it was, anyway, and I had little reason to bring it up. They knew enough. John Leyde, *Janna's* dad, was in a pretty bad car accident this summer.

Sure, people (friends, their parents, my teachers, and coaches) would ask. Regardless, I didn't want to talk about it. And they only cared that he had lived. Gaping smiles, arms stretched open ready to hug me, glazing over as I told them about the rest of summer— about all the details of his hospital stays and the stumbling and throwing and yelling at rehab. All the things that were different, replacing all the things we couldn't have back. Some people were so happy to hear that he lived that I expected them to clap when I finished talking. It made me irate. It's not that I wasn't happy he'd lived. But I was frustrated, too. Especially frustrated when people brought God into the conversation, saying how he had blessed us. *Blessed?*

No one had a clue that my father wasn't well, that he was still struggling so hard. That we all were. But you can't fight the black and white of life and death, at least not at fourteen, in ninth grade. You can nod your head and hang out with your friends.

My friends were in their own worlds, which were spinning in and out of control, like teenage worlds should. I tried damn hard to be right there with them, doped up on our drama. I had a crush on a boy. I didn't get into French class, so I was forced into Spanish. I had best friends and best-best friends and BFFs. I wore shorts that were too short to wear to school and clothing combinations my mother hated. I wrote notes in class and folded them into paper footballs. I talked to boys. I even tried flirting with the ones I liked. I got in trouble for talking, the only thing I ever got in trouble for. I hung out in the parking lot and almost missed Bus 12 nearly every day.

I worried about who to sit next to on the bleachers at the boys' games, who would dance with who at the school dances after the football games, and whose social status earned them a coveted seat on the heater if they chose not to dance. I hated dancing. And why did girls have to ask guys to Sadie Hawkins? Who would I ask? Adam? He was safe.

Adam and I bought a matching Ralph Lauren Polo ensemble: navy blue T-shirts and matching fishing hats, both with khaki swatches with "Ralph Lauren Polo" in black ink, as if they had been stamped on a box of supplies sent to a jungle. Fifteen years later, he still wears the hat, though I "lost" mine. In truth, I tossed it for inexcusable reasons under pressure years ago on the day I moved out.

"What is this, Janna?"

My mom, Nicole, Lisa, and Vicky had been helping me pack up my old room. I looked up from organizing my photos to see Lisa standing over me. She was holding a dildo that was wrapped up like a taco in my Polo fishing hat, the product of a sorority sister and I finding slumberparty.com after one two many spiked Dr. Peppers.

"Uh, just give that to me."

"Just tell me which box it goes in."

"Trash. Just throw it away, 'kay?"

"K." She didn't unwrap it, but waved it in the air like a baton as she walked past our mothers.

"Lis!" I said, blood thumping. "Just pitch it!"

I followed her into the hallway to ensure that she would drop it in the trash box. I still have the shirt, stitched safely into the T-shirt blanket my mother made for me in college.

At fourteen, I hadn't been on a date yet and had no boyfriend prospects. I worried about that, because I thought I should. I also worried about what my friends would think of my dad when they met him—re-met him.

In ninth grade, my newest best friend was Jackie, the blonde girl everyone liked. She always smiled and had no problem talking to the older, cute boys. She was pretty, almost famous for her long, platinum hair and poufy, blunt bangs. Our moms had known each other for years. And this year, we were on the volleyball and speech teams together. My mom wasn't home a lot for dinner, so Jackie's family insisted I join them when I could.

Jackie's dad reminded me of my dad in many ways. He was the blonde version, not too tall, with a mustache and was always happy and smiling. Dinners with Jackie and her parents, younger brother, and older sister were the next best thing to feeling comfortable and normal. Jax and Jans became a duo, a popular blonde and an endearing brunette who did everything together.

I could talk to Jackie about how things were different, unlike most of my friends, whom I didn't talk to about the giant shift that was happening in my life. I wanted to feel like my problems weren't really any bigger or harder or more unfair than anyone else's. In fact, I hadn't even tried to wrap my head around how giant it all was. Maybe my dad was never going to be the same. Maybe both of my parents would be different. It was really unfair. I couldn't try to figure it out.

My mother was working hard to keep our life normal, to keep the regular things going. She started every day packing my lunch and feeding Meagan and Marble. Then she got ready, wearing one of her sophisticated work outfits, complete with peep-toe pumps and a strong spritz of Clinique Elixir. Other days, if she was going to rehab instead of Children's Aid, she'd dress more casually—jeans and clogs.

Every day, she stopped by Gram Mary's to feed her horses (and sometimes ride Jamal if she had not gone to Pittsburgh and there was time) and check on her mother. She had started making arrangements for Gram Mary's care, not even blinking at the mention of Alzheimer's.

I asked her once how she handled everything at that time. She didn't have an answer. She doesn't have answers for these kinds of questions. She just moves through life. She moved forward with Gram Mary—talking to doctors, moving money around, and looking into different options to provide the support Gram Mary would eventually need.

She bought our groceries. She did our laundry. She kept our house clean, our yard cut, and our gardens from overgrowing. She made lists to keep us both on track. She didn't sleep and barely ate. She scheduled my pick-ups and drop-offs, cautiously choosing safe drivers for transportation.

"Do I even need to tell you about this, Janna?" she would ask anytime I had planned to ride with a friend rather than an adult.

"No, Mom. I know."

"I don't do well with this. It's hard for me."

"I know. I understand. But I won't get in an accident. Not every car does. Just because Dad did, doesn't mean I will. It's not fair not to let me go."

"Janna, you—"

"Mom. I know, but you can't just stop me from riding with my friends. I'll be safe."

"I know. It's hard for me."

"It's hard for me, too, but we can't just stop riding in cars and be scared on the road all the time."

It was now common knowledge—Janna and safety in cars. A couple months before, on one of the last sweltering days of our summer freedom, I was walking with Sarah and some other girls from the park to our friend Vanessa's house after swimming at the pool. The lifeguards were cuter than usual that summer. Six of us were walking along Route 58, a swerving two-lane highway where cars picked up speed as they rounded the bend down the hill on their way of out of town. Halfway to Vanessa's, when we were on the crest of the hill, walking carelessly close to the brim as the cars whizzed by us, Sarah grabbed my elbow.

"Jans! What are you doing?"

"Nothing," I said.

I tugged my arm back and kicked up gravel with each step as I stared down, walking as if I were on rocks. One foot in front of the other. The highway, its the asphalt, looked strange up close, like I was looking through a zoomed-in lens. There were pockmarks on pavement that looked black and velvety smooth from inside a car. From this close, the clean yellow lines of paint looked frayed at the edges. I thought about my dad lying on the interstate.

"Stop that!" she said, grabbing me again, yanking me out of a trance. "You are walking too close to the road."

"I'm just walking," I said. "Geez, Sarah."

"Get over here!" She pulled hard this time, pulling me into the weeds at the side.

"What's going on?" one of the other girls asked us.

"If Janna gets hit by a car, Claudia will kill her," Sarah said.

My friends laughed. I laughed, too, because it was funny, I guess. I would be dead if I got hit by a car, so my mom wouldn't be able to kill me.

I could see Vanessa's house about a quarter mile down the road. I knew we shouldn't have been walking on the highway at all. It was stupid and dangerous. "Thanks," I said to Sarah, stopping to examine the weeds.

I pulled up a thick blade of grass, one that would make the perfect woodwind for the perfect shrill whistle. My father had taught Sarah and me how to whistle with grass. He had taught us a lot—how to hold the Frisbee in your mouth for Meagan to jump up and grab, how to ski, how to deep fry crappies, how to go really high on the rope swing, and how to flip over in the hammock without falling out.

"I did it!" I said to Sarah as we reached Vanessa's driveway.

"I heard it. How?"

"Like this," I said, blowing into a sliver of air between my thumbs and a piece of grass until it went from sounding like someone giving a raspberry to a shrill, piercing sound, spit oozing between the webbing of my fingers.

"Gross," said Sarah, looking at my hand.

"Yeah, I know. Oh, well." I wiped it off on my shorts.

"Remember when your dad taught us how to puke?"

"Yeah."

"You were really sick, and we couldn't do anything."

"Whatever, you got carsick on the way home."

Last summer, my dad had taken the two of us to Balloon Fest. New Honda and Nissan City had sponsored someone or something there. We watched dozens of hot air balloons fire up and lift off from up close, the most colorful thing I'd ever seen. When we arrived, I was too carsick to stand up straight. My dad parked the car and then walked the two of us over to the edge of the field, away from everyone.

"Now, just bend over like this," he said, bending at his hips until his head dangled below his waist. "And stick your finger down your throat until you gag. Then you'll barf."

I just watched, doing nothing with my finger. I couldn't. It was too gross. The thought of barf running down my own hand as I pulled it from the trenches of my esophagus was too much for me.

"I can't," I said, wanting to cry from nausea.

"Then you don't want to feel better."

"Dad, I can't."

"Sarah, what do you think?" he asked her as he wiped his own spit from his index finger.

"Just do it," said Sarah. "We're waiting for you."

"I can't."

"We're missing the balloons, Peanut." He ran back to the car and returned with a cardboard carcass from our McDonald's dinner. He stood in front of me. "Janna Marie, stick your finger in. One try."

I leaned over and did as he asked. He waved the empty French fry container under my nose, creating wafts of grease. *Splat!* Milkshake-infused puke spewed out from my mouth, all down my forearm, just missing my Converse.

"Yuck!" said Sarah, jumping back. "Wow! That was gross!"

"How do you feel?" my dad asked, handing me a stack of napkins and a bottled water.

"Better," I said, picking my head up, dizzy but de-nauseated.

"I told you you'd feel better," he said.

I turned away from them, pouring water over the napkins to wash off my face and hands. I was embarrassed, sweaty, and wet.

"Sorry," I said.

"No need to be sorry," my dad said. "Now let's go see the balloons."

I had fallen behind the other girls, concentrating on the tune of my reed. I didn't feel like talking to any of them. Or maybe I just didn't want to talk about what they were talking about.

"Jans! Come on!"

I threw my woodwind to the side and sprinted down Vanessa's driveway to catch up with Sarah.

"Do you miss him?" she asked, looking down at me. Sarah was tall and thin with long brown hair and angled features. Some people called her Skinny Albert. It was hard to see how we were the same age.

"Miss him?"

"Yeah, your dad."

"I guess so, yeah. But he's still ..."

"You know what I mean. Like, the old him? Do you think he'll get better?"

"Well ... I guess so. He will."

At Vanessa's, all five of us jumped on the trampoline and drank Sunny Delight. Five of us at once. My mother would kill me. Sometimes I was surprised my tramp at home didn't have a net around it. Two at a time was our rule. When no one was home, that rule was broken. Sometimes Steven and I got out the hose and the dish soap. Four of us jumping in towers of frothy Dawn.

ON THE WAY HOME FROM Vanessa's, my mom and I picked up wedgies from Fox's Pizza. At home, I set our table for two with two glasses of water, mine with ice and hers without, both of them with lemon. I unwrapped the sloppy wedgies—lettuce, a mayo-like sauce, tomato, and beef between two giant pizza dough triangles—and set them on plates, picking dripping bits of tomato off the one I had claimed.

When my mom and I were home for dinner like this, I'd tell her about my day. Sometimes she laughed or smiled. She always listened intently, always interested in my school subjects, my friends, the boys, the volleyball workouts, and any teenage manifested drama I was willing to share. I asked her about her days. She told me little. I knew there was no one to help her with all that she did. I wished I could be that person for her.

I woke up the next morning in the early hours before my alarm or my mother coming in, feeling like I'd been stabbed somewhere between my heart and my stomach and through to my back. Cramps were still an alien sensation. Womanhood was intrusive. And its entry into my life earlier that summer had been far more embarrassing than puking on my own hand.

"Janna Marie!" my dad had yelled at me from the driveway. "Let's go! We've got the boat all ready, and we're all waiting for you."

"Get Mom for me!"

"Claudia!" I heard him yell. "Janna wants you. I don't know what's taking her so long."

My mother found me in the bathroom. I'd been in there for fifteen minutes while everyone waited for me in the driveway. I had taken off my white suit, wrapped myself in a towel, sat down on the bathmat, and cried.

"Honey, I can't do this one for you," she said through the door. "I'm sorry, but trust me. If you want to go swimming and skiing, you have to do this."

"How?" I sniffled.

"Like it says on the box. It's exactly how. You can read the paper, and I'll wait for you as long as you need. Don't worry about them."

"Did you tell them?" I said, trying to calm down enough to unfold the paper to read the instructions.

"No, no one knows. You're okay. Just take your time. I promise this is the best way."

I held the "device" in one hand and studied the illustrated instructions. It was if someone had made "how to insert a tampon" into a comic strip. I was not ready for this, not even close. Not on a day I was skiing, not with my white suit and a boatload of people waiting in the driveway. I unwrapped it. Ridiculous. This was what women did? This was what my friends were looking forward to?

"Are you okay?"

"Yeah."

"Do you want a pill?"

"For what?"

"Do you have cramps?"

"I don't think so."

"Is it in?"

"No."

"Did you try?"

"No."

"Honey, you have to try. It's really not that bad. Then it will be over, and we can get on the water."

"But what if it falls out?"

"It won't."

"I'll be skiing, how do you know?"

My mom laughed behind the door.

"Why are you laughing at me?"

"Janna, I'm not laughing at you. I'm sorry."

"This is hard. I hate this."

"I know. Just do it, and get it over with. You'll get used to it. The first time is … not fun."

"No kidding."

Ten more minutes, more tears, and a suit change, and I hobbled to the driveway and hopped in the back of the truck. I didn't say anything, and I didn't apologize for holding everyone up. When we unloaded our boat and the Suhries' boat at the dock, my dad stopped and gave me a hug. I didn't hug back. I didn't want to touch anyone.

"Congratulations, Janna!" Vicky said to me once we'd anchored at the dam.

Can people see something? Oh, Christ.

"Huh? What do you mean?"

"You're a woman now!"

I spun around and glared at my mother. "Mom, you said no one knew!"

"Honey, it's fine."

"It's not fine."

I grabbed a beach towel, one of the huge vintage ones that had been around since the '70s, and headed to the bow. I tucked my knees up to my chest and huddled under it.

Now, four months later, I had my first cramps. They hurt like a metal rod poking and prodding my insides. I started sobbing. My head hurt, too. And I missed my parents like hell. I turned over, feeling helpless, staring at the ceiling of my canopy. I wanted to believe what Fred had told me—that the accident was simply one part of my life. But it felt like every part of my life, all the time.

I thought about the second night in the hospital, when everyone else was too busy crying to talk, when Fred had come over to sit with me. He told me that now that the accident had happened, everything might be different. But no matter what, I was still in charge of what happened in my life. The accident would just be part of my story, no matter how it played out. I could not be in charge of how my father acted or of how hard a time he gave my mother, me, or anyone. I could only be in charge of how I acted.

I tugged on the ruffles of my canopy and thought about this. The accident was just part of my story. I was in charge. I wouldn't cry. And maybe if I was a good kid—the best kid—I could make it easier for my parents.

That night, lying on a pillow sticky with tears and snot, I resolved to be a good kid. It remains the most conscious decision I've ever made.

Be good, a good kid—no matter what. Some kids were going down on boys and smoking their older brothers' weed. Or drinking wine coolers and beers and Mad Dogs at parties on the weekends. Some were even tripping on acid, before first period, right after smoking cigarettes in the back alley behind the school parking lot. Others were having sex. Many were breaking curfews and sneaking out. Most were driving. I wasn't doing any of those things. My job was to be the vicarious observer.

My goody-two-shoes demeanor didn't bother my friends. I was open-minded and way too loyal to rat on them. I went to the parties, where I watched people roll joints, chug liquor, and sneak off with boys. Yet never—not even with my let's-please-everyone personality—did I feel the pressure to participate. I'd been watching girls at Children's Aid chain smoke and grow bellies since I was seven. They were real stories, not the poorly acted videos we had to watch in health class about things you could be peer-pressured into. I didn't feel the pressure. I still hadn't French-kissed a boy. I definitely had no plans to trip on acid or have sex. I had never even snuck out or told my parents I was going somewhere when I was actually going somewhere else. I didn't lie, either.

I learned about lying back in fifth grade, when I full-on flunked a spelling test. For whatever reason (I didn't memorize or didn't care), I misspelled well over half of the eighteen words. I told my mom I got a C, too scared to not tell her anything and too disappointed in myself for getting an F. She was okay with it until Mrs. Smith called my house. I don't know why she called my house. I was grounded for two weeks, the only time I'd been grounded—not for failing but for lying about failing.

The truth is that I didn't care what my friends were doing. I was still stuck in the world where lying, riding the horses on the highway, taking the boat out at night, swimming in the strip mines, or interrupting people when they were talking warranted a punishment. I used to get in trouble for those things. But that was before.

Why do stupid things, get myself in trouble, and add to the chaos? Now I shared my parents with a brain injury. The last thing I wanted to do was give my mother a reason to worry about me. I wanted to make my part of her life easy. My dad was would be coming home, and he would get better at home. The accident was behind us, and my mom and I could begin to untangle our lives from it. Then I would focus on me, after the summer had faded away, like history.

But I knew that the accident had already changed us. I was afraid it showed. I imagined people talking about us, the same way you talk about a sad story in an ABC Afterschool Special.

in one ear and out the other

THE SUN SHINES BRIGHTER AGAINST A blue sky in October than in any other month. The crispness of autumn air drugs me with happiness. Everything begins to taste of pumpkin or spice and smells of crunched, fallen leaves and wood burning. Sweaters and jeans. Rich, warm colors. The chill of fall is invigorating. My mother calls it "riding weather." October is my favorite month. "O suns and skies and clouds of June/And flowers of June together/Ye cannot rival for one hour/October's bright blue weather."

My father's discharge date from the Rehabilitation Institute was October 25, 1996. He had not been home in precisely eighty-seven days—almost three months, which amounted to so many weeks that I'd quit counting. The days of chicken salad sandwiches and chairs that hurt my tailbone were long past. So were the days of watching a familiar reality fade away. These days, my mother and I had mastered a perfect illusion of sameness, masking the gap of before and after the brain injury.

My mom winterized the boat, made time to throw sticks and tennis balls to Meagan, and helped me with math homework. I thought her intelligence and perfectionist approach to things would be the trick to algebra, but we were both stumped, bored, and frustrated. She cooked for us, mowed the grass, and kept the garage clean. She went to my volleyball games and chorus concerts and drove me to speech tournaments in the wee morning hours on Saturdays. She lectured me about cars constantly—about riding with my friends and how to pay attention to who was a good driver, who was responsible.

It was as if my dad had been on a long vacation. He could walk in the door and slip right back into our lives, except my mother kept referring to my father as "handicapped, both mentally and physically." She had me prepared to babysit my father—meal times, bedtimes, dos and don'ts, and lists. I was a good babysitter, the kind who gave all the kids on my block secret snacks and extended bedtimes.

Maybe my dad would be like Harrison Ford in *Regarding Henry,* a cold, heartless, intelligent man turned childishly kind and less clever. "This looks like it will be pretty good," my dad had said, bringing the movie home one night for us to watch after work. "I like Harrison Ford, and your mom likes Annette Bening."

Henry was shot in the head at a convenience store. Henry had a brain injury and lost his job as a high-profile, moneymaking lawyer. Henry needed some time to heal in his own home with the help of his wife and only child, a daughter. Henry grew to be a new person; he was different, but it all worked out for the three of them once Henry was adjusted at home.

I would be sharing the bathroom again. My mother had thrown away my dad's bottle of Rolaids. A film of dust had collected on the bottle as it sat untouched on the shelf for months. She replaced the Rolaids with an oblong, transparent blue pillbox that sat on the counter, open and obvious. Each square was marked with bold letters, kindergarten typeface, for every day of the week. In each square, she arranged his medications with same precision as she used to place the Christmas tree ornaments back in their storage boxes. I counted them.

One cotton-candy-pink oblong pill (Paxil: 20 mg at 8:00 a.m.), a Selective Serotonin Reuptake Inhibitor (SSRI) to calm anxiety and reduce obsessive-compulsive behavior.

Three square white pills that looked straight out of *Brave New World* (Buspar: 15 mg at 8:00 a.m., 2:00 p.m., and 8:00 p.m.), another anti-anxiety, the least drowsy drug of its kind.

One round, sand-colored tablet (Desyrel: 50 mg before bed), a Serotonin Antagonist Reuptake Inhibitor (SARI), an anti-depressant.

Three white Mike & Ikes (Risperdal: 1 mg at 8:00 a.m., 4:00 p.m., and 8:00 p.m.), a super low dose of a heavy little drug used to treat schizophrenia and the mixed manic states of bipolar disorder, a mild horse tranquilizer of sorts that slows down the metabolism in the process.

One half white, half sea-green capsule (Klonopin: 0.25 mg at 8:00 p.m.) to reduce anxiety, and in his case, reduce muscle spasms in his sleep.

Two shiny, fire-engine-red pills (Amantadine: 50 mg at 8:00 a.m. and 8:00 p.m.) to reduce the dopamine turnover in his brain. With a Glasgow Coma score so low, he had significantly reduced cognitive functioning, so this drug might be able to help.

One mauve oval stamped with AMB (Ambien: 5 mg at bedtime) to sleep at night.

Twelve pills every day. I wondered how he would take them all. Gram Margaret took her pills three at a time. And Gram Mary hid hers around the house in an attempt not to take them. I'm sure that many tasted awful. Would they get stuck in his throat on the way down? He was always thirsty, but he rarely drank water.

The Rolling Rocks and Honey Browns in our fridge were replaced with cartons of Ensure. Our cupboards were filled with fibrous carbs and the crispers with vegetables and fruits. Healthy, simple things—no Doritos, no Oreos.

"Are you excited?" I asked the day before he was supposed to come home. "He's coming home!"

"Well, yes." she said. "But, Janna, you have to understand that he's going to be very different. He's not the same at all."

"But he'll finally be at home. That's kind of exciting."

"Yes, I know …" My mom didn't seem excited. She seemed more sad or scared. An emotion I couldn't place. Maybe she was just tired.

"But it's good that he's coming home, right?"

"He's going to be very tired, and he's going to sleep a lot. He's not going to be the same dad."

"Oh."

"Janna, he's really not very nice sometimes. It's one of the stages. I just want you know—he sometimes has a hard time with … things."

"Oh."

I didn't expect balloons, cakes, and a living room full of guests with a "Welcome Home, John" banner strung across the beams (though I thought about making one), but I expected something. No one came over. There was nothing welcoming, no hint of a homecoming. On a day like any other, my mother came home after work with my dad. I sat on the back porch with

Meagan, trying to make a blade of grass whistle. We waited to hear the crunch of gravel as the car pulled into the driveway.

When I heard it, I stood up, heart thumping, ready to race down to meet them. I couldn't move. I just stood and watched her pull the car up and park in front of the garage. She got out and came around to unbuckle him and help him lift out of the passenger seat. When I saw him, I realized that I didn't know this man coming to live with us. They walked toward me, and Meagan circled them, tail wagging, panting, nudging my mom with her nose. I played out in my mind when the perfect time would be to hug him.

When they reached the steps in front of me, I backed out of the way. My mom stayed patiently beside my dad as he climbed all three steps, her elbow latched tight around the crook of his arm like a deadbolt. With each step, she gave him a different command.

"Careful." Step one. "Watch yourself." Step two. "John! You have to slow down." Finally, at three, he took a giant gasp and looked at me. We were one foot from each other, and he just stared.

"John, say hi to Janna," Mom said.

"Hi, Dad."

I couldn't do it. I could barely touch him. A hug was out of the question. I didn't know who he was. So I gave him a kiss on the cheek. It was half-assed kiss, like in the movies, just brushing his cheekbone with mine as I kissed air, not flesh.

I opened the door for them, chewing myself out over that fact that I was too scared to hug my own brain-injured father. It was not his fault. Embarrassing. I might break him; his body was stiff and frail, like clay that might crack, under skin that sagged and stretched, desperately trying to hang onto his bones. He was the man in the seventh box of the "Seven Stages of Man" sketch that hung in our basement. An old man, hunched over, crippled. I couldn't hug a man I didn't know.

Meagan greeted him, happy and panting, but he didn't reach out to pat her head. My mother mouthed *very tired* to me as I followed them inside, where he walked around our hallway, lost and confused. It was as if he'd never been there before. He wanted to sit, but he didn't know where. He didn't know to pull the chair out from under my mother's desk.

We had dinner at our kitchen table, like always. My mother tried to acclimate us both to the change and the new way to spend time together, giving us verbal lists of instructions over turkey sandwiches and cut-up cantaloupe. He slumped over, one shoulder dropped awkwardly to the side, and stared at something in his lap. I sat, intently listening, taking mental notes on what was allowed and not allowed with him here, which helped me to block out how petrifying this homecoming was.

After dinner, he fumbled his way through the house. At least he was walking again. There were no bars, no burly men on either side, no walker. He had little patience for himself, which resulted in plowing through space and catching his stumbles on furniture and walls. I was sure he would break our antique chairs with the weight of his falls. He weighed nothing. Nothing ever broke. He got the hang of walking like a normal person eventually.

A few days later, when Ken, his first caregiver, arrived, my dad was disoriented. He used to work with a man named Ken at New Honda and Nissan City, and that Ken was his subordinate. This Ken was bossing him around. So when this Ken wouldn't listen to him, he got mean and very aggressive. It wasn't a question of like or dislike; he simply could not understand the purpose of Ken.

"All he does is watch me," my father said to my mother. "He just watches. I don't need watched."

We tried to explain how that was Ken's job, giving him a myriad of reasons, but to my father, they made no sense. Reasons only aggravated him.

"You're paying someone to watch me do things."

It was not long before Ken got cut and was replaced by Jana, which my mother incorrectly pronounced as Jane-a (with a long *a*). It was an unfairly perplexing situation for him—a Janna with one *n*—sounds the same but spelled different, sounds the same but belonged to someone completely different, sounds the same but bossing him around.

I was also strangely insulted by the fact that his caregiver had the same name. I didn't know anyone with my name. I liked it that way. But Jana was nice, and she was good at watching my dad. He was angry and hostile. But Jana with one *n* knew how to handle him, how to help him go about his days doing what he needed to do.

I didn't know how he spent his days and didn't care. I kept mine separate. I couldn't recognize our relationship. I didn't know how to act.

It helped that I was still allowed to do whatever I wanted, see whatever friends I wanted to see, and stay out late. My father was a just frail, limp, angry, sad, mean man living with us. No one, not friends or family, seemed comfortable in his presence. My friends never came over to my house anymore. I didn't know how to explain to them who this person was, and I was afraid of what he would do or say around them. Nothing was predictable. He yelled a lot. I used to have a fun dad who was loving, involved, and harmless. Even then, I had friends who were scared of him, so I couldn't imagine how they would be now.

The winter before, I'd had a sleepover. Five girls were holed up downstairs under mounds of blankets with the dog, watching movies in the middle of a blizzard. On that particular night, my parents didn't care what we took from the kitchen, as long it was not my father's chicken wings. I was simply asked not to eat them. I relayed the request to anyone who made snack runs to the kitchen, but after we'd plowed through two sleeves of Oreos, Sun Chips, peanut butter cup ice cream, Fruit Roll-ups, and Doritos, Rebecca wanted the chicken wings she had seen in the fridge.

"You can't, Becs," I told her. "My dad said we can't."

"Aw, come on, Janna Marie; he won't care."

"Yes, he will. He specifically asked us not to eat them."

Rebecca brought down the Styrofoam container of chicken wings. My friends attacked them in front of me while I pleaded with them to stop. They just laughed at me.

"Janna Marie!"

I heard him walking across the living room directly above us. We all did—*thumps* toward the top of the basement stairs.

"*Jannamarie!*"

I raced up the steps to meet him at the top. "Dad, they did it. I told them not to. No one listens to me."

"Come with me."

I heard my friends giggling downstairs, giggling and eating his wings.

My father and I went to the kitchen, where we had a firm discussion about chicken wings from Quaker Steak & Lube and sticking up for yourself. He felt the same way about this as my mother did about dog pats and recess surfing.

"Janna, damn, your dad is scary," said Rebecca, licking dry garlic off her fingers. "It's just chicken wings. I would not want to get in real trouble with him."

"Yeah, yikes," said Leah. "He really yelled at you."

"He's not scary, you guys," I said, huffing down into a ball on my covers.

"Janna, you're crying, though," said Amber, who knew my dad was not scary.

I crawled under the blankets. My friends never listened to me, and now they were laughing at me. Sarah lifted the blankets.

"Come on, you guys," I said, forced to resurface, wiping my face. "I asked you not to. You guys never listen to me."

"It's just wings, Jan. He'll get over it," said Amber.

"But he asked us not to."

"Oh, so what," said Rebecca.

But now my dad was frightening to the bones, even to me. He yelled about everything. He was mean. It was supposed to be a phase. Even the dumb book for kids like me said so.

He hit Meagan, too. He whaled on her, right in the face. It made my stomach flip. He loved that dog. That dog loved him. He wouldn't take her out or throw the Frisbee, a stick, or a ball, but it didn't stop her from trying, grabbing her toys and dropping them at his feet like old times, only to be walloped in the face. And he threw the cat off tables, off his lap when she crawled up there, or just because.

He was no longer kind. Sometimes he would raise his hand at me in moments of enraged frustration, but nothing came of it. I just yelled back. I learned how to yell at him. Eventually, we had to hide car keys from him. All he wanted to do was drive. He wanted to drive away and leave everyone. This was his daily, empty threat. So the keys were no longer allowed to hang on the hook above the phone.

As the weeks barreled into the holiday season, I found that it was easy to avoid coming home. Ninth grade in Mercer was a full-time job. I hung out with my friends after school and stayed late at their houses. I ate dinner at the Suhries'. I babysat neighbors. I spent weekends at Jackie's, Vanessa's, or Sarah's. I shopped to stock up on Silver Tabs and flannel shirts and listened to grunge CDs with Amber and Rebecca. Zac introduced me to a new band, a local band called The Clarks. The drummer had gone to our high school. Sarah and I hung out alone in her house and blasted *Clarks Live,* Jimmy Buffett, Oasis, Nirvana, The Eagles, and Celine Dion while we baked things.

I still didn't smoke cigarettes, smoke pot, or have a boyfriend. I didn't drink and didn't have sex. I still got all As and chose responsible drivers. I just didn't know how to be at home anymore. I had disconnected from my parents in a way that made me think that when this all blew over, I'd come back to them. If I thought about it too much, I missed them terribly.

I tried to talk to my father about anything he wanted to talk about. We were the talkers, but the conversation was always taxing and pointless, and he'd turned into a selfish, chauvinist, crude man from a bad sitcom. He told lewd jokes to strangers. He bossed my mother around. He told me I was a selfish little brat. He never called me Peanut or Janna Marie. He never did the dishes. He never offered to help with anything. And he watched a lot of TV.

He swore at me. He ran around the house to get away from me. This made as much sense as when Gram Mary used to do the same thing. She would lock me out of the house and holler at me. I had hidden from her, but I confronted my father. And he was always trying to start fires, like it was his thing. Matches and lighters all had to be hidden like car keys. There was no explanation for it. Many times, it was evident that he had no idea who we were. He didn't know where he was. He didn't even know who he was.

"Maybe it would have helped if we'd taken pictures," my mother said one day when we were feeding the horses.

"Of what?" I asked.

"Your father in the hospital, with his face banged up and all the tubes. I had thought about it, but I just didn't do it."

"I don't think he'd believe us anyway if we showed them to him."

"You're probably right."

He had no memory of the accident. He had no memory of the months after or the months before. In his more lucid moments, he constantly contested the extreme care and concern that we had for him. He thought we were making it all up.

The moments of his old self were so few and far between that they were almost a cruel joke. He'd say a familiar phrase, or we'd recognize something as simple as the intonation he used on one word. He would sit on the porch steps and scratch Meagan's ears. He'd hug Mom. He'd make me cinnamon toast. He'd say "Gesundheit" after I sneezed. It was like watching a snowed-out TV screen play blips of the movie we'd all been watching. Little blips, signs that it all might come back. Motivation to keep on loving him.

My mother thought it would be okay to invite Sarah and Jackie over to re-meet him. Two of my closest friends whose mothers knew and could probably prepare them for what to expect. When they arrived, we had a short conversation in the driveway with my dad. They were polite and careful not to speak to him like he was baby. I had begged them to just be normal. They were. And he was polite, not nasty or lewd.

"Who were they?" he asked after they went inside to put their bags in my room.

"Dad! That's Sarah and Jackie," I said. "You know them."

"I do not know them. Who are they?"

"They're my friends, remember? My best friends …"

"No."

"But you took us skiing all the time, and you—"

"Janna, stop." My mother had come outside.

"Okay, sorry. Dad, Sarah is the girl with brown hair, and Jackie has blonde hair. They are my best friends. You've met them many times before."

"Janna," my mom said. "I said stop."

"But they're—"

"Can it."

"John!" my mom screamed, reaching her hand into the backseat to stop me from keeling forward. *"Slow down!"*

We hadn't even made it out of the driveway. My stomach was stuck in my throat. I wanted to barf. The car was a mix of four splashes too many of Old Spice and my mom's Clinique Elixir. We were going out to eat with Fred and Carolyn. This was exciting. This was something we used to do.

"*Dad!* Please just slow down."

The Explorer hurtled toward the ditch, the back wheel lifting as we made the turn out of our driveway at 45 mph. How one gets from 0 to 45 on that limited stretch of limestone, I'll never know.

Crunch.

"John! That was Suhries' mailbox!"

I could feel us all flying through the windshield, and I pictured broken skulls and puddles of blood to clean up.

Clug. The truck landed.

"What?" my dad asked, annoyed. "I'm the one driving. I am driving."

It was all he had wanted to do for months and months—drive a car. Drive and go back to work. Drive and go back to work. A broken record. This was his big night. Tonight was a test. My mother would let him drive the three minutes it took to get from our house to the Gallos'.

"John! You have to pay attention," she said, putting her hand over his on the wheel. "You cannot just go like that. You need to slow down, and you need to pay attention. Janna's with us, remember?"

He had no idea how not to accelerate and brake at the same time. And, as it turned out, he had no depth perception. He was majorly failing.

"I know what I'm doing," he said, slamming on the brakes.

Once off Delaware Trail, he never broke 20 mph. He could've gone at least 35, but driving extra slow would show us who was in charge. He was. I counted the seconds until we pulled into the Gallos' driveway. My father was livid at having been told what to do.

As soon as we parked the car, I hopped out and ran in through their garage into the house. I didn't say hello, didn't wait for my parents, and shoved Baxter, their giant, slobbery yellow lab, out of the way, racing to the bathroom. I closed the door and stood in the dark with a flickering decorative candle, waiting for my heart to stop beating against the skin of my chest. I heard my parents come in, heard Fred ask where I was, if I was coming. Heard my mother say I was probably in the bathroom.

I sat down on the toilet seat and closed my eyes, breathing in the spiced cookie candle. I heard my father telling Fred a joke about a stripper while they poured drinks in the kitchen. I pictured my dad, face stretched thin, shoulder humped over, wearing a maroon sweater that fit him like a sack. He was laughing his new laugh about the tits in the punch line of this joke that he had told Fred the last three times they were together. I pictured my mom taking a healthy sip of the White Zinfandel that Carolyn poured for her from a box on the dining room table.

"Can I have a sip?" I asked my mother as I emerged from the bathroom.

"You won't like it, hon," Carolyn said.

"Can I just try?"

"Sure," my mother said, handing me her glass. "It needs an ice cube."

I walked over to the freezer, stuck my hand under the dispenser, and pushed "cubed ice." The Suhries had one, and Jackie and the Gallos. Why couldn't we? I plunked two cubes in and walked back to the dining room. I took a sip. It tasted like what I imagined tinfoil would taste like. I made a face and handed it back to her. I went into the living room to search for the bowl of Hersey's Kisses. I picked out three blue and three gold ones and stood, eating them one after the other, while I stared at the Gallos' collection of '80s and '90s movies. I'd watched them all at least six times. I pulled out *Romancing the Stone* and wondered if Cartagena could really be as steamy and romantic as Michael Douglas and Kathleen Turner made it look. Or if it was possible to wheel a schooner down Fifth Avenue in New York City.

"Janna Marie, *mangia, mangia …*" Fred yelled from the kitchen. "Let asa go eeetza."

BY CHRISTMASTIME, WE WERE A different family. We looked like a different family. There is a picture to prove it that hangs in our spare bedroom. I have no idea why my mother has never taken it down. It's still there, and I often find myself staring at it. The picture was taken in front of Aunt Biz's Christmas tree on Christmas morning in 1996. My parents' gaunt faces are a mix of *American Gothic* and Dalí, dripping with sorrow and times changed. I look like a misfit with a bemused half side grin, a smirk, as if I'm daring the picture-taker to actually snap the shutter. Our clothes fit us like clothes fit coat hangers. My mom and I have faces caked in porcelain make-up. I have frizzy hair and braces. The bags under my mom's eyes are a nod to the wars she'd been fighting. My father's mustache takes over his face on a head that is too big for his body, like it could just snap off like a dandelion.

I don't remember anything about Christmas that year. I don't remember the presents or sneaking sips of the standard "White Christmas" drink of frothy vodka and cream soda. We have photos—lots of half smiles and at least a dozen of my father fast asleep on the couch, gifts piled around him. I don't remember New Year's or what I did to welcome in 1997. I don't remember my mother's birthday two days later. There are no photos of that.

In the new year, my dad no longer needed full-time care, so he started to complete lists of things to do around the house involving simple tasks that centered around animal care, snow shoveling, and fixing things. He could cook simple dinners. My mother kept him busy, active, engaged, and for the most part, away from my school stuff. That was a relief.

Eventually he could drive and had passed a driver's test. This allowed a heavily monitored shot at going back to work, a trial to see if the environment of cars and people could kick-start anything. At first, he was good at faking being "old John," but when he couldn't keep track of paperwork and started mixing up sales and customers, it was clear that he couldn't just go back to his old job. He was easily frustrated and was curt, even flat-out rude, to his coworkers and customers. They halved his hours and gave him grade school-level tasks, but his limited attention span and lack of skills and patience were of no use to anyone. People at work had no interest in supporting the steps of his brain injury recovery.

My mother had to find something else for him to do. She's good at that: finding things for people to do, finding things that she thinks they'll actually enjoy. And they do. She has an unassuming creativity.

She found my dad a volunteer job at the Mercer County Historical Society. My father loved history. He lapped up information, anecdotes, and facts about every era. Wars were his favorite. He was most fascinated by the Civil War. And our family genealogy. "Old John," the first Leyde, was buried only miles away. Old John fought in the Civil War. My father used to dress up in a navy blue wool Union uniform, walking around our house with a musket rifle, asking us to take pictures of him.

Three days a week, he went in to the Historical Society to log some kind of county records. Two days a week, Pa took him to rehab (determined too far and too confusing of a drive for him), and my mother took him to his appointments with Dr. Ben Zimmer, the neuropsychologist. Dr. Zimmer was quiet and plump with a gray beard. My father liked him, and Dr. Zimmer specialized in people like my father, the brain injured.

I imagined all the tests, drugs, appointments, visits, and evaluations were what it took to heal someone's brain from the inside out, slowly heal a zillion little cuts, bumps, and bruises on the gray matter so that the person could become himself or herself again. No one had explained to us that his recovery process was nothing like a Band-Aid healing a scrape. It was brain injury in the '90s. No one knew how to explain brain injury to anyone yet.

Just shy of six months living at home, my dad was re-evaluated to determine how to continue with his treatment. Pages of paperwork endeavored to rate and illustrate my father's symptoms and what his injured brain was doing to his life. My dad's report card.

ON PAR/AVERAGE:

Motor functions Walking and moving around with the effort-filled agility that was expected of him. No waterskiing, racquetball, or riding.

Immediate memory span In the moment, he could follow what was going on. He didn't get lost like he used to when we were talking to him—but only in the moment.

Working memory He was confused very easily, always puzzled. His brain was not able to adapt when anything about his surroundings changed.

IMPAIRED/SEVERELY IMPAIRED:

Ability to consolidate new information to long-term memory Everything required prompts: schedules, my friends' names, what we were supposed to be doing that day, that week. Nothing new could stick in his brain. He could respond to people when they told him something, but beyond that moment, he had no way to keep track of what they had told him. In a matter of minutes, he had no clue what was going on.

GONE:

Executive functioning Executive function, a neuro term used to describe the higher-level human skill set that, like opposable thumbs, sets us apart. The beautiful, intricate cognitive flexibility that our brains have to organize, plan, assess, think abstractly, follow rules. How we monitor our own behavior, our impulse control, how we make a decision (the simplest to the most complex), and how we problem-solve (be it in math or daily life). Initiate the proper actions and inhibit the improper. Choose right from wrong.

The first hundred times I'd heard the phrase, it seemed too impersonal and mechanic to relate to human behavior. When people try to describe what happens when executive function fails, they tend to make it analogous to a computer's hard drive crashing. The hard drive is the subconscious part of the brain (a gazillion stored memories and bits of information), and RAM is the conscious part (the information you use in the present moment). RAM is the executive function.

When your computer turns on, what it needs to run your programs is transferred to the RAM, or conscious memory of your computer. When you are finished with a program or application and you close the program, then it is wiped out of the RAM to make room for more applications, but it stays on your hard drive so you can recall it later.

The computer comparison feels stale, cliché. It's not human enough, but maybe that's the point.

Either way, my father bombed the executive functioning portion of his test. The evaluation showed that if he exerted too much mental effort (too much thinking above the level of a second-grader), he became extremely fatigued. It also showed that he constantly misinformed himself. Still, The Rehabilitation Institute at Squirrel Hill hoped that his daily functioning would improve. He had come impressively far for someone with such a severe brain injury—driving, time spent unsupervised, walking, talking, eating, reading. His family hadn't left him. These milestones meant the world to us and to his doctors. They meant nothing to him.

By May, he was bored of the Historical Society, the lists, the appointments, and the time at home. Returning back to work was not an option, but we had no way to get him to understand that. We were just obstacles to getting what he wanted.

By summer, I had a boyfriend. His name was Richard. He was a basketball and track star and was two grades and three years older than I was. I laughed at my father when he tried to tell me what to do. I was always in trouble with my dad, but I never listened to him, because he was three years off. He had no idea how old I was. In his mind (misinformation that could not be dislodged), I was eleven years old, not fourteen going on fifteen. He treated me like I was a fourth-grader, putting limitations on my actions, my bedtime, my time on the phone. Eleven-year-olds don't go out with boyfriends.

Richard asked me out while we were walking through Buhl Park, past the pond where Pa and I would walk to feed the ducks.

"So, will you go out with me?" he asked.

He was tall and skinny, tan from a summer of lifeguarding. I looked up at him and away to the leaves in the trees behind him. I hadn't expected this, and I didn't even know what I wanted.

"Why would you ask me that?" I asked.

"What do you mean, why would I ask you that?" he asked.

"Wait," I said. "Yeah. Sure. Okay."

"Sure? Okay?"

"Yes, I will go out with you."

I was trying to make it more complex than it was or had to be. We met in the same way that I still seem to meet men—when someone else is interested or when, for whatever reason, the odds are against me because of distance or timing.

It was Jackie's birthday party, and everyone was invited—older guys, younger girls, all of our friends. Richard came with his best friend, whom Jackie had a crush on. One of my other friends had a crush on Richard. When things went awry—Sarah's boyfriend's car blew up into ball of flames on the side of the road just before the sky dumped on us—I found myself standing under an umbrella with Richard. We talked, flirted, and laughed. I suppose that's when we started, though according to girl crush code, he wasn't mine to like. I believed in girl crush code like I believed the world was fair.

Richard was nice. My mother liked him.

"Janna, come down here a sec," my mom yelled from the laundry room.

"Yeah …"

"Is Richard here yet?"

"Nope."

"When's he coming?"

"I don't know. Soon."

"Okay, well, I need to tell you something. If you are going to be alone with him …"

" …Okay …"

"You absolutely cannot get pregnant—"

"Mom! What are you talking about?"

"Janna, I'm serious."

"Mom, you've got to be kidding me! I can't even have this discussion." I couldn't contain myself. I sat down on the floor. I was laughing too hard.

"Janna, you know—"

"Seriously! Mom, please don't worry. Seriously, you have *nothing* to worry about. I promise, because we're not, you know. Please. Please do not even worry about this. There is no way I could possibly get pregnant. Like, never. Just, *ugh*. God, gross. Just never."

"I just—"

"I know. I know, but Mom, I promise. Nothing. Not happening. No way. Okay? I know what my friends are doing and stuff. But I'm not. Okay. I don't even want to. I promise."

"Okay."

I heard the car in the driveway. She'd finished ironing the shirt. I got up from the floor and hugged her. I had spoken the truth. They went to dinner, and I made Richard watch *Pretty Woman* for the hundredth time. We made out aggressively. I told him what my mom had said, though I'm not sure he thought it was that funny.

THE SUMMER BEFORE TENTH GRADE was followed by a summer of less waterskiing and more dating than summers before it. There were no hospitals and no rehab centers, but I had no father to take me skiing. Vicky did, sometimes, but it was midday, and the water was always a choppy mess. Occasionally, my parents would take the boat out, but only to anchor at the shallow end and sit in the sun. My mom was tired. My father tried skiing once, and like executive functioning, failed miserably.

In September, Richard asked me to the homecoming dance, so my mother took us all dress shopping. My friends were happy to have her brand of Claudia enthusiasm and opinion. I got a long, black, stretchy dress covered in rhinestones that were spread out like stars down the front. I didn't love it. I didn't hate it. I knew it looked good, accentuating my lean build with growing boobs. The dance was fun, just another thing I should be doing at that age.

In November, one year into living at home, fifteen months post-injury, my father had his second evaluation from Rehab. Unlike last time, they were able to administer a slew of tests with names that ranged from the Very Official to the Nearly Silly:

- The Wechsler Adult Intelligence Scale III (rational thinking, purposeful action, effective ways to deal with surrounding environment)
- The Wechsler Memory Scale III (auditory and visual memory function)

- Category Test (frontal lobe executive function)
- Wisconsin Card Sorting Test (executive functioning flexibility)
- Grooved Pegboard Test (dexterity)
- Finger Tapping Test (motor speed)
- Hand Dynamometer (grip and pinch strength)

The evaluation began with a poorly written paragraph.

> John has returned to work in sales only to find that he had lost patience with both customers and fellow workers. He does not want to return to New Honda and Nissan City. He does chores around the house and volunteers part-time at the local historical society, which he describes as "very boring transcribing." Both wife and daughter indicated that he is not the same husband and father he was prior to the accident. There is a growing awareness that John is not sensitive to his environment—"I go for the jugular" when he is convinced he is right. Furthermore, John has an enlarged aorta and a spot on his lungs, which is adding to complication of his life and emotional impact on his family. But John has his resume ready and has been working with the Office of Vocational Rehabilitation.

According to the scores of the Wechsler tests, my father's IQ had dive-bombed, and his intellectual functioning had plateaued at a level far from what it had been before the accident. He had major problems with "general social situations," "problem-solving," and "planning with unstructured tasks." And his memory was, at best, average: it was extremely difficult for him to "consolidate new information to long-term memory store," and though he could hear, understand, and repeat a conversation, he could not remember it the next day. His "capacity for new learning" was shot.

However, the Wechsler tests also showed that my father still knew how to bullshit and bullshit well. "He can impress an observer as a man with superior intellectual functions, but what the observer fails to notice in a brief observation is that John will have forgotten a great deal of what happened to him yesterday."

And last but never least: executive function, which had now been labeled as "John's greatest handicap." My father could not assess social situations and failed to respond with socially appropriate behaviors. He was losing his friends (even this was noted on his evaluations). Things that were intuitive and obvious to everyone else were not to him. He was losing touch, but it did not stop him from thinking he was not. He had become almost pathologically impulsive. He wanted what he wanted when he wanted it—always, now. He could generate future plans and ideas, but just as quickly, he would discard the current plans and ideas. His passion to "do something" or "say something" was immovable. No room for logical argument. My father was always right.

Seven pages later, his evaluation wrapped up with an equally lazy conclusion.

> John's recovery has plateaued. Few if any improvements can be expected with a passage of time. He can learn and make further accommodations as he struggles for a meaningful way of life, but the major advances will only come from our ability to adapt the environment to the his present needs and level of functions. Getting a job will be next to impossible. He will need a job coach, a job using his already acquired talents, and job that has a low learning curve. Finding and making new friendships outside of his immediate family will be problematic and require major understanding on the part of those with whom he interacts. He will do best with those who knew him prior to the head injury.

In the history of brain injuries, with an evaluation like this one, people leave.

I WAS LEARNING THAT MY father could not express emotions, whether he felt them or not. "Flat affect," my mother had explained. Some people with brain injuries suffered it as result of the depression from the change in their lives, and other people suffered it because of where they got hit on the head.

My father was the latter. He was supremely apathetic in any given situation, unless it was laughing at a dirty joke he was telling or becoming enraged about not being able to drive. Meagan was getting old and having a hard time, yet he hardly took notice and had no patience for her. He made an inappropriate comment about one of my friends. He made Mom cry, made me cry, made Aunt Biz cry. It didn't matter—flat affect. The only thing he could fake was his stupid smile and fraudulent laugh.

"Dad?"

"Janna."

"What are you doing?"

He'd picked me up at school from speech practice. It was December, a whiteout blizzard on a Monday night. He was no sweet and kind *Regarding Henry,* but he could at least pick me up from school. The whole way in from town, we drove through whiteness, slipping and sliding through turns. His driving was appropriate, but the weather was not.

When we got to the boat ramp, he pulled over into the empty parking lot, the headlights illuminating the naked, untarnished snow on the frozen lake. It made me think of the fresh ice-skate tracks we used to make together—his smooth, clean lines on hockey skates and my craggy pattern of blunders and falls on figure skates.

"Dad, why are we stopped?"

He shifted the Explorer into Park and opened his door. He unbuckled his seat belt, got out (leaving the door open), and walked around to open my door. "Because you're driving."

"Dad! No! I can't!"

"Then I guess we're just going to sit here."

"I can't, Dad. No. It's snowing."

"Well, I'm not going to drive."

I started to cry. I told him I'd tell Mom, told him that I was too young, told him it was dangerous. He told me the only way we were getting home was if I drove us there.

"But it's snowing. I can't see."

"*You* can see. *I* can see."

"No, Dad. I can't."

"You can."

It was cold, and snow was building up on the running boards of the open doors to the truck. I kicked it away and got out. I walked around, feeling the snow land on my eyelashes and melt my mascara. I stared at the driver's seat, and the foreign lights of the dashboard stared back at me.

"Well, get in."

I got in. He talked me through it—short, clipped, unemotional steps of where to put my feet and hands. How to turn on four-wheel drive; how to work the wipers; where the brakes were; and what would happen if I went too fast. Then he said nothing. We sat there for five minutes while I sobbed into the steering wheel.

"Dad, why are you doing this?"

"Are we just going to sit here while you cry?"

I wiped the tears and makeup off my face with my scratchy wool scarf. The window had fogged up, so I wiped my scarf on the window. I looked at the window helplessly and then at him. He punched the defrost button. I pushed and pulled at the gas pedal with my foot, feeling for it as if I were reaching into an abyss. I was too short. The truck tugged and jerked out of the parking lot. When I tried to turn onto Latonka Drive, the tires just spun. I hoped they would spin until they found raw, un-iced road, but we just started inching to one side, slipping.

"Dad!"

The tail end of the truck was out of my control, and I could see headlights on the stretch of country road behind us, soon to catch up with us.

"Dad, please! I can't do this."

"Take your foot off the pedal."

I did, and the spinning stopped. He punched the four-wheel drive button.

"Hit the gas."

I hit it, and we eked forward. I couldn't see. I drove blindly into a tunnel of white flurries for what seemed like an hour, never popping the needle above 10 mph. I couldn't see where the road ended. My father just sat there. Silent, with no words of encouragement.

"Why are you crying?"

"Why did you make me do this?"

"You have to learn to drive."

I sobbed, wiping snot off on the mitten that was sitting in my lap.

"Why are you crying?"

"Why can't you understand, Dad? This is so scary."

"No it's not. Stop crying."

"But you won't help me."

"You don't need help. You are doing it."

By the time I pulled into the driveway, my forearms hurt from squeezing the wheel. Salt and snot had dried all over my face, and my clothes were soaked with sweat. I looked at him, and he looked at the garage, reached up, and pushed the red button attached the visor above me. The door creaked open. I looked at him. He looked at the wheel and then at the open garage.

"No," I said.

"Then we'll just leave it outside," he said, starting to open his door.

"No!" I said, leaning over him to swat his hand away from the handle.

I crawled forward in the Explorer, making myself dizzy as I turned my head from side to side to make sure I didn't hack off a mirror in the process. I turned off the ignition, opened the door, and breathed a full sigh of cold winter garage air into my lungs. I handed him the keys. I ran into the house and straight into the bathroom to wash my face off, the sweat, the tears, the entire experience. When had I started this relationship with bathroom escapes?

"Janna, John? Where have you been?" my mom asked, padding into the hallway in a pair of her puffy slippers.

"Dad taught me how to drive," I said through the bathroom door over the running water. I never even went to the bathroom. I would just sit, run water, or look in the mirror.

"John, what?"

"I taught Janna how to drive."

"John, she's not old enough."

"She is now."

"You can't do these things."

"It was a blizzard, too," I yelled from the bathroom. Sitting on the closed toilet seat, feeling steam fill the air from the hot water running in the sink, I began to calm down. I even felt a little proud of my feat.

"John, you can't do that."

"She's fine. She had to learn sometime. She done good."

Done good. There it was—the slight mockery on the English language. I heard it. One of those tiny moments, hidden in a phrase, a taste of the man he used to be, a blip. I knew she heard it, too.

Four months later, I got my own car. It was March 10, 1998. I was still fifteen. It was my father's forty-eighth birthday, and Gram and Pa had come over. The five of us sat in the living room, trying to debunk my mood. I was angry, frustrated, experiencing the typical teenage emotions of rotten friends and a boyfriend who seemed too interested in every other girl.

"Janna, come out to the garage with me, and let me show you something," my dad said.

He had been having more moments of himself in the last few months. We argued less, or maybe I was too busy to argue. He tried harder to remember my friends and understand my age. He told me he was sorry when he thought he had hurt my feelings. But today, it didn't matter. I was angry at my own life, and the last thing I wanted to do was go outside in the dark and check out *something* in the garage.

"You should just go with your father," my mother said.

"Why?"

"Just check it out, Toots," said Pa.

I followed him through the house, watching his slumped shoulder in front of me. It was warm in the house and smelled of the delicious vat of chicken and rice soup my mother had made us for dinner. It was one of my favorites. Outside was March, rainy and cold. The porch was wet, but I was too lazy and walked outside in my slipper socks, fuzzy and blue with puffy white cats playing with balls of yarn that served as treads. My dad stood behind me as I opened the garage door. I could feel the melted snow soaking up the cats and their yarn balls.

"Happy birthday!" he said, reaching in front of me to flick on the light.

It looked just like the convertible that my dad drove when he took Sarah and me to Balloon Fest. He used to drive demo cars whenever he wanted, and the two-seater blue Del Sol had been my very favorite, my dream car. There it was, in red.

"What? Huh? But it's *your* birthday, Dad."

"But we love *you*," he said.

"We couldn't hide this from you forever," said my mom, who had walked out to join us.

"You guys bought me a Del Sol for my birthday and gave it to me on Dad's birthday? Thank you. Thank you! Thank you! You are the best. I don't deserve this."

I jumped up and down, hugged my parents, and told them how much I loved them and the car. I ran around all sides of the car, and my father came over to give me the keys and show me things on the inside, like a little bottle of red paint that he had filled and put in the glove box. He had always been creative and clever, but since the accident, his innovations and attempts at jerry-rigging things were sloppy at best. The bottle of paint was neat, clean, and well thought out.

"We thought maybe this would cheer you up tonight," my mom said.

"Um, yeah. Wow. I'm sorry, like, really sorry."

I was guilty, embarrassed, and happy. Richard had broken up with me that morning, but that night, my parents gave me a red convertible. Life was weird.

"You can't drive it for a couple months, though," my mom said.

"You can ride in it," my dad said. "I'll drive. Richard can drive."

"John. She and—"

"I don't care. It's great. It's beautiful. It's so cool. Wow! This is the best, coolest thing ever!"

The next day at school, I told all the right people that I got a car, a red convertible. I told all the people that would tell Richard. We got back together in a few weeks, probably not on account of the Del Sol, but the attention had helped. As soon as I got a permit, Richard picked up where my mother had left off in teaching me how to drive. She trusted Richard. He told me constantly that I stopped too quickly before turns until I stopped doing it. I made him listen to Jimmy Buffett until he fell in love with Buffett on his own. We made out at a lot of stop signs, and once he dropped the roof (a hardtop that fit in the trunk) in the Walmart parking lot. I spent the next fifteen minutes touching up the scrapes with a tiny bottle of Milano Red paint from the glove box and telling him never to touch the roof again.

By the end of tenth grade, he'd broken up with me twice. The first time, he told me on the way home from the movies that he wanted to see another girl in the grade above me. I cried for two days, and two weeks later, he was driving my new Del Sol. The second time, he pulled me into the gym after lunch to tell me he wanted to take a break, because he wanted to go to the movies with another girl in his grade that Friday.

"What is wrong with you?" I asked, feeling the tears start. I took a deep breath and blinked. I was not going to do this here—not going to cry again. "Seriously, Richard. Are you the most awful person in the entire world?"

"Huh?"

"You couldn't have chosen a better day?"

"A better day, Janna?"

"My dad's open-heart, double bypass surgery is today, Richard."

"What? Oh, God. I forgot."

"Whatever. He could die, and you've broken my heart again. I hope you have fun at the movies. I'm late for chorus."

Sarah and Jodie hid me on the back risers so I could cry. Next period, I went to Spanish, and I cried quietly at my desk. Ryan, who sat in front, angled toward me the entire class and whispered what an asshole Richard was, how much better I could do, how awesome I was, and how much better-looking I was. I sniffled and nodded. He asked about my dad's surgery, and I told him I wouldn't know until my mom got home. He told me everything would be fine. Perhaps with all the brain injury, it only seemed natural that he would live through this.

I walked up the through the yards alone from the bus. I still didn't know how my father's surgery had gone. I didn't want to think about the consequences of not being able to repair an aortic aneurysm. My mother was staying the night in Pittsburgh with my father, but there was a chance that Gram and Pa would want to come stay with me. I prayed hard to a god that I hated against that chance. I saw the green Accord parked at the top of the driveway, under the tree with my hammock, beside Meagan's dirt hole. God hated me, too.

"No. No. No. No. No. No," I muttered under my breath.

"Hiya, Toots," Pa said, walking around the corner of the garage with Meagan. "What's wrong?"

"Please. Please, don't call Mom." I set my book bag down on the ground and ran over to him, wrapped my arms around him, and cried into his plaid flannel shirt.

"What's wrong?" he asked, utterly confused, pulling me off him to see my face.

"I'm fine, okay, really ..."

"What's wrong with my pet lamb?" Gram asked, coming out to the driveway.

"Nothing, nothing. I'm fine."

"What did he do to you?" she asked.

"Nothing, okay. I'm fine."

"You are not fine. I'm going to kill that Richard."

"Stop. Stop that. He just broke up with me. That's all."

But there it was again, involuntarily: the sobbing. She went in the house, and I begged her not to call my mother. I begged her to believe that I was fine. I was just crying. It wasn't a big deal. Just tears.

"How's Dad?" I asked, trying to pull the phone from her hands when we were inside. "Have you heard from Mom?"

"His surgery is over, and he's okay. I'm so angry at that boy," she said, dialing the hospital number. "How dare he?"

"Please! Don't! Don't call Mom. Dad is so much more important today. I'll live. Please. She'll drive from Pittsburgh for this. Please, Gram."

"You are not fine. Look at you. My poor Janna Marie."

"Stop. It's not a big deal. Please, stop. I don't want her to worry about me. I'll be fine."

I couldn't stop her, and Pa wouldn't help me. He took me to the kitchen while my grandmother called my mother over what now felt like the most menial thing on the planet compared to brain injury and heart surgery.

Two hours later, my mother was home. She found me on the couch. I had given up, snotting my way through an entire Kleenex box, my grandparents just sitting in opposite chairs, talking me through it. My heart hurt. My eyes hurt. My chest, my raw nose, and my lip, because I was biting it.

I had started crying because I was so afraid and sad to be without Richard. But I couldn't separate the sadness anymore. I cried for hours about my father. I didn't know how it all happened, and now I didn't know how to love him anymore. I just *missed* him. I missed someone who was living as hard as I would've missed him if he were dead. Gram and Pa didn't know what to do with me. I couldn't tell them how I felt. My heart felt warped.

"Oh, honey," my mom said when she walked in the living room. She came over and sat down on couch and put her arms around me.

"I'm so sorry, Mom. This is so stupid. I'm so sorry and so selfish."

"No, you're not."

"You should have seen her, Claudia, with such a broken heart," said Gram.

"I hate him. I hate him. I hate that you came home for me. I begged them not to tell you."

"I know," my mother said. "It's okay."

"Dad's okay?"

"Yes, his surgery went fine. Are you okay?"

"No. I miss him."

"Janna, he's really not worth this. He's just one boy."

"No, Mom. I really miss my dad."

"Oh … Janna …"

keep a good fight

My FATHER'S DOCTORS DID THEIR JOB. He was home in a few days, fatigued and sore. The aortic aneurysm was taken care of, and my mother had been sufficiently warned. "People who have heart surgery often have personality changes," the doctors told her.

She laughed out loud. I might have thought it was funny, too, if someone had told me that. I thought it was okay for my mother to react whatever way she wanted to. It didn't matter what anyone else thought or felt. Our lives had changed so much, drawing us even closer, almost protective of one another and of the feelings or thoughts we shared about my father, even if they were not in line with everyone else's.

Gone were the days when she yelled at me for wearing skirts too short, clothes that she didn't like, or ugly tennis shoes. Or for running through the house, staying up too late, or staying out too late. All I wanted to do now was to help her, to make things easier.

"I bet you don't know what suit of armor to put on before you leave work," my father said to her one morning when he was trying to get his way about something.

"Well, John," she said. "That is rather insightful."

My mother is the constant helper, the doer. She is a magnet for the help-seekers. She fixes problems and figures out tricky situations for people. She does it all in ways that are smart and kind, without judgment. She knows exactly how to be anyone's caretaker, and she was taking care of everything—her kid, her husband, her mother, her employees, a boat, two houses, three cars, her horses, our dog, our cat, the barn cats, and my father's fish. Just never herself. She let on so little. She was always in action, and I was a teenager.

That June, our dog died, and my mother buried her. Meagan and I were the same age. It was our thing, but dog years don't last as long. She had been in pain for months. Since I'd been a baby, Meagan had slept in my room every night. Before lying down on her rug in front of the door, she would put her head up on my bed to say goodnight every night. One night, just before my sixteenth birthday, she hurt too much to do it. I got down on the floor with her, and she put her head in my lap.

"Pup, why are you trying so hard to hang on?" I asked, rubbing her ears. "You can let go, okay? We're gonna be fine. I promise. It's okay."

She just panted hard.

"You don't have to do this anymore. You're hurting. You've seen the best, been around for the best of us. It's time. And Dad really does love you."

I stretched out beside her, my head level with hers, and put my arm around her belly. Her old age was sad. I kissed into her fur, wondering when it would happen.

I woke up on floor beside her hours later and crawled back into bed to cry myself to sleep. I woke up again around 5:00 to find her head propped up on my bed. I fell asleep with my arm draped over her.

By the next afternoon, I'd forgotten about the night. I was shoving softball gear and clothes into an overnight bag when my mother yelled at me through the screen door. "Janna, you need to come out here!"

"I'm getting ready to go to Amber's," I yelled back. "Why?"

"Janna, I think the dog is dead."

Dead. Out loud and attached to our dog, the word sounded funny, like it was a mistake. No one died. They got ill, severely brain injured, fucked up, mean, or nasty. I felt sick, like I had been lied to.

"She's dead?" I ran outside.

Meagan lay still in front of the woodpile. My mom was crying, patting her head. My dad stood and watched. I heard the wind rustle through the cherry trees and saw the white fur on her belly move. In that moment, I knew she was dead. I understood. I could hear my mother's words, the same words from the day we scooped Marble's mom off the road. Elizabeth had been hit by a car, and we had to use a shovel. Death was simply about moving on.

Things die. People die. Animals die. We all move on. Words her father had said to her that she had said to me.

I knelt down to touch my dog. She felt like a rock that someone had covered in fur, her mouth still open, probably mid-pant. I snapped my hand back, almost falling backwards. My father stood there with his hands clasped behind him.

My eyes narrowed. *"Don't you care?"*

He looked at me. His face showing no feeling.

"Why don't you care?" I burst into tears. "Dad … why?"

"She was a good dog," he said. "A very nice dog."

"You were such a good puppy," my mom said, holding her head and rocking it in her lap. "Oh, Meagan. You were such a good puppy."

I sat back on my heels wondering how she could pet a dead dog. There was no need to take care of her, to nourish her. She was no longer there.

"You were such a good puppy." Pat. "You were such a good puppy." Pat. "You were such a good puppy." Pat. "You were …"

She said it over and over again, patting her dead head. I couldn't do it. I couldn't touch her again, not even one last time. I was too scared of knowing what rigor mortis felt like. I reached behind me, picked up a stick covered in her bite marks, drew lines in the dirt, and cried with my mother. Eventually, she asked me to go inside and get Meagan's favorite blanket while she dug a hole by the hammock. My dad watched her dig. He didn't cry. He just watched her smooth out a hole, deep into the ground, navigating the roots and rocks. His brain was so broken. I was so angry that he wasn't crying. My mother looked heartbroken.

Within weeks, my father was asking my mother if we could get a golden retriever puppy. Every day, he searched *The Herald* for local litters, and every night, he brought it up. Obsessive compulsion. My mother didn't want another dog, and she had been clear about that. My father was not in the position to take care of a puppy, to raise and train another dog.

"But, Mom, I'll help you," I said. "I'll be around to train the puppy. It will be something fun."

"Janna, I'm running out of energy," she'd say.

"You won't have to do anything," I pleaded. "I promise. It's just a puppy. This is something I can help with."

"A dog is not free, Janna."

I knew that since the day of my father's helicopter ride, he had cost a lot of money, money that would blow through the deductible on my parents' private health insurance and money that, given the circumstances, should be coming from New Honda and Nissan City anyway.

Though I had little knowledge and no interest in the judiciary system, I figured the Court of Common Pleas of Allegheny County, Pennsylvania would rule in our favor, because nothing had been his fault. I'm not sure how long it took—days, weeks, maybe a single afternoon. My mother didn't tell me, or maybe I was too busy to pay attention when she was in court instead of at work or visiting my dad in rehab. But in April of 1997, we had received Pain and Suffering, a lump sum that I believed to be a generous amount of money, like $400,000, like an amount that compelled people to play the lottery in April of 1997. My ideas about money were skewed at fifteen.

This large chunk of money was to cover: the physical and emotional distress caused by the injury; the consequences of a limited lifestyle and limited activities for a man and his family; the mental anguish; and any other costs we might incur in the course of his recovery and treatment. More importantly, Pain and Suffering was to replace the monthly checks that Workers' Compensation had been sending us since last July. If it ever ran out, Workers' Comp would continue to pay—at least until he was sixty-five, at which point, Social Security would kick in.

A little over a year after the accident, he'd racked up hundreds of thousands of dollars, draining the settlement money dry. Workers' Comp had to pay for his continuing treatment, the rehab visits, doctors, evaluations, and medications. My mother made sure of it, and they did pay, begrudgingly. His medications, outpatient treatments, and visits with Dr. Zimmer, his new psychologist, were all covered.

His injury was severe, and the recovery process would be long-term, which is not what Workers' Comp had signed up for. He would need constant and permanent care and support to maintain some quality of life directly as a result of this injury.

Things were worse, not better. He was meaner, not nicer. Our life was harder, not easier. He was nothing like *Regarding Henry*.

"SHIT," I SAID WHEN I saw the phone missing from the cradle in the hallway.

My father had it, and now he was going to dial up some ad he found in the paper for something that would inevitably connect him to another country.

"Hey, Dad, you can't do that!" He was on the back porch, receiver pressed to his ear. "Dad, please just don't … don't do this."

He charged off into the yard, and I sat on the steps, willing myself not to cry. "Can we just talk?" I yelled after him.

"No!"

I got up and ran barefoot through the yard. Dusk was just starting to settle over the sky, and I found him standing behind the garage, where the black and yellow banana spiders spun gigantic, sticky webs in the hedge.

"Get away from me! You don't tell me what to do. You're just a little kid, a brat."

"Well, you're a mean father. And guess what? I do get to tell you what to do!"

"You are not my boss."

"Give me the phone, before you call Spain again, like an idiot. Come on, Dad."

He stood his ground, planting his feet and raising the phone up over his head, almost backing into a web.

"I'm not giving it to you. You're spoiled. You get everything you want."

"Ah, Jesus, Dad. Stop it. You have a brain injury. I'm not spoiled."

"You are a little brat!"

And that's how it was with everything. Every time he broke a rule, a battle ensued: over the phone, the remote control, the car keys, who was going to clean the dish, who would have the money. He wanted to make his own decisions, and we couldn't trust him anymore.

"Dad, stop it, please. Give me the phone, and we can just talk about this."

"No!"

"Dad!"

"Get out of my face. I don't want to talk to you anymore."

We were nearing the four-minute mark when things got ugly. There was no one around to stop us.

"Give me the damn phone!"

He threw it. I heard the dial tone when it hit the ground.

"Dad! You're a child. What is wrong with you?" I stood with my arms crossed, and he looked at me. "Well, pick it up."

"No!"

"You threw it."

"No!" He crossed his arms. His defiance was unparalleled. I stared at the phone, out of place in the middle of our yard, humming dumbly. He was wearing me out. A few more rounds of asking him to pick it up, and I'd want

to scream. It wasn't even about the phone anymore or the long-distance phone call. It was about winning, and I was losing. And neither of us would back down.

"Please pick up the phone."

"No."

"Dad?"

"No! I am not listening to you!"

There was nothing else to do but scream. I did it a lot. I'd just stand in front of him and release this blood-curdling, wordless screech, squeezing my fists so tight that my fingernails dug into the flesh of my palms. One long sound until I was sure I'd either burst an eardrum or give myself a brain aneurysm. But nothing ever happened. I'd just run out of breath and crumple, defeated and dramatic, into a weeping heap on the ground. And he would stand there, watching me, as if I were putting on some kind of show.

I looked up, realizing I was sitting in the yard, uncomfortably close to the sticky web. The silk strands, so close, made me shiver. He was walked over to me, his mouth stretched wide, with crazy eyes—*his* screaming face.

"You want to *yell* now!"

"No, Dad, I'm sorry."

"I see. Well then, let's *yell*. We're going to *talk like this!*"

"Dad, please stop. We've been yelling at each other."

"Why? I thought we were *still yelling.*"

"Please, stop it. *Stop it.*"

I pulled myself back up to stand and walked over to get the phone.

I exhausted myself constantly trying to discipline, reason with, and emotionally impale the man all at once. Anger was least effective, but I just couldn't stay calm. His indifference baited me, and his emotionless abyss broke me down. It became my personal quest, my life goal, to eke the smallest sliver of true feeling from his being. Unthinkable. He had apathy in spades.

There was nothing original about the fights my father and I had. They all started the same way, ended the same way, as if every fight had been cut from the same mold. He would neglect or flat-out ignore some disciplinary action my mother had asked me to enforce. *Janna, keep the car keys away from your father.* (He was developing a growing urge to sneak away and drive somewhere alone.) *Don't let him use the phone.* (He called long-distance a lot, friends he looked up or sometimes Spain or France.) *Janna, watch him, and make sure he doesn't hit the cat. Don't let him eat the cake, the pasta, the fruit salad in the fridge. Janna, do not let him go anywhere alone.* Those were the rules. I memorized them, all of them, because he broke them every chance he got. He'd always loved breaking rules. Why should that be any different now?

The keys to the truck were not on the key hook above the phone. I ran through rooms of the house, looking for my dad.

"Did Mom have them?" I asked out loud. "Did I? Shit. I hung them there. Goddammit. Why am I so stupid …"

I found him standing at the top the basement steps, smiling this shit-eating grin.

"Dad, I know you have the keys," I said. "I'm not an idiot."

He stared at me, his face cold and blank. Then he reached into the front pocket of his jeans and pulled out a chunky set of keys. He twirled them around his index finger a few times and tossed them in the air, twirling and tossing with a dexterity that surprised me—like Tom Cruise in *Cocktail,* like Old John. He walked up two steps so that he was level with me, breathing into my face. "What keys?" he asked, smiling his stupid grin.

I snatched at them, falling for his ruse. "Dad, you have them. Come. On. Give me the keys."

"Get out of my way," he growled, sticking out his jaw, an exaggerated underbite, and furrowing his brow. This was his *don't-fuck-with-me* face. Angry but too pitiful to take seriously.

"No, Dad. Fat chance."

"*Move!* I am going to go somewhere. You cannot tell me what to do. I want to drive."

The spit spray and his sour breath sent chills rippling across my shoulder blades and down to my tailbone, and tears flowed down my cheeks in streams. Lately, I was as easy as turning on a faucet. I was losing my strength. He didn't want me to babysit him, and I didn't want to. Maybe this time, I could just give him permission to drive away and do God-knows-what, go God-knows-where. But I would get in so much trouble.

"Dad," I said, grabbing at the clenched fist he was shaking at my face.

"*Move!*"

I couldn't even remember the last time he said my name.

"Get out of my way!"

His balance wasn't great. When he tried to shove me to one side of the steps, he stumbled, and I winced with embarrassment. His face was red, red-pink, like the days before the accident, when right after dinner, around 7:00, he'd wipe the sweat from his brow and chomp on Rolaids until it faded.

"No can do, Dad."

He raised his hand, the clenched one with the keys. I didn't move. He wouldn't do it. He hadn't yet. Neither of my parents believed in hitting. There was no corporal punishment in our house. My mom once tapped me on the butt, and I accused her of child abuse. I was seven. I screamed, cried, and carried on about how she was no better than the mothers from broken families that she worked with.

"Dad!" I screamed, and he lowered his hand.

I sat down on the top step.

"You cannot, cannot drive. I'm sorry. I really am. You have a brain injury, and I love you, and you cannot drive somewhere alone. I'm not driving anywhere. You don't need to. No one needs to go anywhere. You can't. I'm so sorry."

"Get out of my fucking way *now!* I don't care who you are or what you think."

"Really, Dad?" I stood up, recharged with anger. "Really. We're swearing now?"

"Get out of my way."

"Mom and I are taking care of you, and we mean nothing to you?" I grabbed at his fist with both of my hands. "You wanna know what? I don't love you. I don't even care anymore. I'm tired of you. I'm so fucking tired of you. I don't love you. I don't. I can't."

I pulled and pried, his burly fingers losing the fight against my nails. He watched me, perplexed. I was hurting his hands. He let go. I had the prize. He just stared at me as I continued with my gasping, sputtering stream-of-consciousness monologue.

"You know what else? Don't even think about walking me down the aisle. *Don't even be there!* Do not come to my wedding! I hate you."

I knew that I was one of his favorite people in the whole world. I knew how much he loved me and how much those words should hurt him. He leaned against the wall. He was no longer red or angry. Just impassive.

"I'm ... sorry," he said when I'd stopped screaming at him and started crying. "I don't mean to upset you. I'm sorry."

I've lost track of the mean things my father and I have said to each other. At first, his words stuck to me like dead bugs on flypaper for months, years. My words dripped off him in seconds. That's his brain injury. I never regretted anything in my efforts to make him feel something, to hurt him. I think the only person I hurt was myself, and I don't even regret that. That's living with his brain injury.

But that fight—the one on the steps about the keys where I told him I didn't want him at my wedding—that's the one where all the words are still imprinted on my brain. Forever. It's the winner of my top five ugliest memories. So far, I can only count two regrets. One is a rum flight in the winter of 2010. The other is saying all those things to him that day on the basement steps.

I looked at him, his face still completely blank. I got up, walked to my room, and collapsed on my bed. I smashed my face in the pillow, and with the key ring looped around my thumb, tucked the keys under my chest. With their metal teeth digging into my skin, I cried until I couldn't remember falling asleep.

better days in the cards

JUNIOR YEAR, AND NOTHING WAS AS it should have been. Homecoming dances, riding in cars with my friends, boys, dates, movies, after-school jobs, parties, friendships—all were rattled. Worse yet, I was sure I'd be the next kid in the '90s splitting my time between divorced parents.

My parents fought all the time, and I'd eavesdrop all the time. If my family was going to disintegrate, I didn't want it to come as a shock. I wanted to witness it. If they were fighting in the kitchen, then I listened from the porch. If they were in the hallway, I'd stay at the top of the steps. The two of them fought as hard as he and I fought. Our family seemed to be past the point of making choices. Things just *happened,* and I had no choice but to ride the endless wave of fights, broken plans, and my mother's abyss of exhaustion. It didn't leave much room to feel like a kid.

Junior year, and all I had was a tenuous grasp on an ambiguous future. After two more years of high school, I'd head to college. Then what?

I fantasized about hiding away in my bedroom and spilling my fears into my diary in the form of cathartic, insightful prose. But every time I picked up my pen, I filled the pages with angst-ridden missives about crushes, friendships, bad skin, and school dances. Earnest recordings of good grades and victories. Pages about the same boyfriend, but still no sex.

I drove my little red hardtop convertible, leaving the top off well into fall. I blasted the heat and rigged up my Sony Discman, taking my turns slow enough that it wouldn't skip. I bought dozens of CDs and listened to *Under the Table and Dreaming* until it scratched all through "Ants Marching," as if that song would bring something back. It was the first CD my Dad and I listened to together; along with Hootie and the Blowfish, Dave Matthews came highly recommended by my older cousin, Colin.

"Be careful when you take it out," my dad had said, handing me a slick plastic case with a picture of a blurred merry-go-round on it. "Pretty neat, right? Compact discs."

"How do I do it?"

"Keep your thumb in the center, and only touch the sides. Then pull, and it will snap out."

I handed him the iridescent disk, making sure to leave it fingerprint-free. He held it in front of a slot in the dashboard, and in a second, it was gone, as if eaten. CDs seemed so fragile.

"Listen," he said, skipping from the beginning of one song to the next until we were on the seventh track. "Listen to the violin. What a great song, don't you think? You hear it?"

"Yeah, I hear it."

"It's great. We'll have to get some more CDs, Peanut. What do you want?"

"I don't want any CDs, Dad. I like tapes."

He had bought them one after another in the coming months, subscribing to a BMG mail service where you could buy CDs for pennies. When the package came, it was as exciting as getting rolls of film developed from Walmart. His favorites were the spine of my blossoming collection, which I kept in the black canvas sleeve behind the passenger seat. I'd taken some Neil Young, lots of Buffett, and *Under the Table and Dreaming,* because he no longer seemed to care as much about Dave's violin as much as Sarah and I did.

I kept the purple canvas lunch box, toting it around for two periods before I sat down at the cool table, beside the guys' table, with all my same girlfriends. After school, we shopped at the outlet mall or went to Eat N' Park for sundaes or Chi-Chis for free nachos and $0.99 coffee. On Fridays, we went to the boys' games and cheered for their cute butts and the points they earned for the Mustangs, and when we felt like it, we went to dances in the cafeteria. We still had sleepovers on the nights that we weren't with our boyfriends or at parties. The best parties were either at Sarah's house in the woods or in the cornfield behind Adam's house. Epic nights out in the country, full of high school love triangles and cheap booze, neither of which I took part in. Richard, who was a freshman at a nearby college, didn't believe me about the booze. And some of my friends didn't believe me about the love triangles.

I had become close friends with the guys in our group, particularly Zac, who was preppy and dated Amber, and Ryan, who was not preppy and dated a girl no one particularly liked. It was so much easier to spend time with guys—fun, simple, and unemotional.

Ryan lived at the lake, less than a block away from me. He was our paperboy, roaring through the neighborhood on his four-wheeler at 4:00 a.m., thwacking *The Herald* into shuddering plastic boxes. Parents thought he hung out with the wrong crowd, always trying to be the badass, wearing his pants too low and his shirts too baggy, and dating a younger girl. I often gave him rides to school, because his car was broken down, because he had been too lazy to fix it.

The morning of the first big snow of the year, I was jamming to "Ants Marching," tailgating Bus 12 down Latonka Drive, when I hit a patch of black ice. I spun into a 180 and landed in a ditch, stuck with snow halfway up the windows. The kids peering out the back window watched the whole thing as the bus disappeared down the road. Ryan came by on his four-wheeler with a set of chains, and we dug the car out. He owed me, given his recent prank.

"Ryan!" I said, looking at him in disbelief as he sat in my passenger seat.

"Janna!" he said, looking back at me.

"It was you?"

He giggled.

"I can't believe it. It was you!"

He giggled harder, giddy with the brilliance of his masterful joke.

"You mean my car's fine? My brakes are okay?"

"Relax, Janna. The car's fine. It's fine."

"I can't relax about *cars*, Ryan."

"Oh, yeah … shit, I'm sorry."

"It's okay. I guess it was kinda funny."

"Kinda?"

"All right, it was good joke. I'm an idiot, though."

"It was just so easy."

"Oh, shut up, Ryan."

"Aw, come on."

"Just don't do it again, okay?"

"Never."

As I veered left onto the back road to the lake, he reached his hand toward the center console, gripping the e-brake and pushing in the release button so slowly that it was inaudible. He started to pull up as he watched the dashboard for the red light to blink on. Then, he waited.

"Ryan!"

"Janna!"

"Stop."

"You just make it so easy."

ONE WEEKEND IN JUNE, JUST before my seventeenth birthday, we packed up the house and made a thousand and one trips back and forth to Gram Mary's. Richard helped. The Suhries helped. The transition was smoother than I could have imagined, and the house was familiar enough that I could at least sleep at night, even with the ghosts. My new room, my mother's old room, was huge. It had a fireplace, a marble vanity, and a window that looked out over the pasture. I was sleeping in the same bed, in the same room, in the same house as she had when she was my age. I was allowed to pick new wallpaper, so I chose stenciled butterflies in shades of orange, blue, tan, and gray. My father painted the trim slate blue to match.

As a kid, I fought any mention of moving from our lake house, and I was adamant about not wanting to change schools. In fourth grade, when my parents talked about moving to North Carolina when I went to college, I calmed down. Instead, my father got a brain injury, and Gram Mary got Alzheimer's. Moving was a trade of sorts, a way to avoid putting Gram Mary's house on the market and also pay for her to be in a nursing home.

I moved away from the boat, and my mother got to live with the horses. She loved "the boys." We had four: her aging Arabian, Jamal; Thunder; my dad's Morgan; Checkers, my lovable brat of a pony; and now Simba. He was my mom's new horse, a beautiful Palomino Rocky Mountain Horse. She rode him every day. My father had retired Thunder like he retired his skis, so I rode Thunder.

Thunder hated being saddled, hated walking up hills, hated snow, and he bit my butt a lot, but he was my sounding board, my therapist. We took lone trail rides, and I told him everything about my life—crushes, fears, fights with my father, things I was excited about, things I couldn't tell my mother. He made me feel calm. My mother seemed to think he'd been around.

"He's done this all before," she'd tell me. "He's got some lives in him."

It was not long after we moved that the Suhries bought half of Gram

Mary's land, and Pat and Vicky carved a driveway past our house along the side of the pasture to build their house at the end. Pat would do some major work on the barn and add some stalls, and Vicky would buy a horse or two for herself and the kids to keep in the barn. This was beyond exciting. All our fussing, and Nicole, Steven, Lisa and I would be Ditch Kids forever.

The four of us had the kind of parents that you didn't ask the same question more than once with hopes of getting a different answer. Our houses were separated by Delaware Trail. It was first a dirt road, and then when Lisa was born, Delaware had enough houses to be tar and chipped, a messy, smelly, sticky process. So many days had been a careful barter for our freedom.

"Can we go play with Janna?"

"Suhries are outside, can I go over?"

If we didn't like the answers, we simply went outside, sat in the ditch of our respective front yard, and waited for the others. It wasn't crossing the street, and it wasn't technically playing together, so it was technically allowed. Then it became a thing. We just quit asking. When I wanted to play and I knew the Suhries were home, I went and sat in the ditch. And they did the same thing. Until someone came out to the yard or yelled that it was okay to cross.

We made up games in the ditch and brought our toys to the ditch. All we had to do was communicate across a six-foot stretch of road. Nicole and I even made half of our elaborate plans to build a teepee in the woods from our spot in the ditch. Today, she and I still sign cards, e-mails, and the occasional text message with DKF.

By the time the Suhries had dug a hole for their new house, my mom gave in to my father about a puppy. Richard and I went alone to pick out the puppy. I named her Morgan, keeping with the *M* lineage of goldens and as a nod to horses for my mother. When we got home, the Leydes and the Suhries had a welcome home party for the puppy. She made everyone smile, and I took a thousand pictures with my crappy little camera.

The Suhries loved Richard. They made me swear never to leave him for one of my guy friends. He loved them, too. We were going on three years now, and we'd talk about all the big things you talk about when you live in a small town and have dated someone for forever: marriage, college, baby names, how we'd make our differences work. He wanted to open a casino in Vegas. I wanted to be psychologist and live by the beach. We talked about what we wanted for each other. I wanted him to be okay with me going to school far away. He wanted me to love my father more.

My father was alive. He had survived. Richard would always remind me. As if I'd forgotten. He hadn't met my father before the accident. He couldn't know what or whom we were missing. And when I tried to explain how much I really did love my dad, it always turned into a discussion about all the things I missed about him: a long list full of tangible activities and small nuances in his behavior.

"It's like … my dad won't go skiing with me. He doesn't say the same things. He never calls me Peanut. He won't do the dishes. He just—he likes weird stuff."

"Oh, come on, like what?" Richard asked.

"I dunno," I said. "Like, he likes the Beach Boys more than Jimmy Buffett now."

"So what?"

"So what? I hate the Beach Boys. He's supposed to love Jimmy Buffett."

"I like the Beach Boys."

"I don't. Besides, you don't count. You like Garth Brooks!"

"Oh, come, what else? What is so different about him?"

"Okay, fine. He likes cake. Like, he eats sweets now. Cake and cookies and ice cream and chocolate. *Everything*."

"That's not weird."

"Yes it is! It's weird. It's wrong. You don't understand."

"Understand?"

"He never liked cake."

"So what?"

"So what? I hate it. Richard, he never liked cake. I hate watching him eat cake."

"You hate that he likes cake now?"

"I hate it."

"That's weird."

"So?"

"Give him a break, Janna. He loves you."

"A break?"

My mother hated it, too. "John doesn't like sweets," she'd say at picnics, parties, dinners, whenever someone passed her something sweet to pass to him. My father *never* ate cookies, candies, cupcakes, ice cream, or chocolates and always found a polite way of turning down birthday cakes. He didn't even eat Gram Mary's apple pie, which was arguably the best. The occasional licorice sticks, Jolly Ranchers, and peanut M&Ms—that was it.

"Ready, whoever can hold their hand out the window the longest can open the bag," he had said the first time we played the M&M game, reaching over to roll down my window as bitter winter air smacked my face.

"Okay!" I said, sticking my hand out.

"Hey, ya ninny! No gloves!"

"It's too cold."

"Wuss."

We drove around town with our hands out the windows in the thick of winter with the prize, a yellow packet of M&Ms, sitting in the cup holder of his truck. My hand and forearm started to tingle and turn red.

"Dad, it's gonna fall off!"

"Wuss."

"Dad …"

"Ten more seconds."

"I can't. It's too cold!"

"Okay, okay. But I won, so I get to open them and pick the colors."

"Fine," I said, rolling up my window and sitting on my hand. "Just don't eat the blue ones or the green ones. And don't eat them all at once."

"Like this," he said, fake chomping on a fake handful.

My mother and I knew that it was perfectly harmless that he liked cake and probably a little ridiculous how much it bothered us. But it was one of the thousands of signs that he was not at all the same person. He had died. More accurately, the man we knew had died and been replaced by a not-even-close replica. She and I had never talked about that. It was just silently understood. Her husband, my dad, had died, and someone else had taken his place, a stranger. It was just easier to talk about how he never liked cake.

Richard couldn't understand the real loss, or maybe he didn't want to. He wouldn't allow me to have days where I was angry and sad missing someone who sat right in front of me. That was what frustrated me most about him. Other things I could change. He ditched the cargo pants. He went to Jimmy Buffett concerts with me. He quit breaking up with me. Other things I couldn't change, but I could live with. He "walked" his cat. He wore shirts that were two sizes too big. He got unusually quiet after hand jobs. He loved country music. But it killed me that he had such a say in how I should feel about my father. I wasn't lucky, and I didn't want to hear him tell me how lucky I was.

"Janna, what's wrong?" he asked me one night on my couch, his arm around me as we watched a show on the Discovery Channel about TBI: Traumatic Brain Injury. My parents were asleep upstairs.

"Nothing," I said, pushing my face into the crevice between couch pillows.

"Something is."

"Fine. Everything."

I slid off the couch and down onto the floor in front of him.

"Huh? What did you do that for?"

"Nothing," I said, scooting to the middle of the floor and resting my chin on my knees.

The show was a series of vignettes of families dealing with someone with a severe TBI, like my father's—car accidents, motorcycle accidents, ladder falls, snowboarding spills. The last forty-five minutes had been excruciating to watch. All the people had snapped back, one by one. Their memories flooded back to them, bringing with them chunks of normalcy.

"They keep saying *snap. Snap. Snap, snap.* No one *snaps!*"

"What are you talking about?"

"They're all okay."

A sobering voiceover was explaining how TBI patients could experience sudden change—that in the first two years, they could regain their memory, their lost consciousness. They could *snap* back to their old realities.

"Yeah … they are," he said. "So what's wrong?"

"It's been twenty-three months, Richard!"

"Yeah."

"It's been *two years.*"

"Yeah."

"He's never going to snap."

He leaned down to touch me. I moved away, looking up at him, puddles clouding my eyes.

"My dad's not going to be okay."

"Janna, your dad's going to be okay."

"No, Richard, he's not. Don't you see? Don't you get it? He's not okay. He's never going to be okay. These people got their people back. Mom and I don't get him back. It's been two years. It's been too long. He's not going to snap back. It's so unfair."

He stared at me. I was sitting cross-legged in his oversized Mercer Mustangs basketball shirt. He said nothing.

"It's just never going to be okay."

I BROKE UP WITH RICHARD the summer before my senior year. One morning, I woke up and was hit first by consciousness and then by the realization that Richard and I could never work. There was still a lot to untangle, a lot to separate. I tried to make it uncomplicated. We still went to Vegas to see his family, since the trip was already planned.

A week after we got back from Vegas, I was going on vacation with my family to Lake Cumberland in Tennessee, where the water was supposed to be deep, clear, glass: the best for skiing. Zac had always told me I could borrow his wakeboard, so maybe I'd improve my skills on smoother waters. A few days before I left for vacation, Richard and I discussed the fact that despite Vegas, despite staying friends, we were, in fact, broken up—for good.

My cream-colored, Abercrombie baseball tee and cut-off Levis were covered in sand, sandwich, and sweat—a day's worth of babysitting three kids. I loved driving stick, and the board would not have fit in my car, so this was a great excuse to take my mom's champagne-colored Accord. I was meeting Zac at the dock where we kept our boat. It was just past 7:00 p.m. when I pulled to a stop on the familiar patch of grass by the swing sets where my dad had parked his tan truck an infinite amount of times. I pulled the visor down and looked in the mirror, trying to tell myself that I was too tired to care what I looked like. Besides, Zac would be coming from football practice.

I saw him standing on the dock, dressed like he had somewhere to go. I had chopped off my hair that summer—super-short, just below my ears—and in this moment, I felt self-conscious that I had not done anything with it. I mussed up my curls and pushed up at my eyelashes, as if that would elevate my attempt to be cute and carefree. It didn't. I tucked my hair up under a distressed blue Eddie Bauer baseball cap that was sitting on the passenger seat and got out of the car. Walking toward him, I could smell his Cool Water cologne.

"Hey there," he said.

"Hi! Where the heck are you off to?"

"What? Nowhere. I'm hanging out with you."

"What?"

"I thought we could do something."

"Oh, I thought I was just coming to get the board."

"Oh, well, if you're busy. I see you are just using me."

Just weeks before our senior year, Zac was single. I was single. And he was standing in front of me at the lake, asking me to just … hang out. Dressed like he wanted to hang out, dressed to impress me. *Me?* I'd harbored a crush on him for years, probably since second grade, when we were in a school play together and I wore a fluffy yellow dress and he wore a tie and sneakers. Over the years, we'd talked enough that intrusive people thought something was going on. Nothing was ever going on.

"Um, okay. Like what?"

"Movies?"

"I'm too tired. I'd fall asleep at the movies."

"We could get something to eat."

"I just ate."

"Oh, well. Um …"

Don't blow this. Stop being a wuss.

"Well, I guess we could take my boat out. I have the keys."

Completely inappropriate—something I had no permission to do. It was nearing dusk. But we did it anyway. I prayed that the lights would work, that the engine would turn over, and that I would not hit anything. My heart finally free to pound in his presence as we unlatched the ropes from the rusty posts. We putted down to the dam, anchored, and watched mist roll over the water as the stars came out. The ambience was gag-worthy.

We talked for hours about the summer, school, being seniors, my dad, the rumors, the past twelve years, his parents' divorce, our friends, going to homecoming, going to college. It was perfect, a scene of my life so perfectly written that I could have stayed in it forever.

I drove home, through town, past Richard's house with Zac's wakeboard in the back seat, drunk on what happened. I pulled in the driveway, wishing I could run inside and tell my mother everything. I felt like my world had finally changed, had finally gotten interesting. I would tell her tomorrow on the long ride to Lake Cumberland. I still had to pack.

As soon as I closed the door, my mom called down.

"Hey, Richard's here."

"What?"

"I saw his car pull in the driveway just after you got in. How's Zac? Did you get the wake thing?"

"Wakeboard? Yes."

"Good. Now are you going to use it this week? That's a lot to bring down with us."

"Yes. Wait, why is Richard here?"

"I don't know."

I ran out to the driveway. He was sitting in his car, a red Sunfire. Every time I saw it, I thought about how much I hated it, how much I missed his charcoal Subaru, and how much I wished that he'd bought a Honda. He didn't get out when he saw me, so I walked over to his window.

"Hi," he said, looking up at me.

"Hey, *um*. What are you doing here?"

"*You* were supposed to meet me at Eat N' Park."

"I said maybe I would. I was tired."

"Then why didn't you go home?"

"Huh?"

"Where were you?"

"I went to get the wakeboard from Zac, for vacation."

"How long does it take to get a wakeboard?"

"What are you talking about?"

"I saw you drive through town just now. So what were you doing?"

"You're kidding me. I was in my mom's car. How did you know it was me?"

"I know your mom's car. What did you do?"

"I went to get the wakeboard. I met Zac at the dock to get the wakeboard. I just told you that."

"Did you kiss him?"

"What?"

"Did you kiss him?"

"What are you talking about?"

"Did you?"

"I think you might want to get out of the car for this," I said, walking away from his window.

He looked at me like I should take the words back. Like I could, like I should want to. He walked over and sat down on the mounting block in front of the barn, put his head in his hands, and threw his keys in the grass.

"Did you? You did!"

"Yes."

"Did you like it?"

I walked a few steps away to pick up Marble.

"Did you like it?"

"Yes," I said, sitting down beside him with the cat in my lap.

"How? You *liked* it?"

The yelling made Marble antsy, and I held her tighter to me. "I can't answer you how."

"Yes, you can. *How?* It's so unfair."

"Richard, we're broken up. You know that."

"I can't believe you. You're so cold. You don't even care."

"I care."

"No, you're happy right now."

The conversation went on for an hour. Question after question. I answered them all honestly, petting Marble as she sat in my lap. Did I like Zac? *Yes.* Were he and I over? *Yes.* Did I love Zac? *No.* Did I love him? *Always, just … not enough anymore.* Endless questions. Repeated questions. He cried. I didn't cry, and he sobbed. The first time I'd ever seen a man sob. I wanted to run away from him. I didn't run. I just scratched Marble's ears. His sobbing churned my insides. How could I break someone like this? I break, not men. Men don't break. I've tried. I can't even break my father.

"Jaaaaaaanna!"

My mom yelled at me from the open window in the kitchen. I grabbed the cat and ran to the house, leaving him there.

"Why were you running with her?" my mom asked, coming out onto the porch in a pair of green hospital scrubs. "She does not like that."

"I kissed Zac."

"You … Oh, Janna. And you told Richard?"

"He asked."

"Oh, Jesus."

"I had to be honest."

"Oh my. You didn't have to be *that* honest. Well, we have a big day tomorrow. You have to pack. You can tell me all about this in the car."

She hugged me, and her scrubs smelled like soap, like a time when I was ten.

Richard didn't leave until well past 2:00 a.m. We'd beaten the conversation into the ground. There was nothing left to say. He left, face reddened and puffy with tears. He was a good person, but he was a good person for someone else. I went to bed, exhausted, relieved, high.

LIFE BEGINS AFTER HIGH SCHOOL, at least that is what my mother had been telling me. No more love triangle manifestations, no more drama, no more unwanted dates to formal dances, no more people making fun of me, no more crushes on the same boys, no more competing, and no more crying. No more silent treatments, best friend fallouts, or jealousy—at least, not from this crowd.

And no more fights with my father, the skinny, angry man who could no longer drive or hold down a job. He had taught me so little in the past four years. He didn't understand me. I'd grown up certain that I'd go through high school with a father who was cool, who would let me drink a beer with him, teach me about music, intimidate the guys I wanted to date, and teach me about life, the universe, and how to put up with people's shit. No, not the case. And my parents weren't moving to the beach, either.

Loving my dad was hard. It was easier to be angry. Loving him made me miss him, which was a pain I was sure I couldn't handle. Being his daughter became a job. I told him what to do when I needed to, which was often. I got mad at him for the same things that my mother got mad at him for. I yelled at him a lot. Everything about brain injury clung to him, stubborn and prickly as burrs. There was not one shitty symptom, side effect, or deficit he didn't have.

He could only say "I love you," which he did, often. But he couldn't show *love you*. He didn't know how. I'm sure if he truly could have, he would have. But after a while, I lost sight of the line between what he didn't have the ability to do and what he chose not to do. The hardest part becomes remembering that the brain injury is probably doing whatever it is that hurts so much.

He didn't take care of the boat anymore. "Boats are not my thing, Janna," my mother said, reasoning with me when she told me they were going to sell it.

It was another change I couldn't argue. I'd still lived on the water as much as I could, on the Suhries' boat, Ryan's Ski Natique, or Zac's MasterCraft. The boys were all about wakeboarding, but I missed skiing. I still couldn't get the damn board to go over the wake on command. Ryan, with his impressive flips, catching major air, insisted I just keep trying. But I was more interested in teaching myself the grace and precision of one ski, picking up where my father left off. I was my only hope, because he was done.

All the frontal lobe damage, forgetfulness, nasty fights, and incomprehension in the world couldn't have kept my father from sitting in a boat and telling me what to do at the other end of a rope, which is why one afternoon last August had come as a surprise.

"John, Janna's gonna ski," Vicky said, poking him to wake him up.

He fell asleep a lot now—his medication. She poked him again.

"John?" she said a bit louder. "Are you gonna switch boats and watch with us?"

"No," he said. "I don't want to."

"John?" Pat asked. "Really. It's Janna. She's gonna ski."

"No, I don't want to."

And that was it. When he didn't want to do something, he didn't do something. He stayed in the pontoon in the shallow end, and I hopped into the Suhries' speedboat. I sat at the stern, facing backward with my arm around my Connelly Kidder, chin on my knees, watching him get smaller and smaller as we drove out to deep water. I swallowed hard and wiped the tears away with the ski gloves he'd bought for me three years ago for a better grip, because my forearms got so tired. They were a present from the days when he knew what presents I'd like.

I ran the course flawlessly, save one buoy, that day. He would have been proud, but I knew it was over. No more skiing with my dad.

THE GIRLS HAD BEEN ASKED to wear white, whatever we wanted as long as it was white. Our caps and gowns were white. I dressed in a white skirt and a sleeveless sweater. It was chilly that May, so I wore sheer tights with my white patent leather slingbacks—very adult. My parents gave me jewelry as a graduation present—a white gold band embedded with sapphires and sapphire studs for my ears. The Mustangs colors were blue and white.

I drove my little red car to my school for the last time. Taking the turn onto West Butler, I cranked up my stereo and sang along to a song about love and luck. Jimmy Buffett always sang the truth into my life. He was always right.

Seniors had been instructed to meet in the cafeteria, get our caps and gowns, and take time for pictures. It was also a great time to cry, if you wanted to. I saw all my girlfriends, and we gathered and smiled, gathered and smiled, gathered and smiled. We reapplied lip gloss and checked our compact mirrors for running mascara, reassuring each other of our beauty and maturity. I didn't feel any tears coming, so I didn't worry about my mascara.

We lined up in front of the glass cases with the trophies in the hallway. On cue, we were filtered down the aisles of the Mercer Junior Senior High School auditorium, one foot in front of the other to the tune of "Pomp and Circumstance," up to the stage. Speeches were given. Sweat dripped. Fans hummed. We waited for the moment, the place in the program when as one collective, accomplished unit, we stood up and moved the tassels that had been dangling to the right of our mortarboards to the left.

We were the class of 2000—the cool kids, turn-of-the-century kids, all ninety-nine of us kids from the country. Afterward, we gathered in the gym—graduates, students, teachers, family, friends—taking pictures of everyone exchanging hugs and crying. The Suhries were crying. I didn't cry. I was too thrilled for this new chunk of life to start that my mother had promised would be more exciting, interesting, and fun than high school could ever be. Jackie and I hugged our families good-bye and ducked out earlier than most graduates. It was all over. When we got into my car, she took off the hard top, and I tore off my pantyhose. Liberated, we screamed, "Fuck yeah!" as I drove us out of the parking lot. She was going to Penn State, and I was going to Wittenberg University, and life was finally about to begin.

No more brain injury.

another round of brew

I HEARD IT BUZZING. DOWN ON THE hardwood floor, my little red flip phone turned a half-circle with each ring. *Cole calling … Cole calling … Cole calling …* "Shit," I said, face-planting into the pillow. "Nooooo."

This feeling was bliss, and I didn't care that the events of the day had to unfold. I ignored the noise, as we lay there naked, as if nothing had ever gone wrong between us in the last four years. I had just had the best sex of my twenty-two-year-old life. The last thing I wanted to do was leave that cozy bed, scramble to find my things, run to my car, and drive to my sorority house, where I'd have to sneak in through the kitchen and up to my room.

I picked it up. It wouldn't shut up. "Hi," I said. "Sorry. Listen, don't tell Mom where I am. I'm with you at the house, okay? I'm sorry; I'll explain. Yeah, five minutes. Just get in the shower, and save me a place in line." I dropped the phone back on the floor and sighed. "I gotta go," I said, forcing one leg over the side of the bed and then the other.

I stepped into my skirt, a scant swatch of denim. It was what every one of us girls seemed to own. I tugged it up over my hips and laughed to myself about how Pa asked me once if I got it *half-price,* because half of it was missing.

I walked around the room on third floor of the swimmer house in search of the rest of my outfit. It was a beautiful, a sunlit bedroom that belonged at the top of an A-frame. Alex and I did not belong there. It was too mature.

"Need these?" Alex sat up and dangled my shirt from one hand and my bra from the other.

"I hate you," I said, smiling. "This is going to be so hard."

"Stop being so dramatic, Janna. Get going already!"

"Yeah, I know," I said, muffled, as I bit my shirt, letting it hang over my bare chest while I squirmed into my bra. "See ya later."

"You'll see me later if I feel like it."

I stuck out my middle finger at him and smiled. "Oh, you will."

154

He smiled. I ran over to the bed, shoes, purse, shirt, and keys all in one hand, and kissed him. I put one knee up onto the bed, ready to crawl back in. My phone buzzed from inside my purse, and he pushed my knee down and kissed my forehead.

"I will. Now get outta here. You're gonna be late."

I yanked on my shirt in the hallway and raced down the steps in my bare feet, grimacing at the slimy sensation of last night's beer and dog hair. I slipped through the kitchen and gave the giant St. Bernard a pat on his head with my foot.

Outside, the sun hurt. I couldn't fish my aviators—the old pair I'd taken from my father—out of the console of the Del Sol fast enough. They were the key to not puking. Driving up North Fountain to the ADPi house, I prayed for parking, prayed for a spot in the shower line. I would certainly not miss communal living, twenty-two girls crammed under one roof like orphans. I pulled into the one empty spot, a tight squeeze between an SUV and the curb, too tight for normal cars. I ran across the parking lot in my bare feet to the back door. Why did the asphalt hurt so much? Why did everything? *Why in God's name did I drink so much?*

Twelve hours earlier—following a dinner with my parents and Nicole—the night had started by sipping Zimas, followed by taking shots and chugging beers, all to drown the nostalgia that nobody was ready for. At McMurray's, Nicole, my roommate, and I sat around dingy tables splashed in $0.25 beers. I threw away my sobriety with hugs and photos that signaled the end of an era. Krystal showed up with a drove of *her* sorority sisters, and Nicole and I joined them to make the 1:00 a.m. bar hop to Station, where the drinks were stronger and the jukebox better.

Watery Natty Lights turned to Skip n' Go Nakeds, Station's signature pink lethal concoction made from beer, vodka, and a mélange of liquors. Natalie and her friends were sitting outside; we joined them around rickety tables to talk about nothing and everything and watch Mark, the bald, tatted-up bouncer, turn people away. I found more friends, and we bought more pitchers and choked the jukebox with streams of our favorite songs—"Beast of Burden," "Life Is a Highway," "Toxic," "Farmhouse," "Yeah!" "Ants Marching," "Changes in Latitudes." After 2:00, Nicole left to go sleep in my bed. It started to rain. Someone proposed an adventure.

"You've never streaked the hollow?" Krystal asked. "Seriously, Jan!"

Nearly a dozen of us walked umbrella-less up the winding road that led to the hollow: a giant grassy dip in the center of Wittenberg's campus surrounded by hundred-year-old trees. We clumsily pulled off our skirts, shorts, tees, and tanks, throwing them in sloppy piles to soak up the rain and shelter our cell phones. Shoes stayed on, for better traction.

I could hear the rain pattering down on the leaves and the water running down the drains under the sidewalk. I was drunk and naked, standing in a pair of waterlogged Pumas. Someone yelled.

"Let's go!"

We ran the length of the hill, boys and girls slipping and sliding in the muddy grass, rolling around at the basin in intoxicated fits of laughter. We high-fived our daring feat. Soaking wet, caked with dirt and clods of grass, we revived the party back at someone's house with help from a keg and a deck of cards.

When I got bored, I called Alex again—for the seventh or seventeenth time that evening. I'd lost track.

"What's up?" he asked. "How are you?"

"Where have you been?" I filled up a cold beer and walked outside, prepared to argue with him.

"At my house. I told you."

It was raining again, and as our conversation wore on, I choked on tears. People came out and tugged at my shirt, telling me to join their drinking game. Krystal came out and told me not to go. Half an hour later, I was sitting on the porch of the swimmer house, burying my head in the fur of Alex's St. Bernard, whispering to him how dumb this all was, this night, this ending, this porch, this boy. Four and a half years of unhealthy, thrilling back-and-forth that started with inviting him to my freshman formal. My resilience was astounding.

"I'm sorry," Alex said, coming outside. "I couldn't just come get you. We had a Delt thing. I wanted to. It's just—late." He handed me a lukewarm Miller Lite and hugged me, smelling of pot and chlorine. We went inside and joined his friends, who lounged on big couches and passed a bowl around. Eventually, we snuck up to the big bedroom on the third floor.

"What the hell were you doing?" he asked, picking grass out of my hair and brushing caked mud off my shoulder. "What is all over you?"

"We, *um,* streaked the hollow."

"Tonight?"

"Yeah, I mean, I never had, so …"

"You're disgusting," he said. "You're wet."

"It's just some mud. It's nothing."

"You're soaking wet. You can't stay. You'll get me sick. What did you do, roll in it?"

"Oh, come on, Alex. I won't get you sick."

"You can't sleep over."

"Stop being such a wimp."

"Janna—"

I kissed him, and he shut up.

"So, Janna … how was your night?" Nicole asked.

"It was great. I wish I were hungry, though. I'm so sorry I'm so late this morning. Thanks for being here. My head hurts."

"Of course. We have to hurry up. You can tell me about it later." She sat patiently on the couch with her purse hooked over one knee. We had ten minutes until my parents would arrive to take us out to brunch. Makeup was sliding off my face, which was still damp from the shower, and my sopping hair soaked into my dress. I sat down on the couch.

"Janna, let's go."

I was graduating from college. According to my mother, this was a very big deal, a bigger deal than high school. This was college, not just a ceremony and an eight-by-eleven leaf of paper for someone to frame. It was more than that. Now life could begin—again.

When Nicole and I met up with my parents in the parking lot, I felt sticky and unprepared. If I took off my aviators, I might puke or cry. I pushed straightened waves away from my face and tugged at my dress—a low-cut black and white polka-dotted dress that was tighter than when my mother had bought it for me. It now pulled on the side with the zipper, causing the other side to show more cleavage. Afraid my mother would comment, I constantly readjusted the imbalance when I thought no one was looking. When had I gone from flat to full-figured?

"Are you tired?" my mom asked, looking at me through the rearview mirror.

"Nope, I'm good," I lied, looking out the window and trying not to throw up.

"Are you ready?" my dad asked, craning his neck around to look at me. "You look pretty. You are pretty."

He reached back and tapped my knee with his palm. I felt a jolt of energy from such a missed and familiar gesture. I wanted to squeal, but I didn't want to draw too much attention. He squeezed my knee before letting go, and I looked over at Nicole.

"Cole, did you see that?" I whispered.

"That was weird," she said. Just as quietly, she added, "Like old John."

I sat surrounded by beverages as we waited for our food at O'Charley's. None seemed to satisfy me, so I arranged the orange juice, water, and coffee in a row. While my parents talked logistics about meeting up with my aunts and grandparents, I looked at Nicole and blew a bubble in my orange juice. She looked at me and did the same.

"Janna Marie!"

We both popped up erect in our booth at the sound of my dad's voice.

"You might want to stop that, move your orange juice away from the edge, and take your elbows off the table," my dad said, eyeing the orange juice that sat an inch from my elbow, an inch from the edge. "Unless you'd like to spill it all over yourself."

He just yelled at me, but it was different. I looked at my mom, who was looking at him. Nicole was staring at him, too, both of them with wide eyes and open mouths. They'd heard it, too: the slight shift in the intonation of his voice. It was like the knee pat. Thoughts buzzed around in my brain— childhood, hospitals, the show on the Discovery Channel—as I stared at him. He looked the same as when I'd seen him a few weeks ago, carrying too much fat in his belly and sporting an untended bristly pepper-gray beard. But maybe today, fate or God or whatever was in control could pull through, dredging my deceased dad up from the ether and planting him in a booth in Springfield, Ohio. Have him show up the morning of my graduation and tell me to mind my manners, which was code for *Can the hung-over crap.*

For once, it was exactly the way I pictured something. But by the time the eggs came, he was back to forgetting who my friends were.

"Krystal is the one you went on a cruise with?"

"No, Dad, that's Natalie."

"Oh, and she's in your sorority?"

"No, Dad! Amy is the one in my sorority, remember?"

"Claudia, do you think we can stop and get a *USA Today?*"

THE FACT THAT YOU COULD go to a store as big as Walmart and as cheap as Kmart at all hours of the day perplexed and intrigued me. Our freshman year, Natalie and I made a habit of dodging our papers and studies to go to Meijer and buy pints of ice cream at 3:00 a.m. It felt wildly irresponsible, like the lovely recklessness of drinking until I was dizzy. These were things I should be doing, now that I had been let go, released of my duties as a daughter—things my mother never would have done at Wittenberg.

"I don't need to tell you these things, Janna," my mother said to me a few weeks into college. "But I'm going to."

I sat, staring out the window, slumped in a beanbag chair in a dorm room that I shared with a rail-thin pale girl who was obsessed with marching band and Japanese anime. I was happy to have Natalie and Amy on my floor. I listened to my mother as she compiled every piece of life advice into three sentences. "Everything in moderation. Do not drink and drive. Do not get pregnant."

"How poignant, Mom," I said. "Rules to live by."

Everything in moderation. Do not drink and drive. Do not get pregnant.

She made me repeat it.

When I came home for Thanksgiving, I didn't even know who I was. I was ten pounds heavier and struggling in the *one* class attached to my declared major of environmental science. I was losing my self-confidence without realizing it, and pushing my feelings down deeper than before, under boys, rugby practice, and party after party. I had a tolerance for alcohol that I could not admit to my parents and a new longing to share my adventures with my father, and I couldn't seem to get a grip. I was growing up so much like him—without him. While I was away at school, he was at home, flirting with jail time.

"I thought I should tell you before you came home," my mother told me over our weekly phone chat a few days before Thanksgiving. "Your father's been arrested."

"What?"

"Well, he didn't go to jail, but the other night, he got a DUI."

I had friends who got DUIs. One had a scar on his forehead and the other won a battle with the cement pillar of an underpass on a back road.

"He was coming home from a bachelor party, where he'd taken a shot."

"Dad was taking shots?"

"No, just one shot."

"Oh, but if he only took one …"

"You are not letting me finish."

My father's driving again. I should be paying more attention to what is going on at home. "I'm sorry."

"And he didn't stop at a stop sign completely. I told you that's important, Janna …"

"Mom, I know."

"He was pulled over and was given a Breathalyzer test."

"But one shot? He wasn't drunk?"

"No, but that doesn't matter. He had that shot, and that's all it took."

"Jesus …"

"We can talk more when you get home."

"*Um* … okay."

"You and Natalie need to be careful driving. It's calling for snow."

It took Natalie and me twice as long as usual to get home from Wittenberg. We drove eight hours through a white sheet. The next day, my panicked mother bought me a cell phone at the Verizon store. My father wanted one, too, but she told him no.

I came home again at Christmas. My father and I went to cut down a tree, and walking around the lot of trees, I could see how much had changed. The winter air and the walking were hard on his breathing. He insisted on sawing but took twice as long and wheezed his way through it. His winter coat strained to button around his stomach. I pretended to ignore these things. I wished my mother had come with us, or Morgan—anyone to ease the tension of our non-relationship. I wished for how it used to be: the three of us trudging around the field of trees, exploring all the way out to the untouched trees where we made fresh tracks in the snow. We'd circle one tree after the other, each of us, until a decision was made. My mom would hold the winner steady while my dad and I took turns sawing it free with one of Gram Mary's antique saws.

He stopped short at our usual long path to the untouched trees. He looked lost. I could never tell what he was thinking. He told everyone from his sisters to the cashier at Sheetz how proud he was of me, always followed by an arbitrary list of embellished accomplishments. But he never talked to me anymore.

"So what would you like for Christmas?" he asked while we waited for the tree guys to give us change for the tall, rotund, long-needled spruce that was balding on one side, the one that I convinced him needed a home because no one else would like it.

"I dunno, Dad."

"Yes, you do. Pick something."

"Okay, I want a sailboat and a boyfriend," I said, touching my thumb and forefinger together. "Dad, I have sap on my hands."

"What else do you want?"

"Hey, how do I get the sap off?"

"Paint thinner," said the guy who owned the tree farm as he handed me a $10 bill.

I did this a lot. I reacted to my dad's compulsion for something with one of my own. I knew exactly how to take the sap off and that I couldn't deal with it until I got home. But I wanted him to tell me how—not the tree guy. I was testing for old John.

"Come on, Dad, we gotta go."

He had started talking to another customer, telling him all about his daughter in school in Ohio. "Have you heard of Wittenberg?"

"Hi, sorry about that," I said to a man I was sure was someone the Suhries knew. "Merry Christmas!" I climbed into the driver's side of the truck, and he ambled over, pulling himself into the passenger seat.

"Why do you do that? You just talk to whoever you want? That guy doesn't care about me or college."

"Do you want any CDs?"

"Um, not really."

"How about Destiny's Child? Now they're a good group."

"Are you kidding me? No, they're not. No way."

We said nothing else on the ride home.

On Christmas morning, before we packed up to head to Columbus, I opened one of several packages from my dad. This one, unlike the others, was wrapped with mismatched ribbons, and the *To:/From:* was written on the paper rather than on a tag. The shape told me it was CD.

"I thought you'd like it," he said, smiling at me.

I looked at my mom, who was looking at him. She looked defeated.

"Dad …"

It was Destiny's Child's *The Writing's On the Wall.* I still have it, but I don't think I've ever listened to one track. Sometimes my friends find it and put it on, but I take it out right away. But I can't throw it out, either. I've even consciously added it to my iTunes library. My hate for it has since spread to Beyoncé and most R&B.

"Yeah, I don't want to listen to that one," I'll say.

"Why do you have it, then?" I'm always asked.

"My dad gave it to me for Christmas."

"Oh."

"Yeah. He stole it from Walmart."

Would it have been better if he had stolen *Is This It, Mad Season,* or *White Blood Cells?* I don't know.

The Writing's On the Wall.

It's almost funny now.

I PLEDGED A SORORITY MY second semester, wore a lot of black, lit candles, memorized things and stood in a line with my new sorority sisters while drunk freshman guys kissed us on the cheek—or, disgustingly, full-on made out with us. I changed my major to Spanish and signed up to spend a summer in Mexico. I chugged whiskey from a boot, got two mild concussions, and broke my little finger in rugby. I talked my way into off-campus parties and walked past the kegs to find liquor in the kitchen. I e-mailed papers to professors, who all gave me good grades. I had regular sex and a relationship—not exactly one full of I-love-yous and commitment, but one with a guy who I thought understood me in ways people had yet to, and I was overwhelmingly attracted to him. I popped birth control like every other nineteen-year-old college girl. My boobs were two sizes bigger, and I had a ridiculous tattoo, which was pretty much on my ass. It still takes at least a beer's worth of conversation to justify and explain why it resembles a sperm but is not a sperm. I did Jell-O shots, keg stands, and pulled all-nighters. I un-curbed my swearing, quit being a sugary sweet doormat to everyone, and learned about sarcasm. I was cool. I didn't share my lunch.

The day before everyone was leaving campus for the summer, our first collegiate summer break, I was hanging out with Natalie and some girls in her sorority. We all lived in Ferncliff Hall and were mixing liquor in Dr. Pepper when the idea of riding around campus in a van became more exciting than anything else.

"Come with us," Natalie said. "You'll like it."

"Like it?"

I watched my friends pinch dusty, crumbling bits of green from a plastic baggie and expertly roll them into a neat, white joint.

"Yeah, come on, Janna Banana," said our friend, Mary.

Mary was pretty, always kind, and down-to-earth in the way I wished I could be. She wore Birks and tie-dyed shirts, and her long, curly hair never looked unruly.

"All right, what the hell."

Getting stoned in a red van, I felt like my father's daughter. He'd been smoking pot since he was a kid, and he'd been doing just fine. He was really smart and funny, and everyone loved him. I was not pregnant, did not have a DUI, and was living in moderation. I was really starting to have some fun. I had no plans to tell my mother about anything—the tattoo, the sex, or the weed—unless, of course, she asked. Or maybe years later when she wouldn't care, like the coffee stain on the stairs.

"JANNA, DO YOU KNOW HOW many calories are in a pancake?" my mother asked me, setting her fork down.

"I hadn't thought about it."

"John, do you?"

"No, why?"

"Well, you two certainly eat a lot of pancakes. It's a little piggish."

The night before I had just come back from Cuernavaca, the middle of Mexico, where I had spent the summer practicing my tan, my love for tequila, and the Spanish language. I didn't waste time. Just hours after I stepped off the plane, Ryan and our friend, Matt, picked me up, and with a bottle of mescal in tow, we headed straight to a campout party at Adam's.

A few days later, and I had only one more month until I was back to

Witt. I had a simple itinerary for the rest of the summer: lay in the sun, hang out with Sarah and Jackie, play on the water with the boys, show up for my part-time hostess gig at Iron Bridge, and craft the perfect e-mail to Alex to see where we stood when we got back.

"How many?" my dad asked.

I looked at the copper and silver bracelet he was wearing that fit too snugly around his wrist. I had brought it back from Mexico, a gift for my dad and his zany brain. It had been blessed by the Oaxacan Indians for him. I'd never thought of my dad as a big man, so I chose what fit a man I thought to be his size.

"You just have to watch what you eat," my mother said. "Both of you."

I stared at the bracelet on his now chubby wrist. I could see where it dug into this skin. My father was bigger. He was slower and lazier than I'd ever known him to be. Complications seemed to unfold one after the other as soon as I'd left for school. He still fought us and forgot nearly everything he was told to remember. He sat at home doing nothing but eating and watching TV. He'd been put on and taken off medications. He bought huge quantities of weed from his friends. And he walked with a limp after a back surgery a few months ago that he'd had to correct scoliosis, which had become increasingly more painful after the accident. The pain was gone, but the surgeon clipped a nerve in his back that cut off feeling to his left heel. He had to use a brace, a cumbersome white plastic half boot. "Drop foot," he called it.

My mother desperately wanted him to get back in shape, if anything. And now she was sitting at the kitchen table, telling us both, in so many words, that we were fat. The truth was, we were, sort of.

"Okay, I'll finish, and then I'll go for a run."

"Janna, it's late," she said. "It's getting dark. Don't be ridiculous."

"It's fine. I'll take Morgan. I'll just run on the Suhries' driveway."

"Well, that's not what I—"

"It's fine. I'll run." Looking at my plate, which was littered with gobs of soggy, syrup-soaked pancakes, made me want to gag myself. "May I be excused?" I scraped the contents of my plate into the garbage, rinsed it, and put it in the dishwasher.

"Where are you going?" my dad asked.

"To run. Duh."

As I walked down the Suhries' long driveway, I calculated—four lengths of the driveway equaled a mile. I could run it sixteen times, and that would be four miles. No, twenty times, and that would be five.

I was on length seven. I could still feel the syrup in the corners of my mouth, sticky like tree sap. Sweat stung my eyes, ran down my face and into a river between my boobs. My thighs chafed, and the little toe of my right foot throbbed. Morgan was panting. I had at least nine more to go, and it was well past dark. I couldn't breathe. I looked up at the sky shimmering with a thousand tiny pinpricks of light and took a gulp of air.

Glop. I stared at it, my pancake dinner splattered like cow cud at my feet.

"Get away from there!" I yelled at Morgan, who had stuck her nose in it. "That's disgusting."

The last time I threw up without being hung over or carsick was in eleventh grade, when our volleyball coach made us run endless suicides for losing to Sharpsville. I did have a weak stomach, and it had been a long time since I had run that hard, I reasoned. And now my stomach was empty. No more calorie-infested pancakes. I ran one more length. My head was too light, so I stopped. We walked back to the house, and I felt better. I felt accomplished.

"Bigger boobs, skinnier waist, prettier face."

Alex and I had just finished having sex on floor of Natalie's and my spacious sophomore dorm in Ferncliff.

"Wow, that is quite the poem," I said. "You're an original. Um … thanks."

He laughed and stood up.

"I was afraid you wouldn't want to see me," I said, peeling myself up to his level, feeling punchy. Ohio air was always too stagnant and muggy, as if it had nowhere to go and was trying to suffocate you.

"Are you nuts? Of course I did. I just had swim practice and had to sit with the team at dinner. You were with your sisters anyway."

"True. So we're cool?"

"Yes, Janna. We're definitely cool."

We started out cool. Everything did—friends, new friends, lots of parties, lots of drinking and a French professor that scared the shit out of me with her passion for government holidays, khaki pants, and butch haircuts, all of which played into her sexuality, which also scared me. But the woman taught me the power of memoir and remembering, and for the first time, the intricate way you can identify memories with feelings. I read Proust. I wrote about Proust. I drowned in Proust. I aced Proust.

Krystal liked French, too, and like me, she liked boys and their uncomplicated relationships. And she liked food, and she didn't like food, just like me.

"You were the girl who lived in Ferncliff that I always wanted to talk to," I told her. "But then you rushed Chi-O, plus you were all skinny, blonde, and pretty, and I didn't think you'd want to talk to me."

"You are crazy," she said. "I thought *you* were, with your brown curly hair, and you always dressed so nice for class. I thought you'd want to nothing to do with me."

When I found out about Alex and one of my sorority sisters, I ran down the hallway to Krystal's room. Well, first I hurled the phone into the wall, shattering it into irreplaceable pieces, and tore off the piece of notebook paper that had been taped to the inside of my vanity, and then I ran to her room.

"Hey Jan!" Krystal was sitting cross-legged on her bed, buried in a bio book. "What's up?"

"Remember the list?" I shoved the paper at her, exasperated.

"Oooh, yeah, *the list* … "

"Yes," I said, closing the door as if that would stop the impending tears. It didn't. I sat down on her roommate's twin bed and slapped myself in the forehead. I didn't want to cry. I really didn't want to. Krystal closed her book and waited for me to find space between sobs for words. "Well, she does want to be me. She plays rugby. She's a Spanish major with a business minor. She's an ADPi. She cut her hair … "

"And?"

"We should have put 'sleep with Alex' on the list."

"*What?*"

"Yeah, I just got off the phone with him. It just *happened*. She just went over to his dorm, and … took her clothes off. It just … "

"Oh … Jan, I'm so sorry."

We talked and I cried for hours, and when Natalie came home, I cried more.

Christmas vacation came and went, and when we were back in school, they were dating. *Dating*, that thing that Alex didn't want to be doing with anyone. I hurt and hated for months. I was broken, oblivious to anything at home. I only called home to whine to my mother about how hard life was and how unhappy I was. She kept telling me to lose ten pounds and asking where my confidence had gone. It didn't really matter to me that my father was arrested for stealing newspapers. Goddamn, he loved the newspaper, so what was one more arrest?

I KNEW IT WOULD HAPPEN. I knew they wouldn't get on a plane to Europe. I knew they couldn't, because if they did, something would happen to Gram Mary. I talked to my parents every Tuesday, perched on the arm of the sea-blue couch, toying with the lace curtains, looking out the window over all of Seville. Every Tuesday, it smelled like *jabon,* because it always smelled like *jabon* in Spain. I had two more Tuesdays until I was home for Christmas, back in America.

In the past half year, I had ridden a camel, celebrated Thanksgiving in an Irish pub, weathered a storm in the Canary Islands, *bottellon*-ed on steps of the cathedral in Seville, stuck my feet in two oceans at once, watched a man fight a bull, eaten fish off the bones, dreamed in another language, wrote a marketing campaign in another language, partied for four days straight in Paris with Natalie and Mary, danced in Roman ruins, kissed a guy I'd just met on a bus, met the Green Monkey, rode an Andalusian, windsurfed, regular surfed, danced flamenco, debated life with psychologists in Germany, walked around a Christmas fair drinking *gluvine*, and experienced Proustian moments with German toys.

"I wasn't going to tell you this," my mother said.

"Tell me what?" I could hear my father breathing on the line, which annoyed me.

"I just thought I should wait," she said.

"Wait for what? Mom?"

"Gram Mary died."

"What? When?"

My butt slipped from the couch arm, and I fell into the cushions, snapping the phone cord so tight that I almost lost my international connection. I hadn't spent time with Gram Mary in years. When I had visited her in the nursing home, she was a shadow of the grandmother who had taught me about jewelry and pie and animals and style and gardening and Christmas.

As much as it had occurred to me that she would most likely not be alive when I got back from Spain, it never occurred to me to miss her.

"Janna, she was not doing very well at all. You would not have wanted to see her."

"Hija!" said my señora, who came in when she heard me crying. *"Hija mia? Que paso? Con tu mama? Que se diche? Es tu papa? El cerebro malo?"*

"No, no," I said. *"Esta bien. Voy a decirte despues. Te promiso. Esta bien. Tiene que mas tiempo?"*

"Hija! No estas bien. Digame."

"Sorry, Mom, hang on. Please, just—"

"Mi abuela ha muerto. Estoy bien, es solamente …"

She brought me a box of Kleenex and left the living room to put on a pot of tea for me, shaking her head and mumbling about grandmothers and death.

"Mom, are you okay?" I started to cry. I wished for a teleporter. I wished I could remember something about Gram Mary beyond the slumped form, with brittle hair and dried spittle that I had left. I wished I'd said a better good-bye. I wished I'd visited more or tried harder to love her when she was like that. I wished I'd never sworn at her, not ever in my entire life—not even when she chased me, yelled at me, or swore at me.

"She's been cremated, but there will be a memorial service. We'll wait until you get home. Janna, it's okay …" She was crying. "Go to Italy."

"Rome is stupid. I can come home now, really."

"No, no. Gram Mary would have wanted you to go. Go see Rome. Do something she would like to do."

"I can't, Mom. I should be at home."

"Go to Rome, Janna," my dad said.

All the way across the ocean, I was leaving my mother alone with this death. A death that was so much more than the dog. I hated the world. I hated it for my mother. I told my señora how much I hated the unfair world and brain injury over tea. She told me I was strong.

"Fuerte, hija," she said, putting her hand over mine. *"Fuerte, tan fuerte. Y inteligente. Que te vaya bien, hija. Que te…"*

A week later, I threw a coin in Trevi Fountain and wished that my mom could be happy again. I threw another and wished for a man of my own. I threw another and wished someone could teach me how to love my father. I threw another and wished to someday make sense of all the loss.

Rome was dazzling at Christmastime, swathed in fragrant green pine boughs and trimmed in red. Gram Mary would have loved it. My father would have loved it. I was thankful that, even in all the muck of brain injury and all his fucking things up, he had always gone to visit Gram Mary when he could still drive. I was excited to go home and see Christmas at my house.

"You have to eat this pretzel," Krystal said, handing me the same rod she'd been trying to get me to eat for the last hour of our trip. "Jan, you have to eat something."

"I *can't*," I whined. My feet dangled unsafely out the passenger window of my own car. I'd pulled my dress up to my hips and curled into a ball, trying like hell to make my hangover nausea disappear. "Why did I take all those shots?"

"Because you turned twenty-one. Sit up straight. You'll feel better. Drink your water, and seriously, Jan, eat the pretzel! Just one!"

"Christ. It's because the boys dared me to chug a beer."

"We all know you can chug, Janna. Why did you need to prove it?"

"I don't know. Maybe because I wanted to end the evening topless on the bathroom floor puking my guts out."

"We need to change this CD, Jan. And I can't drive once we get beyond the tunnels. I'm not driving once we get into Pittsburgh, okay?"

Two hours later, we met Ryan and my parents at Bucca de Beppos. Ryan and my mother were on their second glass of wine and had demolished the first breadbasket. The pasta settled nicely into my stomach, and Ryan slipped my wine into his glass. It was a good birthday dinner. The old Italian men at the table next to us gifted me with a jug of Chianti for the road. And after dinner, we all took the incline up to show Krystal the view from Mount Washington—one of the best views in country. Around 10:00, after my parents headed home, Ryan, Krystal, and I met up with Sarah, her new boyfriend, and some of Ryan's friends from Pitt at a bar in the Southside. It was a good birthday.

The next morning, Krystal and I went to Primanti Brothers, where we gorged ourselves on overstuffed sandwiches at the counter. We were in the thick of the Sunday church crowd. People stared at us as we sat sipping beers, wearing boys' basketball shorts, too-big Pitt tees and heels, with last night's makeup smeared below our eyes. We hadn't bothered to pack.

I GOT THE GRIP I was looking for my senior year. I planned ambitious parties for the ADPi house, got the boy back, quit throwing up, and worked part-time at the Gap. I toyed with applying for an MBA, but I decided my time was better spent having fun than studying for the GMAT. I didn't even know where to apply. I lost my grip, or maybe the one I had no longer applied. I didn't know what to do. I didn't know how to go back home or how not to.

My mother could use my help. Eight years after my father's brain injury, it had become ingrained in our lives. The father I'd once known existed only in old photos or the video recording of my third birthday party. This father was in AA. He was blindly addicted to pot. He'd been smoking every day of his life, but thanks to a combination of no executive functioning and a buffet of brain meds, he was dopey and sluggish nearly every time I saw him. He couldn't get a job or get his life back, so he would smoke weed.

"It just feels good," he told me. "I don't need a reason."

One of my sorority sisters and I used to smoke out of an apple sometimes. It didn't make me think better or even relax. It just made me crave Doritos. I could take it or leave it.

"You can't keep doing this," I told him. "I don't care, but you're hurting Mom, and you're hurting yourself."

"No, I'm not."

"Dad, you're stealing money for weed."

He was. He'd been lifting twenties from my mother's purse or letting his parents pay for lunch when he was supposed to, pocketing his lunch allowance. He'd build a stash and blow it on grass.

He smoked like he ate cake: all of it, all at once. He smoked until he couldn't stand or until he drove the tractor into the pond. As soon as it was gone, he'd want more. And when he couldn't smoke, he ate. His fingers were nubby, and his knuckles were dry and puffy. I stared at them as I listened to his list of excuses. I stared at his ring finger, the tan line empty of a wedding ring. I couldn't believe what his brain had done to him—or maybe what he was letting it do. My mother lived in a constant struggle to move from one day to the next.

"You know, I'm gonna take a pill when I'm sixty," she said often, joking.

"I'd shoot myself, but that would be too messy, and you'd have to clean it up."

I hated when she said that, but I had no inkling of how in God's damn name my mother could continue with this life. Even her horse, Simba, her daily riding buddy, had recently broken his leg in the pasture and had to be put down. And her husband, a man who had become so hard to like, but whom she'd always love, had just traded for pot the few precious possessions that connected who they once were. His thick gold wedding band, a gold watch she had given him, and her father's bloodstone ring were all hawked for $50 worth of dried-out skunkweed.

It couldn't hurt to spend the summer at home. Figure out what the hell I was supposed to do with my life, since I wasn't going to be a vet, or a psychologist, or a meteorologist, or a Spanish interpreter. I could at least come home, get a job at the outlet mall, and help my mother keep an eye on my father.

she's my next of kin

I WAS BORN AT PRECISELY 7:20 P.M. on Monday, June 28, 1982. Fair of face and born with the sun in Cancer, I had blue eyes like my mother and the beginnings of brown curls like my father. And just like my mother—and every other little girl born in 1982—my middle name is Marie.

My dad filmed everything. He was so happy to have a baby girl. He filmed the nurses suctioning mucus out of my nose. He filmed himself severing my umbilical cord. He filmed me, my pink, slimy little body being wiped clean and wrapped in a towel. He filmed my mother, exhausted but smiling. Then he put the video camera down and took pictures with the Nikon. My scrunched-up face, his scrunched-up face mocking my distress—our two red, wrinkled faces are smashed into a photograph forever.

Mom and Dad brought me home to a welcome party full of neighbors, friends, family, tables of food, balloons, and an "It's a Girl!" cake. I was passed from person to person like a birthday card that everyone wants to read—Pat and Bill, then to their three kids, Danny, Keith and Leah Ann, and on to Vicky and her husband, Pat, who were the new couple living across the street, over to each of my parents' friends from work and from forever, handed back and forth between aunts and grandparents, all of whom were new at being aunts and grandparents. All new faces and hands to me, but I didn't cry.

Two months later, my parents bought a puppy. They borrowed the Riegs' station wagon, piled the three kids in the backseat, strapped me on top of Leah Ann, and drove over an hour to pick a puppy from a litter of golden retrievers. On the way home, we had a tubby seven-week-old golden retriever crawling all over us. My father named her Meagan—a girl, a golden with an *M* name.

When I was three months old, Aunt Biz bought me a white Christian Dior baptism dress, and one of my father's childhood friends, fresh with a Unitarian ministry degree from Harvard, trickled water over my head at the same altar where my parents were married. At the small ceremony, Pat and Bill became my legal guardians—my Godparents—to care for me in the event that something happened to my own parents.

"They were good neighbors and had good kids," my mother had said when I asked why they chose Pat and Bill. "We could trust them with the most valuable part of your life. They would not spoil you. And they would always make sure you kept in contact with your family."

When my mother returned to work, the puppy spent the weekdays in the care of the Riegs' kids, and my grandparents traded off on watching me.

Gram Mary and I spent time with the horses, the barn cats, and her German shepherd, Greta. We did yard work in our bare feet and picked apples and rhubarbs for pies we baked from scratch. On busier days, we ran errands or visited friends, and we always stopped by the beauty shop on Friday mornings for the ritual of fuzzy Velcro curlers and pod-like hair dryers.

"You are my favorite person in the whole wide world," she would say to me. It was her favorite thing to say. I keep it with me, on a shelf of good memories, for the days when I need to feel like someone's favorite person.

When my dad dropped me off at Gram and Pa's house, our days started very early. They would be waiting for us in their den-like basement, where a morning talk show perpetually hummed in the background and the smell of instant coffee drifted down the steps from the kitchen. I was Gram Margaret's pet lamb. We made cupcakes and casseroles in the mornings when we weren't shopping or helping out with an event for the church. Afternoons were for sitting on the breezeway or walking through the neighborhood to count the birds on the wire with Pa. (In 1983, Jack Leyde became Pa, because his granddaughter could not be bothered with "grand," and shortly thereafter, neither could anyone else.)

I slid right into the lives of the adults, like I had always been there. At thirty-two, my parents were older than other people with kids my age. My mom tells me that they were more patient with me than they would have been years earlier. Both were naturally good caretakers and had educated themselves about raising kids. They weren't scared to take risks. They taught me one skill after another. They had fun.

Six months: riding. I rode with my mother on Jamal, the skittish purebred Chestnut Arabian that my father had bought her. Perched on the crest of the saddle, Jamal's head bobbing in front of us, her hand holding me tight to secure my wobbly little body, we went on trail rides together. My dad rode beside us on Dodger, the stocky black Quarter Horse my mother had bought him. My dad rode Western, that un-sleek and un-polished way with an embellished, hefty saddle piled on top of bulky blankets. We rode English.

Nine months: swimming. My dad carted me to the pool at Buhl Park so we could splash around with other parents and their children, the same pool he'd spent a few summers as a lifeguard in high school. I was almost too young for the lessons, but I floated on my back, paddled, and kicked. And I stuck my face in the water—under the water—just like the other kids.

One year and six months: creativity. I took all the shoes—pumps, peep-toes, huaraches, sneakers, loafers, sandals, and boots—from my mother's closet and lined them up in an arc. I took a ballpoint pen to graffiti Gram Margaret's good sofa, the one that sat beside all the decorative bells and birds I wasn't allowed to touch. I added milkweed and ragweed to Gram Mary's wildflower bouquets.

One year and nine months: waterskiing. This was the activity the swimming lessons had prepped me for, and I was prepped: fastened into a bulky orange life jacket with straps that itched; practiced in doggie paddling skills; able to go underwater; forewarned that this might be terrifying. And I had been promised that this would be fun.

My dad hoisted me onto his shoulders and eased us into the water by way of the invisible two-rung ladder at the stern of the boat. We floated past the monster-like motor that spit and growled. I thought if I fell off, it would eat my feet. I wrapped my arms around my dad's head and neck and held tight onto his face for fear of sliding off. With one hand, he held my torso in place, slick with sunscreen from head to toe, and with the other hand, he held his ski steady to slide his foot into the boot. My mom threw us the ski rope handle, and he caught it.

"Hold on tight, Peanut." He craned his neck to look back and wink at me. "And close your eyes. *Hit it!*"

I heard a roar and felt us go up in the air. When I opened my eyes, my mom was just a speck driving the boat, propped up on seat cushions so she could see. (She could never see over the window, which is something that will always perplex me.) The ski under us swooshed through the water, my dad steering it in big swoops from one side of the boat to the other. We got good at it that summer, going around the lake once, sometimes twice. And sometimes my dad gave my mom the thumbs-up signal so we could swoop just a bit faster.

"You learned fast and were very imaginative," my mother told me. "As soon as your dad and I mastered one developmental stage, you were on to the next. You were hard to keep up with—a very entertaining parenting challenge." My mother often uses the word *entertaining* to describe me. I think it's her euphemism for "too much" or "very intense," or maybe "takes a lot of energy."

I didn't like to sleep. I rarely cried. I wasn't scared of things. I liked other people and animals. I wasn't fussy. I had opinions and eventually a lot to say. *No* was my first word, followed by *Daddy, dog, horse,* and *Mommy.*

Perhaps *no* was my favorite word. I exercised it a lot. I had to. My father was always pushing me. He was constantly challenging me, taking me to my limit. Always making me do the thing that was too scary, too loud, too hot, too cold, too high, too wet, or too new. And just before I was at my breaking point—puckered up and ready to wail—he would save me. He'd scoop me up in a hug and kiss my face with his tickly mustache. He'd tell me how much he loved me and how proud of me he was.

"Nooooooo!" I screamed, tottering away from the edge in my fuchsia polka-dot bathing suit with the ruffles.

"Stop being a wuss!" he said, arms outstretched. "What's wrong? It's just wet."

He tapped at the pool water to make it splash. I shook my head and covered my mouth with my hands. He looked different to me. His hair and mustache drooped down, dripping with pool water, his eyes covered by a huge pair of aviators. His face and chest were bright red. He was scary, standing in the pool, splashing around and making snorting noises when he wiped off his mustache.

"Peanut! Jump!"

"Nooo! Dad, noooo … I don't want to."

"Do it!"

I did. He didn't catch me. I sunk to the bottom. Water filled my nose and leaked into my ears. I kicked and punched in all directions. I kicked and kicked and puffed up my cheeks, and then something pinched under my armpits, and I was shooting straight up into the air, sputtering, spitting, and kicking as he held me up above his head.

"You did it!" He squished me into his skinny frame and hugged his hairy arms around me. Then he lifted me up in front of him and kissed me on the forehead before plopping me down on the side of the pool where the bricks were too hot on my feet. I stamped my feet and rubbed my nose.

"Let's do it again, Peanut! This time, plug it." And we did it again, and again and again. We did it until it was fun, until my mom told it us it was time to take a break.

The next summer, we conquered the waves of the Atlantic Ocean. They hurt, too, beating me down headfirst and filling my every gasp with saltwater until my dad would put me on his shoulders and we'd go out to where he could barely touch. We'd roll up and over the big waves together, and he'd tread water for both of us.

WHEN I WASN'T SAYING NO, I was an inquisitive kid. I wanted to know things. I talked all the time, incessantly. I loved to be outside. I loved being active. I loved animals. And even then, I could be excessive.

I had stuffed animals in droves—dogs, horses, big cats, small cats, owls, a woodchuck, a skunk, a caribou, a frog, a mallard, two unicorns, a camel, bunnies, a lamb—endless creatures, an obnoxious amount, really. I wanted every one that I saw in every store, and I got them. With the exception of Barf Monkey, who had been christened as such the day I projectile vomited all over him in the passenger seat of my mom's Jetta, my stuffed animals were all girls with "people" names like Mona, Tabitha, Elizabeth, and Meredith.

The very favorite and most special was Priscilla, commonly known as "the butterfly" (or "bofly" or "flutterby"). I was obsessed with the Monarchs that we saw on trail rides. Priscilla was like a rainbow Monarch, with her plush black bug body, green bug eyes, and floppy, colorful wings. She was one of those learning toys, a gift from my parents for my third Christmas. We did everything together. And you could unzip her abdomen, flip her inside out, and tuck her wings in, and she turned into a blue corduroy caterpillar with sixteen nubby black legs. *Metamorphosis*—a hard word to say. Learning toy.

Priscilla and I didn't like taking naps. If I was sleeping, I might miss something Mom and Dad were doing, something the adults were doing. I dreaded preschool naps—a bunch of kids lying, bellies to the ceiling, on a Crayola-colored rug that smelled funny. I stared at the inside of my eyelids, silently singing made-up songs about ponies that jumped over your head.

But bedtime was worse than naptime. People all around me got to stay up later than I did. They got to watch TV, talk, or play with the animals while I had to go to sleep. Sometimes it was still light out, in which case, Meagan would not lie down on the carpet beside my bed. After a few years, I had the dexterity for shadow puppets, so going to bed was not as brutal. There were a lot shadow dogs and shadow wolves. If my dad caught me making puppets for too long, he'd switch off the hallway light.

The sooner you go to bed and get to sleep, the sooner tomorrow will be here.

My parents said this to me all the time, the first mantra in my overactive little brain—Mom and Dad's little psychological trick. I always wanted to know what was next. I wanted to know our plans, what we would do that day, where we were going, who we would be seeing.

"What were we *keeping* forward to?"

"You need to get some sleep, Janna," my mom said, tucking me in, wrapping me tight in the summer sheet, too tight to move my arms and hands. "You have a big day tomorrow."

"Sleep tight," my dad said. "The sooner you get to sleep, the sooner tomorrow will be here."

"What are we keeping forward to for tomorrow?" I asked, again.

"You'll see," my dad said.

"You'll like it—it's exciting," my mom said, leaning over to give me a kiss. "Now go to sleep. I love you."

"What is it?"

"You'll see," my dad said. "I love you, Peanut."

The next morning was chilly, shivery chilly, and everything was still too wet. The boat cover sagged with rainwater, and when we pulled it off, the floor of the old tri-haul was soaked and littered with tree droppings. Back then, the boat was a good boat, almost reliable. It could do at least two essential things—pull a skier and go in reverse. In the summers that followed, it lost horsepower, lost reverse, and one day, the motor cover fell off and sunk to the muck at the bottom of Lake Latonka.

I cringed as my toes squished into the blue AstroTurf. I was six. I knew this day was coming. I'd heard about it, saw the red skis in the garage, the ones that the Riegs' kids had learned to ski on. Where were the ropes? All the other kids got to tie their skis together.

"You want me tie your skis together?" my father had asked me as we were discussing this forthcoming lesson.

"That's what other kids do it like," I said. "Vicky said she learned it that way. Why can't I?"

"Because life's just not fair, is it?"

"No," I said.

The boat floated serenely at the deep end of the lake. My parents looked at me, waiting.

"Dad, we're too close," I said. "Please can we move? It's too close to the thing."

"Janna, you're fine," my mom said. "We are not going to float over the dam."

"But … please …" I said, dancing around at the back of boat. "Please, it's too close!"

"Let's go, ya ninny," my dad said. "Just get in the water."

"But the thing—"

"Janna Marie, come on," my mother said. "We are not going to go over it."

I stuck my hand in. The water was uncomfortably cold, and now I had to pee. This happened every time I got nervous. I immediately had to pee—a rush so immediate it was sometimes shocking, a true telltale sign I was scared shitless of what was going to happen next. It happened before every single trail ride, too. We'd have everyone tacked up and ready to go, and I'd feel it and have to drop everything and run into Gram Mary's downstairs bathroom.

"If you have to go to the bathroom, get in the water," my mom said. "You can do that here!"

I strapped myself into my new blue and purple lifejacket and walked to the back of the boat, trying to stay balanced as the waves rocked it. I wanted to cry. I wanted to pee. I hated the life jacket and thought the strap under my legs was for babies.

"Dad …" I said, dancing again.

He handed me a ski. It was clunky, its red paint starting to chip and flake, what things look like when they've been around since the '70s. Nicked up with love by every kid since my dad who had been forced to learn to ski on them. No holes for ropes.

"I don't want to," I said.

"Okay, fine," he said. "I'll give it to you when you are in the water."

"Dad, I'm really not ready."

He set the ski down and picked me up, walked over to the side of the boat, and held me suspended five feet over the water. He was laughing.

"*No!*"

"John!" my mother said, suddenly alert from her sunbathing post at the top of the bow. "John, come on, now. Stop it!"

"*Nooo!*" I screamed. "*It's soooo cold! Pleeeease don't do it!*"

"John, you don't have to do it this way," my mom said. "Go easy on her."

"*It's gonna get wet!*" he yelled, dangling me lower.

"*Daaa—*"

He dropped me. I surfaced, wet and angry. A blob of seaweed bobbed on the surface a few feet away. I fought the life jacket to swim away from the slimy strands. I paddled my way over to the back of the boat, where I looked up to see my father holding two skis, one in each hand, as if they were light as toothpicks.

Splat! The ski glided like a spear across the water, right up to my face. I stopped it with my palm and tried to swing it around but let go when I spotted the seaweed that was even closer.

"The only way to get away from it is to get up," my dad yelled from the boat.

I swam for the ski, which thankfully was making its getaway in the opposite direction of the green mass. I grabbed it by the rubber boot and shoved the back end in the water. Tip up. I'd practiced these movements a million times on land—in the driveway, sitting with my legs dangling off the back of the pickup. I had wiggled my feet into the boots, remembering that since it was land and not water, I had to be careful not to scratch the skis during my self-taught lessons of how to get my foot in the ski boot and keep the *tips up*. In the water, the boot was too slippery, and on top of that, the ski was trying desperately to get away from me. I was fighting. I was losing. The seaweed was encroaching. I started to cry.

"John, please help her."

He cannonballed, plastering me with a wave of lake water. "Watch me," he said, grabbing the stray ski. He moved away; grabbed the ski with two practiced, strong hands; tucked his foot up to the boot; stuck his face in the water; blew bubbles; and surfaced with half of his crinkly foot in the boot, ski secure, tip up. Then he took it off. "Now you try it."

I took the ski, struggling to get the tip up. I stuck my face in the water and pulled like hell on both sides of the boot. I came up for air. Nothing. I tried three more times. I pushed and wriggled my toes as far as they would go, held my breath, and pulled. Blew bubbles and pulled. This was far less fun than saddling a horse, and I didn't think there was anything in the world that would require more pulling than buckling a girth. I pulled and pushed, pulled and pushed, until I felt my foot jolt forward and the rubber cut into my ankle. It was on. Even with boot's notches adjusted for the smallest foot, it was still a fraction too big for mine.

All that work, now my arms were burning. I looked up at the sky. My leg with the ski was twisting awkwardly, making it hard to do anything but float helplessly.

My mom tossed the other ski. It hit the water and zipped toward us with the same accurate glide of my father's throw. He nabbed it and handed it me. Then he swam away, leaving me to fight this one on my own. After two tries, it was in. Too easy. My other ski had fallen off. I had to go through the whole process again. I hid my tears and blubbered my complaints underwater.

Finally, I reached out and grabbed the rope. My parents stood at the side of the boat and watched me—my tantrums, and eventually my success. Rope in hand, I was no longer cold, no longer nervous, and no longer worried about the seaweed attack. I was embarrassed. I was terrible at skiing.

"Hey, ninny, you still have to try," my dad yelled out at me from the boat. "You have the skis on now. That's the hardest part."

I watched the boat pull away, allowing the thin nylon snake to slither between my palms. By the time I gripped the handle, the boat was far away, a whole ski rope's length away. Jet skis and other boats roared by, creating waves that smacked me in the face and whipped my skis around. If I lost one, I'd have to start all over. I stayed curled up, knees up to my chest, tips up and butt down—as instructed.

"*Let's hit it!*" I yelled at the boat.

The rope lurched forward with a giant tug. The tips of my skis disappeared in front of me. A gush of water pulled my legs apart, so wide it hurt from the insides, wider than I imagined my legs could go. I lost one ski. I face planted on water that felt like concrete. I didn't let go of the rope. A gallon of water flushed into both nostrils and filled up my chest cavity. Still holding the rope. I lost the second ski. I couldn't let go. My armpits were stretching, and my legs were battered. This was too weird, a feeling more complicated than pain. I let go.

"Wooooooooo!" I heard cheers and claps coming from the boat. My eyes and ears were clogged. My head hurt. Feelings I'd never felt were invading my consciousness. I had no idea what had just happened.

"Good try!" my mom yelled as they circled back. "You almost had it!"

I looked up to see that my dad had corralled the rogue skis.

Splat! Woooosh … he tossed a ski. It was like an arrow, perfectly aimed at me. *Splat! Woooosh …* the other. They bounced off my tiny palms.

"I hate this," I said, gathering the slabs of wood in front of me that clacked and clattered with the tiniest movement of water. "I have water up my nose. It hurts. My ears hurt."

"Oh, you're all right," my dad said, folding over the side of the boat and skimming his hand over the water. "We're not done yet."

After three treacherous days, it happened—forty-five seconds of whizzing along on a smooth, solid surface until the skis picked up more speed and pulled me toward that giant hump of frothy water, my very first wake. I panicked. My legs pinged straight. I lost my balance. The water ripped the skis away and shoved the bottom half of my suit so far between my butt cheeks that I looked like I wasn't wearing any bottoms. My toes snagged the surface of the water, and I flew into a sloppy cartwheel.

Stunned, I rolled onto my back and watched an airplane cross the sky, leaving a cotton-white trail as water lapped at my ears. I couldn't locate my muscles, and I was afraid to look around for fear of finding that my appendages had been ripped loose from my body.

"She's down, John!"

I turned over and felt warm streams of water leave my ears, possibly one of the best sensations I'd ever felt. I blew my nose and looked around.

"Nice job, Janna Marie!" my dad yelled. *"Woohoooooo!"* He clenched his fist and pulled his elbow back, as if sealing his own victory. I'd never seen him so excited.

"Janna, that was so good," my mom said. "How do you feel?"

I coughed.

"John, I think she's had enough."

"Nice work, Peanut," he said, leaning over the side of the boat and holding out a ski. "Again?"

And I did it again. Again and again—for the rest of the summer. I think I might have been the worst, wimpiest kid, the wimpiest person, who had ever learned to waterski. I fussed and whined. I cried. I took forever. My father was endlessly patient.

One day, I just got it. I got up every time. And I even crossed the wake. Eventually, in summers to come, I crossed it with grace and ease.

"You ready to do it on one?" my dad asked when I was nine.

"Can I drop the ski?"

"We'll see," he said. "But if you ski on one ski, then you should learn how to get up on one ski."

If I was going to ski like my father, to be *that* good, I'd have to learn the way he wanted me to learn—goofy foot, no whining, and no dropping skis.

waking up in a foreign land

Song lyrics, quotes from movies, titles of books, authors, lead singers, blogs, bands, bars, *asanas*, grammar rules, actors, actresses' baby daddies, yoga teachers, cross streets, restaurant names—endless bits of concrete information that I struggle to recall. But the sensory stuff snaps right to mind. The conversations I've shared, connections I've made, outfits I've worn, feelings I've had, interactions, experiences, sensations, discoveries, tastes, smells, thrills, and fears are neatly filed away in a card catalogue of nostalgia, where I can sort through the memories as if my life were a library.

Then why the gaping hole of memory I can't explain? What the hell happened to the months sandwiched between college and adult life? Did they get sucked into a black hole? Were they erased? Did I lose the journal? These were days at home, spent with my parents, my family, my friends, and yet I remember them like I remember that one line in that one Delta Spirit song I like: "I'll give you my love but not my ...? Tattered and torn, beaten and ...?" Mixed up. Incomplete.

I feel guilty, as though somehow I've avoided things—the ugly feelings that come from sorrow and sadness and all the painful words and sentences exchanged in the fights. I salvage what I can. Had it been my choice, I'd have every single one of those memories logged under 2004–2005 with all the rest. Instead, I'm left with hazy scenes of birthdays, holidays, family vacations, parties, dinners, discussions around the kitchen table, and decisions analyzed on the back porch and out in the barn. Scenes that float around in my brain, tethered to one chunk of time by three plane tickets, two white envelopes, and one bag of weed.

I came home from Wittenberg with clear intentions. Be an adult. Spend time with my dad, and develop our father-daughter relationship. Learn about his brain injury, and help us live with it.

Unlike my mother, at twenty-one, I had not tapped my well of patience. My uncluttered days had room for this commitment. This time at home would give me the chance to reboot. I could finally figure out what the fuck I was going to do with my life. Over the years, I'd ruled out one occupation after another. Vets have to put animals down. Psychologists should not have their own issues. Meteorology involves way too many numbers. *Janna the interpreter* sounds boring as piss. Business of any kind also involves way too many numbers and has the potential to become intolerably boring.

No one had told me that Wittenberg was a drug. When I came home, I came down. Within days, I was wracked with emotions that I could neither define nor control. I'd been away for so long that I'd forgotten what I was coming home to. This was not life at the lake circa 1995. I was a victim stuck in an undeserved reality where my indolence was shifting to resentment. I fought with my parents—both of them—all the time. I was angry with the world, angry with my parents. I was angry with myself for being angry.

I was angry at the brain injury. I hated that brain injury, that insidious little bastard sibling. I'd been watching it take bits of our old way of life and crumble them for almost a decade. I no longer had the courage to wrap my head around what my mother was going through. Four years ago, I'd left her to go gallivanting into adulthood, chugging beers and making grades. I left her, and her horse had died, Jan had died, Gram Mary had died, and old John had definitely, unquestionably died. My mother was more tired and sad than I had remembered. Life was just one insurmountable obstacle after another—change, death, money, medicine, time, and the insurance company. What the insurance company would and wouldn't approve would become a running dialogue for the rest of time.

Before December of 2004, Workers' Comp had been covering all my father's medical expenses: surgeries, hospital stays, doctor's visits, outpatient treatment with Dr. Zimmer, his own MSW for behavior management, therapists, treatment plans, and dozens of prescriptions. According to the settlement, this was the plan—for Workers' Comp to cover all medical costs related to the injury—until he was sixty-five. He was fifty-four.

That December, Dr. Zimmer had recommended Dr. Terry Heltzel, a new psychologist who could treat my father specifically for his traumatic brain injury. Dr. Zimmer also prescribed Namenda, a new drug that had shown positive results in fledgling studies with Alzheimer's patients. Namenda blocked glutamate, a natural chemical in the brain that's believed to be linked to dementia. It was an off-label usage, but Dr. Zimmer was confident that Namenda would improve my father's memory and awareness and increase his ability to perform daily functions.

Despite several letters of medical necessity, Workers' Comp refused to pay for both Namenda (only $500 a bottle, a pittance among neuro drugs) and treatments with Dr. Heltzel, as Workers' Comp considered both "unrelated to treatment of work injury."

A few months later, Dr. Heltzel referred my father to Dr. Crush, a psychiatrist at Psych Care, whose behavior management counseling would enhance his treatment regimen.

"He's a little guy, like John," my mother said.

"Who?"

"Doug Crush ... he's like John."

My parents had started this habit of referring to one another by their names to me. I did not like it.

"Like?" I asked.

"Like your dad. I used to work with him. Doug has a personality like your father, a little guy with aggressive speech and actions. And he has had a head injury!"

"Really!" I loved this, the idea that there were others like us. I felt a rush at first. *Oh! My dad has a TBI, too! It's frontal lobe, executive ...* And then it loses its luster, this uncommon thing in common, because you realize you're cheering about finding out that someone else has a brain injury.

"Yes, so I think he may be able to really help John."

I made a face.

"Your dad walks all over people, Janna."

It was true. If anyone could bullshit a brain injury, it was my father. He would smile, tell a bad joke, or say whatever he needed to get the keys, money, or permission he was after, whatever he wanted. He could bullshit his way through his treatments.

"He needs someone that might be able to relate to him, someone he'll like."

In May, just weeks before I graduated from Wittenberg, my mother had filed a petition to review medical treatment coverage. Workers' Comp was not only refusing to cover the cost of Namenda and Dr. Heltzel, but also Dr. Zimmer and Dr. Crush. The hearing was scheduled for July. Three weeks before the hearing date, Workers' Comp appealed. The hearing was rescheduled for two months later, and three weeks prior, Workers' Comp appealed—again. Like clockwork, this reschedule-appeal pattern persisted throughout the fall and into the next year, allowing Workers' Comp to forgo almost all medical coverage related to my father's treatments.

Brain injury treatment is ongoing and expensive. The first year cost an easy $400,000 in acute care, medical bills, treatments, medications, and Squirrel Hill, which alone cost a whopping $1,200 a day. And due to the Pennsylvania Workers' Compensation Act (passed on June 24, 1996), the state now required that the family pay back 84 percent of all first-year medical costs. The year 1996 cost us roughly $336,000. In years that followed, my dad's monthly medical care average was give or take $3,000. Few salaries can sustain these costs. My mother's was not one of them. My dad's planned recovery slowed until it eventually reached a hiatus. While my mother went to work, my father sat home. He was bored stiff.

Bored stiff: perhaps my worst fear in the world. I grew up with my family's endless suggestions on how to remedy the problem. My mother was always practical: "You could do some yard work with me." Gram Mary was never practical: "Go stand on your head in a corner and spit wooden nickels." Pa would suggest a conventional adventure: "Let's go for a walk to count birds on the telephone wires." Aunt Biz was fun: "Wine spritzers." My father proposed the obvious: "Well, go and find something to do."

But now, that old, obvious part of his brain was missing. He could never find something to do. He just sat. He lacked anything resembling drive; he slumped in front of the TV and ate his way through bags of pretzels, cookies, and chips. Sat and sat, his boredom feeding his cognitive sequelae (that elaborate term to describe the compilation of symptoms attached to his particular brain injury). Boredom morphed him into a person we didn't recognize.

He lied a lot. He lied about what he did during the day, where he drove the car, and the fact that he didn't smoke—or for that matter, grow—pot. He stole money from my mother's purse and occasionally nabbed the tips off tables at restaurants when he was deft enough to pull that stunt off. He was aggressive, compulsive, and impulsive when he wanted his way. He was depressed, but he didn't know it. And when he smoked the pot he was not growing or buying with stolen twenties, he smoked it until he couldn't function. He got the kind of high that mixes up verbs and nouns, that makes you trip on air, that makes you think a half-ton tractor will float.

There was no more waxing and waning to his recovery. No more hope that the fragments of old John would piece together. He was fixed on a monotonous track from okay to worse, and I wanted to know whether there was one health care professional out there with the balls to admit the inevitable truth of his brain injury—"old John," "John before the accident," my father, was not coming back.

I picked up my own ways to cope. When Sarah wasn't in a grad school class down at Pitt, we'd pick up our high school friend, Amelia, choose a restaurant, and order something fried. Sarah would drink bourbon-and-Cokes; Amelia and I went with tall, frosty Yuenglings. On more exciting nights, Adam—who was back from Virginia Tech selling gym equipment—would dust off the old spot in the woods behind the cornfield, invite guests, ignite the fire, and provide an endless supply of IC Light.

"I'll probably end up at Adam's," I yelled to my mom, sprinting down the steps, keys in hand. "I'll be home before eight."

"Okay … just don't drive if—"

"I know, Mom."

"Home before 11:00?" my dad asked.

"Fat chance, Dad."

He leaned in to kiss me good-bye.

"8:00 a.m.," I said, tilting my cheek to the side, willing myself to be warmer or nicer to him next time.

Adam's campout parties devoured the hours. When the crowd grew smaller, we'd move the festivity to the back porch, play music, and soak in the hot tub. Many mornings, I found myself at his kitchen table, realizing the sun was coming up and wishing for coffee. When the clock in the kitchen said 7:00, it was time to drive home and crawl back into my own bed.

I can't imagine this behavior was okay with my mother, but she never said otherwise. Instead, she focused on my chubby cheeks. They bothered her in the way that seeing myself in a bathing suit bothered me. My closet was filled with clothes that didn't fit. I'd filled the hollow leg of my youth and then some.

I lived a sad cliché, every day trying on a single pair of jeans. They were my favorite, a positive byproduct of college and my relationship with Alex. One morning during sophomore year, I had gotten up angry over something he had said or done, so I drove to Columbus and exhausted an entire day drinking black coffee and thrift shopping. I spent the night at Aunt Biz's, watched a thousand *One Tree Hill* episodes with Annie, and returned to Wittenberg the next evening with a pair of boot-cut J. Crew jeans from the '90s that made my ass look like asses should look in jeans. Now I couldn't squeeze my thighs into them.

I told myself anything was worth doing if it burned calories—half-assed bits of yard work, weeding or mowing acres of grass, pounding the elliptical at Cool Springs Fitness Center, which was the fancy new gym overlooking Mercer County's only winery. I even joined Curves, because Sarah worked there, but all we did was wear out Rob Thomas's solo CD and cut into menopausal women's workout times.

I needed to do something to feel productive, so I got a job working at the Banana Republic at the outlet mall. I spent mind-numbing hours board-folding shirts and schmoozing half-hearted discount shoppers. Eventually, I was managing the visual merchandise. This gave me the idea of working at Gap corporate. I was driving back from Columbus when the call came. Somewhere near Akron, I turned down a chipper woman offering me a coveted Visual Merch internship too far away in San Francisco. I cried the rest of the way home.

I TRAVELED A LOT THAT year, because I could. Because if you didn't have one of those on-track-to-become-a-such-and-such plan, that is what you did. Or maybe I did it for my parents, because they couldn't. Because someone should be doing something fun.

In July, I flew to Florence to study Italian and fashion design. For two months, I lived in a sunlit room with two younger girls. I ate twice my weight in pasta, developed a taste for red wine, and designed a chic collection centered on gold lamé pieces. My parents looked right past me at the airport. I'd like to think it was because my mother had made friends with a woman who was waiting to pick up her boyfriend, the drummer from U2, but it was my caramel skin, platinum bob, and fuller figure.

A week later, Alex called and flew me out to California for Labor Day weekend. I couldn't believe my mother let me go. He was living in a house in the Hollywood Hills with an Infinity pool. He shared it with his brother, his brother's girlfriend (who'd been on *The Real World San Diego*), and his St. Bernard. They had wild parties every night. Steve-O, from *Jackass*, taught me how to twist off a beer cap with my forearm. I talked Proust with the guy with the dreads from The Black Eyed Peas. I took shots with spindly girls working in fashion who applauded my premature musings on moving to New York to write for magazines. Meanwhile, my mother—and everyone at Children's Aid—waited for the phone call to announce that I would be staying. *Staying?* No way. Not in the place where everyone lived in a state of aspiration. The only two things I cared about in California were seeing Alex and sticking my feet in the Pacific. I saw Alex, at least.

I returned from LA to the healthy stack of MBA applications I'd left sitting on my desk. I moved them from my desk to my bed. I laced up a pair beaten-up Adidas and ran until my feet burned. Six miles. I came back, showered, and sifted through the stack. I made three piles and put sticky notes on them in the hopes that it would help me take the whole thing more seriously.

business schools
non-business schools
non-business (journalism?!?) schools in New York City.

I had stacks of writings on literature in three different languages, but I had no experience in journalism. Well, there were a few articles in the *Wittenberg Torch* and all the Mercer High School photos I'd captioned for the yearbook. If I was taking this seriously, that was nothing.

I enrolled in two newspaper-writing classes at Slippery Rock University. I didn't make any friends but earned As on my stories. My professor told me I was a good candidate for grad school—even for Columbia—if I got an internship, so I helped out at *Views & Voices,* a local women's magazine in its infancy. In October, I spent the better part of a Saturday in a dingy, chilly room in the *Pittsburgh Post Gazette* building that was packed with people who sniffled and coughed throughout the GRE. I wanted to get them Kleenexes. I wanted them to be quiet. Studying for this boring exam had been grueling in that oh-God-I-don't-care way, and every time someone sniffled, I forgot some bit of trivia or some grammar rule I probably never really knew.

A month later, my scores proved how far-fetched my New York idea was. I excelled in math but had verbal scores embarrassingly low for someone wanting an advanced degree in writing. New York was nothing more than the next pipe dream, and I couldn't even find the energy to give a shit.

Two days later, I boarded a twenty-one-hour flight to Melbourne, Australia, cashing in my college graduation present from my family—the plane ticket. A few weeks into my stay, I tore into the second package my mother had sent me and found a letter.

Dear Janna:

Though we appreciate your interest, New York University does not accept incomplete applications …

I stood in the lobby of *The Age,* Melbourne's biggest newspaper, and waited for my friend, Sam. I was all the way on the other side of the earth, and NYU admissions had never received—read: lost—my test scores, personal statement, and college transcripts. Sam and I watched while her mother helped my mother fax the missing materials to us so that we could rush an envelope emblazoned with Australian postage to an address in Washington Square. I gave it to the mailroom man and kissed NYU good-bye. It was January. I stayed in Melbourne until March, writing, windsurfing, eating, drinking, and traveling up and down the southeastern coast of the continent with Sam and her friends.

I came home a brunette with an intercontinental best friend and an affection for Vegemite. Two months' worth of mail and magazines were separated into neat piles on my bed. I've come to expect this and to appreciate it. No matter how long I've been away, my mother's self-categorized piles of magazines, envelopes, printouts, clippings, and papers, many topped with sticky notes, are like Cliff Notes to my life back home.

One envelope was set off to the side, a pile unto itself. It was thin. A strip of Scotch tape served as the seal and showcased a thumbprint, alluding to the importance given to it by its sender. I took it downstairs to the kitchen, my hands shaking and clammy. My father handed me the silver letter opener that he'd gotten from the porcelain cup that sits on top of my mother's desk, special for the occasion. He'd been waiting for this for a week.

"What do you think it's going to say?" he asked. He rubbed my shoulders, making it harder for me to concentrate on slicing the tape. He leaned closer as I opened it.

"I don't know." I walked away and faced him. "Why would you ask me that?"

"I'm just curious."

"Don't be."

Dear Janna:

Though we appreciate your interest in the Columbia School of Journalism, at this time we regretfully inform you …

My insides collapsed. I ran out to the barn with the letter. *"Mom!"*

"Jan?" She was unsaddling Jamal as I pounded through the side door of the barn, scaring a smattering of cats. I stood still and said nothing, as if not moving kept it all from coming true.

"Janna?"

"Columbia didn't want me." I walked backward a few steps until I bumped into the gate.

"Honey, I promise you … this is not the end of the world."

I couldn't hear the rest. I ran back to the house to get my phone. I sat under the maple tree I used to climb as kid and called Krystal. I told her over and over again how silly I was—thinking I could do this. I sobbed into my phone until my chest hurt. I asked her why things like this happened to me. I repeated the questions so many times that I was sure she'd have different answers, answers that would change the situation. Instead, she reminded me about NYU. I reminded her of the lost paperwork.

"You never know, Jan," she said. "Your dad's wife's friend … or … dad's—"

"Dad's-friend's-wife's-brother *was* the president," I said.

"See, you have that."

"Oh, come on, Krys. That's weak. You know that."

"Well, Jan, if you're meant to go be a writer, a journalist, in New York, you will. You have to trust that things work out."

A few weeks later, I came home after work to find my father standing on the side of garage where I parked the Del Sol.

"Dad! Move! What are you doing?"

"Something came in the mail for you today." He was holding a white envelope in front of his face, hiding that shit-eating grin that sent me into a fit of annoyance.

"Dad!" *Just be nice to him,* I told myself, turning down the stereo. "Please move. I really don't care."

He stood still, feet cemented into my parking spot. "Why don't you open it?"

"Move. Come on, Dad. Please. I'm trying to park the car. I don't care about the envelope." I inched the nose of the car into the garage, but he didn't move.

"What if you got in? Don't you want to know? I think you do."

"No!" I killed the ignition and left the car parked half in and half out of the garage. He followed me into the house, holding the envelope.

"What if I know you got in?"

"Stop it. What are you talking about?"

"I'm talking about how you got into NYU."

"Oh for chrissakes, Dad. Come on."

"What do you mean come on? Ray called me today and he said Judy told him that Dave said that—"

"Jesus, Dad! You don't know what you're talking about. I didn't get in, all right? Stop this. Stop being annoying. Don't you get that I'm upset about this? That I don't know what the hell I'm doing with my life? That my plan didn't work? *Don't you ever get it?*"

"I'm so proud of you," he said, putting his arm around me and handing me the envelope.

His touch made me want to bolt. I was so angry—at him, at the future, at myself. I didn't like this version of myself, but it was all I knew. Just fight and hate, and then you can be tough and survive. I took the envelope from him and set it on the kitchen table.

"Please, Dad. Stop."

"Well then, open it."

"No." I asked him to make a half-pot of flavored coffee, and we sat in the kitchen, listening to it brew until my mom came noisily through the door, a bag of cat food wedged under one arm, with her purse and a plastic bag bursting with toilet paper, chips, cereal, and bagels dangling from the other.

"So, did your father tell you?" she asked, distributing the items across the counter.

"Why do you have to use plastic bags, Mom?" I asked. "Doesn't anyone get it? They are so bad for the planet."

"Janna. I forgot the market bags in the car. I drove the truck. Give me a break. Now did you open your letter?"

"No, I did not open my letter," I said, handing her a cup of coffee, only half-full so it wouldn't get cold, the way she likes it. "I didn't get in, okay?"

"You don't know that. Come on. How do you know that?"

"It's too thin," I said.

"Open it," my dad said.

"You're being ridiculous," my mom said.

The two of them stood there, waiting until I tore at the edge of the envelope. I didn't want to be told that some school hundreds of miles away in a city that I hadn't been to since I was fourteen didn't feel that I was worthy. I pulled out a single sheet of paper and unfolded it. I took a step back from my parents.

Dear Janna:

Congratulations …

Wow. I handed it to them and smiled. My mom pulled me toward her. Her hugs were so rare and so warm. I closed my eyes. I could feel relief wash over both of us. My dad smiled at us. A smile that felt as old and familiar as her hug.

I watched inflated cumulous clouds roll across the sky. I tried to discern whether I was hungry or thirsty. My head hurt. I closed my eyes. Beads of sweat trickled down my temples, over my rib cage, and into the crevice between my boobs. Everywhere it touched, it tickled, shattering my sensation of stillness. I'd been like this for hours, baking in the late June heat with *The Sun Also Rises* splayed open under the shadow of the chair, its story of love, rot, and drinking in old Spain split down the middle.

"*Janna Marie!*" my dad yelled.

I looked up. The hum of the mower had put me in a trance.

"*Janna Marie,*" he yelled again, neglecting to turn off the engine. I could only see his mouth move.

"What?"

"*Janna Marie!*"

I thought about the roots of the poor cherry maple the blades were severing. He had the deck set too low—again. I sat up. My empty, grumbling stomach pushed more pressure to my head.

"Dad, turn it off," I yelled. "I can't hear you."

I can't hear you, he mouthed, spinning the mower in a circle around the small tree.

"*Turn. It. Off.*" I made an exaggerated twisting motion with my wrist. I watched as he reached down for the key. As the sound died, he held up his hands like a "no hands" kid on a bike and rolled to a stop next to me.

"Happy birthday." He grinned. "How is your day?"

"Dad, it's the same as it was half an hour ago." I rolled my eyes.

"May I ask you a question?" he asked.

"What?"

"What would you like for your birthday?" He had been asking me this same question since early that morning. His compulsion infuriated me, so I'd started counting.

Nine.

"Well, what can I get your for your birthday?"

Ten.

"I told you already. I don't want or need anything. I want it to be simple. I don't need presents."

At precisely 7:20 that evening, I would be turning twenty-three. As a rule, my mother made little acknowledgment of my birthday, never a proper wishing, until that very minute, which made my father's persistence maddening.

"I know that, but what can I get you?" he asked again.

Eleven.

"Nothing, Dad."

The last time I remember wanting a present for my birthday—the last time I asked for one—I was fifteen. I wanted a WaveRunner. I'd wanted a turquoise WaveRunner since I was twelve. When I turned eight, I got a pony, every little girl's dream. But my pony bucked me off every chance he got. When I turned eleven, after I won a spelling bee, I got a slalom ski, a Connelly "Kidder," but I had wanted an O'Brien. Sixteen—a red convertible, presented three months early on my dad's birthday. I never got the WaveRunner.

But I didn't want material gifts anymore. I wanted people to wrap up boyfriends, careers, or life plans and set them under my Christmas tree or beside my melting ice cream cake. It was easy and rather amusing to want things that no one could give.

"Just think of one thing you'd like to have," he said. "What can I get you?"

Twelve.

"Okay, fine. Do you know what you can get me?"

"Tell me."

"For my birthday … I want you *not* to smoke pot today, not any. Not one tiny hit. Do not be high at dinner. *That* is what you can do for me. *That* is the only thing I want for my birthday. Can you get me that?"

"Okay."

We were going to The Iron Bridge, my favorite restaurant, to celebrate with the Suhries and Gram and Pa. Lately, it had become common for us to find my father too stoned to function. He would sneak away and smoke himself to the point where his motor skills failed, his speech drawled, and his eyes closed mid-conversation.

My mother told me that he'd been getting high his whole life, probably smoking every day, which didn't seem to bother her. Apparently, for someone like my father (who can get "pretty wound up"), smoking pot calmed him down. She explained it to me as his way of self-medicating. I thought of it as his hippie version of Ritalin. I never even picked up on it as a kid. Back then, pot was something that never affected him or other people, something that he got away with early in the morning when taking the dog out or playing racquetball with his buddies or before dinner behind the garage. But let's be real: my father was a bit of a pothead.

Pot was something my parents didn't need to share. My mother wasn't interested. Simply ingesting it made her hyperventilate. I asked once, "Have you ever?" It was one of my clever segues that would allow me to casually admit that I occasionally smoked pot—only *in moderation,* of course.

"I ate brownies once."

"Mom ..." I said, smiling, thinking this segue would be more clever than I'd planned. "*Special* brownies?"

"He didn't tell me it was in there, and I ate three."

I chuckled. "You ate three pot brownies?"

"It's not funny. I told your father I'd try it once, but not smoke it. So one day, he made brownies, and he didn't tell me he put it in."

"And you ate *three* of them." I couldn't stop myself from laughing. "Jesus Christ, Mom. No wonder you hyperventilated."

"I couldn't breathe. It was very scary. I do not like it. And he *lied* to me, Janna."

"He just didn't tell you. I mean—"

"Your father knows how upset I am about that."

More than pot, my mother hated lying.

After the accident, getting high was no longer something my father could control. In fact, my father is the only person I know who can get stoned the way other people get shitfaced.

"Just please don't smoke pot today, Dad."

"Oh, no. I won't do that."

"For my birthday, promise me you won't get high."

"I won't get high. I promise." He started the mower and mowed away.

"Thank you, Dad!"

I laid back down into the slick of my own sweat, noticing where the plastic weave of the faded chaise had carved an unflattering pattern into my skin. The stench of sun-scorched horse poop and my own body odor hovered over my nostrils. I needed a shower, so I packed up my oasis and went inside.

I ran the water and waited until the shower was piping hot. (It doesn't matter the weather; showers and coffee should always be hot.) I stayed under it until the pads of my fingers started to prune. Afterward, I wrapped my splotched body in a towel and examined myself in the mirror. I wasn't sure if this was how I should look at twenty-three. No detectable lines in my face. No gray hairs. No stretch marks. Yet I did not recognize who I was looking at. Maybe it didn't matter.

I opened the bathroom door, and an overpowering smell of skunkweed hung in the air. I threw on the first pair of shorts and shirt I could find in my room. Braless and dripping shower water, with my hair wrapped in a sloppy towel turban, I ran down to the kitchen. *"Daaaaaad!"*

My father stood, facing the microwave, hands interlaced behind him.

"Dad?" I walked closer to him. "What are you doing?"

"Nothing," he said, startled.

"What is in the microwave? What smells?"

"Nothing."

"Nothing?"

"Nothing."

"Well, that's not what it looks like. I'm not stupid."

The microwave dinged. He turned to face me.

"Dad, come on. What do you have in there?"

"I don't have anything," he said. "It's none of your business."

"My business? Come. On."

He pushed the button to start it again. The humming was loud; I swore it was vibrating. I was sure he was going to blow it up, that weak little excuse for an appliance that I'd brought home from college to replace my parents' ancient box.

"You are going to break it."

"I'm not going to break it."

I walked up to him and peered over his shoulder. The window was fogged with condensation. I opened the door.

"Don't do that!"

The smell from the pile of wilted green leaves on a paper towel choked me. I slammed the door shut, and it starting cooking again. "Dad! How could you?"

"How could I?"

"What on earth do you think you're doing?"

"I'm drying them out."

"I'm aware."

"I don't need to tell you what I'm doing."

"Oh, but you do. Jesus!"

He turned around to remove the plate and tended to his leaves. I put my hand over my eyes and shook my head until my brain rattled and the towel turban unraveled. I watched him move the saturated paper towel off the plate and place it on the counter.

"Come on, Dad. You're cooking a pile of weed in the microwave!"

The leaves from the young marijuana plant had begun to furl at the ends.

"It's cannabis," he said. "And I'm not *cooking* it."

"Do you think I'm stupid? Are you fucking kidding me? How could you do this?"

I walked out of the kitchen and threw the wet towel on the phone stand, sending bits of papers, notes, and all of his lists into a flurry. "Fuck you, twenty-three," I said to myself in the mirror that hung above the phone. "Fuck you." I flipped off my reflection. I took a deep breath, promised myself I wouldn't cry, and rewrapped my wet hair in the towel. I wrapped it so tightly that it could safely hold all my rage inside. I walked back into the kitchen. Sunlight streaming in from the open window above the sink highlighted the wet footprints on the hardwood floor where I'd stood minutes earlier.

"Weed? You are drying out a pile of weed in the microwave?"

"No."

"Dad!" I stomped my foot. I felt like a child.

"So, do you know what you would like for your birthday?"

"I ... don't ..." I stopped talking. He was spreading out the leaves on a new paper towel. He then transferred the leaves to a plastic baggie. It was as if I stood in the kitchen while he made a sandwich. "So ... you'll get me *whatever* I want for my birthday?"

"Yes, of course," he said, not looking up.

"Absolutely anything I ask for? Promise?"

"Anything. I love you." He stopped his project and came over to stand behind me. He put one hand strategically on each shoulder and began to squeeze and pull at the muscle fixed to my bones. It hurt—a pain that unearthed pockets of tension.

"You love me?" I asked.

He squeezed and pulled. "Yes."

"Ha. Sure ya do."

"Yes, I do."

"I want that," I said, pointing to the baggie of weed. "For my birthday."

He stopped, hands dropping to his sides.

"You can't have that."

"Yes, I can. Dad, you said—you *promised*—I could have *anything*."

"Why do you want that?"

"It doesn't matter why I want it. That is what I want—from you—for my birthday."

"But what are you going to do with it?" he asked.

"It doesn't matter. Nothing."

"Then I'm not going to give it to you."

"Yes, you are," I said. "You said I could have anything I wanted. I want all of it. I want *that* for my birthday."

He picked up the baggie, folded the ends over, and looked at me.

"I want all of that pot for my birthday."

He handed it to me. He wasn't giving. I was taking.

"Thanks for my present." I left him in the kitchen and ran upstairs. I sat down against my dresser, and tucked my knees up to my chest. Before I could give in to an onslaught of tears, I snapped open my red Motorola flip phone and pushed down on the *K* key.

"Happy birthday, Jan!"

"Thanks …" I said, swallowing hard. "But, Krys, do you have a sec … to … "

"Jan? What's wrong? What happened? Are you crying?"

"I'm sitting here with my birthday gift from my dad … and …"

"And … what did he get you?"

"A bag full of fresh weed."

THE SEVEN-MINUTE DRIVE TO SARAH'S house is bucolic. Countryside sprawls out from the wide two-lane highways that squeeze and snake across three narrow bridges and past farms and woods and twisting back roads. I often stop and take pictures on my way. It's the best way to show anyone who's not where I'm from what it's like where I'm from.

It was my last night Mercer. I cooked one of my inventive pasta dishes for dinner, and my parents and I sat around the table talking well past our clean plates. It had been fun. And I was a little scared. My dad's truck and my car sat in the garage, stuffed with dishes, chairs, clothes, end tables, lamps, a dismantled antique bed—all the goods for my new home. After dinner, I drove my mom's car to Sarah's. I stopped on the one-lane bridge over the creek that curves in front of the entrance to the horse farm where Ralph Lauren and the blonde guy from *Queer Eye for the Straight Guy* board their horses. I watched a blue heron stand on a rock and lost track of time. My phone rang. The heron heard it and flew away.

"Where are you?" Sarah asked.

"On my way, seriously, five minutes."

"Get movin', woman."

"It's my last night. I didn't want to rush dinner. You know we eat late, anyway."

Sarah lived alone in a small house on a back road in Amish country. Her fiancé, Ken, was in Iraq, and she was finishing her master's in Speech Pathology at Pitt. I parked beside Amelia's Miata, let myself in, and found them on the back deck that overlooked her yard and the woods beyond it. We situated ourselves in Adirondack chairs, opened fresh Yuenglings, and talked and drank until Amelia had to leave.

"Hey, Jans ..." Sarah said as we waved Amelia good-bye from the driveway. "You know what I still have?"

"Um, no. *Yes.* Oh, shit. You still have that?"

"Do you want it?"

I gave her funny look. Did she think I'd take it to New York with me? I had given it to her months ago—having it in my possession made me sick.

"Like, want it now?"

"Why not?"

"Can we go in the hot tub?"

As we considered our celebratory plan—her engagement, my NYU acceptance—things became evident. We had nothing. No bowl, no papers. She had brownie mix, but the idea didn't appeal to either of us, so we drove her car out to the gas station out by the interstate. I bought three different pints of ice cream, and she bought two packs of Marlboros. On the way back she smoked one cigarette and then another and I deejayed Buffett songs.

Back at her place, Sarah crafted three fat, wrinkly joints while I turned on the hot tub and tore through her drawer of bikinis in search of one that could cover my boobs.

"Good grief!" Sarah said, sliding into the water, passing the stubby cigarette from her thumb and forefinger to mine. "This shit is good."

I swore I was the only person on the planet who could never get properly stoned. I seldom *felt it.* I inhaled, handed it back, and eased into the hot water. I stared at the two others, sitting side by side on the railing. I pondered how we would handle it if a raccoon snatched one or if they rolled off in the wind that wasn't blowing. If we didn't find one, would it be littering? At least there was ice cream.

We settled in, the water like liquid fleece around us, warm and cozy. We talked about our high-school boyfriends. We talked about the first time I got drunk, silly and stupid—the night six of us girls chugged strawberry wine coolers and played hide-and-seek outside of Sarah's house, buck naked, almost getting caught by her older brother—the middle of summer, a week after I had turned fourteen. We talked about all things we did wrong and all the things we wouldn't change. We talked about the many times that she would visit me in New York. We talked about her fiancé. We talked about Adam and Ryan. We talked about what I would say to Ryan if we ever talked again. We finished a second joint and talked about the universe, about God, and about our own personal psychic abilities. We talked about my dad and his brain. We talked about becoming or not becoming our moms.

"I love water," I said, dipping my head back into the churning froth to sweep the hair away from my face. I looked up and saw Ursa Major stretched across the sky. "My mother would kill me for this."

"Dude, you're high."

"I hope my parents will be okay. I hope they know how much I love them. I'm gonna be something—for them, ya know."

"Quit worrying about it. You're high. They know." She climbed out of the hot tub." Ice cream?"

"Yeah ... ice cream."

"Which one do you want?"

"Peanut Butter Cup ... *gracias.*"

"You bought it."

"No, I mean *gracias* for this night. It's perfect."

"You should thank your dad."

a jungle out there

THE ARMHOLE CAUGHT ON MY NOSE, and the thin fabric clung to the sweat on my forehead, plastered there like wet papier mâché. My struggle with the cotton tank had become embarrassing. I threw it on my bed, took a breath, and unbuttoned my shorts. Another struggle. I tugged at the hem of the khaki cutoffs that were stuck around my thighs. "Sonofabitch." I had never wanted to give up so hard on the simple act of undressing.

I stood up and yanked. The shorts fell to my ankles. I stepped one foot out, teetered on one leg, kicked them into the air, and overshot the bed. Standing in the center of my apartment, I snapped at the pink elastic waistband of my underwear, French-cut panties covered in butterflies. They were playfully sexy, according to Victoria's Secret. *Panties.* Awful word.

Hot air drifted in through my open windows. It flirted with cooling my clammy skin, carrying with it my aunt's voice from the street and the city's summer stench. I hated the air outside. It was sweltering and sticky, a different stickiness than North Carolina beach air. New York City air was putrid. I took another deep breath, but it failed to reach my lungs.

I wove through boxes and suitcases to my closet. My mother had arranged every item by color, the way she did with her own. I pulled out a new pair of linen pants from the white section. I'd recently bought them from the Banana Republic on Fifth Avenue, where I'd be working. I paired them with the same sleeveless sweater I wore for my high school graduation. I heard keys jangle in my door as I hopped back to the open space in my apartment to get dressed.

"Janna?" my mom called through the door. "Janna, what are you doing? Everyone is waiting outside for you." She walked in and set her purse on the arm of the leather loveseat she'd loaned me. She picked up my tank and shorts, folded them, and placed them neatly on my bed. "It will get really hot if you leave these open." She walked over and shut the windows. "What is taking so long? I thought you were just going to change clothes."

"I can't—"

"What's wrong? Everyone is waiting for you."

"I can't breathe. I can't do this. I don't know what I'm doing here."

She knelt down and put her arm around my shoulder. Droplets of our sweat mingled.

"Mom, I can't. I just can't."

"Can't what?"

"I just can't do this."

"Do what? Janna, you have to tell me what's wrong."

I closed my eyes. Only half an hour ago, I'd asked everyone—aunts, uncles, parents, grandparents, cousins, friends of cousins—to clear out of my small studio apartment so that I could get dressed. What the fuck was wrong with me? My whole family had come here to move me into my new life, into this tiny space that could barely fit one person, let alone six liters of pop, shopping bags, pizza boxes, newspapers, maps, purses, and one dozen adults. Why couldn't I breathe? I pushed at my temples, hoping to get my lungs to work. I could feel my mom watching me. I wanted her to fix it for me. More than once in the past, I'd overacted, been Janna-dramatic, specifically so that my mom would have to take care of me. This was not one of those times. I started to cry.

She had gotten up to choose a purse from the "PURSES" box. She had decided that I needed a purse.

"I don't like that one," I said as she slipped my wallet and phone into an orange clutch. "It doesn't match."

"We're all here," she said, holding up another option, and I nodded. "And this is what you wanted. I don't understand this. Do you want a pill?"

"Why would I want a pill?"

"A headache pill," she said, handing me the glass of water that had been sitting on the counter, growing warm. "You're *sure* your head doesn't hurt?"

I looked up at her.

"Just take a pill, for God's sake. Janna, you are too hard on yourself." She handed me a generic Tylenol from a tiny wooden pillbox in her purse. She had gotten me one of the same variety last Christmas. I was sure it was packed away somewhere. Maybe I would start keeping headache pills in it. I took the pill and the water. "Now, are you okay?"

I nodded and stood up.

"Do you know how to get to Little Italy? That's where everyone wants to go."

I started to cry again.

"Janna Marie …"

"I know. I know. Just give me a second. I'll be fine."

"This is a big second."

I managed an actual laugh as I followed her out, the pill sticking in my throat as I locked the door. Outside, Pa grabbed my hand and squeezed, pushing my knuckles closer together than I thought they should be.

"Ya ready, Toots?"

I smiled a fake smile.

"Hey, sorry about that," I said collectively to my family, who had amassed at the corner of Thompson and Prince. "You know me; I can't choose an outfit in a hurry to save my life."

"I'm hungry," my dad said, wrapping his arm around my shoulders. I could feel his sweat.

"You're always hungry," I said, sidestepping out of his reach. I didn't want his sweat to touch me.

"The big city, huh?" he asked. "I think they call it the big *apple*."

"Yeah, Dad. I know."

His forehead was bathed in perspiration droplets, and his shirt was stained with the ink from a *USA Today* that he'd been carrying around for hours. Ink streaks stretched across his belly. It was too hot for him. It was too hot for everyone.

We met my dad's cousin, Diane, her husband, Jim, and their teenage son, Bryant, somewhere on Mott Street. They knew the city and where to go, so we followed them into Little Italy. We walked past countless men singing their restaurants' entrees. The street was loud and crowded, and it looked like Christmas in July with red, green, and gold tinsel strung above the streets, connecting the chaos one block to the next.

At a place Jim found with enough outside seating for all, the host crammed four rickety tables together. My father recited facts and stories he'd already told us. Gram Margaret fretted over me. Aunt Biz, Diane, my mother, and I pulled ourselves through the conversation one glass of chilled Pinot Grigio after another. Things got weepy.

"I can't believe you live in New York City now," said Annie on the walk back. "Like you're here."

"Yeah, a whole whopping five hours," I said. "We'll see."

I said my good-byes to everyone outside of a parking garage on Thompson Street. I didn't cry. I wanted to. I wanted to leave with my mother. I watched them all pull away and then walked to my apartment.

My mom had left a fan blowing, and the stacks of maps and papers that had been sitting on my counter were in all corners of the studio. I hung my keys on a hook that my dad had pounded into the drywall by the door. I took off my sweater, carelessly tossing it over the arm of the couch, hopped onto my bed, and opened *Where Is Joe Merchant* to my favorite chapter. I fell asleep around midnight listening to the footsteps and voices coming from the sidewalk outside my window.

The next day was sweltering. I stepped out of my apartment and found myself in thick of SoHo, where the streets buzzed with non-Americans, models, and presumably non-models who were still a breed of intimidatingly good-looking Americans that I could not face. Did any of these people sweat? I ran, almost as if sneaking, across the street to H&H Kim deli and bought pints of ice cream and boxes of pasta. And mangoes—because you could buy mangoes at any deli, at any time, if you lived in New York City.

Krystal and our friend, Jamie, came to christen my first weekend. Despite our big plans, we never got beyond a ten-block radius of my apartment. But we got drunk. We got drunk on wine in my apartment. Drunk on cheap beers bought by old men at Kenny's Castaways, where someone played a banjo and everyone threw their peanut shells on the floor. Drunk on rail drinks two doors down with a bartender who went to Columbia j-school, to whom I argued that NYU's liberal approach was better than Columbia's stuffy one. We wandered, drunk, to MacDougal Street, and got drunk on drink specials at Off the Wagon where we played beer pong with the city college boys who did not play by Wittenberg rules.

The heat persisted. I was wearing a white shin-length skirt splashed with giant blue flowers and a cobalt blue boat-neck tee that matched the flowers—all from the Gap. My cropped bob was pulled back with bobby pins, and I wore my aviators. Well-planned outfits give me confidence, but that day no one else had dressed up.

Bill Serin, the gruff newspaper professor who headed up the grad program, led us—the three dozen newly minted NYU j-school students—around the Village, telling writerly tales of the city. Sometime after McSorely's Old Ale House (the oldest bar in NYC where both blonde and brown pints were $4), I had grown tired of the cheerleader type yipping at me about her internship at Fairchild Publications.

"Hey there," I said, walking closer to a girl who wasn't talking to anyone. "I think Professor Serrin's giving us a break. You want to get some coffee with me?"

She said nothing, didn't even look my direction. She was wearing Sevens and thick leather flip-flops—Rainbows, like the pair I'd almost bought one year at the beach. Smooth auburn waves framed her face, but a pair of giant sunglasses hid it. I assumed she was pretty.

"Hi," I said with a bit more pep, or maybe too obnoxiously, because it was hard to imagine that she hadn't heard me, easier to imagine that she was ignoring me. "I'm getting some coffee. Do you want to get some with me?"

"Hi," she said, taking off the sunglasses and squinting at me. She looked a little like the girl from *Mean Girls*. "Hi!" she said again, less confused. "Yeah. Sure, I'd love to. Do you know where we can go?"

"Maybe there?" I pointed to a sign scaling the corner of building with its red-pink neon letters that read: *Coffee Shop*. "Coffee, I would think."

"Probably," she said.

The entire rest of the day, it was as though Lauren and I shared a conversation on speed. By the time we were two glasses into a bottle of red at the only place I knew to go to in Little Italy, we had agreed that we could survive this city if we had each other.

Lauren and I became friends fast, good friends, like sisters. We shopped, ate, studied, watched movies, and explored together. She was an LA native, fresh from four years at Tulane, close with her family, as non-attached to her own religion as I was, and she missed the beach and riding motorcycles through the canyons with her boyfriend, a guy named Dan who sent her meticulously thought-out care packages. She lived just two blocks away in NYU housing, where she shared a square with a girl who only spoke Taiwanese.

In time, we found our regular spot, the place where we were the people closing down the bar. It was a plush, New Orleans-themed nook called the

Bourgeois Pig on MacDougal Street. Growling jazz singers played on repeat while we emptied bottles of wine, sitting at our spots on opposite ends of a velvet couch. We dipped bread and fruit into vats of cheese and chocolate on the marble table in front of us. We talked about classes, the friends we were making, writing, parents, boyfriends, beaches, and brain injury.

I invited her home with me for Thanksgiving. Home to the country, to my high school friends, and our cheap bars with fried food. Home to meet my amazing mother and my father's amazing brain injury. We shopped to buy her a warm coat, and my mom paid for our flights. I had let my dad sell the Del Sol to a history teacher at a rival high school for $3,000. He still honks and waves every time he drives by. I missed my car, and his drive-bys made me jealous.

DURING MY SECOND SEMESTER AT NYU, I had a full course load, worked practically full-time at Banana Republic, and hunted hungrily for a magazine internship. Yet I never missed a late night out with my friends. Bars stayed open until four. Fueled by residual energy from college, I stayed up until sunrise, writing articles for professors who wrote articles for *The New York Times, Esquire,* and *New York* magazine. They wrote books, too. Whole books.

My thoughts were becoming more structured, and I felt a sense of obligation to the written word. I reread old books my father had once loved, seeing them from a new place. The summer before I left for New York, he gave me a copy of *The Electric Kool-Aid Acid Test.* The present had been one of those rare blips.

My mother thought I was "spreading myself too thin," and she thought I needed to "stop putting the social stuff first," to "stop being so much like your father." She was rarely wrong.

"Your father still has a brain injury," my mother said to me one afternoon as we caught up over the phone.

"Huh?"

"Apparently we have to keep proving that he has a brain injury. Workers' Comp is making this very difficult, and he really needs more treatment. I'm trying to figure out what to do."

Moving to New York (or maybe just going to grad school, or both) had cast me as an adult in my mother's eyes, as someone she could talk to, vent to. Now I was invited into the Workers' Comp and TBI treatment conversations. Now I was privy to what was really happening.

"But I thought you had a good attorney."

"He is, but this is just very complicated. They do not want to pay for his treatments. Dr. Zimmer had to write a letter of medical assessment proving that John still has a brain injury."

"That's nuts."

"Workers' Comp will not pay for his treatments, and I can't continue to. We don't have any money."

"How can—"

"How's school?"

Just when I thought she needed answers from me, she'd flip subjects. Maybe she just wanted to vent about my dad and not be judged. Maybe something in my tone told her I couldn't handle it yet. I wasn't very good at being this daughter. I didn't know how to help her.

"Umm … it's good. It's hard. It's hard to live here. But I love it. I'm never bored. There's so much energy, so many interesting people. I really, really love it." I couldn't tell her that it was killing me, that I was tired of this city kicking my ass, or that she was right about my schedule spreading me too thin.

"Have you met any interesting boys?"

"What? No."

"None?"

"Mom …"

"Did you think about going to therapy like I'd asked you to? It really won't hurt you, and NYU will pay for it—"

"I tried it. Last Friday."

"And?"

She was a younger woman, too close to my age, who wore a pencil skirt that fit her like a pencil skirt would fit an elephant's leg. She was chunky with thick legs and should have chosen a different skirt. She looked at me a lot and took notes. She pushed up at her bangs a lot, as if it was hot and she was trying to get them off her forehead. But the office was cold. We talked about brain injury. I didn't have a brain injury, but that was what she was most curious about—my dad's brain injury. I assume she took notes on frontal lobes, executive functioning, and throwing things.

"I'll tell you later. I have to go to work. I love you!"

"Okay. I love you. I'm going to ride."

The following Friday, I didn't go back to the woman with the bangs. Instead, Adam came to visit me from DC. We watched a blues band at Scotland Yard in Hoboken with a buddy of his from college. We drank beers until we were too hungry to think. Then we met Lauren and more of his friends in the city for dinner and drank more beers in crowded East Village bars. The next night, we rounded up my friends and holed up in the back room of Spring Lounge while the first snow fell. At 4:00 a.m., I made a snow angel on the sidewalk outside the bar, and the intimidatingly good-looking humans looked at me with perplexed faces.

Two weeks later, exactly a week before Christmas Eve, I flew to California with Lauren to stay for a few days at her parents' house. It was decked out in Hanukkah silvers and blues. We had brunch at Paradise Cove, where we ate pancakes and eggs with our toes in the sand. We laid out in the back yard, and hung out with her older brother. And the day after Dan's Christmas party, he and his friend took us on a motorcycle ride so I could see the Pacific Ocean. We ate breakfast at Neptune's Net and wound up, down, and around the canyons, just like every scene in every movie.

"Hey, Jan!" Dan yelled, pointing west. "Loooooooook!"

I stumbled off the motorcycle, trying to take off my helmet, yanking at the red globe fastened to my head. I wanted to break my neck if it meant getting it off.

"You okay?" Lauren asked. "Just relax for a minute."

She unhooked my chinstrap. My face was white. My eyes were watering. She took my wrist and led me over to a pile of rocks by the side of the road.

"What's going on?" yelled Dan's friend.

Lauren held my hair with one hand and my helmet with the other while I emptied my insides all over the rocks. *Pancakes. Hilarious.*

"Do you feel better?"

"Yeah, I will," I said, tearing open the zips and snaps to free my torso from the riding gear. "Leave it to me to see the Pacific for the first time and puke my guts out."

I'd never seen an ocean from so far away before. The Pacific was endless. I could smell its salt air for miles. I looked north up the coast and thought of the times my parents had driven up the PCH to San Francisco, the times before me. I would tell them both about it tomorrow, when I saw them at home on Christmas Eve. I'd tell them the first thing I did was puke, too. They would think that was funny.

I HAD JUST GIVEN AN abominable speech in front of at least three hundred wedding guests, many who knew me. I clutched the half-empty bottle of champagne and weaved through the audience to the bar at the back, where I found an empty stool. I set the bottle down and put my forehead on the counter. Just thirty seconds, and then I would move on.

"Hey there, Janna."

"Wow," I said, unable to pull any other words out. "*Um,* I mean, hi," I said, my thoughts staggering all over the place. "Hi, Ryan."

I felt foolish for my head-on-the bar dramatics. He looked so different, like an older, crisper version of himself, and I felt self-conscious about the buoyancy of my boobs, which had been squeezed into Sarah's idea of a bridesmaid dress—tight, taffeta, tea-length. All the yoga in the world, and I still looked like a shapely burlesque hooker.

"You gave a nice speech," he said, pulling over a stool to sit down beside me.

"Oh, come on, Ryan. It was inaudible."

"It was good, Janna, very heartfelt."

"Oh, please. The mic was off, and everyone had to hear every word twice."

"The audio is not your fault. Do you want a drink?"

"That's what I came to the bar for."

"Hey, I wasn't sure. It looked like you came to take a nap."

I laughed. It was deserved. "I don't take naps, Ryan."

"Do you take shots?"

"A shot? What is this, college?" I smiled, ordered two shots of tequila, and asked for limes and salt.

"Okay then, Janna Marie."

"Dude, my best friend just got married. I gave a speech that was all kinds of crap, and I'm wearing this stupid dress—"

"—You look very nice—"

"—And, now, well … you. I haven't seen *you* in years! This calls for shots."

We held up our stubby bar glasses. We licked the soft skin between the index finger and thumb, the place where the salt is supposed to stick, and then downed them. The tequila lit up my empty stomach like gasoline. I bit the lime, hoping to cool off.

We caught up. He had finished grad school. I had almost finished grad school. We took another shot, which felt *nice* on round two. He worked with numbers—I, words. One more. I asked him about his girlfriend, pretty and blonde, looking angry as she sat at his table without him. He asked about the men in my life and my dad. We got beers for ourselves, I ordered a Chardonnay for my mother and a gin and tonic for my father, and we headed over to my parents' table.

While my mother asked Ryan about school, my father finished a cupcake in two bites. I watched him with a disgust that caused me to chug most of my beer.

"See this," my dad said, having unbuttoned and rolled his shirtsleeve up as far as it would go. "It's my new tattoo."

"That's nice, Mr. Leyde," Ryan said as I shot a look of embarrassment to my mother, who was shaking her head.

"You can call me John."

"That's nice, John."

"Do you know what it is?"

"It looks like a mushroom and palm tree."

"It is. Do you know what it stands for?"

"I don't."

"Jimmy Buffett and Jimmy Hendrix."

"Niiiice," he said, drawing out the word the way you do when you want to express the absolute awesomeness of something. Ryan had thought it was both funny and clever. My mother hated it. I hated it.

"Dad, we have to go," I said, finishing my beer. We walked back to the bar for one more shot before joining a good chunk of the class of 2000 on the dance floor.

"He's just being nice," Ryan said. "You are so hard on him."

Hours later, just as the sun was coming up, I pulled in the driveway, tired and sober. Before taking a shower, I called Sarah and left a voicemail about having "boatdrinks" on the beach, because she got to go where it was warm.

"Good morning," my dad said, coming into the kitchen still in his pajamas, wearing a tattered, camel-colored monogrammed robe over them like a cape. "How was your night last night?"

"It was good," I said, wishing I'd gotten at least an hour of sleep.

"What did you do?"

"Just went out after they left for the airport."

"Who left?"

"Sarah and Ken."

"It was a nice wedding," he said, walking behind me to rub my shoulders.

"Yes, it was."

"She looked pretty."

"She did."

"Who was that boy that came to our table?"

"Ryan, Dad. It was Ryan."

"From the lake?"

"Yes, from the lake."

"He's a nice fellow. You have nice friends. I'd like to meet some more of your friends from New York. Like your neighbor, Laura?"

"Laur-*en*."

"Yes, Lauren. I like her."

"I know, Dad."

"John, you need take the dog out," my mom said as she emerged from the basement.

"She'll be okay," he said.

"John, she needs to go out," She filled a travel mug with coffee, one of the ugly ones, a plastic one from Sheetz. "It won't hurt you to go for a walk with her." My mother was always trying to get him moving.

My dad seemed like he was always groggy. He slept a lot, falling asleep in his chair covered in pages of newspaper, in front of the TV while it blared. He watched stupid shows, like *Real TV,* where people sent in videos of stupid shit. They made my dad laugh his stupid, inauthentic laugh. I blamed the medication for his lethargy, or maybe it was the pot. He had more doctors than I could remember the names of, all of whom referred him to other doctors with more names to not remember.

Workers' Comp paid for nothing, so my mother fought them. She filed petition after petition that she knew they would deny. She scheduled and rescheduled hearings that she knew they would cancel. She got my dad as many treatments as were feasible under the circumstances either by billing his private insurance or paying in cash.

"Really, Dad. It won't hurt you to take Morgan out."

I filled a coffee cup, handed him Morgan's leash, and ambled out to the barn, where I found my mother opening and shutting grain bins with the speed of a tornado. Watching made me dizzy.

"I think I'm gonna write a book," I said, shoving a metal scoop deep into the cat food. I liked the sound of scooping. I liked the feel of the grain, too—smooth and cool. I picked up a handful and watched it pour through my fist.

"Why?" she asked, lining up tins filled with everyone's breakfast.

"I think I might be a good writer."

"I see. Well, what would it be about?"

"Dad."

"Your father?"

"Yeah, you know … tell the story."

"Good luck with that." She laughed, and handed me a tin. "Here, give this to Thunder."

It was a slow summer Friday in Manhattan. Everyone in the office had bolted for the Hamptons or pools in Jersey, and my boss had left me to my own devices in the beauty closet of *Marie Claire*.

"Happy birthday, babe!" she had said, handing me a medium-sized shopping bag before she left. "Just fill it up! Whatever you want!"

Didi was slender and pretty. I loved every second of working for her. It was as if she sparkled. We had met one night when I was closing the shoe section of Banana Republic. She came in with a gift card burning a hole in the pocket of her trench. We spent the next hour talking espadrilles, wrap dresses, patterns, schools, and writing.

"So would you be interested in an internship?" she asked as we waited for her Banana Republic credit card application to process. "Can you do that at NYU?"

"Yes, of course we can—and yes, absolutely!"

"Well, I work in beauty at *Marie Claire*," she said, sliding her business card, popping with pink font, toward me. "I absolutely love you, so call my editorial assistant tomorrow."

Five days and zero formal interviews later, I started.

Deep in the beauty closet, I filled the bag—Nars, Mac, YSL, Dior, Shiseido, and Chanel, compacts, pallets, tubes, and brushes like toys. Descending the Hearst escalator, I felt satisfied by the heaviness of the bag filled with birthday makeup. Wasn't I living every girl's dream? I was turning twenty-four, and my life felt steady. I was finishing my master's and working at a fashion magazine. I was growing cultured. I had great girlfriends at NYU. "A regular United Colors of Benetton ad," Adam had called us.

Enough post-class happy hours, and the seven of us had become real friends.

I met Lauren first on the walking tour. Then I met Katie, tall and blonde, a Michigan grad from a small town outside Detroit, at an uneventful j-school mixer. We regaled each other with familiar, comfortable college memories of Jack Daniel's, Midwestern boys, and sorority life. Katie lived in Stuyvesant Town in the East Village, near Samina, who might be one of the most beautiful people I know. Samina, Indian, but born in Canada, had recently moved to New York to pursue journalism once she'd realized her law degree would make her money but nothing else. Samina had class with Alejandra, who I remembered but didn't talk to at orientation, because she had been talking to Katie, and both girls had seemed too pretty and smart to approach in my state of ice cream hangover. Alejandra, who grew up in a country town on the outskirts of Boston, was born to Spanish and Peruvian parents into a family of seven, and reminded me of Amber. And Alejandra and Lauren had both made friends with Cristina, Puerto Rican, with dark, shiny hair, and from Miami—Southern Florida, that part of the world I pictured myself in. Cristina and Katie had been hanging out with Courtney, tall with a pixie cut, and from Morgantown, which made her as Pittsburgh as I was. Courtney and I would end up writing partners in Professor Norman's novel-writing class second semester, spending many nights in her Upper West Side apartment discussing our words surrounded by Hunter S. Thompson's widow's house plants, which she had strangely come to own.

I CALLED MY MOM FROM the street in a fit of histrionics.

"You need to slow down, because I can't hear you!"

"Mom! It's not me. It's the traffic."

"Well, you need to slow down and stop crying. I can't understand. *What is wrong?*"

"He gave me C, Mom!"

"I thought you said he gave you a B-minus."

"Whatever. That's basically a C."

"Why are you so upset?"

"Because I don't get C's."

"Janna, it's okay. You go to a hard school."

I crouched down against the coarse brick wall of NYU's Bobst Library and cried.

"Janna, you have to get a grip here," she said, as though she could see me. "This is not like you. You are doing exactly what you wanted to do. You moved to New York, and you work at *Marie Claire,* for God's sake!"

"Internship." I slithered back up the wall and wiped my nose on my hand. I had come to consciousness with my dramatics. I never carried cash or Kleenexes. I looked at my hand, glistening. *Disgusting.*

"What?"

"It's an *internship,* Mom," I felt the second surge of tears. "Besides, he told me he was being generous."

"You need to can it. Now stop. Can you go talk to him? I thought you really liked this professor."

"Yeah, I guess so."

"What do you mean you guess so?"

"I'm not cut out for this." I fell into another inarticulate fit of sobbing a block from the subway. "See, all I do is cry. This stupid city just makes me cry all the time. I don't know what I'm doing. Half the time, I can't even take the right train. And I can't even get good grades."

"Janna, I don't understand this behavior." Her voice had the firm tone I dreaded. "I really think you need to talk to someone. I think that would help you. You get so intense and hard on yourself."

"All they do is talk about brain injury."

"Not everyone! So you go talk to someone else. How's the weight?"

"Mom."

"Have you lost any? I'm telling you, if you lose ten pounds, you will feel so much better."

"I know, I just—"

"Janna, I think you are beautiful. But imagine how much better you will feel without ten pounds. Are you doing the yoga?"

"Yes, when I can."

"Okay, go to talk to that professor. I'm sure he's just pushing you. Sometimes you need pushed."

"I know."

"And do the yoga. I want a report—on the yoga, on the professor."

"I know."

"I love you."

"I love you, too."

"You should call your dad. See what he thinks."

"Tomorrow."

I got on the crowed E train to Hell's Kitchen, where Lauren and I crammed our lives and all of Gram Mary's miniature antiques into a teensy two-bedroom apartment with a beautiful kitchen just west of Times Square. We slept on Jenny Lind beds and shared a makeshift closet built into the corner of my room.

We had fun living together. She had broken up with Dan, and we were two single girls living in Manhattan, trying to make our magazine internships into magazine jobs in a world where magazines were either dying or changing, depending on which professor was talking. Lately we had a habit of eating our dinner sitting on the kitchen floor. We would stay there, talking for hours as though it was impossible to run out of words to share. Some nights we finished a bottle of wine, and some nights we never opened one.

I walked in, hung my coat on the rack, and went straight to the bathroom. I closed the door and yelled for Lauren to please make us eggs. I splashed warm water on my face, melting away a cracked layer of dried tears. Lauren has an exquisite way of scrambling eggs.

"White or red?" I asked as I came out of the bathroom and stared at the wine rack filled with bottles Adam had given us.

"What's wrong?"

I showed her six leaves of paper stapled together, some paragraphs slashed through with red pencil.

"Oh, boy," she said.

"Yeah, how about red?"

"Sure," she said, pulling the fry pan from a narrow cupboard.

THE NEXT DAY, I DIDN'T call my dad. Instead, three days later, my mom called me. "Do you have a minute to talk?" she asked.

I had been walking around my apartment, sorting through summer clothes. "Yeah," I said, setting a pile of yoga clothes on the top of the dresser. "What's up?"

"It's about your dad." She was using that tone. I hated that tone. I was scared of it. It was the precursor to finding out something I wished I didn't have to find out.

I sat down. I could feel it coming—insides expanding, every organ inflating with fear and uncertainty—that unnerving sensation that had become so familiar over the years, the one that followed all the other phone calls when she used that tone. Calls that had told me that my father had gotten arrested for possessing marijuana, for a DUI, for stealing; that he had sliced open his hand on a band saw, a tractor blade, a circular saw; that he'd stolen something from the store, from the neighbor's mailbox, from her purse; that he'd said something to offend the wrong person, their friends, my mother; that he'd broken something, a rule, a bone, a promise.

"Are you there?"

It really was no big deal that my insides were going to start to ooze out of my throat. I would be fine. I was always fine. I wondered if it was healthy to have such metaphorical reactions to reality. When had my imagery become so violent? "Yeah, yeah. I'm just listening. I'm here."

"Okay."

"So what happened?"

"Well, first of all, his psychologist died a few weeks ago—"

"Dr. Zimmer?"

"He had a heart attack."

"Oh ..."

"Anyway, that's not even it. Your dad is in quite a bit of trouble."

"Oh."

"I had to go to Harrisburg for a board meeting on Monday, so I left him alone for one night. I gave him a list of things I needed him to do. I thought that would keep him busy and out of trouble. And that night, he was supposed to go to Methodist Men with Pa."

Methodist Men was a social group for men held by my grandparents' church. Everyone agreed that it would be "good for John to go with Jack, good for the both of them." To me, Methodist Men seemed like a poor man's Kiwanis Club, though to this day, I still have no idea what Kiwanis is and why my father was a member. When I was a kid, I liked to think it was secretive and special. I knew nothing of Methodist Men. I simply saw it as the lesser version of something—the same variety of lesser as the Beach Boys were to Buffett, as *Real TV* was to Gallagher smashing watermelons, as Coke was to Rolling Rock—just post-accident lesser.

My father did not go to Methodist Men that night. He went to a party.

Both of my parents told me the story of what ensued. First I listened to my father's version, which he told like an eight-year-old boy would tell a story about getting in trouble.

"I drove to Sharon early before meeting Dad," my father explained. "I had some things to do. I got an estimate on the sweeper. It's not suctioning right. I bought weather strip for the doors. And then I went to Sharon News Agency, because I wanted to look for a book for you, for Christmas." He told me what happened, one clunky detail after the other. He met Ned at Sharon News Agency.

"Who's Ned?" I asked, knowing that most times he thought if he knew something, we all knew it.

"I used to play racquetball with Ned before work."

One of those buddies, I thought to myself. *Pot-smoking Ned* needed my father to give him a ride home. *Great.* On the way home, they ran into a buddy of Ned's who wanted to borrow the truck for a few hours.

"Why on earth would you let someone borrow the truck?"

"He said he'd fill up the truck and bring me back a case of beer."

"And where were you supposed to go?"

"Ned said I could go stay with him at his place. He was having a party."

"Ah, Jesus, Dad. A party? Really."

It was one of those hypocritical moments of becoming an adult. Why would your parents want to go to parties? What do they do at parties? I know mother does not like—in fact, hates—parties. And given how much

I am like the person my father once was, who was I to judge him for going to a party?

"But those people never came back to get me," he said. "I asked everyone at the party where they went, but they didn't know."

"No one helped you," I said, my voice cracking.

"I wanted to find the truck, and no one would help me. I waited for three hours. No one came back, so I left his place to see if anyone around knew."

"You left? How? You had no car."

"I walked to a Sheetz."

"Then what?"

"Someone told me that my truck had been towed to Lowery's, because it had been in an accident."

"Lowery's?"

"Lowery's," he said, annoyed, which was my cue that I was running out of clarifications. "The auto shop in Farrell."

From there, he walked to the police station, where he thought he could get help. But he doesn't remember much after he talked to two cops in the parking lot and gave them his plate number. They would not help him. It was obvious that he'd become fatigued. There would be no more explaining, so I asked him to give the phone to my mother.

"Apparently the people who took the truck had gone to go buy drugs and were involved in a hit and run," she said.

"What? Good Lord."

"And they figured this out because the license plate number your dad had given them matched a hit and run from earlier that night. They told him the truck was impounded, and they couldn't help him, but he didn't understand them."

"Wait. I don't understand. *Dad* didn't get in the accident ..."

"No, but—"

"—And they impounded the truck? Why?"

"Yes."

"Well, did they at least try to help him? Did anyone get hurt?"

"Janna. You are not letting me finish ..."

"Sorry."

"No, I guess it was a parked car, so no one was hurt."

I listened to the whole story without saying a word. My mother's voice was heavy with disappointment and exhaustion. She told me all the facts that she knew—a mélange of the police report and my father's account. It was 10:30 by the time my father walked up to the police station, approaching the building from the back, having come from the nearest yard. He wandered around the parking lot, looking for an entrance.

"Restricted Area: Authorized Personnel Only" is a sign on a door that prompts most people to stop and think before pushing at the metal bar. People with failed executive functioning just see a door and push.

In the front parking lot were two police officers loading equipment into cruisers. They have names, but the truth is, I dislike them so much it's best if I don't use the real ones. For the sake of story, I call them Officer Turner and Officer Hooch.

Turner and Hooch had been loading some stuff into their cruiser in the front parking lot when they noticed a man lingering by the side door. They watched for a while until he left.

My dad couldn't get in, so he walked around to find another way. At the front of the building, he found two officers by their cars. He walked right up to them and interrupted their conversation to tell them that he'd been in the area and flagged down by a man requesting a ride—a lie. He told them that the man requested he follow his friend to a location where he lent his truck to some men who promised they'd return it with a full tank of gas—a half-lie. He told them that he had waited at the apartment, and the men never returned with his truck—a truth.

Officer Hooch, who had been listening to him, cautioned him about the "risk of injury or robbery" when you lend your vehicle out to people. This warning neither interested nor made sense to my father. He wanted them to help him find his truck. He couldn't understand why they wouldn't stop what they were doing to help him. They were not doing their job. He demanded they do their job and help him find his truck.

Hooch and Turner couldn't see his brain injury. No one can. No one knows how extremely agitated—sometimes to the point of confusion—he becomes when he doesn't get his way. The brain injury snaps him into a state of aggression.

"Why can't you help me find my truck?" he asked. He stepped forward toward Hooch.

Hooch asked him to step back. He stepped forward and leaned close into Hooch's face, telling him that he didn't have to step back, that they had to help him find his truck. An inch closer, another demand—"You have to help me find my truck!" Hooch braced himself, and my father raised his hand.

I'd been in Hooch's shoes so many times before. I wish he would have known how harmless that gesture was. It's what my father does when he's really angry, but there is never a follow through. I wish Hooch could have seen the brain injury.

Hooch shoved at my dad's chest. It was barely a push, but enough to knock a brain-injured man off his two feet—the one with the brace and the one without. He fell backward onto the pavement. When my father falls, he's like a turtle that can't flip over and hop up. It's uncomfortable to watch.

Now Hooch and Turner were standing over him, ready to pin down the man lying on his back in the parking lot of the Sharon Police Station. I couldn't imagine someone trying to hold down my father—that kind of stuff doesn't make sense to kids, not even the grown-up ones.

My dad picked up his legs and tried to kick at Turner and Hooch, who were attempting to cuff him. From the ground, he grabbed Hooch's leg, holding on the same way a little kid would, until Hooch fell over and had to break his fall, which caused him to suffer "immediate pain and discomfort to his right hand."

Hooch got up, and the two of them held my father down by his neck, smashing his face into the asphalt, while his hands flailed wildly at his sides. Still not able to get handcuffs on him, Turner and Hooch called for back-up, repeatedly telling him that "he needed to remain still, because he was under arrest."

It was the first time my father had ever been handcuffed. Apparently he is pretty hard to handcuff. Apparently it takes four Sharon Police officers to cuff a brain-injured man.

Once handcuffed, my dad refused to cooperate. He would not walk to the building and would not do anything that was asked of him. He was innocent, and when he'd gone to get help, they arrested him. He had just wanted to find his truck. He wouldn't get up and walk, so Officer Turner and Officer Hooch locked their arms around his elbows and dragged him into the station. They sat him down and forced him to answer questions so they could fill out their forms. He began to cooperate. Other officers witnessed that the man that Turner and Hooch had arrested was struggling to keep his balance.

My father told everyone inside that he had a brain injury. As they processed his arrest—CPIN (taking his photo) and Live Scan (fingerprints)—he tried to explain to anyone that would listen that he had "a brain injury, a severe injury to the frontal lobe." No one was interested.

He was charged on four counts:

- *Simple Assault*—knowingly and recklessly causing bodily injury to an officer; attempting to kick (twice) at the legs and in the groin, grabbing the officer by the leg and causing him to fall, which resulted in injury to the officer's right hand.
- *Aggravated Assault*—all the above, specifically to a "police officer on duty."
- *Resisting Arrest*—trying to resist arrest, to keep a public servant from doing his lawful duty, which put said officer at the substantial risk of bodily injury and caused for substantial force (back-up) to overcome the resistance.
- *Disorderly Conduct*—intent to cause public inconvenience, annoyance or alarm; recklessly creating a risk; engaging in fighting or threatening behavior.

THE CONSEQUENCES OF LENDING HIS truck and losing his balance were momentous. My father spent the night in jail. My mother came home to find his bail set at $5,000, which would ultimately cost her $500. But with our Explorer Sport impounded, the total came to $3,500, and court dates were set.

THE FOLLOWING WEEK, DR. PUET recommended a TBI rehabilitation facility called ReMed. *ReMed.* I Googled it.

It was the best of the best—around since 1984. The facility took the long-term effects of TBI seriously with ongoing rehabilitation plans designed for both the clinical and home environment. And ReMed believed that having a TBI not only affected the life of the survivor, but also greatly affected the family of the survivor.

It was 2006—ten years later—and ReMed was the first opportunity for my father to receive a treatment plan specifically tailored to traumatic brain injury survivors.

In early 2006, MSNBC ran a two-night, two-hour segment called *TBIs: Signature Wound of the Iraq War.* It was my generation's Agent Orange. If you didn't screen soldiers, you'd miss it.

2006, and NPR's *Morning Edition* had become peppered with news of soldiers and their TBIs: nearly 1,000 had been treated for brain injury, a statistic that only alluded to the number of untreated brain injuries. I got up, made my coffee, got ready for work—NPR on, ears perked to reporting on brain injury rehabilitation, neurobehavioral science, cognitive disabilities, lobes, hemispheres, and head injuries. I was a regular TBI news junkie. It had cracked my top issues of concern, right up there with global warming and any threat to the environment.

It was 2006, and I wanted to be involved.

"Brain injury rehabilitation isn't just what we do," I read off the home page of ReMed's website. ReMed treated all kinds—mild, moderate, and severe on short-term, long-term, or episodic bases. "It's all we do. And we do it to support every journey, even the longest journey."

The interface was cheesy, scripted blue letters floating on white backgrounds. Pictures of trees and open skies, old and young people smiling in wheelchairs or gripping metal bars in a gym. But the fonts and photos weren't important.

"Our passion is to change lives." Finally, a group of people who stopped using the world *recover* No one really recovered, but no one admitted that. Perhaps ReMed would. Perhaps they had a solution to not being able to recover. Perhaps my dad would get a chance.

NEAR THE END OF 2006, my father was put on probation for three misdemeanors—Resisting Arrest, Disorderly Conduct, and Simple Assault.

My mother wrote a long letter to the attorney that Brenda McBride had suggested, asking for more extensive treatment and a psychiatrist, which was even more crucial now that Dr. Zimmer had died. In the interim, my dad's long-time physician, Dr. Sartori, agreed to prescribe psych meds and referred him Dr. Santiago, a psychiatrist he knew. However, Dr. Santiago would not accept Workers' Comp insurance (too hard to work with) so my mother paid more out of pocket. Dr. Sartori and Dr. Santiago agreed with Dr. Puet and wrote letters to the new attorney, recommending ReMed.

Everyone wrote their version of my dad's need for ReMed, which would fulfill his need for evaluation and treatment of his significant frontal lobe brain injury: intensive short- and long-term neurobehavioral rehabilitation, treatment in conjunction with group therapy, vocational assessment and rehabilitation, and individual attention to his psychological needs. And all the letters came with the same string of meds for his diagnosed conditions, which included but were not limited to: high blood pressure, scoliosis and back pain, heart aneurysm and aortic repair, hearing loss, closed head injury, cognitive impairment, and of course, the all-inclusive compilation of deficits that come with simply having "frontal lobe syndrome."

Things quickly became complicated. Dr. Puet moved away. Workers' Comp requested a utilization review (to prove that my father still had a brain injury); refused to reimburse any prior appointments with Dr. Crush, Dr. Heltzel, and anything involving Psych Care; and discontinued coverage for any future health costs. Anything my father got was poached from his Social Security or came straight out of my parents' bank accounts.

In December, we got our degrees. I didn't go to graduation, and I didn't go to the cap and gown photo session, as my mother had requested. I finished my last assignments, sent them to their respective professors, and went out with the girls. The seven of us celebrated by dancing at dingy Uncle Ming's in the East Village and eating tacos at 3:00 a.m.

I came home for Christmas with a master's degree—a good gift for my parents, for me. My mother found a frame for my oversized diploma, and my father hung it on the wall in my bedroom, covering a swarm of butterflies, just to the right of my degree from Wittenberg.

"Ya done good," my dad said, looking at my wall.

Blip.

"Yup," I said, smiling at him. "Thanks, Dad."

could i just get it on paper

THE BOTTOM DRESSER DRAWER IN MY bedroom at home is filled with an assortment of journals—a pink journal with a gold butterfly lock and gilt-edged pages, something spiral-bound that looks like it was from a Lisa Frank collection but wasn't, one covered in clouds and cherubs, journals with cats, astrological sun signs, trees, and ocean waves, and one made from leather and bound with a string. And in New York, under my desk, more are accumulating—a *Thank You* journal, two "treeless" notebooks, another meant to inspire the principles of the *The Secret,* a travel journal, and a Jimmy Buffett one themed around latitudes and attitudes.

No one has ever asked me to write in these journals or to put my scrambled, worried, harried, compulsive, frightened, heartbroken thoughts on paper. In fact, it's hard for me to fill them, because I picture other people's journals to be neater and nicer than mine: journals filled with clean sentences crafted from smooth pen strokes. My ugly journals take effort. My hand cramps. My sloppy cursive and erratic, scribbled sentence fragments often feel like last-ditch efforts to cope with or analyze the episodes of my life.

In the new year, my father's psychiatrist suggested he start keeping a journal. Nearly a requirement, his journal was a way for his doctors to suss out his thoughts and feelings on arrests and lying, rehab evaluations, his wife, daughter, and the people in his life, the mental and physical shape he was so out of, and his new treatments, new doctors, and new to-do lists.

> Today is the 6th of February 2007. I did something wrong today. I took the truck without permission. I got into Claudia's purse and took her key. I left her with one that didn't fit the truck. I didn't like being stuck at the farm all the time. So I had the truck and went for a ride … I didn't go anywhere, but I did waste some gas for nothing. I took it after Claudia left for work and was back before she got home. But she knew I had gone somewhere.

We had a long discussion about how I wouldn't go anywhere off the property until I have her trust. I'm not sure I'll ever have it. Time will tell. I also sealed the basement walls and painted the shelves. I may finish the walls and shelves tomorrow.

I must remind my self every day to be trustworthy loyal helpful friendly courteous kind obedient cheerful thrifty brave clean and reverent. If I can do these things Claudia may come to enjoy my company.

Like my father, I had every intention to start my 2007 journal for the new year on January 1, but life got in the way until February. I made excuses: nothing to say, no good pens, too tired. Finally, I chose from my collection— one that my high school friend Grant's wife gave me. Grant and I met up for drinks often, and his wife Sarah worked at *Glamour*. The year 2007 would be recorded on oversized pages edged in gold with *GLAMOUR* stamped onto the salmon-pink leather cover.

Saturday, Feb 4, 07 2pm-ish,

Maybe I am doing it wrong.

I talked to Krystal for an hour today, snuggled under my Amish bedspread avoiding the frigid west side wind blowing in through my open window. Manhattan pre-war apartments are saunas in winter and the cold wind felt less suffocating.

Krystal and I talk quite often. We have a close friendship that transcends the distance we put between us after college. It works, because there is no pressure, no lines to cross or uncross, just us. Life is never simple, so I think we try to be. And we just always know what to say. Today we had one of our serious talks, one that lingered around the beer-soaked college memories and the unforgiving ambiguity of our futures. "I was thinking the other day—you know when you were talking about the cookies you were making," she said in her chipper I'm-getting-things-done-while-I-talk-to-you voice. "I was thinking that you and I should've opened a restaurant. We'd be great together. We could've had a healthy, chic natural food place together."

"We still can," I said, in half yawn, yet completely serious.

By the end the conversation I'd dragged my Mac I-book under the covers to email her song lyrics that I thought represented the feelings of my life. Some were about exes, others about my dad—Buffett, Ryan Adams, Rolling Stones, Indigo Girls, and Band of Horses… Not only did she understand me, but Krystal understood the men in my life. After we hung up, I stretched out and hung my head over the end of my bed. The cold city air slapped my face. I lay there thinking about the absurd amount of pot I'd smoked in Brooklyn the night before at Katie's.

Yesterday had started out as one of the dreadful days in the city. New York's a great city, but being jobless with a severe lack of vitamin D in the middle of February tends to bring it down to dreadful.

Lauren and I woke up around 11am and then spent the entire day in our apartment glued to our laptops. By the time 4pm had rolled around we were in hideous moods and left our apartment in complete silence. Ninth Avenue was an uninviting throng of Friday traffic, and we had to dart between buses, tourists and angry commuters to get to the other side. It was a grueling walk from Times Square to Herald Square. People moved like sludge and no matter which way I held the bag of cookies and wine, passersby knocked into it. By the time we got to Sephora to meet Courtney, Lauren and I were yelling about everything. It was a dumb idea to meet there, surrounded by beauty products. I stood there, in my aged puma sneakers, jeans, a blue polo sweater, carrying around my calf-length chocolate brown down coat, an outfit that only seemed to accentuate the weight I had gained.

I stared at a NARS blusher/ bronzer duo. I was swimming in rejection. "I know I may not have liked Cosmo," I said to Courtney as we waited for Lauren to find us. "But Jesus, what do they want? I worked so hard on that stupid beauty edit test thing. I actually felt like I had a chance."

"I know, sweetie," Courtney responded.

We were all fresh from NYU with masters degrees and no jobs. I was no different, and really deserved no sympathy.

The Q to Brooklyn was miserably crowed, so much so that the four of us, now that Cristina had met up, had to stand centered around a pole. All I kept thinking about was that we'd soon be high. Days earlier I'd wanted to hug Lauren because she'd given in to two things for me—adopting a sea turtle and agreeing to smoke pot, for the first time, at Katie's, on Friday.

When we got there, we ordered in, watched a You-Tube video of our NYU professor being his intelligent sexy self on the Stephen Colbert Report, and lit a bowl. I smiled at the burning, choking sensation of my first hit. It had been so long since I'd been high that it zipped my brain back to the hot tub with Sarah and before that to all the times with Alex. I hacked, the smoke feeling like razor blades on my insides. I remembered my dad's probation and everything going on at home and how nothing was right anymore. Nothing had been right since I was fourteen. I was trying to make it right, but life was falling apart. While my friends puffed and gossiped about celebrities and debated words and told hook up stories and pondered employment, I stayed silent. I couldn't open my mouth for over an hour.

Now I'm crying.

I've never cried upside down before. Tears were running into my hairline as my nose plugged up. It feels like water up your nose. I almost choked.

Enough of this.

If my mother had a journal, I certainly didn't know about it. It's not like her. She likes the present moment, not pages dripping with nostalgia of things remembered. Though I imagine if she had one, it would be frighteningly consistent and exquisitely legible. And there would be pictures of horses or zebras.

My father bought his journal—his purple one-subject Mead Five Star notebook—at Walmart. His entries, which ran from roughly February to April of 2007, were nothing comparable to my dramas of life in New York: musing on my new job working for a website that was part of *National Geographic*, complaints about the dry well of available men in the city, thoughts on my friends and their relationships, worry about my non-relationships, hate toward my weight, and synopses of our drunken adventures.

No one read my journal. Everyone read his, and it read like the diary of an uninterested eleven-year-old boy. He showered, ate cereal, and took his medication, not knowing what exactly for. He refilled bird feeders, watered the horses, and walked and brushed the dog. He painted things: stairs, walls, chairs, floors. He cut grass—a lot of grass. He laid bricks and shoveled the walk. Sometimes he went to the gym or ran errands with Pa. He ate hot dogs a lot and slices of cheese—a lot.

Had he not been a man with a brain injury, I would have found his journal mind-numbing, but the simple sentences about his days scrawled in his lefty all-caps were endearing and heartbreaking.

Upon rereading them—in order to weed out the literal record of his routine—I was introduced to his slivers of thought, thoughtful sentences buried in the mundane. These sentences were evidence that he was trying to discern black from white, wrong from right, where he was trying to pull shreds of reasoning away from the tedious complexity of his injured brain.

> Today is Saturday, the 17th of February: Claudia and I went to see Rod Stewart at Mellon Arena today. I didn't tell my probation officer I am going to Pittsburgh. I guess that is okay.

> Today is Sunday, the 18th of February: I asked her [Claudia] about getting the keys for the truck back. She said I badgered her about those keys. The cost of the replacement is about $200. I think the justice will have the person responsible for their loss replace them.

> Today is Tuesday, the 20th of February: Claudia tells me I should volunteer at one point. She was going to find someone to drive me on Meals on Wheels. That hasn't happened yet.

> Today is Monday, the 26th of February: Not a good day … Claudia says by the end of the day I smell. So I must take a shower before and change before she gets home from work. I don't want to smell … Teresa [a therapist] wants me to write about what I think. I think the different person I am is not different. I must work on understanding this.

> Today Tuesday, the 13th of March: When you write Janna Leyde in the Google Search engine it tells of her work at NYU. How Nice.

> Today is Wednesday, the 28th of March: I think Claudia is upset with me all of the time.

There are a lot of pages and sentences devoted to *pot* and *driving*, perhaps my father's two compulsions, his two unrequited loves. He wrote about how he wanted to *drive* by himself. How he would *drive* anywhere just to not be bored. How he would *drive* to go buy a newspaper or visit a friend. How he'd break the rules and *drive* around Sharon, looking for *pot*. How *pot* made him feel—good, happier, better. How he stashed the money that he'd been given to buy his father lunch so that he could buy more *pot*. How he'd always be over in Sharon, *driving* around, looking for *pot*. How he is supposed to think about life without *pot* but didn't know how. How he can smoke *pot* and not get caught. How he has always been good at that.

His last entry is about my parents' trip to see me that Easter. I have one about that trip, too.

Tuesday, April 10, 07 Sometime after 9pm

My parents came to the city. They stayed for one night and the next morning we (I) drove out to Long Island, all along the deserted beaches of the Hamptons. Adam's right. The Acura is a car that "drives." We took back roads to get as close to the abandoned houses as was possible, and Mom explained all the different styles of houses. She even asked Dad to chime in because some recorded facts, like architecture, are apparently still intact. She and I discussed what life would be like if we'd lived on Long Island year round. Like North Carolina, but colder. The weather was beautifully dismal.

At one point we parked the car, got out and walked on the beach, the bitter cold Atlantic in April, empty and serene. When we couldn't drive any farther (in Montauk, where I hear they have great surfing) we stopped and had crab cakes looking out over the ocean, smooth and flat, like gunmetal. That day felt as close to the three of us before the accident than I've ever felt. It was one of his good days. The next day we had Easter dinner at a small Italian restaurant with Diane and Jim and Bryant in Ardsley, family I need to spend more time with because I live so close. The next day Dad slept too much, ate too much, and said too much of the wrong stuff.

I think I've fallen in love with winter on the beach. I could live where a few months out of the year you wear chunky sweaters and ocean air bites your face.

I have to stop writing to do my taxes. What a drag. I hope TurboTax is legit.

His journal entry was much less about Long Island than it was about the broken CD player. He wrote three sentences about the trip and seventeen about taking the Acura to Flower's Radio, and then to the Honda dealership, and then calling in a part, and then calling Flower's, and then …

IN JUNE, I GOT A new job—a sales assistant at a small, luxury lifestyle magazine group that was owned and run by Harold, a gruff, old Jewish man who had launched dozens of trade publications in the '70s and '80s while palling around with Warhol. Of all the applicants, I had the most personality.

The first day, I settled myself at my desk in and attempted to make sense of a thousand documents filled with foreign magazine jargon. I had been paging through last summer's copies of *Hamptons Cottages & Gardens* for mental breaks when I heard yelling—no, screaming. I walked over to the water cooler to be closer to the screaming. The door was open, and I saw Harold leaning over his desk, spilling stacks of paper, fuming red, so angry that he was spitting as he yelled at a tall man with wiry black curls, our group publisher.

"*Well, fuck you!*" Harold screamed.

I stood there staring, holding an empty paper cone. The tall man said nothing.

"Get out of my office. *Get out!* You're a waste! A fucking *waste!*"

The man left, nodded his head when he saw me, and walked out. He was the only connection I had there—a weak one, from a magazine where I'd interned for two months two years ago. It had since folded. I never saw the tall man again, and his office was barren when I came back the next morning.

"Good morning," said the sweet blonde woman who had hired me. "I'm so happy you came back. It's really not like that here, I promise. You just have to get used to him."

"Morning," I said. "Don't even worry about it. I can handle yelling. Apparently he was very angry. It happens, right?"

Caitlin wore bright lipstick and looked like she plucked her outfits straight from the window of Anthropologie. Her Williamsburg apartment was no different. She was older and my boss, but we hung out a lot outside of work. Dinners at her place with her friends, Brooklyn bars, and steamy nights at Bembe where we'd dance to island beats and cool down with mojitos. Caitlin had been with the magazine company since its inception— Harold's first hire. She showed me how exactly to get on his good side, handle his temper, and decode the torn leafs of yellow legal pad that he'd casually throw on my desk so that I could come up with a marketing piece.

Those yellow pieces of paper were the hardest challenge I'd had in a long time. Real deadlines.

When I got my first paycheck, I went down to my old SoHo neighborhood to buy myself a birthday dress, something edgy, something out of the realm of J. Crew and Banana, something to show off the yoga.

I was going to be twenty-five that year. It was a huge birthday, and birthday celebrations in New York had to be thrown with the utmost finesse. There seemed to be a formula: look fabulous; choose a restaurant to invite a carefully chosen number of good friends (not fewer than five or more than twelve) to that is not too cheap or too fancy; expand the invite to the rest of your friends and everyone's friends and their significant others to the well-chosen drinking and dancing establishment—not too much club, too much rock, or too much house and conveniently located near late-night food (tacos, pizza, falafel).

It was easy for this all to spin out of control by becoming too complicated, stressful, or expensive. Thankfully, Ale's boyfriend, Ryan, who had just moved in with her from California, had a birthday three days before mine, so we decided to combine celebrations—the Twenty-Fifth Birthday Extravaganza. We invited our closest friends and some of Samina's friends visiting from out of town to dinner. And then afterward, everyone else we could think of to a bar chosen by Samina, which guaranteed good ambiance and good dancing. Samina was a master at choosing venues, booking dinners, talking us to the front of a line, and getting through doors without paying a cover.

I found my dress in a boutique on Spring Street. It was royal blue with the chalky sheen that comes from being made from 100 percent silk. Draped on the hanger, it looked more like a man's short-sleeved beach shirt than a dress.

"$387, with tax," said the petite woman behind the counter. She was dressed in all black, and the blue hue of her pixie cut matched my dress. "Happy birthday!"

The blue dress was easily the most expensive thing I'd ever bought myself. There was no way to rationalize the purchase. It was more than my friend's mortgage, more than any prom or formal dress, more than I'd admit to my mother. But I'd never been so in love with a dress before. I felt like Lauren Hutton and wore it with a gold chain belt and espadrilles. I felt fabulous from dinner to tacos.

A few days later, I told my mom it was the best birthday ever. I shared every detail (with the exception of the cost of my dress) with her. And I told her that my life in New York was perfect. She gave the phone to my dad so I could give him the abbreviated version of fish entrees, belts, friends, shoes, songs, and drinks—and the perfection.

I DIDN'T COME HOME AGAIN until Thanksgiving. It had been almost a year, the longest I'd ever been away from home. I was looking forward to wintry weather, seeing my parents and family, my friends from high school, my dog, and riding my horse. Flights were expensive, so I arrived in Mercer by way of DC. I took a bus down to spend an evening with Adam and Ryan and see one of our favorite bands, and I rode home with Ryan the next morning.

The first night I was home, I cooked chicken stir-fry for my parents. My father didn't eat the broccoli, and he'd asked me the same questions he'd asked me every week since I had moved to New York: "How's the big city? How's Lauren? How do you like your job?" Then he announced that he was leaving the table to go watch TV.

"Dad, can you clean up for us?" I asked.

"I don't want to clean up," my dad answered.

"Well—" I continued.

"Janna, let it go," said my mom.

My father put his plate in the sink and walked into the living room.

"Someday I'm gonna just take him out," my mom said.

I laughed. My mom made a gun motion with her fingers, aimed at nothing, pulled a trigger, and laughed at herself.

"I miss Marble," I said, taking the conversation to a new angle on death. She had been put down my last semester in grad school. I never said good-bye. My mother called me the morning it happened, and I told a bunch of people in my class, people who clearly didn't feel the same way about cats as I did. I cried on the train home, trusting that my mom knew she had been too sick and old to be happy in her cat life.

I hopped off my stool and walked over to the microwave. I reached my hand behind and pulled out a bottle of Little Penguin Shiraz. "You want some?"

"Sure, I have some chocolate from work. It's buried in the freezer. You might have to dig. I have to hide it from your father. He'll eat the whole damn thing."

I secured the chocolate and poured us two glasses while she rinsed our dishes and put them in the dishwasher. That night, we sat at the kitchen table and talked for hours. My mother divulged, revealing things to me about my father for the first time: how their marriage worked, his addiction, his arrests, the petitions she'd filed and the hearings she'd attended to help get him treatment. How it wasn't working and how we were now losing money because Workers' Comp would not cover anything.

That night, we finished all the chocolate and a bottle and a half of Shiraz while she told me absolutely everything that was happening to him and to her. Her fear showed vulnerability that both excited and unsettled me. I asked endless questions, doing my damnedest not to interrupt her. It was no different than when I was a kid hell-bent on mastering a subject through the knowledge of my parents—the galaxy, metamorphosis, bulimia, photosynthesis, animal phyla. This was just "TBI 201: Effects of Traumatic Brain Injury on the Family."

For years—away at college, across the world, in the city, or at home in my backyard on the rusting chaise lounge—it had been easier to pretend things were okay, that nothing was actually happening to the degree that it was, that is was my job to be away and living it up. I couldn't do it anymore. I wanted to be knee-deep in it with my mother, helping her in a way that I hadn't had the chance to. *I* wanted to find solutions to improving his poor quality of life. *I* wanted to fight Workers' Comp. *I* wanted to write a letter. *I* wanted to be the daughter who called from New York City to bitch, eloquently and constructively, about her father's care. But she wouldn't let me. I suppose helping me help them would have been too much for her. But it would be my support—something an adult can give her parents.

He was wearing her out, wearing their marriage to shreds. Not even sixty years old, and my dad looked seventy and acted fourteen. He had become a hard man to like, and it was growing harder for my mother to remember how much she loved him. Most of the outside world—his pot-smoking buddies, the general public, insurance companies—had no idea that this man would not make it one week on his own. To the two of us, it was glaringly obvious. He had no means to provide a life for himself, a brain that wouldn't adhere to reason, let alone a budget, and no friends who understood who he was.

He had Wayne, who called from Fort Lauderdale to check up on him every few months and always on holidays and birthdays. Wayne was one of his only friends left. He acknowledged that he had a brain injury, yet continued to be my dad's buddy, same as ever, just as if they were still in their early forties. He wanted to provide my father with some semblance of how things used to be, so they'd meet up with old buddies in Sharon or down in Florida and get beers or smoke weed and comment on things like tits, women, wives, daughters, the cars and bikes they used to drive, and the golden retrievers some of them still had. Wayne never wanted to treat my dad like he had a brain injury, which sometimes got the two of them in trouble. The brain injury was hard to accept.

"But, Mom, what can I do?" I asked, swirling the last puddle of wine in my glass. "There has to be something."

"Nothing, Janna," she said, smiling and shaking her head. "I'm not asking you to do anything. This is not your responsibility. He is *my* husband."

"Mom! He's my *dad*—"

"Janna. *We* are *your* parents. The only thing I, we, want you to do is enjoy your life in New York. Get a good job. Have a good time. Find a nice man. You are very smart and pretty and very capable."

"Well, I can write this book," I said, swigging the rest of the wine down.

"If you say so. I don't know anything about writing books."

"You read more books than anyone I know—more than some of my friends, and that's a lot."

"I would not want to do that. Not at all. I live this *book*."

"Then I guess it's my job."

We could hear my father snoring—long, loud, thunderous snores from the living room.

"Go to bed," I said. "I'll rinse these out."

My mother never got sleep because of his snoring. It didn't matter which special pillow she bought for him, Breathe Right nasal strip he wore, or medication he took. I would hear her in the middle of the night, sleepy and frustrated, telling him to roll over—first a whisper, then a yell. Anytime I heard him snore—in backseats, on my aunt's couch, in the living room chair, in bed, in hotels—my whole body tensed up. The sound was infuriating, a reminder of how unhappy my mother was and how unaware of it he was.

"I love you," I said as she left the kitchen.

"I love you, too," she said, coming back in to give me a long hug.

Six hours later, my dad came upstairs. It was 6:45 a.m. "I came to wake you," he whispered. "Your mom told me to tell you she's out in the barn."

I got up and plodded to the bathroom. With a toothbrush hanging out of my mouth, I rifled through my top drawer to find my old barn jeans. They buttoned—barely—for the first time in years. I pulled on a sports bra and a Jimmy Buffett T-shirt, put the toothbrush away, and went down to the basement, where I could layer up and choose a pair of my mom's riding boots, which were always a half size too small, so they pinched a little. I heard my dad making coffee in the kitchen.

"Good morning," he said. "Would you like some toast?"

"Um … sure," I said, not even close to awake.

"Would you like some peanut butter?"

"Yeah."

"Okay, I'll make it for you."

"Thanks."

The early morning hours seemed to be his best, his most alert, when he was most kind. They were my worst. I was a mute. I filled two travel cups with hot black coffee, and with one in each hand, I bit the toast off my plate, held it in my mouth, and walked out to the barn. There was no snow, but the dew was frozen and crunchy. I hoped it would snow later—my first truly conscious thought.

The barn was quiet and cold. We listened to NPR, and I listened to my mother give me tacking instructions: use a blanket, Thunder uses *this* bridle now, hold Ex (Exceptor, her newest Arabian) for me. The ride was a rejuvenating experience as we walked the field and woke up with nature. With each step, the horses' hooves broke frozen blades of grass like porcelain. It was a short ride. I had grocery shopping to do, and my mother had to clean before people arrived tomorrow, which made no sense, because everything was always clean.

"Are you sure you don't need me to help?" I asked her that evening. "I don't have to go."

"It's fine; go out with your friends," she said.

"But it's just Adam's."

"It's fine. Really, you made two pies and did the grocery shopping. That was plenty."

"Okay, all right. I don't know when I'll be home, though."

"You'll be home by 9:30," my dad said, walking into the kitchen.

"Yeah, right, Dad."

He laughed, and I looked at my mother.

"I'll be home in time to help you put the horses out in the morning."

I kissed them good-bye and headed out to meet Sarah and Amelia for dinner. At Benjamin's, there were chicken wings and beer, and it was a good place to see what everyone else was doing the night before Thanksgiving. People from our class and the classes right below us and above us started to fill the tables and booths around the bar. We talked about Sarah's marriage, a boy Amelia was dating, and the older guy from work that I had a mega crush on. He was in a band. Richard came over to our table to say hello with his petite fiancée. I'd met her the summer before at a Buffett concert. She barely knew me yet was tipsy enough to tell me the entire story of their engagement, a narrative of country music and red rose petals.

"Are the boys coming?" Sarah asked, biting into one of my onion rings.

"Why do you care?" asked Amelia.

"Because she does," I said. "Just because they're not your friends doesn't mean they're not ours, Misses Melia."

"That's what my autistic kids call me, fancy-pants New Yorker. So how's your dad, being home and whatnot?

"Oh boy. I'll tell you later," I said. "You know, I love that Yuenglings are only $2. God, I miss this place sometimes."

"Move back," said Sarah, laughing.

I couldn't move back. I couldn't tell them about my dad. I couldn't even tell them how scared I was. My phone beeped, and I flipped it open.

"Adam will be here in a few minutes," I said.

"What about Ryan?" Sarah asked.

"So ... Amelia, are you coming to Adam's with us later, or what?" I asked.

"We'll see," Amelia said, giving us her *severely-annoyed-with-this-conversation* look.

Later, everyone was at Adam's. Eventually, around 3:00 in the morning, Sarah and Amelia left. I had quit drinking hours ago, and it still hadn't snowed. In two hours, the sun would be cracking the horizon, so I said my good-byes to everyone gathered around the Bertis' kitchen table.

"Hey, can I get a ride?" Ryan asked, getting up.

"You want a ride now?" I responded.

"You'll be home to feed the horses. It's not even six."

I'd taken my mom's Acura. She always let me drive it wherever when I was home. The night before, I'd parked in the yard on crunchy frozen ground, but this morning, it wasn't as cold. We buckled up, and I shifted into reverse, tapped the gas, and the wheels started spinning. "Shit! I think I'm stuck."

"You're not stuck," Ryan said, dealing with his own concern and cranking up the heat.

"It's too hot for Thanksgiving weather. I hate this. There should be snow!"

"It's global warming, Janna."

"Shut up! That's terrible. It's fucked up that the seasons are messing up. And now I'm spinning out in Adam's yard, getting my mother's car dirty."

Pressing harder on the gas, hearing flecks of mud hit the sides of the car, I thought about the mess I'd leave in the yard and the muddy car I'd ask my father to clean as I pulled forward and drove through the nice part of Adam's yard, leaving tracks.

"Janna!"

"Shut it."

Driving the back road back into town, I thought about how I shouldn't have left the tracks in the yard. Now I'd potentially pissed off two moms with teenage behavior at twenty-five. *Great.* The windows fogged up, and I slammed at the defrost button. I was sweating, groggy, and angry that I'd stayed up this late again at Adam's. Ryan put his hand on my thigh. I looked at him. I wondered if my face showed surprise or disgust.

"You know what I was thinking about last night?" he asked, taking his hand back.

"Last night, like at Adam's or Ben's or what?"

"Well ..."

"Ryan, what? I don't know what you're talking about."

"It's been awhile since we've ..."

"We've ...?"

"Since we've ..."

"Since we've kissed, Ryan? Oh, so I should just pull over, and we'll make out on the side of the road at 6:00 a.m.?" My acerbic sarcasm never fazed him. I liked that about him. That, and that we could argue tirelessly.

"Actually, it's 6:30."

"Ryan, it's 6:00 in the morning! Are you nuts?"

He said nothing, just looked at the windshield. I pressed harder on the gas, cut a familiar hard right, before passing Trent Reznor's family's industrial plant known for space heaters, and headed down a country road. I swerved to the right and pulled the car off the road onto a patch of gravel.

"What are you doing?"

"Richard and I used to make out here." I put the car in Park.

"Janna ..."

"Well you—" He grabbed my face. His hands were warm, probably from holding them in front of the heater. I unbuckled my seat belt. He tasted a little like cigarettes. I pulled away and got out of the car with the intention of walking down the path toward the natural gas well. I wanted to cry. I leaned against the front bumper. I wanted to go back in time, to summers on the lake. He got out of the car and stood next to me.

"Janna ..."

"I think you're still drunk," I said.

"No. I'm not. Are you?"

"No! I'm driving. Jesus. But this is—"

He kissed me again. This time I felt dizzy, a good dizzy, and I dropped the car keys I'd been clenching in my right hand. I forgot about time, and it started to rain. He pulled the chunky wool turtleneck sweater I'd been wearing up over my head and threw it on the hood. It started to pour, the rain soaking through my pale yellow tank and his white T-shirt like wet rags. I could feel yesterday's makeup sliding off my face in the rain. I was shaking, my skin rough with goose bumps, but the rain felt tropical and warm.

"We can't do this," I said, pulling him over me, throwing my arms around his neck and kissing him hard through my words. I stopped.

He kissed me on the forehead, which I had determined to be one of my favorite things from guys that I liked. It made me wonder if I *liked* him. He wrapped his wet arms around me, and I put my head on his shoulder and shivered. The tips of my ears had started to burn. Maybe it was wrong. I didn't know, but I felt safe and happy all at once until the raindrops started to sting.

"Ryan?"

"Janna?"

I looked up at him. "Ryan, it's snowing!"

The air started to speck with snowflakes that melted when they hit the ground.

"Wow," he said, handing me my sweater from the hood. "You must be freezing."

I pulled it over my wet skin. The inside was dry and warm.

"This is so crazy," I said, running around to the passenger side to get his sweater and throw it at him. "I freakin' love nature!"

The sky was now teeming with swollen snowflakes.

"You can hear it," he said, walking over to me. "Listen. When it hits the ground."

"It's like the first couple minutes when snow falls in the city. It's so quiet, you can hear snow fall."

We made out until my hair turned crunchy, until we, like the trees, the car, the gas well, and the ground were covered in a layer of white powder, until we couldn't feel our hands or faces. I had to fish the keys out of three inches of snow, and when we got in the car, it was well past 7:00. He turned the heater on high, and we drove in silence with his hand on my thigh until we got to his driveway.

"That was …"

"Pretty incredible," he said.

I wondered, hoped we were talking about the same thing. Yet I didn't even know what I was talking about.

"You can stay for Thanksgiving if you want," he offered.

"Ryan, you're nuts."

"I'm not nuts, Janna."

"You are, and thanks, but you know I can't."

"I know. You could come in and say hi."

"It's 7:00! And I have to be home to—"

"—the horses."

"The horses, yes, and my grandparents and, uh, well … Happy Thanksgiving."

"Happy Thanksgiving, Janna."

"Tell your parents hello and Happy Thanksgiving."

"Same to yours. See you later."

And then we kissed good-bye in his driveway the way two people too familiar do, quick and direct. I drove home, distracting my feelings by devising a plan to wash my face, change my clothes and get out to the barn in the least amount of time possible.

"JOHN!" MY MOM YELLED AT him. "Come on now. Stop it. How many times do I have to tell you?"

He quickly stashed away the hard candy he'd been pawing. My mother was angry, and half the contents of the jar on my grandparents' counter were now in my father's jacket pocket, sticky bits of yellow, green, red, and pink clinging to the lint and lining. With nothing more than a stoic wave good-bye to my grandparents, aunt, and cousins, my mother grabbed her coat and purse and headed to the car. She looked at my dad in disgust. He stood there, his free hand holding two slices of ham, cut thick as slices of bread, the other hand in his pocket, protecting his candies.

"John! Let's go!"

He shuffled to the door, engulfing the ham slices in three bites as he went. I followed him, and Pa grabbed me on the way out. His old hands were rough and his fingers swollen. He cupped my hand and squeezed so hard, my rings pinched.

"See ya, Toots," he whispered, pulling me close to kiss my cheek. "Happy Easter."

It was chilly, but I'd thrown my coat in the backseat. I didn't want to feel the constrictions of the cinched belt and the narrow shoulders of my cranberry trench while driving home. I adjusted the seat settings and mirrors in my mom's car without saying a word. My dad collapsed into the passenger seat, released the seat back with little concern for my mother, who sat directly behind him, and promptly went to work fishing out his linty, sticky candies. I wanted to puke from tension.

"*Janna!*" my mother screamed from the back. "You are going through a red light!"

"Jesus, Mom! It's—" I started to reply, inching the car into a left turn.

"It's a stoplight," my dad said as I eased into the middle of the empty intersection. "It's blinking red."

"It's fine, like I'm going to go through a red light," I said. "I can drive, Mom."

Silence—again. I desperately craved the selection of alternative music on the car's XM radio. All I could hear was my dad sucking and crunching on those bits of damn disgusting candies. It was dark, and the country road's street signs were shiny and blurry. I knew I should have been wearing my glasses, but I also knew Route 62's curves and turns by heart, and at this point, I couldn't imagine troubling either of my parents to find them for me. My mother would have had to dig in my purse, which I had thrown somewhere in the back seat. I cranked up the seat heater and drove the rest of the way home squinting and repeating the refrain of a Jack White song in my head, nodding as if the drum beats were audible.

I took as many items as my hands could carry into the house and set them on the kitchen table. I raced upstairs to beat my mother to the bathroom, where I felt like I could breathe again. I had every intention of crawling into bed and forgetting about what I was feeling, but I got distracted reading old journals that I came across in the bottom drawer of my dresser. Twenty minutes later, my mother came in. She had put on her robe and washed the day off her face, and we started talking, holding a whole conversation standing on opposite sides of my bed.

"There is no way out," she said.

I had been pulling at the yarn fibers of my carpet with my big and second toes, some dramatic action that reminded me to breathe. It wasn't working, so I started pushing my knee into the iron frame of my bed. I pushed so hard into the iron that I had to switch legs and do it to the other side.

She stood leaning over my queen-size antique bed with her arms crossed, holding her Easter clothes in them. She sniffled and blinked, her eyes red behind her glasses. "Death. Death is the way out. Either I die, or he dies. That's it."

I couldn't push into the iron hard enough. I felt an immense heaviness like the weight of my entire life sitting on my shoulders under the force of all gravity. Too fucking heavy. My brain stopped. There was nothing I could think to do or say, nothing that had prepared me for this. What is there when one of your parents—in so many words—wishes death not on one or the other in particular, or even in any malicious sort of way—just death, on whomever it came easier?

"I know," I said, half expecting the words to come out in sobs. "I'm not arguing with you."

"Janna," she said, stopping me with her authoritative tone. "I am going to be sixty next year. I am absolutely exhausted. I don't know how I am going to do this much longer. He is taking everything out of me. I want to be done. I have nothing left."

I leaned up over my bed, finally alleviating the pain of the iron frame, to crawl my elbows closer to her, trying to think of something, anything, I could say.

"What the fuck am I supposed to do?" she asked, setting the clothes down on my bed and starting to cry.

I swallowed, feeling like I was pushing a golf ball back down my throat. My mother never said *fuck*. Well, very rarely did she say it. I'd only heard it a couple times: when she was unbearably angry or in the presence of her rather hip adult nieces from her first marriage. As a little girl, any swear word was petrifying. I still remember the first time I heard my mother say *fuck*.

We were eating dinner in Gram Mary's kitchen, just the three of us—my mother, her mother, and her kid—gnawing on ears of corn. We'd come in from riding, and my father had a work meeting. Corn on the cob was my absolute favorite meal. At some point, my mother and Gram Mary had started arguing about my Aunt Pamela. My mother stood up and hurled a shiny, buttery, half-eaten ear across the kitchen. "You always fucking do this!" she yelled.

Then she walked over and picked up the corn, rinsed a dishrag to clean the mess, and started crying. I don't even remember what it was about. I just remember my mother's hand covered in butter and salt and the greasy handprint she left on the red and white paisley tablecloth.

I use *fuck* like a sailor, like a casual verb or adjective. In fact, Jackie and I once determined that *fuck* was our favorite sounding word. Yet I will always balk at my mother saying *fuck*. Like how she was saying it now.

"I wish I knew," I said, sighing and still surprised at my lack of tears. "I wish I could help you."

"There is nothing you can do, and that's okay," she said, directing the conversation into what had recently become very familiar dialogue between mother and daughter—love, money, the accident, responsibility, life. And it always resulted in the same practical, civilized conclusion. My mother loved my father, and she believed in their marriage enough. And, yes, *enough* was the exact word to use here, not *so much* or *more than,* but *enough.* She knew that she had given up her own life, wants, and needs to do what she could to maintain some semblance of normalcy and to provide a safe life for him. It was that practical—*that* was how much she loved him. They were never going to get divorced. I was no longer afraid of that.

As a kid, divorce had been one of my worst fears. It was the kind of fear that leaves your mouth dry and your heart palpitating—divorce, bears, and one of my parents falling asleep at the wheel. It was the '90s, and I was an only child in what felt like a minority of kids whose parents were still together. I remember being at the lake house, hearing the muffled arguments, keeping around a corner, out of sight. My mother would grab her coat from the hallway and slam the door with such force that it sent the door chime falling. I'd hear her speed down the driveway and look for my father, who was inevitably in the kitchen, cracking open a Rolling Rock and pouring it smoothly into a frozen mason jar. He'd head downstairs, as if all was normal, and promise me that she'd come back. "Sometimes she just needs to cool off," he'd say. I would go in my room and cry, staring out the window until she came back. I don't know where she went, but she always came back. During the few fights they had before the accident, he never left, got upset, yelled, or even slammed a door. Once I found him crying into his palms, sitting on back porch steps. He stayed there for hours.

I didn't know what it would take for them to get divorced. I just worried about it the same way other kids like me did. Exasperated fits of worry—*everybody's-parents-are-splitting-now-mine-are-too.* Who would I live with? What would happen? Who would take the animals? I didn't know the strength of their marriage until college, until after the accident.

It was winter break, and I was crouched on the upstairs landing, just outside my room, listening to a conversation between my mother and father escalate. I lay flat and still like a spy. My dad had started yelling, the way he'd yell at me. I had never heard him yell at her so much.

"Fine!" he yelled, stomping with exaggerated stomps on the slate tile to the back door. "Maybe I shouldn't have worn that seat belt! Maybe I'll just leave and never come back!"

I army-crawled backward into my room, wishing I'd never heard that. It was too strange. The leaving lines were my mom's lines, fiery but harmless.

My dad never fought back, not with emotions and threats of leaving. He never fought her.

"John," she had said calmly.

"What?"

"Let me tell you something. I love you. I don't like you very much sometimes, but I do love you. I will never, ever, leave you, no matter what you do."

He had stopped stomping and yelling. I crawled back to the landing, put my cheek on the carpet, and looked down over them, seeing the tops of their heads as they stood in the entryway. He held the door partway open, and she stood a few feet back, hands at her sides in fists. "I will never leave you, John. But, if you walk out that door—ever—don't you ever, ever come back."

He closed the door.

"I am not going anywhere. This is not your fault and I love you, but *you* walk out that door, and it's over. It is over, and we're done."

They have a different kind of marriage. I've never heard of anything like it—or at least anything like it lasting more than the length of a movie. No part about it seems real. For the last twelve years, their marriage has been smothered with an infinite amount of unhappiness on her part and apathy on his. It is exhausting to watch. And there is nothing I can do.

I leaned into my bedspread, thinking about all fights I'd witnessed, thinking about how this was just another. I put my head down and closed my eyes. They were dry and burning. I took a moment to let the liquid of my eyelids soothe them. I could see why she was exhausted. I could understand. I couldn't argue.

"Now … why are you closing your eyes?" my mom asked. "Are you crying?"

"No, Mom," I said. "My eyes are just dry, that's all." And it was the truth. They were dry, and I didn't want to cry.

"Janna, I just can't do this anymore. I can't fucking do it. I'm sorry."

These are my parents, I thought to myself. *My mother and my father, the two people that I love the most. The two people who have cultivated a wonderful life for me, who are smart and kind and fun. Two good people who simply do not fucking deserve any of this. I cannot help them, and I feel broken.*

"Don't be sorry," I said, scooting closer to her. "I am not asking anything of you. In fact, I support whatever you decide to do. I don't know how you do it, do what you do. I will support you no matter what. I will, always. But, please Mom. You have to start to do things for yourself. You have to …"

"With what money?" she asked, leaning back from my bed. "We have no money. No one will pay for him. He needs treatment. It's impossible to change anything without money."

"But—"

"My father used to say, 'Don't listen to anyone that tells you money is not everything. It is.' He used to say, 'No matter what, you can buy things, pay people to do things.' He's right. You better find a man with money. You better think twice about you-know-who. Money makes things work."

She walked away and into the bathroom. I put my hands over my head and smashed my nose into my bedspread. It smelled like her. She was right. She was wrong. She was tired. I knew she was running out of ways to try to help my father, running out of energy to think. She was sick of the budgeting, sick of worrying about money. And now she was worried that I was too picky with men. I wondered if her frustration was reality or the consequence of quitting Lexapro cold turkey. It didn't matter. I just wanted to support her in whatever she did, however she felt.

I stripped my clothes off and left them in a pile on the floor. I pulled on pink fleece sweats and an old sorority T-shirt and climbed into bed. I loved my bed at home with its crisp, clean cotton sheets, always piled with billowy pillows, thick with blankets and puffy quilts—perfect that night to fight off the cool country spring air that seeped in through the old bricks. I nestled in with stuffed animals and a book that Lauren was reviewing for *DailyCandy* about the lives of Oberlin College kids trying to escape the bourgeois lives of their families by surviving in low-rent digs in Brooklyn in the '90s. Maybe it was all about money.

My mom came back in almost half an hour later. "Goodnight," she said, leaning in under my canopy to kiss my forehead, smelling like something almond-y. "You do know I love you very much."

a woman goin' crazy

I WAS TWENTY-FIVE, AND I HAD IT all. Life was one epic adventure after the other. My friends and I ate at Top Chef restaurants and any place that *New York* magazine told us to try. We discovered indie bands and boutique shops. Our nights were fueled by the libations from dive bars, beer bars, rooftop bars, or the latest mixologist haunt, and the nights bled into the early hours of dancing, cabs, pizza, and bagels from the bodega. It was the year I fell in love with brunch, eggs benedict, 4-inch heels, pencil skirts, good whiskey, craft beer, Thai food, and a new band called Delta Spirit.

I lived with Lauren, my newest best friend, and Lauren and I were always with the girls from grad school, our New York best friends. Krystal came to visit at least twice a year. I'd just spent a week in the Bahamas with Natalie. Adam, Ryan, and I hung out at least every other month. I never missed a major holiday at home, and I worked a lot.

The hours were long, but the small regional magazine boasting regional luxury lifestyle paid good money, and I had good work friends. We couldn't complain that our job required us to pack up, hop on the Jitney, and spend weekends in the Hamptons at Harold and his wife's sprawling house in Amagansett. The walls were mosaics of his contemporary art collection, enough capital invested in that art to fund a small country. We swam in his pool, walked his dog on the beach, cooked in his kitchen—all for the price of dressing up and schmoozing with advertisers at parties.

MY WHITE SHORTS WERE FAR too short, especially with the heels I was wearing. I was entirely aware of the inappropriateness of this outfit as I sat down at my desk almost an hour late. It was Friday. I turned on my computer and didn't take off my aviators for another four hours, not until Caitlin and I came back from lunch. It was my birthday. The inappropriateness was excusable. One more year older, and I felt like shit. Hangovers lingered, and

I had lost count of how many times I'd watched the sun come up on my way home.

I was twenty-six, and I was developing patterns.

"Meet me at the beer garden @ 6. Can't wait!!" I sent the group text to my friends around 2:00. It was the most productive thing I'd done all day. My head felt like someone was setting off firecrackers from the inside, and all I wanted to do was throw up. I sat at my desk for the next three hours, willing myself a second wind, almost regretting the night before—girls dinner, tequila, bull-riding, and hookah bar with late night *Bhangra*. A little after 6:00, my phone chimed one text after another. I didn't respond to any of them.

"Where have you been?" Courtney asked, nudging up to the bar beside me. "And *what* is *he* doing here?"

"It's my birthday," I said. "He wanted to celebrate. What is so wrong with that? I waited for him, okay?"

"Well, I'm surprised he showed up, that's all. Aren't you going to come over and say hi? We're all here, waiting for you. It's been two hours, Jan."

"Yeah, just gimme a sec."

"Happy birthday, Janna!" Jonny, Courtney's boyfriend, switched places with her at the bar. "How is twenty-six treating you?" He handed me dark beer that sloshed over as people bumped into us. Jonny was lean and wore vests, all hipster-cool with a voice that dripped with that perfect British cheer, a birthright from the other side of the pond. He was getting his doctorate in philosophy.

"Thanks, Jonny." I clanked my glass to his, wondering why in God's name he was being so nice to me. "I will be over soon. I will."

"Babe, what are you doing?" Samina asked, squeezing through people we didn't know to find me still at the bar half an hour later.

I wiped whiskey off my lips, the splash of a shot poorly taken. Samina had to catch a flight to Toronto, and I appreciated that she was being diplomatic in trying to coax me back over to the place I belonged—with my friends, not hanging around, trying to talk to some guy from work I had a crush on. She and I both knew he wasn't worth it, but I had glued myself to the bar—his general vicinity—convincing myself that he could be.

"Come and hang out with us. I have to leave for the airport, and we've barely seen you. We want to celebrate with you!"

"I know. It's just that everyone is mad at me, because he's here, and because I came really late with my work friends, but I don't want to deal with it. It's my birthday. I just want to be with people who are fun tonight."

"Honey, these are your friends. They want to see you. That's all. No one is mad at you."

"Min, come on. I know they are. They hate him."

She shook her head and grabbed my wrist. Back at our table, I sat on the end. I felt sorry for myself—late to my own party, and all my friends deep in conversations that started without me. I convinced Ale to come meet my work friends. To meet the guy I worked with, the one I liked so damn much.

Over the last few months, I'd drug almost all of the girls, one by one, out on random weeknights to see his band when they would play grimy East Village bars splashed in PBR and Christmas lights. I'd ask whomever I was with to stay a little later after the show, to meet him, to give me my chance to show my undying and misplaced support. He was ten years older and had a girlfriend, none of which mattered, because we had a strong intellectual connection. So strong that Lauren had to scrape me off the kitchen tiles when I'd come home drunk and in tears because of something he did or didn't do. My friends all hated him, hated all the unnecessary drama, hated that they couldn't get it through my head that there were better men out there.

"Jan!"

I held the phone—Lauren's voice—away from my ear. "Where are you? What are you doing? Do you know we're still here?" It was past midnight, and I'd just left a handful of my friends at the third karaoke bar of the night. My friends had been chasing me chasing him all over the Lower East Side. It wasn't my fault. It was my birthday. I hadn't asked anyone to come with me. Of all the days of the year, *today* was the one when I could do whatever the fuck I wanted.

"I left." Nerves and carsickness were mixing my insides. I held my breath to keep from throwing up. "Everyone is mad at me," I said, thinking about the consequence of hanging my head out the window to barf. "I don't want to be around those people. I just want to have fun. I didn't make anyone follow me around, okay?"

"I know you didn't ask everyone to follow you around—"

"—No, I did not. I didn't ask anyone."

"It's just ... kind of rude. I mean ... everyone is out for your birthday, and we just love you. No one really cares that he came, but you won't even talk to us. We're your friends."

"Laur ... I just—"

"—I just called because I was worried. I didn't know where you had gone."

"I'm fine, okay? I have to go. Stop worrying. Just stop fucking worrying about me!"

"Okay, Jan. Okay. Just ... be safe. Please."

I got home with the sun and slept through Saturday. Two of my friends didn't talk to me until Tuesday. Two didn't talk to me for weeks. Things were different after that night.

That fall, the magazine nearly went bankrupt. Our salaries were halved, and we moved offices from Manhattan to Connecticut to avoid folding. Those of us who were not laid off made the commute on the 7:50 train from Grand Central to Westport each morning. In the evenings, I rode home with him, a gesture that seemed to only solidify our connection. No one liked this—not my friends, not his girlfriend. In February, all but six people were laid off. I was one of them.

"I should be mad at you," my mother said. "I can't believe you. You have everything you want. You live in New York City. You work at a magazine, for Christ's sake. What more do you want?"

She was right—*Harper's* freakin' *Bazaar*. Why change the subject? Advertising assistant was a rung or two down the corporate ladder from where I had been, but now I worked at a fashion magazine. The associate publisher, who liked my eyes, or my personality, or maybe it was my education, had told the ad director that she should hire me.

"Sit," Martin had said when an assistant ushered me into this office for my third interview. "Just one sec."

I sat down. I tugged a frizzy curl behind my ear and smoothed the morning's raindrops into my black shirt-dress. I watched him shuffle through papers. I waited. The phone rang.

"Shit! Can you hang on a second, sweetie?"

"Take your time. I'm in no rush."

He picked up the phone and smiled at me. I smiled back. I was annoyed.

Just days ago, I had finished seven rounds of interviews with my dream magazine only to have the sales rep from *Esquire* nonchalantly dump me over a lukewarm Starbucks—because they wouldn't be filling the position after all.

"Ah, come on. What the fuck is this? No … no … are you serious?" He slammed the phone down, rifled through some folders and looked up at me, as though he was surprised to see me still there. "I'm sorry about that," he said.

"Well, good morning," I said. "I see you are having a lovely one."

He laughed. "So, tell me about this grad school stuff. What the hell are you doing here?"

I talked up sales and down journalism. A colleague walked in to hand him a paper. "Sorry," he said again. "Just a second."

"No problem at all."

They discussed the paper. "Look at her." Martin interrupted his colleague. "She has the most beautiful eyes."

The man with the paper smiled, waved, and walked out. I wondered whether I should feel uncomfortable or empowered.

"You do," he said again.

"Hey, it's whatever gets me this job." I threw him a shameless smile. "I mean, *thank you.*"

A few weeks later, I was stationed in a cubicle on the twenty-fourth floor of a glass tower, and the most enjoyable part of my job was putting together outfits for work. For the five minutes each morning that it took to turn on my boss's computer and set up her office, I would pretend her floor-to-ceiling views of Manhattan were my own. Renee was nice, but a little neurotic, and always wearing four-and-a-half-inch Pradas and the biggest diamond ring I'd ever seen in person. Life might as well have been a movie.

Renee called me "Almost Birthday Girl" until I turned twenty-seven on a rooftop in the East Village in a tomato-red strapless dress that was shaped like a tulip. It was a redo of twenty-five, a perfectly planned evening with my friends in an attempt to make up for twenty-six. Amelia flew in to celebrate, and the night started with tapas at Las Ramblas and ended at the Delancey, where we all danced in a huge circle to Michael Jackson in honor of his recent passing. It was hardly my choice in music, but I had promised myself that I would be nice to my friends *this* birthday.

Five months later, I was twenty-seven, and I felt like I had nothing going for me. How could I tell my mother that?

"Mom, it's just—well, you're right," I yelled into my phone as I power-walked through the Hell's Kitchen crowds.

"What?" she asked. "It's so loud. I can't hear you! Where are you?"

"Ninth Avenue! I'm on the same street I was before. In fact, I'm on 43rd, standing outside the nail salon where Lauren is. It can't possibly be louder!"

"What?"

She was getting frustrated. She hated when I called her walking down Ninth Avenue. She had to sort my words away from the traffic, horns, and people walking by.

"*You. Are. Right,*" I yelled into my phone. "I work at *Bazaar*. I should be happy."

"Yes. Now what is with this ridiculous behavior? It's time to stop. You really need to see this pattern you are developing. Do you not see what it is doing to you?"

"Yes, Mom." I had spent the fourteen-block walk home from Hearst listening to my mother tell me that I needed to stop liking the men I couldn't have. *Exhausting.* To stop making everything about dealing with my father. *I was?* To go to therapy. *No.* And, of course, to lose ten pounds. *Maybe fifteen. She hadn't seen me in while.*

"Are you just saying that to shut me up?"

"No, I'm not."

"And I really think you need to talk to someone. I do. Can't you do some research? You have good health insurance with Hearst."

"Mom, come on. That doesn't work."

"You've tried two people, Janna. You need to give it a chance. And it's been a few years."

"They'll just want to talk about brain injury. And then I'm just answering all these questions about the frontal lobe and explaining executive functioning. I don't need that. That doesn't help me. I *already* understand it."

"Then don't talk about your father."

"Mom."

"No one said you had to."

"But—"

"Stop! You are not letting me finish, Janna. You are wasting all this opportunity dwelling on this shit. You live in New York. That is exactly what you want to do, but you are blowing it. Is that what you want?"

"No, it's not. It's really not." I slumped down against the cement wall of the building of the nail salon. I wanted to sit on the sidewalk, but it was cold and wet. I squatted, feeling tingles shoot into my knees. I started to cry.

"Come on, what's wrong? I love you."

"Nothing, I just …"

"I want you to be happy, but you have to stop this nonsense over guys. Please, Janna. I know you are smarter than this. Where is this coming from? You must not want to be with someone right now if you keep liking the men you cannot have. You do that a lot. I don't understand where that comes from. You need to move on."

"It's Dad. Because it's so messed up. I miss him, you know what I mean?"

"Janna …"

"I don't know. I need to get my career going, before I focus on that, on men."

"Then do that, and stop dwelling, okay?"

"Okay. I need to go, Mom."

"What are you going to do?"

"I'm going to change."

"How?"

"I'm going to stop dwelling."

"Okay, you have to do it then."

"I gotta go. I'm late. I'm always late, and Lauren hates it. I love you."

"I love you, too."

I threw my Blackberry in my purse and tugged open the door to Ivy Nail Salon. I hoped that the hostess-like Chinese woman with pumps higher than she was tall wouldn't say anything to me as I walked by to find Lauren.

"Long time, no see, no?" she said, stopping me and looking at my hands.

I smiled at her.

"You want color? Like your friend? Long time."

I shook my head and smiled harder.

"What do you think?" Lauren asked, holding up her hand and waving at me from the row of chairs. "Fiesta pink. It's your Essie bottle. Nice for a bachelorette party in Vegas, right?"

"It's pretty perfect." I sat down while they finished the VIP treatment on her hands. We talked about our long weeks at work. We stopped at Gallo Nero on the way home and splurged on a cheese plate, dinner, and two rotund glasses of Multipulciano. Our friendship was perfect. She left early the next morning for Vegas.

I spent the entire day inside, jealous and sulking, and then the next day doing the same.

Dusk, finally. I was tired of the sunlight invading my mood. I curled up on my bed to think about what my mother had said on the phone. I sat up to open the window; the air inside had turned stale—or I had. I swallowed, my tongue dry and coated in the flavor of spicy basil noodle from hours earlier. I lay back down and ran my palms across the flannel sheet, letting my fingers drag and catch on the hard puffs of mattress quilting beneath. My mother had been right. She was always right.

I pulled the sheets over my shoulder and looked out my bedroom window, past the fire escape, and out over Midtown. The horns and sirens blared their constant, obnoxious running dialogue down on Ninth Avenue. I stared. I wanted to lie in bed until something shifted. I was stubborn, stuck with the lazy feeling of waiting for something great to smack me in the face, something as easy and enjoyable as my father's accident had been heartbreaking and painful. I'd lost sight of where I stopped working hard for things and where my sense of entitlement kicked in.

On August 2, 1996, I had *promised* myself that I would *never* feel entitled, *never* be the girl with the dad with the brain injury, *never* expect my life to be easy. I even wrote down the promise in one those damn journals. What the fuck happened?

I hated my job. I didn't hate the people or the magazine, and I did love my outfits, but I hated how utterly and completely unfulfilled I was counting advertising pages day in and day out. This hate oozed into the rest of my life, contaminating everything. I showed up late to meet my friends. I stayed out too late. I paid my bills late. I got up late every day for work. I never listened to NPR, never made my own coffee, rarely cleaned my room, rarely went to yoga, and the only things I wrote were snippets of marketing copy between counting ad pages.

I was breaking, feeling a loss lonelier than losing first one parent to an accident and then the other to the caretaking. I was crumbling, stuck in my own apartment, dwelling on how to carve out accomplishment from a mess of apathy and over-expectation.

I got up to brush my teeth, the first time all day. It was Sunday evening. I'd lost hours of my life, an entire weekend, to take-in Thai and HBO series. I took a long shower, hoping to wake up some motivation.

I crawled back into my unmade bed, sopping wet, and mentally ran down a list of things that I thought I could change. *Something, anything.* I had to make a shift, had to quit waiting.

This would have to start tomorrow.

Get up
Make coffee
Turn on NPR
Walk to work
Count pages
Do yoga

Yes, I would go to yoga tomorrow. Tonight, I would to cry myself to sleep, because above all else, above all other men, I really missed my father.

"IT'S THAT FEELING OF WHEN your elbow skims the water," Eddie said. Or maybe he didn't say it exactly that way. Eddie and I had been talking on the phone for at least two hours. In the last week, I'd started becoming familiar with the way Eddie talked, the way he used words, his intonations, the sleepiness of his voice after a long day.

Maybe he said something like, "I love it when …" Actually, he probably said love. He loved that word—*love*. He was the kind guy who was comfortable with using it. I was not comfortable using it, at least not with him. It was too much enthusiasm for someone I hadn't met in person. But now he was talking about slalom skiing, so he kinda had me.

We had started talking late on a Sunday night after one of the Sundays that I had chosen to stay in all day, get sleep, save money, and watch the

Steelers. During the night game, I was bored of my own company, bored enough to call Dan in California. Dan and Lauren had broken up long ago, but we all stayed friends, calling him on speaker to entertain him while we got ready, made dinner, or drank wine on the kitchen floor. Lauren liked that he and I were friends, and sometimes, when she wasn't around, he and I would share in our miseries of unavailable relationships and muse about our commonalities—Ohio and Lauren.

Dan texted after he didn't pick up my call. "Sorry, can't talk—driving back from a race."

"No worries."

"What are you up to?"

"Stop texting me. You're driving. Unsafe!"

"No Dan is driving. This is Dan's friend Eddie."

"Oh. Hi."

"Hi. What are you doing?"

"I'm watching football."

Two—maybe three—days of texts made their way from inquisitive to flirtatious, followed by a series of pictures on Facebook that Dan recaptioned specifically for me: "This is Eddie." "Janna, meet Eddie." "Janna stop staring at Eddie" (where Eddie was playing beer pong, shirtless, showing a tattoo that can only be described as an argyle sock on his bicep). Then we sent e-mails. Then came an actual phone call during which I discovered that talking to Eddie was easy and addicting. He made me smile a lot, the stupid kind of smiles that hurt your face.

He called me on Halloween, when I was Jennifer Beals and he was Connor, the cuter Boondock Saint. I was searching the Duane Reade across from Samina's apartment for a mixer to go with vodka when he told me that since he had the means to get on a plane, he should. He would.

Five days later, I could not stop my heart from pounding. Anxiety was eating me alive. Eddie hadn't mentioned his idea to visit New York since Sunday and I started to wonder how much of it was in my head. It had been a long week at work capped off by a Friday that had me in the office until well past 8:00. I almost missed the UPS slip stuck on our door.

Shipper:

Converse Inc.

North Andover, MA

I grabbed my purse and the slip, power-walked to 11th Avenue, and sat in a dingy waiting room—the kind that looked and smelled like you're waiting to get the tires rotated or the brakes fixed, not pick up a package. An hour slipped away with my giddiness. I wondered if they'd be black, but hoped they'd be navy. I tore into the box at the corner of 11th and 43rd.

Black Chucks, size eight. The color no longer mattered—I had never been this excited about a pair of shoes. They were exact replacements. The month before, I'd carelessly set mine outside the door of my apartment. There were caked in mud from All Points West, and I let them sit while I thought about how to salvage them without clogging a sink—for days. A neighbor threw them out.

"Eddie!" I squealed into my phone on the way home. "They're perfect! But how did you know what size?"

"You told me, silly."

"I did?"

"Five foot six, blue eyes, and size eight, remember?"

"Oh, yeah. Well, I just love—"

"—My plane lands at 5:03 next Friday," he said, casually interrupting my sentence. He had me giddy all over again. We could have talked for hours, but we both had plans.

I got off the phone and called my parents. I mass texted all of my friends—this charming, photogenic, decent man was flying all the way across the fucking United States just to see me. I changed my outfit so I could wear the Chucks with a skirt. I practically skipped to the dessert bar on Ninth Avenue, where I met my friend Dustin and gushed to a bunch of people I didn't know over champagne and chocolate. People smiled and nodded. It was the kind of story that dissipated peoples' skepticisms and reservations. It made people happy, made me happy. And they all said, "Eddie. That's such a great name."

I couldn't process a thought for a week.

"WHOA. WHAT'S THE WITH THE bat mitzvah outfit?" Martin yelled at me as I walked over to my desk. "You have a hot date tonight or what?"

T-minus nine hours.

"*Um,* yeah, you could say that," I said, trying not to indulge him as I went

257

through the routine of swapping black flats for black booties and turning my computer on.

"You've got to tell us what is going on," he said, coming over. "Look at you. You look so sexy. Fucking incredible."

I couldn't stop smiling. My cheeks hurt. I was wearing my red birthday dress with a black sweater that was cut out like a doily in the back. My hair was curly in an unruly, sultry kind of way, and my eyeliner was dark.

I ignored the continuing questions and went into the pantry to make a cup of instant black coffee. I found Cate, the other assistant, and filled her in on the four-day-long blind date. I sipped it, feeling it slosh around in my empty stomach. It was the color of motor oil and weak as water. As soon as I started my day, it flew by. By 3:30, the whole office was in puddle at my desk, counting down to his arrival.

"Hi," he said.

"Hi," I said, twisting the cord of my office phone around my fingers and spinning my chair around so that I could shoot Cate a crazed smile. We'd become close work friends.

"*Ohhh* area code 805… it's boyfriend," Renee said. "Look at her. You better be careful."

"Do I need call your father?" Martin asked. "I should talk to your father."

This stopped my breath. I swallowed. No one needed to call my father. He was not the kind of father who cared about this kind of stuff. In that second, I wished that he was. I wished that Martin could have a good old dad-to-dad chat, but I didn't have that kind of father.

"*Nah,* my dad's cool with this."

"Do not sleep with him," Renee said.

"Jesus! I gotta go!" I threw my shoes into my bag and backed out through the glass doors to the elevator bank. "I'll see you all on Monday." The doors closed on their voices.

He had landed. It was raining. I had already calculated the time to deplane, walk the length of the American Airlines terminal at JFK to the place where the cabs line up, wait for a cab, and cab it into the city in the rain on a Friday. If I ran-walked the fourteen blocks home, it would give me plenty of time to reassess the impression our apartment would make and to calm the fuck down.

I barged into my apartment and tossed my bag and coat in a heap at the door. I lit four candles and sat down on the couch. The drizzle had weighted down my hair—I could feel it. I went into the bathroom and sprinkled on Aveda Hair Potion. It was as if I was rubbing baking soda into my roots, but it made everything a little messier, a little bigger. I looked into the bathroom mirror. *Fine, good enough.* I was nervous. I had to pee.

"Dammit!" I said to no one. "We never have toilet paper!" I grabbed the keys off the hook, dug my phone out of my bag, and ran to the Duane Reade downstairs. I paced the aisles and called Sarah, holding a four-pack of eco-friendly toilet paper. "He's not even in Manhattan yet, and I'm freaking out."

"Jans, relax," Sarah said.

"Yeah, okay. Shit! He's calling me. I'll call you back, because I'll probably hang up on you accidentally. I can't figure out switching over—"

"Go!"

"Hi!" *Wow—too excited.* "Hey."

"Hey, I'm, *um*, on 10th Avenue turning onto 44th," he said.

"What? How? I thought you were in a cab?"

"I took this black SUV," he said. "It was a lot faster. I wanted to get here and see you, silly."

"I'm, *um*. Well, you'll see me in like two seconds. Look for the Gallo Nero sign. It's a red and black rooster. That's beside my apartment. And you can't miss me. I'm wearing red and black, and I'm holding toilet paper. I guess I match it, the sign, I mean. The rooster—"

"Toilet paper?"

Shit. "Yeah, we were out."

He laughed. I cringed. My heart was pounding, and my hands fumbled, trying to find change to pay the man at the register. I called Sarah back. She couldn't stop laughing, telling me to buy my toilet paper and remember to call my mother.

I stood under the eave on the front steps of our building. It had stopped raining. When I saw the black Escalade pull up, I squeezed the bagless toilet paper under my arm. A bag might have been less embarrassing. When the door opened, thumping bass beats poured into the air. I couldn't move. I just watched him step down and heft a massive duffle bag behind him.

Eddie was skinnier than I thought he would be, wearing jeans, a white

T-shirt, and a green hat. I thought the hat was dumb, but he was very cute. We said hi but didn't hug. My hands were still shaking as I scrambled to unlock the doors. He waited behind me, patient. I offered to take his bag, and he looked at me like I was crazy.

Once inside, we sat down on opposite ends of the little leather love seat and looked at one another—an evaluation. I poked him. He told me I had beautiful eyes. I told him he was very good-looking. I asked him about the tattoo, and he proceeded to explain the colors of the Portuguese flag and Scottish tartans to me. He was nervous.

"I brought you presents," he said, getting up from the couch. He fished around in his bag and then handed me a chocolate box and a gray T-shirt from his company. "I don't even know if you like chocolate ..."

"I love chocolate!"

We heard the door click. Lauren came home, a thankful break in the tension. He gave her a huge hug, a hug that he hadn't given me, and the three of us went into my room so I could decide if I wanted to change. She sat on my bed and tore into the Godiva box, interrogating him and handing me the ones that she knew I'd like, like coconut. When we were halfway through the box, she hopped down, grabbed a cardigan, and left for dinner with her boyfriend. I stayed on my bed, dangling my feet over the edge, feeling like a little kid, while he changed shirts.

"I really want to kiss you," he said, walking up to me, his face now centimeters from mine.

I set the box down and slid off my bed to stand. "Then do it," I said.

He stepped closer. He smelled good. Our lips came together. It didn't feel right, didn't feel like I'd wanted it to feel. I opened my eyes and found his to be closed. We stopped. It was awkward, or maybe it wasn't. I didn't know.

"So, dinner's downtown on the Bowery," I said as I grabbed a black tube of mascara from my makeup tray and walked out to the living room where the full-length mirror was. "We should take a cab."

By the time the cab had pulled up in front of a quaint, farm-to-table place called Little Giant, I was carsick. It was hard to talk.

We squeezed up to the crowded bar to order drinks while they readied our table. He asked if I was okay—why I was being so quiet. I apologized and told him I that I was fine and that this was all very perfect—because it was.

It didn't need all my words. At a table near the kitchen, we shared mussels and both ordered the pork chop on special. It was one of his favorite meals, which I knew, which was why I chose the restaurant. We talked incessantly. We barely touched dessert. We waited for a cab in the rain and held hands on the West Side Highway. All I could think about doing since mussels was kissing him again, really kissing him.

THE AIR WAS THICK WITH a December drizzle. The signs of the restaurants and bars of Hell's Kitchen hung suspended in the black night, as if they had been drawn onto it with smears of neon. I watched the round toes of my beige pumps make graceful, slow clips between the cracks of the sidewalk. Fixating on the cracks helped me to walk slower, to keep my arm looped through the crook of my father's elbow. I had walked block and after block alongside his laborious, uneven gate.

"It looks like it is raining," he said in an observant tone that he used to point out the painfully obvious. I hated it. It made him sound artificial. I didn't say anything. I was lost in the thought of the consequence of letting go of his elbow. Walking was hard for him, so hard that I had to concentrate for him. When had I neglected to notice that? His shoulder used to slump down to one side. That Christmas, Aunt Biz had told me that watching my father leave a room is one of the saddest things she's ever seen. Now that shoulder slumped further down than ever before, as if it would slide right off his body.

"Yeah, it's pretty gross out," I said a block later. "I wish it would snow. It should snow this time of year. It's nearly December."

He said nothing, allowing all my other thoughts to be buried by one— how my father walked. One foot pitched forward, splayed like a duck's. It landed with a *clomp.* The other foot had to be pulled across the asphalt to meet up. There was no lift, no grace—just a big drag. And he kept his hands interlaced behind him, resting on the small of his back. This forced his belly to jut forward, a misalignment that added to the pitching forward of his every step. His balance was shot, and in this sea of people, it was anxiety-inducing for everyone but him. I looked at him, trying to place just exactly who my father was.

His forest green sweater stretched across an ever-expanding stomach. His breath was audible. A Band-Aid crossed the bridge of his nose. It had a crimson splotch, wet with blood that had been seeping through. My mother had only one in her purse that day—it would have to last the entire evening.

My mom had called me earlier. "Well, we had to go back to the hotel. Your father fell today."

"Fell? Is he okay?"

"He's okay. But he broke his glasses."

We made dinner plans, and I hung up. Parents falling isn't right. When other people fall, it's funny—sports fumbles, friends who trip, people who have imbibed too much alcohol to stand. But when my father fell on 42nd Street, right beside Bryant Park, it was alarming. Flat on his face, slicing open the bridge of his nose, helpless until strangers helped my mother help him get up.

I looked at his nose. Had the splotch grown in just two blocks?

"Have you heard from Lauren?" my mom yelled from behind us.

"No, not yet, but she's probably still at work. Can we go to the M&M store? It's only a few blocks away." It was *ten* blocks away, but I hadn't heard from Lauren, and I wanted to get M&Ms in specific colors to send to Eddie.

"Sure, that's fine. I guess."

My mom was carrying a bag full of glass Christmas trees (Christmas gifts from a shop near Rockefeller Center), her purse, and an Anthropologie bag stuffed with my cranberry trench. I loved that coat. She didn't, and despite a lengthy conversation about finances—how easy it was to blow $600 on food and drink in the city—she bought me a new winter coat. It was gray with bell sleeves and a silk bow that cinched it together in the back. We had switched duties—she with the shopping bags and me walking my father.

Times Square was a clusterfuck on a Thursday evening. I immediately regretted my request. The three of us stood on the first floor of the M&M metropolis, tourists and grouchy workers bumping into us. My father—no different than the kids in the store who were lured away from parents by shiny plastic toys and rainbows of chocolate-covered candy—wandered off. I could feel my mother's anxiety rise. I watched him and pulled out my Blackberry.

"We're in Times Square and I think my mother's gonna lose it," I texted Eddie. "Hey, where are you?" I texted Lauren. "What's the score?" I texted Adam.

"Janna!" my mother said, grabbing my elbow. "Where is your father?"

"Mom, he's right there," I said, pointing two feet away to where he stood, watching kids play a game. "He's fine." I slid my phone back into my pocket.

"I don't do this well. He is hard to keep track of. And it's even more difficult in this city!"

The Blackberry chimed, and I pulled it back out. "I'll meet you wherever in 40 minutes," texted Lauren.

I grabbed a plastic bag from a dispenser and hurried over to the M&M wall. I knew I had to do it fast, like within five minutes. My mother looked furious.

"Mom, I have the candy, so we can go."

Chime. I pulled the phone out again and looked at it. She glared at me. "Stillers!!!" It was from Ryan.

"Janna, I'm losing my patience here. Where is he now?"

"Right there," I said, pointing again to him as he walked over to the wall of candy where I had just been filling up my bag.

Chime.

"Janna!"

Chime. Chime. I looked down at its lit screen. "We're up by 14." Adam. "See you there!" Lauren.

"Okay, I'm just going to leave," she said.

Chime. I looked again. "What are you doing taking your mom to Times Square?" Eddie.

"But, Mom—"

"I don't need to be here!" she said. "The two of you are impossible. He won't listen or stay in one place. And you with that damn cell phone!"

"Mom, come on …"

Chime.

"You won't leave it alone. You have looked at it every five minutes since we got here. It's rude, Janna. I'm chasing him around. You won't get off your damn phone. Now how am I supposed to feel?"

Chime. Chime. Chime. She looked at me. I looked at my phone. "Where are you guys? Where can I meet up?" Lauren. "TD. Harrison." Ryan. "She prob hates it there!" Eddie.

"See! You can't leave it alone. I should be at home with my horses. You don't want me here. You're making *that* obvious."

"Come on, Mom," I said, feeling tears well up. "Please don't say that. That's not true at all. I love you. I miss you. I want you here."

"I don't like this. I don't want to be here, keeping track of him, keeping track of you. I'm too tired."

"But I'm texting Lauren about dinner," I said, looking at my phone.

Chime. Chime. She walked away from me. I looked at. "I would hate that place!" Eddie. "Are you watching this?" Adam.

"We need to go," she said, having returned with my father.

"Did Janna get her candy?" he asked.

"Yes, John! Now we're leaving."

"*Oooh.* We should eat some."

Chime. "Is it snowing there?" Eddie.

"Mom!" I grabbed at her elbow as we walked outside. I wanted to touch her, to hug her. "I'm sorry. I love you. I won't get the phone out again. I mean, I just have to tell Lauren where we're going. She won't pick up if I call."

She was angry. Rain was pelting. People were shuffling. This was my hell and hers. I couldn't remember the last time the three of us had a good time. I got us a cab, and my mother arranged the pile of bags, umbrellas, and my father into the back seat. I gave the cross streets to the driver and pulled out my phone for the last time that evening.

"LB! 45&9." I texted Lauren. "Can't talk now. Got in trouble for texting. No snow. Have a good night in CA!" I texted Eddie. "Hola amigos. Go Stillers. There in spirit. Can't watch. Parents in town." I texted both Ryan and Adam.

I felt stupid and selfish. My heart didn't stop hurting until my mother and I were on our second glass of Riesling. My father and Lauren did not drink at dinner, which annoyed me. When did everyone stop drinking? Where did all the fun go? I couldn't think of a way to apologize for my juvenile behavior, so I tried to erase it with wine and pasta.

"Hey, why haven't I heard from you?" I texted Eddie the next day.

Chime. "Because your mom's in town. I don't want to get you in trouble, silly."

Chime. "I'll see you in a few days. I'm so excited!!!!!!!!!!!!!!"

IT HAD RAINED FOR FOUR days straight, which made California look like Ireland. I liked the rain. I lay in Eddie's bed, thinking about how amazing the day had been. Breakfast with his friend's family at their country club and a trip to a house in the canyons to pick up a painting, where he bought me a beaded cobalt necklace that would never not be one of my favorites. Then we had dinner on the beach, after which I insisted on putting my feet in the water, which involved taking off my tights. This California was colder.

Lying there, I thought about my dad. I used to think that I had much to say on the matter of my father. I had a great, big, tragic, evolving story about brain injury that I would share with people who most likely hadn't even uttered the words *brain* and *injury* together in a sentence before meeting me. Now, I didn't know what I had. I just missed my old dad more than ever. I was such a goddamn lucky little kid. I had started to resent the happy memories. I was growing bitter—hateful. How was it that the last secure, warm, and happy relationship with a man had been my father—twelve years ago? Eddie had me frightened of my feelings.

This relationship, despite the distance, was escalating to a serious place. I found myself wanting Eddie in the rest of my life with the same intensity that I wanted my old father back. I wanted the two to meet, to hang out, to *not* drink beers together. He, like most of the men I had liked, reminded me of my father—similar in their lust for fun and their complete and harmless self-centeredness.

But Eddie was different than the others. He had been the only person that I hadn't rushed to tell my tragedy. We talked about other things, ourselves.

"I'm really pretty smart," I had said the first night we talked for an hour. "Well, I mean, I'm not that smart."

He told me to quit talking in contradictions. I liked him. I wanted him to know me without my past, so I told him the watered-down version of my dad, as if there were such a thing. There isn't, so I invented one: it was hard, but totally livable; my mom is amazing, but anyone would be; it was actually pretty bad, but it could definitely be worse; I wasn't going to tell him it all now, but maybe I'd tell him about it all later.

This—California—was later. I sat up in bed and told him the whole story, starting from the afternoon it happened and every gory detail I could think of. Arrests, falls, weed, tractors, newspapers, orange juice, hospitals, pills, fights, poems, cars, tears, cake, Buffett, hearings, hearing aids, barfing, bleeding ...

He listened and asked the same questions that everyone asks, and when there was nothing else to be said, I laid my cheek down on his chest and closed my eyes. I felt calm and emotionless, like I'd just told a story about someone else.

"I can't imagine going through any of that," he said.

"You don't want to."

He pulled me up, kissed me on the forehead, put his arm around me, and squeezed. I felt my shoulder blades pinch together. I felt safe.

"You are amazingly strong."

"No, that's my mother."

I FELT SICK. NAUSEATED. My stomach was in a perpetual knot that left no room for an appetite. My mind was uneasy at all hours.

"I just keep thinking about what Lauren told Dan," Eddie had said. "This is not the kind of relationship you want, because you need someone there every day with you to remind you how much they like you. I like you. I can't be there to tell you every damn day."

"Oh, come on, Eddie," I said. "That's not true! I wish I hadn't told you about my father. I just miss you, like, I want to see you. That's *normal!*"

We had stayed up late talking, mainly about why he thought I needed therapy and all the reasons he thought we would and wouldn't work. Eddie talked as much as I did, but now it was as if someone had put a cap on his emotions when I wasn't looking. It was like talking to my father—someone who can only see the world in black and white with zero sense of empathy. And what did he know? I wasn't the only one with issues. He hadn't talked to his father in fifteen years and never flew home for holidays. It didn't matter. Our conversations reeked of the familiar frustration of trying to get through to a brain-injured man with a flat affect. And my tears. He couldn't hear them, but they slid down my cheeks anyway. The entire relationship was draining my sanity and my happiness dry.

I tried hard not to ask for anything, not to need anything from him. I tried to keep at bay all the things I could say that would most assuredly drive him away.

Self-discipline. Lately I needed more of it, according my mother—and especially when it came to men, because I could be *a bit too much* for some people. I needed to *relax,* to *live in the moment,* to *leave well enough alone.*

There are very few things I have a decidedly hard time with, but relaxing was fast becoming one of them. I had no clue how to do it. I couldn't accept that something—read: a male relationship—could be positive or trust the future, trust that things simply pan out more often than not. It was easier to worry about the inevitable, because life was either not going to go my way or was going to go exactly my way and subsequently crash and burn. That's how I knew it—lose-lose.

Here I was in my late twenties, and all my fears were surfacing violently. I was changing who I was, denying that I was weathering an emotional tempest. I was determined to ride it out while no one was watching. I kept telling myself I could handle anything, that I already *had.* Eddie could get as cold and angry or as understanding and warm as he wanted, but I was determined, I *knew,* that I could make it work if I dumped all of my own energy into us.

I did need therapy. There was no one I could burden with this. My one-of-a-kind sob story kept bleeding into everything else. My mother's e-mails—long musings on how to deal with Eddie and my fears—no longer felt like Xanax. I was a little crazy, after all. *Daddy issues.*

"HOLY SHIT, JAN!" ALEJANDRA SAID when we met on the corner of 56th and Seventh Avenue. "You are so fucking skinny! You look amazing. What have you been doing?"

"Hi, Al," I said. "Not eating, I guess."

We hugged, and she swatted my thigh. I hadn't worn my thrift store J. Crew jeans in more than a decade, and I had a collarbone, two collarbones. Visible clavicles—I had wanted those for years.

"Damn, girl."

I was happy to meet up with Alejandra. It had been ages since we had shared a post-work coffee chat at Dean & DeLuca. We ordered dirty chai lattes and cookies and sat under the fluorescent lighting with the intent to dissect life. I broke pieces off my gingersnap cookie, setting them down on the wax paper like a puzzle.

"Honey, what's wrong?" Alejandra asked. "Babe, talk to me."

I couldn't eat it. I couldn't eat anything. Food meant effort to me. For the first time, I understood how my mother could not eat for days after my dad's accident. The guilt of comparing my life to hers was bewildering, but I understood now.

"It's fine," I said. "I'm fine."

"Look what he's doing to you. Jan!"

My mother is always right. If I'd quit eating, I'd lose the weight—those nasty ten pounds since grad school that were apparently weighing down all my fun and success. I didn't eat and lost that and more in two weeks.

Eddie had canceled, or maybe not even booked, two flights to New York since December. His broken promises and un-bought tickets were driving me emotionally, certifiably crazy.

"Al, I'm going nuts. Nuts. I don't eat. I can't eat. This is killing me."

"Honey, it would be killing *anyone*. It's not just you."

"It's too much. I had to leave my phone at home today."

She sat with me for the next two hours, listening to me ask the same things over and over and watching me not eat my cookie. Coffee was always digestible. It had been the same with my mother. Alejandra assured me that I wasn't *crazy* and that it was okay to be crazy, if I was. Anyone would be. And it didn't matter anyway, because none of this was *fucking cool*. And he, like Ryan, Adam, and Samina had all said, had too many *red flags* anyway.

I wanted so badly for these things to sink in, kind words said by my countless smart friends. I felt disconnected from the whole world. All I really wanted was a missed call from Eddie when I got home to check my phone. I had two.

"I HATE THIS DISTANCE THING today," I said to Lauren.

She ignored the comment and handed me a black Barney's bag. She ignored those kinds of comments. "I got you something today," she said. "Sorry I put it in a *bag*."

"What!" I yelped. "This is amazing!"

"I know," she said. "This is why I buy you gifts, so you won't move to California."

"But, you …"

"*DailyCandy* gave us gift cards. I know it's your favorite and you've been out. So you better not move."

"You know I'm not going to move. I mean, I'm not going to … not in the next few years. Why would I, anyway? This is *New York*."

"Eddie."

"Come on, Laur."

"Though I don't know what you're going to do out there. You'll be bored out of your mind watching movies, playing with a dog, and eating Carl's Jr. every night with a bunch of Republicans. You'll hate it."

"He's supposed to visit in a couple weeks."

"*Woo. Hoo.*" She adjusted the folds of her Sanchez jersey over a black tank top and looked at me.

"It looks good, for a Jets jersey," I said to her reflection in the mirror.

"Have a good time at WD-50," she said gathering her things. "Wish Cristina a happy b-day, and tell her I'll see her on Saturday. And enjoy your mascara!"

"Oh, I will!"

The apartment still smelled like a freshly baked cake after she'd shut the door. I carefully discarded the mascara packaging in the recycling basket in our kitchen, along with the baby Barney's bag it came in. I borrowed her distressed leather belt to dress down the strapless red dress. I put on black flats and a coat of Shu Uemura.

Chime. My phone vibrated on the coffee table. "I love you." Eddie.

I stared at the grey bubble, trying to figure out what to do next. Three stupid words typed up and sent from some Bavarian ski town nestled in the mountains of Washington, bookended by texts about snowfall and my boobs—what was he thinking? I put on a second coat of mascara. I called him and left a frantic voicemail agreeing in a "me too" sort of way without actually saying it.

Chime. "At dinner." Eddie

I put my phone in my purse and put on my coat. I felt it vibrate twice. I waited to read it until I was in the cab.

"Go with the duck." Eddie.

"Have fun!" Eddie.

We talked about it later that night in the way that you talk about something that happened to someone else at some other party. I felt like we were both crazy and that there could be something functional to that.

tension and suspension

ON THE FIRST DAY OF 2010, my parents' attorney, Michael Joanow, filed a brief, an incomprehensible (to me, at least) law document contesting Workers' Comp's numerous and consistent appeals to pay for my father's treatment. The brief targeted the latest appeal, where the *Employer* (Workers' Comp) had failed to properly process payment for reasonable, necessary, and related medical care of the *Claimant* (my father). Mr. Joanow had caught Workers' Comp's mistake—something that can be best described as missing paperwork.

My mother liked Mr. Joanow, who was as pushy as he was polished. She said he knew how to use his mouth, and she called him "a good politician in that sense." She had always wanted me to be an attorney. She still does, because it would be a good way to use my mouth.

I didn't go to the hearing. Not that hearing, not any. The courtroom is the part of the accident that doesn't belong to me, only to my parents. As if I'd feel more whole having seen my father testify or my mother argue. I am left to imagine my father slumping over in one of those hard chairs made of dark wood, forced to tell the judge about his brain injury—sparse stories and superficial feelings. He can't access what we experience. And then there is my mother, indubitably wearing one of her sharp skirt suits and smiling in a way that shows she is not to be messed with.

I suppose I could've asked to be included, and after enough asking, selling myself, my mother would let me, but I've always assumed that my being there would only complicate things. Besides, I'd probably talk too much during my testimony. Preparing my father for the hearing was enough.

For this particular hearing, my mother had asked my father to make a list of reasons he wanted to receive further treatment. It took him just under an hour to type his list. He folded it in two halves and put it in his notebook, and it stayed there until the day of the hearing.

My father brought the folded paper with him to the stand, where he admitted to (partaking in and being arrested for) purchasing and processing marijuana, shoplifting CDs, and stealing newspapers from the neighbor's mailbox. He admitted to driving to dangerous areas to purchase drugs; lending his car to acquaintances, which led to criminal charges; having no control over his actions; and relying on his eighty-year-old father for transportation.

He asked for an opportunity to get better. He unfolded the piece of paper and read his list out loud. When he was finished, he refolded the paper and slipped it between the pages of the book he'd been reading that particular week.

My mother testified to his need for a specialized brain injury treatment program. She mentioned ReMed, the brain injury rehabilitation program that had been strongly and consistently recommended by my father's PCP, psychiatrist, and several therapists and clinicians. There he could receive the necessary and comprehensive inpatient and outpatient rehabilitation for his particular and significant frontal lobe injury. A treatment plan had recently been submitted to Workers' Comp: a thirty-day trial at $965 a day that covered a medical director's services, therapy services, behavioral analysis, physical therapy, occupational therapy, counseling, neurobehavioral counseling, nursing, and all meals and board. Should he need further treatment, additional months would be arranged.

"John Leyde was an appropriate candidate for our program," the director of the program had written in several letters that Mr. Joanow shared with the courtroom. And when Mr. Joanow asked them directly, the Workers' Comp's expert witnesses agreed that "John was exercising poor judgment and impulse control, which has put him in grave danger of harm and/ or arrest, which has virtually placed him in a prison in his own home." Therefore, he was indeed, on all accounts, "an appropriate candidate for a rehabilitation program."

Yet Workers' Comp had appealed, denying coverage for this treatment. However, as Mr. Joanow shared with the courtroom, they had done so *incorrectly*. The fight was no longer about denying the necessary treatment plan—a fight hard to win. It was about catching a mistake. Workers' Comp had not filed a Utilization Review Petition within the proper appeal period of thirty days.

The presiding judge saw a greater need for a brain-injured man to receive treatment than for an insurance company to keep its money, and the Review Medical Petition was granted along with the additional request that the *Employer* pay reasonable attorney's fees for an unreasonable contest and penalties for violating the act.

By the end of the spring, all compulsory paperwork and applications had been put through and approved. The next step was ReMed.

THE DAY THE SAINTS WON the Super Bowl, I left Lauren and her boyfriend at a bar and walked forty-nine blocks home, where I cried through the fourth quarter alone on the couch. I hadn't heard from Eddie in more than two days. I knew it was over. I knew he wouldn't call, text, or write another e-mail, and he would certainly never get on another plane. That didn't stop me from calling him over and over for days. I left messages. I apologized for being too emotional, too needy, too crazy, and too girl-with-the-brain-injured-dad. I apologized for liking him too much. Other times, I didn't leave messages, as if I was trying to hit the right strategy, the one that would make him pick up and talk to me. I tried texting, but my texts started to string themselves together like e-mails. And my e-mails stretched into novels. In response, I received nothing. I'd begun to refer to it as radio silence. "Asshole" was how everyone else did.

I called my mother every day and cried. On my lunch breaks, I called my father and cried while he read me sections of the newspaper. I called Krystal, Sarah, Amelia, Natalie, and Nicole and cried. I called Ryan, Adam, and my cousin, Annie. It was a cycle: go to work, go to yoga, call someone, cry, go to bed, cry. I quit eating. The cycle kept me alive.

Six days later, I woke up inexplicably grateful for the first weekend day in days. Lauren had left, so I dragged myself to the deli, bought a pint of Haagen-Dazs pistachio ice cream, came back, and sat down on the kitchen floor. With my back to the fridge, I sat, holding a spoon in one hand and the ice cream in the other, and cried. Fifteen minutes later, my phone rang.

"Hey, Ryan." I dumped a green puddle of melted ice cream into the sink, put the rest of the pint in the freezer, and slid the untouched spoon back in its drawer. "I'm eating ice cream. Pistachio."

I walked to the living room, listening to him talk about the squirrels in the park behind his apartment and the girl he was starting to like a lot. I stretched out across the leather loveseat. My head hung over one arm and my legs over the other. He asked how I was really doing. I told him I was debilitated. It had become my favorite word—*debilitated*. Like dead, but alive.

"You know there's something about him that's not right," Ryan said. "I thought this from the beginning."

And then it started: me asking the questions no one could answer. *Why? How could he? What happened?* Questions turned to sputtering, fragmented, gasping bits of conversation that lasted for more than an hour. *Will he come back? What does this mean? What did I do?* Pointless questions. Answers that changed nothing.

"Promise me you won't change," he said, cutting me off.

"Huh?"

"Just don't let this change you. You've always been so honest, so able to express your feelings ..."

"You sound like the therapist I should've have gone to a long time ago. Ryan, come on. You know me—I'll never lose touch with my melodramatic, misdirected feelings."

"I'm serious, Janna. Don't let this close you up."

Wow. I really did have everyone fooled. My emotional openness was my sly slipcover to hide what was really going on. I was scared shitless. Perhaps I always had been. Who was I kidding? Eddie was proof enough that I was trying to fill a pit of need, loss, and fear with men.

We hung up. I put in season one of *Friday Night Lights*.

The following week, my friends had to force me to come out after work, where I'd cry into my drafts or goblets of red wine. There had to be an expiration date for all this, for the crying and for their tolerance. I willed myself to keep distracted with work and ferocious amounts of yoga, but every night, I'd run the conversation over and over again in my head. The one we'd have if we ever talked again, where he'd apologize for being absent and thoughtless—an asshole—and I'd apologize for being needy and overemotional—a crazy female.

More than a month went by without me being able to finish a meal. I'd lost twenty-five pounds. Food made me want to throw up, which was a habit I'd worked too hard to break. It became so easy not to eat, because sensations, feelings, and connections all made me want to throw up. But it was time to be done being sick. In three days, I was leaving for vacation with my parents.

The whole day at work, I daydreamed about my sweaty *vinyasa* class. Maybe I'd actually balance on just my arms today. Yoga never made me sick. I craved yoga. My craving had morphed from time spent on the mat to lose weight into time on my mat to gain sanity. My practice had moved from the physical body to the mental realm, but I didn't care. I just *needed*. After class, I crossed the street from the studio and stood in a long line at McDonald's.

It was probably the seventh fast food burger of my entire life. I hopped up on my counter and unwrapped it, inspecting it as I pulled the waxy paper away from a filmy bun oozing orange goo. I took a bite. It was sweet and salty. I hoped I wasn't tasting ketchup. I hate ketchup. I took another and another, and by my fourth bite, I wanted to throw it up. I couldn't finish. I was still heartbroken and angry. I'd convinced myself that I would be broken until I heard from him. But finally, I was hungry. I called West Way Diner and ordered a chicken salad sandwich.

The Pell Newport Bridge is a suspension bridge, and it appeared suspended in the night sky, connecting nothingness to nothing. I had been watching it grow bigger and brighter as I drove closer. My parents had fallen asleep. The panorama was remarkable, as if a cartoonist had drawn it on the darkness with the clean blue lines of a glow-in-the-dark Sharpie.

It was a relief to be away from the city, to be spending time with my parents. I had missed them. It was a relief to be away from work and out of my apartment. It was a relief to be away from my friends, who had spent the past two months telling me in various forms to let go: move on, fuck him, get over it, fuggedaboutit, and reminding me that I was amazing, worthy of someone so much better, so strong, and not going to care eventually.

The car ride had been quiet, and when we got there, my mom got our room keys, and my dad and I schlepped the suitcases into the small B&B-like unit in Newport. We were too tired for talking. I took a shower and passed out on top of my sheets. Nine hours later, my only responsibility in the world was to be in Newport, Rhode Island, a kid on vacation with her parents—that, and to get the hell out of my pajamas before the entire world woke up.

"Janna!" my mother called through my closed door. "You're just going with your parents. It's not a fashion show."

I stood on tiptoes in front of a mirror. The mirror was working in my favor. In jeans and a black cowl neck, I looked perfectly skinny, but the sweater reminded me of Eddie. I had bought it at the Gap in Times Square. I had debated between black and eggplant while listening to him yammer on about Republican ideals.

"The bus is leaving," my mother said, opening the door.

I pulled on the neck of the sweater, waiting for her assessment, just like her kid getting ready for school again.

"You look really good." Was that jealously in her voice? Maybe. "You look skinny. Those jeans look good."

Those damn J. Crew jeans, my absolute proof: *skinny*. Skinny was the only thing that felt good that year. I smiled.

"I'm sorry you are just here with your parents."

"Mom, don't say that. Please don't. I love you guys."

She'd planned this vacation a few months ago and had reserved a separate room for me and maybe someone else. "Are you going to send him a postcard to show him what he's missing?"

"No way in hell."

We laughed. "Ready? Can you help me with your father?"

I nodded, slipped into my cranberry trench, and slung my bag over my shoulder.

Newport was chilly and gray, and the morning sun was buried behind a soupy layer of nimbostratus clouds. Its off-season sidewalks were barren. I walked ahead of my parents. With each step, I could feel it coming.

"Janna!"

I spun around, head down, hands in my coat pockets.

"You're going to have to slow down. Your father cannot walk that fast. And neither can I. This is not New York City, okay?"

I was cold. I was aching to get to a destination with hot coffee, and walking in sync with my parents was too much brain injury reality for me. For years, my attention had been so focused on the constant malfunctions of my dad's mental capacities that his physical deterioration had slipped by me. Now looking at him made me cry. Did it even matter? Everything made me cry.

There was not one iota of finesse left in the way my father approached life—how he ate, spoke, slept, and moved through his days. It was all sloppy and cumbersome. His posture dumped all his weight into his lower back, which added to the pain he felt but couldn't or didn't bother to explain to us. He hobbled with his foot brace and hobbled without it. His stomach ballooned over his waist as he walked around like one of those men who allow their beer bellies to lead the way. But my father wasn't supposed to drink beer anymore. Some days—like this one—I hated him. I hated him for how he looked, how he moved, and how he made my mother feel.

"I need to call Vicky and check on the horses," my mom said, digging through her purse in front of a café on Thames Street. "Can you take him inside?"

I nodded.

"Go in and get us a table. And make sure he watches that step."

"Step," I muttered. It was such a half-assed warning. Hating him made me hate myself.

Inside, the line was long, as if it were—and it probably was—the only café open at noon on Palm Sunday in Newport. My father and I talked about muffins. I paid for three black coffees, two banana nut muffins, and one chocolate chip cookie. My mom came in, and we sat down at a table littered with newspapers, the only table free of resident college kids. The muffins were gone within minutes. My mom held her warm coffee cup to her cheekbone, and my father sifted pages out of a *USA Today*. It was drizzling. No one was in a rush. I snapped my cookie in pieces and made eye contact with a guy who reminded me of Eddie, or maybe Ryan. I hated that I had become one of those girls who broke things in bites rather than just eating them.

"Dad!"

He had been folding and refolding a section of the newspaper in order to create a perforation. He had always been good at it—he had an enviable ability to make a couple folds that would tear paper as clean as scissors ever would. I could never do it. I didn't have the patience.

"What are you doing?" I halved a cookie piece. "Why do you do stuff like that?"

He held up a square of paper to show me. It was an ad for a music website. My mother and I exchanged looks that bounced silent communication between us.

What the fuck is he doing?

Janna, just leave it alone. I deal with this shit all the time.

Tearing sections out of the newspaper was one thing he did with finesse.

When we got up to leave, my father walked over to a table of college guys. They all held Gatorades, probably willing the electrolytes to cure their hangovers by osmosis. I'd been there before.

"What did you do with the money?" my father asked a beefy frat boy.

I looked around for my mother, who had already gone outside.

"What money?" the kid asked.

My dad leaned over the table of boys. "The money they gave you for whistling lessons."

I rolled my eyes so hard it hurt. When had this kid been whistling? I hadn't heard him. The kid smiled, confused, hung over. My father smiled his goofy fake grin and leaned in closer, his way of demanding an answer.

"I whistled it away with beer," the kid said with a confident chuckle.

I refused to hear the rest of it. "I can't believe he does that," I said, hopping down the steps to join my mother on the sidewalk. "He just walks up to total strangers and starts an invasive conversation."

She gave me her *I deal with shit all the time* look.

"Like what in the world does he talk about to people he doesn't know?"

He would talk to everyone—waitresses, mailmen, shop owners, guys pushing babies in strollers, couples, old fishermen—about anything, but nine times out of ten, the conversation revolved around me.

"I'll be over in this candle store," my mother said, pointing across the street. "Can you just wait for him, or go in and see what he's doing?"

I nodded. Ten minutes later, we found her standing before a wall of scented candles packed tight and shiny like leather-bound classics in one of those home libraries designed to spark dreamy envy.

"Smell it." She handed me a jar the size of a shot glass.

"Dirt?" I asked, turning it over to read the label. "Come on. What does *dirt* smell like?"

"Smell it!"

I sniffed. The brown wax smelled exactly like dirt. It smelled deliciously like *earth*, that rich black soil that Gram Mary moved around with a trowel to replant bulbs. The candle's smell linked me to a string of memories that I hadn't thought about in years—planting Mother's Day flowers with my mother, weeding with Pat, taking the Rototiller to a patch of our yard for my herb garden—a slew of Proustian moments. I walked up to the register, where my father and a bubbly woman were deep in conversation about me.

"That's me," I said, interrupting and setting my candle on the counter between them. "The one who works at *Harper's Bazaar,* who would rather be at *National Geographic.* I have no doubt he's told you everything."

"Why yes, he has." Her eyes were veiled in thick coats of mascara to offset her loud lip shade, and when she spoke, the bangles on her wrists sparkled and rattled. "You've got quite the proud father here."

I smiled one of my fail-safe, customer-service smiles. "I suppose I do." I took over the conversation—candles that smell like dirt, how life imitates art, how the beach in the winter is inspiring—just bullshitting with some stranger, the same thing my father does. I just do it better.

My parents were waiting for me to leave. For the next few hours we shopped up and down Commercial Street. My mom bought a ring, gifts for the Suhries and Fred and Carolyn, and a hat for my dad. She bought me a bracelet that resembled a piece of gold chain mail and a little black dress, just another addition to the sleek and black pieces that hung in my closet above my 4.5-inch-heels, just another something for the job I hated. But she insisted, because the dress looked good, because I fit in things now.

When the clouds cleared, we drove to the end of Ochre Avenue to see the Breakers Mansion. No tours, we decided. We explored on our own, finding the Cliff Walk, the three-mile winding path that snaked along the shore on the other side of a wall that kept the estates separate from the gray spray of the ocean. I watched my parents walk ahead of me, my father walking like an eighty-year-old man, my mother's arm looped through his elbow. I stayed behind. I wanted the distance, to stay in my own world of blustery salt winds smacking me with sea spray—my world of disconnect from my father and all other men, freezing cold and lonely.

We ate dinner on the second floor of the Red Parrot, where the service was slow and the plastic menus were sticky with the residuals of the blended, sweetened frozen cocktails that brought families and friends to the Red Parrot on drizzly Sundays. My father complained to my mother that the bathroom was downstairs. I asked her if we could order a Key lime pie, because this seemed to be the kind of place.

When the waiter set the pie down in the center of the table, my dad asked him if he'd ever been to New York City. He had. Pittsburgh? No. The waiter looked at me. *Why could nothing ever be normal with him?* I turned the plate crust-side away from my father. It didn't matter. When the interrogation was over, he took a fork to the wall of crust, and I watched the entire structure of the pie crumble with his first bite.

"You really should send him a postcard," my mother said. "Just write, 'You could be here.' You have nothing to lose."

I laughed.

"To who?" my father asked. "Lauren?"

"No." I could feel my forehead wrinkling in the crease just inches below my widow's peak. I swore it had deepened over the last few months. Maybe someday I'd be able to afford Botox, if I wanted it.

"Seven-two-four six-nine-nine three-one-one-two," I said.

"What?" my mother asked.

"It's what the postcard should say," I said, pulling the pie plate closer, away from my father for the last bite.

"And …" she said.

"That's her phone number," my dad said. "She thinks he forgot it. If the phone doesn't ring, it's me." He looked up at me with a smile so familiar, a smile that had grown so foreign that it stung. "It's *him*. It's *him*."

My father touched his middle finger to his tongue and used the spit like an adhesive to pick up the graham cracker crumbs left on the empty plate. I wondered whether this action bothered my mother. He had always cleaned up the crumbs, before and after the accident. He had always quoted Buffett lyrics before the accident, but never after—until just now.

A FEW WEEKS LATER, MY parents had picked me up from the airport. We stopped at Bahama Breeze for dinner. The "Jimmy Buffett place" had become part of the airport routine. Even our orders became routine: my mom's "fun" drink, my father's fried seafood choice, and my two Aruba Reds (their signature brew, always on tap). If it was nice, we'd sit outside with a view of the parking lot, and if not, we'd settle into the big red booths inside. I'd always point out the one in every ten songs that was a Buffett song and comment on whether it was one of our favorites. And when dinner was over and our lives felt a little more in sync, we split the mediocre Key lime pie. My mother would always let me drive home, and ten minutes into the drive, somewhere on Route 60, I'd switch to my music.

"Mom, have you ever had to … you know … get over someone?" I asked as I merged onto 60. I stopped talking and punched the fast-forward button on an Eddie-heartbreak compilation CD. I'd made it for myself, an act of unrepentant wallowing. My mother never would have gotten herself into what I had with men—unrequited and completely unavailable non-relationships. She was too practical.

"Him." She pointed her thumb at the back seat. "You know what his newest thing is?"

The freeway was long, dark, boring, and familiar. I was happy to have her company and conversation for the ride home. It didn't happen enough anymore. Maybe something was shifting.

"He wants a divorce. He wants his freedom. He wants rid of me."

Fuck—instant tears. I was glad for the darkness.

"His freedom?" I asked. "What in the world does he think he is going to do on his own?"

"Well, he's going to get an apartment."

"And that would last, like, two months. He'd be on the street, Mom."

"I know. He cannot make decisions. But he wants his freedom, because he has no stimulation all day long. I can't give it to him, though. I can't. I know he has no one to talk to all day. That's why he gets himself in so much trouble."

"I can't even imagine how he feels. I think I'm more like him, more than you are. I would go crazy."

"Just think about the power of the brain." She told me about how she had been reading about early-onset dementia—a probability for someone who grew old with a TBI. I told her about how when Gram Mary first got sick, she used to swear and scream at me and lock me out of the house. And I told her about the screaming fights I used to have my father. I had never really told her about these things before.

"I know," she said, unsurprised. "I'm so sorry. Do you see what the brain can do?"

"I've loved them no matter what though. I had to. I have to. No wonder I go all-out when it comes to putting up with people I like."

"What do you mean?"

"Like … with guys—"

"Janna, you have to stop doing that. Not everyone is going to be your father. And if you don't learn to quit, you're going to get yourself in trouble. Have you thought about therapy?"

"Mom. The list of therapists in New York is ten miles long. What do you want me to do?"

"I want you pick someone. Pick ten people, and then e-mail Fred. See what Fred says." She faced the window and closed her eyes. I turned the volume up. We got home just in time to go to bed.

I opened *Nine Stories* by J. D. Salinger, the book that my mother had left on my bed with a Post-It that read, "Exceptionally good! You need to read at least one!" A folded piece of paper fell out. I opened it. "Michael Joanow" was written at the top in my father's all-caps. The rest was typed.

List—

I would like treatment because I have no life to speak of.

I sit at home every day and watch TV. No more no less.

I am not allowed to drive a car alone. I may go out and get in trouble.

I need taught how to find meaningful things to do and do them. I need to learn how to stay out of trouble.

If I could drive alone I could find somewhere to volunteer. That would be interesting.

I could drive to exercise at Coolspring Fitness during the day.

I am mean and driving everyone away.

I am going to have nothing left.

I am going to kill myself because I think that is the way I can end this problem.

I have done everything I am supposed to do. Go to hearing and doctors and the insurance company is denying me treatment. They are in breach of contract. I want to sue them. They are supposed be helping me.

I read it again, tears dripping all over the folds and coffee stains that were already there. The paper was ugly. I folded it back up and slipped it into the paisley cloth sleeve that held my laptop.

"I need a hug," I said, leaning against the doorframe of my parents' room.

My mother looked up from the book she was reading. My dad was still downstairs. I was wearing her clothes, a pair of gray sweats and an oversize

Buffett T-shirt that said, "We are the people our parents warned us about." The clothes were soft and clean and smelled like her.

"Please," I said, sniffling and wiping my face.

I walked around to her side of the bed, and she reached her arms up and smiled. I leaned down and put my head on her shoulder. I rarely got her hugs anymore. At first it felt awkward, but I held on. I started crying.

"Oh … come on now," she said. "Do you want to sit next to me on the bed?"

I nodded.

She was using the voice normally reserved for animals and children: soft and warm, with drawn-out words. I sat beside her, and we talked for a long time about my broken heart and my broken dad. I cried, and she consoled. My phone rang.

"Maybe it's him," she said.

I ran into my room to answer. Amelia wanted me to come out to meet her new boyfriend. It was 1:00 a.m. I told her I'd see her tomorrow. I ran back to my mother, ready to restart our conversation, even though I knew there wasn't a whole lot more to say. But it had felt so good, and I wanted to keep living in that moment. I sat back on the bed next to her.

My father, who had come up to go to bed, walked out from behind his closet door and took off his robe. He walked to his side of the bed, balancing on one foot with one hand on the nightstand, and bent over to look for his glasses, which he had dropped. He was completely naked.

"John!" my mom said. "You can't just do that."

And then I hated the moment. I hated when he did that, had no regard for his nakedness. Didn't he think about the fact that he had a daughter and that his disregard was just fucking weird and disturbing? He looked at us, and I looked at the fern pattern on the sheets.

"John, you have a daughter. Your daughter is in the room. She is not supposed to see you like that."

"Oh," he said, and he walked back over to his closet. "I wasn't thinking. I'm sorry." He came out and kissed me on the cheek, having put on a pair of briefs.

"John!"

I got up, slinked away to my room, crawled under the sheets, and read Salinger.

HE TEXTED ME A COUPLE months later, stupid and simple. "Hi Janna, it's Eddie."

We talked on the phone a week later, and he gave me a weak apology smothered in enthusiastic promises to visit me again. For a few months, we bounced around plans, but more than anything, we texted a lot. I hid it from my friends for a while, and then I finally told them one by one that I was fine with giving him a second chance. He made a few more plans to come to New York but canceled them all.

On my birthday, he wished me a happy birthday with a thousand exclamation points. I wore a purple polka-dot dress and red lipstick, and I went out to dinner with my six friends and some of their boyfriends. When the check came, I put a wad of cash on the table and walked out.

"Honey!" Samina said, chasing after me down the sidewalk. "What are you doing?"

"I'm going home," I said, wiping wet mascara onto my knuckles. "Just go have fun without me. Just go with everyone."

"Okay, you have to stop this," she said, grabbing my shoulders. "I am not in Chicago right now with my fiancé, because I stayed to celebrate with you!"

It was like she was my mother. She was right. And now I was too embarrassed, and I just wanted to go home, to cry in my shower. "I know," I said. "Okay? I know. I'm trying. I don't cry at dinners anymore, do I?"

"No, but you're crying on a sidewalk outside of a bar, on your birthday. You have to see what he is doing to you. Honey, you know I love you, but you have to stop talking to him. You are just doing it to yourself now. So you have to stop. Just stop."

"Okay, okay. You're right, Min. But I can't go back in to everyone."

"Yes, you can. Everyone is out here celebrating with you. You can't go home. That's selfish. I know you have a lot going on right now, but you have to see how talking to him makes things this much harder for you. This is not *you*. You are one of the most optimistic and fun and beautiful people I know. You always know how to have a good time and how to find the best in things." She looked at me and shook my shoulders. "But, Jan, you are losing all that."

"I am?"

"Yes, honey. So *stop*. Stop it with him. I'm serious." She handed me a tissue from her purse and I got out my lipstick. I didn't have a choice. I pulled my hair back in a ponytail, and we went back into the bar. Before we found my friends, she ordered us a shot.

"Here's to twenty-eight, babe! A whole new year!"

"And to never again leaving my friends at bars on my birthday." The tequila burned and made my head fuzzy and my mood a little lighter. "I'm so sorry, Min. So, so sorry."

"I know, honey. Don't worry, because now it's done."

It was 6:30 a.m. I curled up on an empty chair in the American Airlines terminal of JFK with two hours to go until my plane took off for Burbank. I had missed my super-early, perfectly planned flight to California for Lauren's brother's wedding. It was too early to text her. I just sat there with my freshly cut blunt bangs hanging in splits around my cowlick. My mother had told me this would happen, that if I ever got bangs they wouldn't work with my cowlick, but I needed this major change.

I sat, silent. I thought about getting up to get coffee. I thought about the men in my life, because that was what I did in moments of free time. I thought about what my father would have thought of me—*my father,* the one who had yet to his head on another man's head.

He'd call me a "ninny" and tell me that missing the flight was my own fault. It was. I had taken my time this morning and then got on the wrong train. He'd tell me it wasn't that big of deal anyway, and he'd tell me the same about the boys. We'd have black coffees and peanut M&Ms. He'd be reading a *USA Today* and asking me questions about things in the paper and things in my head to test my intelligence. He would have probably told me I was pretty, too. He used to tell my mom and me that we were pretty all the time.

I had grown up to be so much like who I knew him to be. I think I had done it on purpose, completely consciously. I chased fun like he did. I loved music and books, because he did. I liked to argue and to figure other people's opinions out. I liked water sports and golden retrievers and had made a place in my heart for Jimmy Buffett. I liked to drink beer and sometimes smoke pot. I liked to be right. I liked to push. I liked to talk a lot, to anyone.

My phone buzzed. "Hi, Mom."

Her early morning conversation had an agenda. California was first. Was I wearing the black dress with the gold? *Yes.* Was I going to see Eddie? *No clue.* Tell Lauren hello. *Of course.* Next was my father. He would be admitted to the ReMed facility in Philadelphia in October.

"Do you want to talk to your dad?" she asked. "I have to go to the barn."

"Sure," I said.

I answered his regular stream of questions and listened to him tell me about an article on cars. Then I asked him what he thought of me, if I was ever going to get what I wanted. What the hell—I'd spent a coffee-less hour and a half sitting and thinking about it.

"We never get what we want," he said.

"Well that's great …"

"Well, when you get something you don't want it anymore."

Oh … "So what do we get then?"

"I don't know what we get," he said. "But it's not what we want."

There were times when my father would say things I found shocking, as if nothing had changed and he lived at home and I was in New York and no one had a brain injury—a fantasy of mine. I would tote those words around for months until they became so thin and worn out that I had to convince myself they had never meant anything. I heard the woman announce my gate changing.

"Dad, I gotta go," I said.

"What? Are you—"

"Dad! I'll talk to you later. Love you."

"Oh, okay. I love you."

I got up and pulled my little red suitcase down the terminal to my new gate. I sat down and thought about my mother. She had traded her whole life to help him. I had no idea why. I hoped it was for love, which made me realize how much I didn't understand anything about finding love. My phone buzzed.

"I can't wait to see your hair!" texted Lauren.

"Why in god's name are you up?!? It's nearly 4am there!!"

Buzz. "New York time. I can't sleep. Text me when you take off."

"Will do. Stupid Mercury Retrograde—Sorry!"

Buzz. "Hahaha. Don't worry. See you around noon!"

I looked up at a TV. Hurricane Earl was ripping up the Outer Banks. I had time to grab a black coffee and maybe some M&Ms, because that is what my father would have done. I'd eat them on the plane and make wishes on all the blue ones, the way Jackie and I used to do in high school.

a fairly nice maze

Our place in Hell's Kitchen now had an elevator, the product of a year and a half's worth of busting apart the marble staircase, leaving us with a grim little lift that looked like it belonged in the back of a warehouse and a crude staircase. After it lost its novelty, I went back to climbing up the three stories, which was better for the planet anyway.

I tucked a fat stack of mail under my arm, took the steps two at a time, and tore open the corner of a puffy manila envelope with my free hands. By the time I had reached the fourth floor landing, I was out of breath, and my black pants were covered in the dust of the cardboard batting. I dropped my purse and the rest of the mail in a heap on the living room floor and dug into my envelope, which was stuffed with CDs wrapped in bubble wrap.

I found a white piece of paper folded in three. At one point, the message had been typed, but since the printout was too faint to read, the message had been written over it in blue felt-tip pen.

> Somehow I missed June 28th. But I didn't forget forever. Now is Septemebering and I'm remembering. I thought you were coming home this weekend. But your mom says no. I hope we see each other soon. Until then I hope all goes well for you. My love never ends.
>
> Your Dad

I sat down crossed-legged on the floor and re-read it. Then I unwrapped each CD: Fleetwood Mac, *The Dance; Monterey Pop;* Led Zeppelin, *I* and *II;* Cheap Trick, *Silver;* The Rolling Stones, *Exile On Main St.;* The Rolling Stones, *Bridges to Babylon Tour '97–'98.*

Two of the cases had been cracked and another taped shut. None of the CDs were new, all having been burned and written on with a smudged black marker, their cases filled with makeshift, printed-out attempts at the oringal artwork. I already owned *Exile On Main Street* and *Zeppelin I,* having taken them from my father's collection long enough to slip them into my computer and download them into iTunes when he wasn't paying attention. The others were albums I'd never thought twice about.

I put the CDs in a basket under the TV with DVDs that Lauren and I hardly watched and called my parents. I left a message saying that I got the package and thank you. I wanted to call Eddie. I called Ryan and hung up before his voicemail. I'd see him in a few days anyway. I called Adam, Sarah—voicemails.

I pulled a *Cosmo* from my bag. Jess, my friend who worked in the marketing department, had given me the latest issue when we met earlier that day for lunch.

"Vajazzling" was hot that October. I stretched out on the couch, picking up where I'd left off at my desk. *Esquire* made me want to be a better woman. *Cosmo* made me angry that I was a woman who wasn't having sex. Two articles later, I still felt empty. I threw it down, grabbed my keys and wallet, and ran to the bodega. I bought a pint of chocolate peanut butter Haagen-Dazs and a container of organic blueberry yogurt. *Cosmo* had said to use organic.

I put the ice cream in the freezer and took the yogurt to the bathroom, where I took a long, hot shower. Wrapping myself in a towel, it occurred to me that what had been an exciting idea twenty minutes ago now felt pretty stupid. But I had committed.

I pulled off the tinfoil yogurt lid with my teeth and stirred the chunks of blueberry with a fine-toothed comb until the yogurt turned dark magenta. Then I slathered it, first meticulously, and then sloppily, all through my hair, starting at roots and squeezing it down to the tips. Yogurt plopped into the sink and on my feet. Inky, chunky gobs splattered all over the white porcelain and on the bathroom tiles. It was the sound of bird shit hitting pavement.

Steam from the shower had fogged the mirror, and the bathroom smelled like warm milk and fruit pies. I stood, half-naked, scrubbing my head furiously and piercing chunks of berry with my fingernails until they squished out their natural dyes and dripped down my temples.

I never tried beauty tricks in women's magazines. This was just something I could do to completely occupy myself, and hopefully (hardly expectedly at this point), I would be left with softer, healthier locks and a slight twinge of auburn.

It couldn't hurt—it something, anything to eat away at my alone time. The mess took seconds to wipe up, the yogurt only cost $1.39, and it engaged my brain for a good twenty minutes.

"What is that smell?" Lauren asked, standing in our living room, having dropped her bags and coat in a pile. "Ugh, God! It's like grandma smell and fruit."

I didn't have the energy to tell her that in trying to get over the guy—again—I was doing things like dyeing my hair with yogurt because *Cosmo* said so. I didn't know how to explain that behavior to anyone.

I'd been here before—once, twice maybe. It had taken me days, weeks, maybe months—I didn't remember—to get over these feelings. And here I was again, with the tears and debilitating helplessness, my own personal trauma that would eventually shape me into someone new. Here I was again, wanting to spend the rest of my life with a man whose actions led me to do things like dump blueberry yogurt on my head.

In the end, the guys didn't matter. I always healed, and I found ways to get better at getting over them. Even if better sometimes meant sillier. It was as if surviving the pain was proving something.

THE NEXT MORNING, I GOT up and hauled myself to yoga. Back home with midday pasta and a movie, I couldn't shake my guilt. Lauren was with her boyfriend that weekend, and I should have gone home. Everything was about to change, and here I was, spending a plan-less weekend in my shoebox of an apartment, dwelling on boys. I had been lazy. I could have scoured the Internet for a cheap JFK-to-PIT flight.

On October 4, my father was moving to Philadelphia—well, Paoli, to be exact—to have a team of therapists, psychologists, neuropsychologists, behavioral analysts and clinicians (all specific to traumatic brain injury) treat and find solutions for his ongoing deficits: significant drug-seeking and addiction, mood instability, persistent cognitive sequelae, inability to self-monitor behavior, poor social skills, and poor impulse control and decision-making.

My father hadn't had specialized TBI rehabilitation treatment since April of 1997, and that had been post-acute treatment, which is a totally different animal. Not to mention, it had been fifteen years ago. So far, Workers' Comp had agreed to pay for only thirty days at ReMed. Ongoing treatment would be subject to further evaluations.

This was his last weekend at home. It was the beginning of a new chapter, and I wouldn't even be there. I sat on our baby couch, braless in a graphic tee and a pair of Joe's Jeans, coming down off five hours' worth of Showtime series, and feeling sorry for myself. I thought about what I'd be doing if I had gone home.

Coffee. Yes, coffee in the evening. I had brewed a pot between episodes three and four of *Nurse Jackie*. It freaked me out how much Edie Falco could look like my mom. I thought a few cups of strong, black coffee would help me enjoy my Janna time a little bit more than I had been. It didn't. I should've gone home.

At home, my dad would have brewed a strong half pot for my mom and me after we came in from riding. He'd ask what flavor. I would choose French vanilla, and my mom would chose hazelnut, and he'd brew the hazelnut. The coffee would be dark and strong, and the plastic horse-print tray would catch the water that inevitably leaked from the coffee pot. Our kitchen hadn't seen a reliable or functioning brewing system since the Bunn died one day in the late nineties. My mom and I would change out of our barn clothes, sit on the back porch, drink the coffee, and talk. She would hold the cup up to her cheek, bracing the hot ceramic against the bone of her eye socket. She had been doing this with hot coffee cups for as long as I could remember. I did it now too, especially when I was tired. It made me wonder whether my mother had always been tired.

At home, I would have ridden my horse. Thunder was getting old. His black coat was dusted with white along his nose, mane, and hindquarters, and his eyes were cloudy. His back was starting to sway, and he had to eat "old guy food" that he could digest. Thunder wasn't even really my horse. I had taken ownership of him when my dad quit riding.

I should have gone home, had coffee with my mother, and ridden my horse around the field—just once. I should have gone home for my father, too. I had no idea what we'd do or how our time would be spent any differently. My last weekend with *my* dad was fifteen years ago. We'd just gotten back from visiting his cousin and her family in New York, just the two of us. We got home, unpacked, mowed some grass, grilled steaks for dinner, and spent the weekend on the boat. We threw the softball in the backyard—at least, I'd like to think we did. We did that a lot that summer. I wondered which way or how far a softball would go if he tried to throw it now.

If I had gone home, he would have asked me mundane questions about my job, my friends, and the city, and I would have answered each with a lack of enthusiasm. Maybe we'd talk about the Steelers or a movie he had recorded on HBO. He'd show me something in the paper. He'd ask me to take the dog out when we both knew that was one of his "chores," and I'd always say no.

"*Aw* come, Janna, look at her," he'd say. "She wants you to take her out."

"Dad, you take her out," I'd say. "It will be good for you. You both could use a walk."

"Please."

"No, I can't. I'm on my way to …" *Sarah's or Amelia's, Adam's or the bar or to eat, somewhere, anywhere.*

And he'd always rub my shoulders. His clumsy, calloused hands would work to pinch and lift up the muscles that folded over my shoulders. He'd slashed a mower part through his right hand a few years ago when he was high, and now three of his fingers didn't quite work. He couldn't even make a fist without effort, but he'd still rub my shoulders, ending the twenty seconds of painful bliss with a back scratch, something popular on the Leyde side of the family.

I felt sad for him, sad that his daughter, his one kid, wasn't even coming home. I felt sad that at rehab, he was going to miss the most simple things— taking care of the dog, zonking out in front of the TV, his lists of chores, and mornings making coffee with the leaky coffee pot.

Katie had told me that my dad going off to rehab would be just like a kid going off to school. He had to pack up enough things to make a small one-room space feel like home. He'd bring clothes and maybe some pictures, books, and other things on a list he had been given by someone at the facility. Thinking of his personal possessions made me cry. He was my father, and he was not responsible enough with his things to own one quarter of what I did. It was 2010, and the man did not own a cell phone, a car, or a computer. And now he was going away, to live somewhere near Philadelphia, so that he might have the first chance in more than a dozen years to learn how to be more responsible. Like a kid, he thought he was going somewhere to learn.

Higher education—a major in responsibility. He didn't see any of it being about his brain injury, no matter how many times we all told him.

I called the diner, ordered a bagel with lox and then called my mother to tell her that I should have come home.

She chuckled. "Are you rich?"

"Um, no."

"Well, then, you have to stay there," she said. "You don't need to fly home for two days for $500."

"I know. I just wish I could've."

"Janna, it's really no different. You're not missing anything."

I could tell how tired she was. It was in her voice. We talked for an hour about my father, the man who was and wasn't in my life, my father's family, and how she was feeling. I did a lot of listening.

My mother will always say that she doesn't have a lot of words, that she doesn't like talking, or have much of anything interesting to say. It wasn't true. She is always interesting. People are always listening to her and listening to the way her stories of the days and weeks unfold. If anything, she was modest.

"I can't really talk about him with people, except Debbie," she said.

"You do know you can always talk to me about Dad." But she couldn't. How could she tell her daughter how sick of her husband she was? Who could?

"I'm so tired of it," she said. "I'm starting to wonder why I ever married him. I know that's probably not really how I feel, but I don't know how to feel right now. He's so nasty and hard to live with. I feel like I'm in prison."

"Prison? You can't call it that. You did nothing wrong." But I knew, for reasons that I couldn't comprehend, that she felt like she did do something wrong—like there was something she could have done, something different to help him recover better, something different to make the brain injury less for all of us.

"I just don't think I know how severe his brain injury really is. And I cannot understand why I can't pick up on signs of addiction."

"But, Mom, you—"

"I should have seen this sooner. I'm at a complete loss. I can only hope that something—anything—will change during his [now extended] ninety days of rehab. I cannot keep doing this. The pot. The nastiness. The eating.

The laziness. He just doesn't care about anything. I hope they will see that."

"Well, maybe this can be as good for you as it is for him ... you know, give you time to figure out what you want without worrying about him ..."

But she changed the subject to Annie's "brush with death," having fallen asleep at the wheel of my mother's Honda Accord, a hand-me-down gift for her sixteenth birthday. Annie had renamed the Accord Hewie, and she had just smacked Hewie off a guardrail somewhere near Columbus and rolled him into a totaled mess. She walked away in shock with a sore knee and a few bruises from her seat belt. It reminded me of Herman Stillman.

She changed the subject, again, to Eddie. My mother was the only person on the planet who didn't waste energy hating him. While I dwelled on the future and the past, my mother didn't dwell on anything. "Weird, weird behavior, don't you think?" she asked.

"Yeah, maybe. I guess. But everyone is weird. I don't expect any of this to be easy."

"Expect what?"

"Relationships. Since when did people think they were supposed to be that easy? Nothing worth anything is that easy."

"It should be in the beginning, Janna."

When we hung up, I lay sprawled on the apartment floor, sweltering in the Indian summer heat.

I would have to visit my father at ReMed. I hoped it wouldn't be like visiting Gram Mary at the nursing home. I used to take my time driving there and sometimes lie about the amount of time I spent with her. We would just sit. I would wheel her out of her room or away from her lunch, a tray of half-eaten, smashed food. My mother would remind me to make sure she got outside if it was nice. I'd have to punch the buzzer and drag the wheelchair through heavy double doors before the alarm sounded. Sometimes I'd lose, which would create chaos, sending workers running to see who was trying to escape. It was just Mary Eckman and the scowling, twiggy teen struggling with the door. I didn't like interacting with anyone who worked there. I was sure they could smell my hatred.

I would find a spot near the brick wall in the sun, lock the wheelchair brakes, and climb on top of the wall with my legs dangling down the side. Gram Mary never said anything, just slumped to one side with her thick glasses barely balancing on her nose. Her hands, though always manicured and clean, were cold and shook constantly. She was sick, and her brain was numb, and all that was left of Gram Mary was a goofy smile. I should've done more with her, been a better granddaughter in the end. I could have told her stories or painted her nails red.

I would try harder when visiting my father. I would smile, talk to the staff, and engage in whatever there was to engage in. I pictured physical fitness, group activities, and cafeterias. I had no idea what you could do with a sixty-year-old man with a severe frontal lobe TBI and an addiction to pot. What could anyone possibly do for him in ninety days?

The door buzzer startled me. I gathered cash for my bagel.

"Seriously, what can they do in ninety days?" I asked out loud. "Fuck you, Workers' Comp. Only ninety days. Fuck you."

"Dad, you are not going to *care* about *bread-ed chic-ken*," I said into the phone for third time, over-enunciating so he could understand through the cell connection.

"What?"

"Dad! Don't write in a journal about what you eat! Write about what you feel!"

"Oh."

Calling my dad after work or yoga had become part of my routine in the past two weeks. Many times, it was taxing, listening as he told me what he read in *Rolling Stone* or about the puzzle he was working on or what he bought at Walmart.

We even talked about my mother. I was pissed and whiny, because I thought she had no help. The most recent problem was Gram and Pa and how they had called her from Columbus to be picked up, which led into a bigger discussion about their need for care. My aunts wanted my mother's help. I got it. It was hard. I didn't get what it felt like to be burdened with deciding how to care for aging parents. Sure, my father's situation was a unique emotional difficulty, but it was my mother who took the real responsibility for him. I didn't get what it was to be in my eighties, or what it was like to see my parents in their eighties. But I understood difficulty. And I didn't want to see my mother take on the responsibility. I was ranting.

"Yes, your mom needs to have a break," he said. "She is always the one to accept the burdens. I worry how she got to Columbus to pick them up."

I was speechless. I'd have to call her later: Dad cared.

"So, how's the new job?" he asked.

"Oh. I don't start until next week. I think I'll be happier, though."

"I guess you can just go into the lobby on Monday, and they'll tell you where to go," he said.

"Yeah, Dad. I guess so." I laughed.

"So you will be doing marketing work, for *Veranda?* And you think you'll like that better than advertising?"

"I do. I'll miss *Bazaar,* but this is a better opportunity. I have to take it ..."

"I think it's good what you are doing. You never know what will happen, but I think this was a good move."

This conversation was one flabbergasting thing after the other—first the brain injury talk, then his empathy for Mom. And how did he put all the pieces together to know that I had a new job in the same building but at a different magazine? He even referred to my mother as "your mom" rather than "Claudia." Who the hell was processing his thoughts?

"I know I am different," he said.

"I know, but do you actually feel that way? Do you really understand how?" I had to push it. Why did I always have to push things?

"Oh yes, yes. I do. They are helping me. I used to think that a brain injury was something that other people wanted me to have. I used to think everyone else was different. I'm starting to understand that now. They are helping me understand the brain."

Holy shit. He was speaking with a conviction I hadn't heard in years—using real sentences without prompts. I wondered what the people at ReMed were doing with him each day to catalyze such profound changes. He'd barely been there two weeks, and he was expounding on the frontal lobe, executive functioning, and finding coping mechanisms. He told me about the seat belt and about how it crushed eleven ribs and caused his brain to rattle around inside his head, creating multiple bruises. He told me he had a "—diffuse brain injury," we said at the same time.

My mom had been waiting for me at the Amtrak station in Paoli. The rain was depressing and our coffees weren't hot enough. After some navigating, we found Paoli Pike and then ReMed.

"This is it?" I asked.

"It's actually pretty nice," she said. "They live in rooms in separate buildings at the end of this driveway. There is a nice pond out back and a deck."

I couldn't understand. Nothing about what I was seeing matched what I had seen on ReMed's website. We drove up a dirt path, past a backhoe, past a dilapidated house and parked in front of a few buildings that looked like they had lived in trailer parks at a KOA campground in some past life.

As I unloaded the trunk, my father came outside to meet us, his hands wrapped and clasped around behind him, resting on the small of his back. He was smiling, hobbling toward us. I watched my parents exchange an awkward kiss and followed them into his building, carrying too many things in both hands.

"Do you know where we're supposed to meet?" my mom asked after dropping his bags in his room.

We were having a family meeting. Given that the surroundings were not as pristine and medicinal as I'd pictured, I wasn't surprised that the meeting took place in one of the therapist's offices. It was crowded with folding chairs arranged in the center of small room and a desk, a desk chair, and a giant desktop computer. One wall was crammed with books. The other held a collection of framed degrees and certificates. There were dozens of people on his team, but only three were there, seeing as it was the day before Thanksgiving.

My father's psychologist, one of the clinical specialists, and the clinical director sat down with my mother, my father, and me. I sat on my folding chair, sipping a now-cold cafe mocha, and listened to everyone fill us in on how he was doing. Everyone seemed to like my father and enjoy his company. Everyone thought he was smart.

They told us that he had been verbalizing motivation to change, showing some insight into his difficulties. But this worried my mother, their instant belief in him. In her own words, she repeatedly told them, "He's an excellent bullshitter." *He was.* And my father—still with his drug-seeking, lying, stealing, lack of motivation, mood instability, persistent cognitive sequelae, and poor social skills, impulse control, and decision-making—told us that he wanted "the staff at ReMed to change my brain."

The team at ReMed established a treatment theme of sorts for him: to understand that his behaviors were putting him at risk to lose his primary support system—his wife, who had been feeling "emotionally and verbally abused." They also put him on a medication trial period, back on Risperdal to address his problems with executive functioning. It was evident that these people cared, that these medical professionals knew what they were doing, knew about brain injury. They were not simply prescribing antidepressants and sending him home to hope for the best. They were trialing cognitive behavioral strategies to help remind him of his acceptable behaviors. He wore an elastic band—not a rubber band, but something more like a LiveStrong band—around his wrist to remind him that he had a brain injury. And he used a written cue card to help him remember his acceptable behaviors.

Since his arrival, he'd been showing signs of progression. He was making conscious decisions regarding appropriate conversation topics and telling fewer bad jokes and crude stories. He did laundry and kept his room clean. He did jigsaw puzzles, drew pictures, and painted with watercolors. He had been pleasurable on outings to the store and to the movies. And he could correctly count his change.

I sat in the room, my legs cold from the metal of the chair, sipping my cold mocha, listening to specialists discuss my father's numerous deficits and improvements. It was oddly too familiar. I felt like I was having an out-of-body experience. I was fourteen, watching an older, more articulate version of myself ask intelligent questions and point things out about our father, discussing his treatments and the effects his injury had on our family. These things were easy to discuss in front of my family, but here, being received as an equal, it was strange to see all my suggestions warranting head nods and notations. I looked out the window and over the pond. This afternoon made me feel like his accident had just happened.

The meeting lasted three hours, the last hour of which I really had to pee, which was a welcome distraction from my maudlin emotions. I didn't want to miss anything, so I just tapped my heel on the bar of the chair.

After we finished, one of my dad's housemates suggested we have dinner at the Paoli Diner. The three of us ordered sandwiches and talked about my father's brain injury, his life at rehab, and his list of behaviors to improve upon. He didn't appear frustrated by any of it. We ordered dessert and talked about my life in New York and my new job. When it was time to leave, my mother gave me money to pay up front and went to the bathroom. She said something to my father after I'd gotten up from the table. He joined me at the register, handed me a mint, and we waited for my mother.

"Did you leave the tip there, John?"

"Yes," he said.

"Janna, did you check the table?" my mom asked.

"What do you mean?"

She went back to our table and returned, livid. "Can't you learn anything?" She walked up to him and held out her hand. "Give it to me!"

He reached into his pocket and handed her seven crumpled dollars. She gave me the wad of cash. I walked it back to the table, trying to block out her lecture to him, which got louder as they stepped outside. I was embarrassed. It had never occurred to me that he would steal a tip right in front of me, right after we'd discussed "this type of behavior."

"Mom, I'm sorry."

"You have to watch him, Janna. I told you. He lies, and he steals."

Back at the Embassy Suites, my mom and I didn't talk much about what happened. I told her stuff about my friends, and she told me stories about the Suhries. We rented *Going the Distance* and fell asleep in separate beds while it was still playing. The next morning, while my mother met with one of Dad's behavioral counselors, I went to his room to make sure he was ready to go. I found him sitting at the communal card table with the jigsaw puzzle, wearing stained blue pants and a sweatshirt.

"Dad, you can't wear that," I said. "It's Thanksgiving. You need to change."

"Okay, you tell me what to wear."

I picked out a pair of khakis and a green sweater that I'd seen him wear before. His clothing options were scarce, like the rest of the stuff in his room. Three books—*Scarlet, 1776,* and something by James Patterson—were on his night stand along with an electronic *New York Times* crossword game my mother had bought him, two rubber bands, one pencil, one pen, his planner, and a Kleenex box. His digital camera and a pair of family photos sat on the windowsill. An empty hamper sat at the base of his bed, which was made up with a Beatles throw from our living room couch.

"Those don't fit me," he said, putting the khaki pants on the single wooden chair between the closet and the window.

"Sure they do; I just saw you wear them."

"They don't fit," he said, lifting his shirt and smacking his bare stomach to show that the navy pants were also too tight, barely held in place by a belt in which he'd crudely punched an extra hole for more room.

"Well, can you try?"

He sat on the bed and took off the blue pants. He stood up, wearing only briefs, and retrieved the pair of khakis. He struggled to put one leg in and then the other. He was breathing hard, red in the face. He looked up at me, helpless.

He stood, tottering, and sucked his stomach in while tugging at the waist. He grunted and sighed in his first unsuccessful attempt to button the pants. He hobbled over, grabbed the belt from chair, and threaded it through the loops. With the button and zipper still undone, he cinched the belt on the last hole. Then he put on the green sweater and tugged it down well past his hips.

"Dad, you can't do that."

"Do what?"

"You cannot wear your pants like that and cover it with a sweater."

"Sure I can. I am right now."

"Ha." *Literal. Funny, Dad.* "Fat chance."

"What? I have the pants on, the pair *you* wanted."

Oh, he didn't mean it to be funny. "Dad, you can't wear your pants like that. You just can't. I'm sorry. How is it even comfortable?"

"It's not."

"Let's try another pair," I said, handing him a pair of jeans.

For ten minutes, we went through the same process. He asked for my help with the buttoning. It was harder than saddling Thunder. We both gave up, and I sat on his bed and started laughing. The whole event was so sad and pathetic that it was almost hilarious. He stood there, looking at me, wearing a green sweater and a pair of baggy briefs. Laughing was better than crying. There was nothing either of us could do. He was not my father. Well, he was my father. This man was my father.

Quite an epiphany—this man was my father.

wild occupation, strange situation

IT ALWAYS SMELLED LIKE PINE AT Christmastime at Gram Mary's house. Even though it was our house now, it still smelled like pine. It made me happy. I was happy to be home, happy for the coffee and the snow on the ground. Happy to be away from my job. Happy—at this moment, at least—to be out with Amelia, even if being out meant watching her get her hair cut. I'd agreed to come in exchange for stopping at the outlet mall so I could pick up one last gift for my mother. Tomorrow was my favorite day of the year, Christmas Eve.

"What are you doing, you dork?" asked Amelia, who sat dutifully upright, hair wrapped in a towel.

"Nothing," I said, unscrewing the top to a shampoo bottle and sticking my nose in. "I'm smelling this. It smells like home."

"You're a weirdo."

"So what's *this*?" her hairstylist asked me, reaching over and flicking my bangs out of place with his comb. "You know, with a widow's peak like you have—"

"—I know. I know. Trust me, they work." My bangs did work. It wasn't like I was hearing this for the first time. Besides, this morning, my hair had been lathered with Suave Professionals, rinsed with well water, and styled with whatever poor excuse for a round brush I could dig out of my mom's collection.

"You could try a straightening iron," he said, cutting apart my thoughts with more hair advice I wasn't going to consider.

"It's not like I'm on a date this morning," I said. "You gotta give a girl's bangs a break."

He laughed, and the topic of conversation quickly shifted from hair to boys. As the stylist chopped layers into Amelia's blunt ends, he schooled us on the fail-safe ways to find a man—a "mate," in his words.

"You girls gotta play the game, and you must avoid social networks."

"And texting, right?" I asked, pulling out my Blackberry.

"Yes!" He flicked the comb in my direction.

"It's 2010, and it's the only way that people talk anymore," I said. "It positively sucks."

"See you tomorrow," I texted my dad. He had just gotten a phone. It was nothing like the smartphones my friends and I now had, but its existence proved that he, too, existed in this technological world. I had no idea who, if anyone, texted him, so I made sure I did.

"I'm not going on any dates if boys ask me via text," said Amelia.

Buzz. "I miss you. U, your mom, the dog and the horses." Dad.

"I miss you, too," I texted back.

He was supposed to miss those things, us. And I was supposed to miss him. I told myself that I should. It was the holidays, and he was far away from his family. I sat, staring at the back of Amelia's head, zoning out to the hair guy's rant about Facebook. I bounced it around in my mind—the missing of my father—a thought that flails between missing him now and missing who he was fourteen years ago.

Buzz. "I love you vry much," Dad.

"Love you, too," I texted back. Then I texted the boy from DC about snowfall in western Pennsylvania.

Buzz. "We have some too. Driving the diesel :)" the boy texted back.

I blamed my attachment to him on Lauren. She had told me to give him a chance when he had started a conversation with me at Adam's annual Nog and Hog Christmas party a few weeks ago. Lauren had convinced me to keep talking to him, because he was *so nice*, because *I needed someone nice*, and because *it's not about types, Jan.*

I had convinced Lauren to road trip it down to DC with me, explaining that we both were due for a weekend away—a little testosterone fix, a break from dates gone wrong, long work hours, intense Manhattan, and a chance for me to kick this Eddie thing for good. She hated Eddie.

And I was busy hating the thought of spending the second holiday—Christmas—in horrible Philadelphia. I wanted to be strong, to buck up and quit complaining, but I couldn't. For this, I hated myself. All the hate had left me exhausted and angry. I needed DC and needed Lauren to come with me. I needed to wear a cocktail dress and hang out with the boys. I needed enough booze to make me forget about Eddie. I needed enough booze to make me forget about brain injury.

Nog and Hog turned out exactly as I had hoped—festive and boozy, full of friends, food, wine, and ugly sweaters—an evening that bled into the morning. Around midnight, I found myself out in the driveway with Adam's friend. It was cold and spitting rain, but after our talk of watersports, football, and hatred of plastic bags, he'd wanted to show off his low-emission truck. When it got too cold, we went back inside and remained inseparable until the next day, when Lauren and I had to leave brunch in the third quarter of the Steelers game to head back to New York.

It rained the whole way. It didn't matter. We sang along to a Gin Blossoms CD that Annie had made me, reminisced about the '90s, and recounted the weekend.

"Look at you, Jan," Lauren had said, poking me in the arm.

"What? Look at what?"

"You. You're happy."

"*Ha.* Maybe. I mean, I'm hung over. I mean … I'm not hungover, I'm tired. Really tired."

"Oh please. You're happy. I told you."

"Yeah, yeah. I know. He's just the kind of person that makes me re-believe in stuff. I needed that. Whatever. It's amazing not to be thinking about my dad or *Veranda* or stupid old Ed—"

"—I know. *Exactly.* See what happens when you listen to me."

"Fine, yeah. *You* told me so. You sound just like Claudia."

She smiled and poked me again.

"Keep your eye out for a Dairy Queen," I said.

"*Blizzards!*"

"*Gin Blossoms!*"

Lauren had been so right, I thought, now bored with the haircutting. I couldn't remember the last time I enjoyed talking to someone so much or if I ever had. Talking to this guy made me want to forget all the crap, all the emotional garbage from my past. He was different, simple and grounded. He was sweet, and something about him made me want to pursue things rather than fear them. But we didn't talk about that.

"Who are you texting?" Amelia yelled into the mirror.

"My dad," I said, lying. I was happy to still be talking to Adam's friend.

Buzz. "I miss you." Dad, again.

I did miss him a lot. I missed the way he'd sip a beer; the foam would cling to his mustache, and he'd wipe it clean with his thumb and forefinger. I missed the way he used to wrestle the dog, Meagan, getting her overly excited by swatting her head back and forth between his palms. I missed how he'd tap his thumbs on the steering wheel to every single drumbeat the song on the stereo had to offer. I missed his old wardrobe—shirts, ties, and wool sport coats with khakis. I missed his pancakes and his crappies in the deep fryer on the front porch and his well-done steaks. I missed his love of poetry, the way he'd make me memorize everything from Longfellow to Silverstein. I missed watching him hug my mother, wrapping his arms around her whole body while she leaned her head against his chest. I missed arguing, waterskiing, and playing backgammon with him. I missed his jokes—the ones that were funny.

"Stop being so quiet!" Amelia yelled.

"Sorry, checking my work mail," I said, lying, again. "God, this job blows."

"Where's your dad, again?"

"Paoli, PA," I said. "Close to Philly."

"Why is your dad there?" asked the stylist.

"Oh, ya know. He's in, um … rehab," I said. "Not for booze. He has a brain injury—a TBI, a traumatic brain injury."

Sometimes that came out so easily it was awkward for other people. In fact, I had no idea why I told Amelia's hair guy this—maybe to shut him up about my bangs or boys. I hated Paoli. I could barely take it seriously, it and all of Philadelphia. I didn't even know if I missed him at all. I didn't want to spend another holiday in the Embassy Suites.

"What's out there?" Amelia asked.

"Oh, not much," I said. "It's no Pottstown."

Pottstown was where her dad lived. I'd spent a few days out there with her two summers ago. During the day, we drank daiquiris concocted by her stepmom and bummed around luxuriously by the pool. At night, we drank beers and hung out with people we didn't know. I liked being that close to the Yuengling plant, but we never visited.

Paoli, Pennsylvania was a pike, a town, a two-hour train ride southwest of New York City. I had met a girl at my friend's holiday party a few weeks ago who had compared the train to Paoli to a warm holiday drink, a welcoming to friends and relatives. I thought about how I had stood in the kitchen of the people throwing the party, leaning against a fridge, sipping on a bottle of Sam Adam's Winter Lager, wanting to vomit as this very nice girl who was about my age talked about how much she *loved* going to Paoli for the holidays. Instead, I smiled and took mental notes on where my parents and I might be able to have Christmas Eve dinner. To me, the train was the opposite—a steel tube transporting me to a puzzle of suburban roads that unearthed a feeling that made me want to cry with each sign and turn. Paoli was suffocating. Paoli, Dad's rehab, the last place I wanted spend the holidays. It reeked of conversations that I hated having revolving around topics that were now all too familiar: Risperdal, executive functioning, caregiver, cognitive sequelae, behavioral tips, therapists, money, stealing, weight, driving, pot, puzzles.

I hated the puzzles. I hated hearing him talk about how he fit the pieces in that day, how this day he had help, how that day he bought another one at the Walmart on their trip to the movies. The puzzles made me want to vomit. These days he talked about puzzles instead of his brain injury. His understanding of that had been relatively fleeting. Or maybe I was asking too much. It didn't matter—I was never going to like puzzles.

"And you leave tomorrow?" Amelia asked.

"You betcha."

"Do you think he's sad?" I asked my mom the next day as I drove us across Pennsylvania. It was a dismal day.

"Yeah, I don't think he likes being there," she said. "I just hope he changes, just something. I'm pretty skeptical."

"I don't understand why it's taken this long to get him the right kind of treatment. It's been fifteen years."

"The insurance company, Janna."

"I know. I know. But it's unreal that they were able to keep putting this off."

"People don't understand brain injury. You can't see it. You can't see how bad it is."

"Who cares? They are supposed to pay for his treatment, his care, his medications, right? Who cares if you can or can't see it?"

"Right, but they are still trying *not* to. This is the first time they've had to pay in a long time."

And now we got to have Christmas in Paoli, I thought, but did not say. *It was exactly where we should be, for my father, lugging bags of wrapped presents up to our drab, Christmas-tree-less room at the Embassy Suites.*

When we got there, we picked up my dad and went to dinner at an Italian place that my friend's friend had recommended for fish on Christmas Eve. After dinner, we took my dad back. He had wanted to go to the movies, but he had a 9:00 curfew. At the hotel, my mom and I sat up and talked for a while. Then we watched a movie that was so crappy, we couldn't remember it the next morning.

The next day, we ate our Christmas meal at a Bucca de Beppos. As best I could tell, it was us and a few Jewish families taking advantage of the fact that this one restaurant was open. The last time I'd been to a Bucca de Beppos was my twenty-first birthday. While we sat waiting for the breadbasket, I asked my dad whether he remembered it. He didn't. Neither did my mother until I told them the story of how they'd waited there with Ryan, how I had arrived late with Krystal, how I hadn't done my hair, and how we got a free jug of wine from the Italian men who sat next to us. She nodded at some of the details and apologized "for not remembering *everything* anymore."

I picked at the mound of spaghetti bolognese on my plate. It was sticky. I excused myself to the bathroom. I wound around the empty rooms of the restaurant, following a sign path of pointing fingers. In the bathroom, I locked the door, stood at the sink, and stared into the mirror, trying to cry. I thought I should cry, because I was sad, and this was sad. But Christmas in Philadelphia felt more like reality, like something I was so familiar with that it was impossible to cry anymore. I rummaged through my pocketless giant purse, looking for my phone. Someone knocked once, and then twice on the door. I had hoped to see a Merry Christmas text from the boy. I did. I reapplied a bright red lip gloss, unlocked the door, and left. At the table, my mother had ordered me a second glass of wine.

We talked about my dad's continuing treatment and the impending move to a different ReMed facility in Pittsburgh the week after Christmas. My mom would have to drive back here and pick him up on her birthday.

The Pittsburgh treatment team would proceed with many of the same goals as before: behavior management, "stopping and thinking," drug-seeking and addiction, poor impulse control and decision-making, and persistent cognitive sequelae. They would continue working with his biggest cognitive barriers, which were his lack of awareness and memory impairment. My father still saw himself as fine, though (whether he agreed with it or not) he was beginning to recognize that others saw something wrong with him. His pillbox would remain abundant with capsules and tablets for daily intake: Risperdal, Paxil, Propranolol, Depakote ER, Prilosec (the high blood pressure had come back), Namenda, Miralax (something new), and a multivitamin.

The team in Pittsburgh would also monitor him for signs of depression and investigate options that would support his goal—his wife's goal—of losing weight. He had gained more than twenty pounds at ReMed, where he was encouraged to exercise every day and eat well. Encouragement was clearly not enough. Marital counseling with a therapist (one who specifically worked with TBI couples) and AA and NA meetings, all once a week, also came highly recommended. And no more naps—his schedule would keep him active from 9:00 to 5:00 so that he could "develop a tolerance for daily activities."

After dinner, we drove back to the hotel, turned on the local NPR station's selection of Christmas music, sat on the beds, and opened our piles of Christmas presents in the chilly, Christmas-tree-less hotel room at the Embassy Suites.

MY MOTHER HAD NEVER LIKED her birthday. Once, when I was kid, my father threw her a surprise party, which led to a big fight. I didn't understand why or what was so terrible, but I took her side, because it was her birthday, and it had made her unhappy. She will tell anyone that she does not like surprises.

Sixteen birthdays after that, my mother drove to Philadelphia to pick up my father. He didn't wish her a happy birthday, didn't buy her a card or a present. He didn't even acknowledge it. Before she dropped him off, they went to lunch or maybe dinner, where she mentioned that he could have at least said *something*, seeing as how she was spending the day switching him from one rehab place to the other and doing a lot of driving.

"It's your birthday," he said. "You can spend it however you want to. I'm not going to stop you."

I had called to wish her a happy birthday from New York. She had sounded fine on the phone, though she later gave away how nasty he had been that day. He'd been angry, as if he thought if he did well enough in Philadelphia that he could get out of going to ReMed in Pittsburgh. I was so frustrated with him that I quit calling him every day. I chose to stay out of his rehab business and concentrate on my own life, which was unraveling at the start of 2011. I had a new job and recently a new boss, the latter of which had me perpetually frazzled, and any expectations I'd set for this new year had dissolved into a constant fight to make my job situation, which was slipping into unbearable, manageable. I was losing myself, disenchanted with everything.

Krystal came for the long weekend over New Year's. We celebrated with my friends, all of us expectant and eager for the newness that came with one decade rolling into the next. A new year, a hopeful stop to the unraveling.

But a few weeks into January, I was searching for a new job, my mother was fighting the flu, and my father was punching people.

I hadn't talked to either of my parents over the long Presidents Day weekend. Lauren's brother had been in town, and we had spent the weekend brunching, dancing, and drinking to celebrate her birthday. Now Tuesday, back at my desk, I tried to caffeinate away a headache with a weak cup from the Hearst Cafeteria. I switched from my work e-mail to Gmail and saw an e-mail from my mother: "Weather and your dad and etc ..."

I opened it, and a novel filled my computer screen. I cut and pasted the 577 words from my very personal-looking Gmail account into my very professional-looking Outlook account. My mid-level marketing job had morphed into an entry-level joke, and I was tapped out of the mundane tasks for the day. I closed all the other programs, sipped on my coffee, and started reading.

HI!

Got to work today—after the doctor and some medication ...

Something told me your dad would have problems in this new facility, and he is. It is very structured. I'm not sure he is up for that. It is kind of a long story, but someone accused him of swearing at them and slapped him in the face. First wrong move. Then he hit them back—second wrong move. Hit them hard enough that they were knocked down and went to the hospital and had a concussion. Really not good. So your father is being ostracized by the residents. I talked to the caseworker for about half an hour this a.m. He has been staring at people, flipping people off, mouthing f/u, etc. Real passive aggressive and intimidating … stuff we've seen bits and pieces of. But the swearing surprises me. He's telling them that no one likes him, which I am surprised that he even cares about. So now he is making sure that no one likes him. I think the person he hit was a resident, but I am not sure. I also think he is with higher functioning residents than in the last place and he is feeling his deficits, so he is going to feel intimidated. We don't compete with him most of the time, so he doesn't feel the need to be "the best." I don't know. Not that I want him to behave that way, but I'm feeling a little confirmation about my observations of his behaviors over the years. I am feeling a little less crazy.

Of course the story he told me was the very tip of the story. And I was too sick to really push him or actually care.

The case manager kept saying he was exhibiting brain injury behavior and that actually it was good this was showing up so they could work with him. Doesn't make it appropriate, but it is not unexpected. Of course they contacted Philly, and they had seen none of that behavior. He was on his good behavior there! Here I am not sure he is ready for the challenge. When challenged he gets mean instead of trying to get better. This will be interesting—more "stuff" for your book!

Don't get all worked up about it. This treatment should have happened a long time ago and his behaviors should have been challenged a long time ago. Wonder if they will get his time extended. Don't tell him he can't come home if he doesn't get it together, because he will cover stuff up then get away with it. We need to figure out what he can and cannot control.

Don't forget the therapist!

XO

Mom

My mother had voiced the same concern to the team in Pittsburgh as she had to the team in Philly—to please be sure that he did not just float through his stay at ReMed. "He's smart, and he will act the way he needs to get his way," she told them. "And please help John find things to do that help him lose weight." He had gained forty-five pounds since he'd left in October, which infuriated her.

For most of the first week in Pittsburgh, my father was oddly antisocial, sitting in the community center with his arms crossed, staring at the other residents. When anyone asked what he was doing, he looked at them with the glare of a madman and silently mouthed obscenities. He was described as antagonistic.

On the fifth day, he got into an argument with another client. It was over something trivial, but the man, who felt antagonized, slapped my father in the face. My father hit him back, knocking him to the floor, which resulted in a concussion. In the days that followed, my father had to meet with the various members of his team until he was able to admit that he was partially at fault (the antagonizing) and to realize that hitting back was not the way to respond. He told them that he would no longer antagonize other clients or mouth obscenities. A few days later, he voluntarily apologized to the man he had hit and to the other residents.

Once again my dad's brain injury was lost on him, so in Pittsburgh his ongoing deficits and current barriers were tackled with more forceful and tailored strategies—new treatments, implemented by a new team. It was now clear to everyone involved that my father would need ongoing home support after his scheduled discharge date in March. Someone other than my mother needed to monitor his activities, sobriety, and behavior on a daily basis.

Now that he was closer to home, he was able to leave on weekends for "home visits," but at home my mother did not see the improvement that she was looking for. He was not able to initiate tasks on his own and did not attempt to make up his own schedule for the day. It seemed like he was regressing, significantly. She asked him to write a list of five things he needed to quit doing. She thought a simple list might trigger the new behaviors, the ones he had learned about in ReMed in Philadelphia, the behaviors that he was supposed to be practicing at home and at ReMed in Pittsburgh. He wrote them out on a piece of computer paper and carried them around in his pocket—his "Don't List."

Don't Lie
Don't Steal
Don't Overeat
Don't Preach
Don't Use Drugs

At rehab, when asked to recite his Don't List, he couldn't remember it without looking at it, so his therapists helped him chunk the list into "things you do with your mouth" (lie, overeat, preach, drugs) and "the thing you do without your mouth" (steal), but that way of remembering also proved ineffective. Further breakdown was necessary: "things you take in through your mouth" (overeat, drugs), "things that come out of your mouth" (lie, preach), and "the other thing" (steal).

When he told me about the categorizing of his Don't List, I got confused. Wasn't there some therapist who could come up with a mnemonic for this?

In truth, the Don't List was about practicing boundaries and behaviors around other people. When seen this way, it became a slightly more tangible concept for him, as it was in my dad's nature to want to interact with people. He wanted interaction with anyone: family, strangers, friends, servers at restaurants. The Don't List—his outlawed behaviors— was understood as "what *not* to do around other people." Understood, but still a hard-won concept on my father.

IT WAS ONLY THURSDAY, ONLY the fourth day of one of the most trying weeks so far that year. Thank God for Spencer. She was my friend and coworker at *Veranda,* one of the best work friends I'd had at a job since the luxury magazines. Spencer and I had planted ourselves on the barstools at Bricco, the Italian restaurant with the radioactive-green olives, across the street from the Hearst Tower. Having just drained our trillionth glass of Pinot Noir, we realized they were closing and that we were being kindly kicked out. It was all of 10:00 p.m., and neither Spencer nor I wanted to go home. But staying out later, like we did the night before, might not be worth the dual hangovers at work tomorrow.

Home. It was woefully decided.

I bundled my scarf around my neck twice and cinched the belt of my black wool coat so tight it jabbed under my ribs. I walked a few blocks, studying the sensation of the belt, thinking about how at least I'd managed to stay skinny. It was the yoga that allowed me to stay skinny and sleep harder and think a little more clearly.

I remembered my mother's e-mail. I had not written back. I bit the fingertips of my red leather glove and pulled it off my hand. It was cold, snowing, almost too cold to hold an exposed hand up to my ear, but there were pieces of life, details that we needed to exchange—my dad in Pittsburgh and my meeting with Human Resources.

"Hello?" She was groggy.

"Hi!" I was drunk.

I had woken her up. I took my phone away from my ear to look at it. It was 10:34 p.m. "Oh, I'm sorry," I said. "You were asleep. You can go back bed. I just thought I'd call you on my walk home. Spencer and I got wine, again."

"No, you're fine. I just fell asleep reading, that's all."

"What were you reading?"

"Just a book. ... How was the meeting with HR?"

I had made the appointment, because everyone had said that it would be a good idea to go to HR to simply inform them of the situation. The situation was that my new boss was a lunatic. She seemed to have no sense of work/life balance and possessed a penchant for mistaking nonsensical rants for constructive criticism. In short, I hated her. I hated her perverse wants and needs as a superior. I hated her red wine-stained lips and her pleather trench coat that squeaked like cheap plastics rubbing together anytime she took a breath. I hated how she was always reminding me about her undergraduate education from NYU. I hated her arrogance.

I hated that because of her, I couldn't do it anymore, couldn't do magazines with their hierarchical climb to the top. But perhaps secretly I didn't hate it, not fully. Maybe I loved having a real reason to get the fuck out of Dodge.

"It was fine, completely in confidence, and purely to inform them, as you told me to." I tried my best to give my mother a description of the forty-five-minute meeting with the cheery, plump woman wearing a red patterned blouse and black pants. I was running out of meaningful details. The rep and I could have discussed the situation into the ground, because absolutely no action would be taken. She had advised me to keep a positive attitude and to keep looking for other jobs.

"You just have to keep a good attitude, no matter what you do, no matter what other options you explore," my mom echoed.

"Mom, I know that," I said. "You know I know that. Even she told me that."

"You may know that, but I want to make sure that is what you are doing." I could hear her voice starting to wake up.

"Well, I am. I'm keeping up the positive attitude. It's just so exhausting, and I hate this woman, and I'm so tired of all of it."

I was whining. I was drunk. I thought about changing the subject to something less frustrating—like therapy. I had a therapist now. He let me come in early on Mondays, because that was the only time I could fit it in. Eight a.m., before work and before any of his other clients. He was older, old, and wore a lot of tweed, which perfectly complemented his dim, den-like office on the Upper West Side. I liked knowing that he had started this gig on his leather chair long before the Internet and text messaging and Gmail had taken over how we talked to one another.

He and I talked more about the men in my life, and my talents—writing, yoga, talking, adapting, making friends with guys, understanding others—than we talked about my father. After a few sessions, I introduced him to the brain injury I lived with, but we always talked about me, no matter how mundane or trivial my life seemed in comparison to the never-ending intricacies of my father's rattled frontal lobe.

I didn't experience any revelations in his office—no *a-ha* moments, no tearful breakthroughs. But slowly, through stories of boys, friends, and the magazine industry, he helped me admit to my unhealthy patterns.

I chose "non-involved involved" men. As soon as he uttered this potentially made-up phrase, I got it. I so beautifully understood what he meant that I wanted to hug him, or maybe applaud him. I chose men who wanted to be a part of my life, to talk, flirt, laugh, argue, challenge, and plan things with me. Whether it was for their own confidence or for real, it didn't matter, because the second I showed emotional vulnerability, *poof!* They were gone. So I would board up my feelings and needs, and there we were again—talking, flirting, laughing, arguing, challenging and planning.

Sure, these men were involved in my life, but in a way so lackadaisical that I could now look back and see that I was the idiot for seeing commitment where there most obviously wasn't. I had myself fooled, thinking that if I could tone down my emotions (or whatever it was that was *too much* for them) then one of these men would stay. I had high expectations, but I found a zillion reasons to lower them when it came to men. Lowering my expectations was a talent my therapist wanted me to drop.

He told me to quit my job. He told me to quit the industry. He told me to write. He pumped me so full of self-worth in that office, digging up my long-lost self-confidence, that same confidence my mother had been asking me about for the last decade.

Before I brought up therapy to my mother, she changed the subject for me. "Well, have you had any hits?"

Hits—her favorite way to refer to job prospects—and, in the coming years, online dates.

"No ..."

"Where have you applied? How many places?"

"Oh, you know, like ten. It's exhausting. I just want to move to DC. Everyone is there. All kinds of stuff I like is there. All the boys." I was carrying on about DC and the boys and nature adventures while simultaneously planning my bodega bagel order in my head. *Toasted pumpernickel bagel, lettuce, tomato, salt and pepper. Roast beef—no. Chicken salad.*

"You can't just up and move there, Janna."

Here we go, I thought, yanking open the bodega door and smiling at the Indian man behind the counter. I leaned against the wall behind the row of baked goods, produce, and Doritos. This conversation had now become a discussion, and it was too cold to stand outside, and I really needed this bagel sandwich in my life.

"You cannot just decide you want to up and move," she said while I silently pointed at the ingredients behind the counter and handed the man a bagel. "You need to keep looking where you are, and apply to jobs everywhere. Have you looked in Florida, or what about North Carolina? Stop beating yourself up over this. You wanted to work in magazines. You wanted to move to New York. You've realized that dream, and maybe it's just not what you thought it would be. That's okay."

"Mom, I know. I just—"

"You're not letting me finish!"

"Okay!"

"You need to calm down about this and stop having such a negative attitude."

I looked at the time on my phone—11:12 p.m. I was tired, hungry, and drunk.

"Fine, I will stay positive, and I won't show my apathy, but know that I really do not care what my boss thinks of me," I said. "I understand that the best idea is not to get fired. It's not high school. I'm not a doormat. I promise you. I don't let people walk all over me anymore. No one pats me on the head."

"And you need to can it with that DC guy." She'd flipped subjects on me again. "He probably *is* very interesting. But are you being very interesting right now? Would you want to be talking to you like this?"

"He is!" I said, picking up a bag of Cool Ranch Doritos. "He really is, so … yeah, I know. No I wouldn't. I'm not so hot right now."

"No, you're not. Come on, Janna."

"Not what, Mom?"

"You know this behavior is not interesting."

"I know. Okay. I know. I'm a mess. It's this job, or I don't know. I'm just not fulfilled."

Outside, bagel sandwich in hand, winter near the West Side Highway was slapping me sober. I started to feel bad, bad for calling my mother when I was drunk, and bad for ordering food while I was on the phone with her. I unlocked my door and threw my coat at the coat tree. It fell to the floor. I didn't bother to pick it up and ignored Lauren who was watching TV. Still on the phone, I went into the kitchen, filled a glass with water, and sat on the floor with my sandwich.

"I wish Dad were here to tell me what I should do." Such a ridiculous thing to say. I'd been silently wishing it for fifteen years, never saying it out loud. There was no point to actually talking about it. I had really drunk way too much pinot.

"He'd say it's not work if you're having fun."

"That's stupid. You know what I mean." I slouched against the refrigerator and propped up my boot-clad feet on the face of the dishwasher, aligning them as if they were in the rubbery binding of my slalom ski. I tapped the chunky heels on the metal. It was as inappropriate as my childhood habit of tapping my feet against the glove box of my mom's Jetta.

"You have to let that go," she said. "Your father's dead. My father died when I was twenty-four, and yours died when you were fourteen. Let it go, Janna."

I pulled my knees up to my chest and felt the wine slosh against the empty walls of my stomach as I straightened my back. It burned, and I felt sick. I set the tightly wrapped sandwich on the floor, still warm, and put the palm of my free hand to my forehead, as if that would help stop the tears.

"Janna, he's gone. It's time now for you to get over this. He's not the same, and he's not coming back. You have to remember everything that was good about him."

"Mom, I can't." I curled into a fetal position on the floor, eye-level with the sandwich. My insides hurt.

"Now, stop. You have to learn to relax."

I was sobbing.

"Your father would not want you to feel like this …" It kept going and going. Her words, painful and acutely truthful, were suffocating. I let her pour them all over me, acting like they were new to me, like what she said was shocking, like it made no sense. But it all made sense. They were all conclusions I'd come to on my own over the years, things that already lived inside my brain. He—that dad I grew up with, that dad I had planned on growing into a woman with—was dead. He was dead. It didn't matter how many stars I'd wished on or how hard I'd believed. That was it. He was dead.

And it was time for change. It was time to admit to this loss my mother and I had been feeling for so long and had never talked about. I stopped crying, and we stopped talking at almost midnight. I told her that I was fine, that I felt better. I wanted her to hang up so she could go to bed and get some sleep. I wasn't fine.

I laid my forehead on the floor. It was cold, and I pressed it into the tile. Lauren came in and handed me my abandoned glass of water. I sat up. I felt carsick. I unwrapped my sandwich and told her that my mother had told me to accept that my father was dead.

"Jan, I'm so sorry," she said, sitting down beside me.

I put the heels of my palms into my eyes. My head hurt. I wanted to throw up. I didn't want to cry anymore. Not ever again.

"You know that, though. You know what she was trying to say."

"I know. I just wasn't ready to hear it. Not with all the shit going on."

"You need to eat that bagel."

"I can't. I can't go to work tomorrow."

"I know. But you're stronger than anyone I know. And you know you're a champ. You can."

"I'm so tired of being a champ, Laur."

jugglin' verbs adverbs and nouns

THERE ARE THOSE MOMENTS IN LIFE when you can say, "I feel like a million bucks"—unironically, without a hint of cliché or hyperbole. It's when everything—no matter how big, small, life-changing, regular, or routine—is perfect. Moments with no trace of brain injury. I want to bottle those moments, keep them in glass mason jars. I want to have them all forever—sunny days on the lake, playing with kittens, playing the M&M game, taking a train ride through New Hampshire, ice skating in front of the PPG building, writing poetry on a plane, rounding slalom buoys, pots of rich fondue, trail rides, stretches of ocean, stretches of New York City sidewalk, stretches of Spain, live music at The Bowery, dancing at Uncle Ming's, Bloody Marys at the Caribbean Club—to pour all over the days when all I want to do is take a shower forever.

I had sprinted down Ninth Avenue, sweating, weaving, and hopping through the neat and tidy tourists and brunch goers. I ran up four flights two stairs at a time, burst into our apartment, shucked off Lauren's Uggs, and slammed the bathroom door shut behind me.

"I'm hurrying!" I yelled over running water. "I promise. Sorry! Oh, and thanks. I just borrowed your Uggs to go to yoga."

"You're fine," Lauren yelled. "Relax."

While she stood at the mirror, contemplating the way the folds of her new green sweater fell, I ran past her, wrapped in a towel, leaving wet footprints on the hardwood floor on the way to my bedroom. I was always late, and Lauren was always on time, a combination that often created tension for both of us. I ripped apart towers of sweaters in search of a particular kelly green, short-sleeved top. I was still wet, dripping on everything I touched. I threw it on and squeezed into a constricting pair of J Brand jeans. Ten minutes later, neither one of us perfectly satisfied, we were out the door. Twenty minutes later, we stood elbow to elbow, swaying in a sea of people, some sober, some wasted, and most wearing green.

"Your sunglasses make you look really angry right now," she said.

"They make me less train sick."

"Yeah, that guy knows what you are talking about it," she said, pointing to the guy who had started singing, 'I wear my sunglasses at night so I can, so I can ...' "Three more stops, Jan. You'll make it."

"I'm gonna vomit all over someone, and I can't decide whether I want a beer or a bagel."

"I'm going to get there and be like, food, come to my mouth."

I unwound the checked green scarf I was wearing, noticing that sweat had seeped through my sweater. The train lurched and swooped around whatever underground track dipped under the Hudson and emerged on the other side. Wafts of my honey-jasmine shower gel, now sickly and cloying, only made the remainder of the ride worse.

The walk from Water Street to Second was clogged with drunk people, but the air was brisk and the sun shining. *Fresh air always helps.* I could hear my mother's voice. We walked by two girls fixing their make-up in the reflection of a car that was stopped at a traffic light. When it rolled away, they threw a fit. Laruen looked at me, repulsed.

"Where are we?"

"Hell." I fake coughed. "I mean, Hoboken."

When we opened the door to Cristina's boyfriend's large apartment, we were enveloped into a college-style party. Tons of people crammed in the kitchen, spilling out onto the balcony.

"LB! Janna Banana!" Katie yelled, motioning us over to the countertop that was serving as a bar for the day. Among the army of vodkas, rums, red Solo cups, and sticky shot glasses, Lauren and I foraged for leftover breakfast food. We found some cheese and two mismatched halves of a baby bagel.

"We're those girls," she said, shooting a sideways glance at me. "Food ..."

Cristina handed me a Miller Lite. I cracked it open with one hand and shoved half a baby bagel into my mouth with the other. We tapped our cans and smiled. I washed down the train sickness with most of my beer, willing my stomach to handle the hard liquor that was coming.

Katie, Courtney, Cristina, Lauren, and I formed a huddle, and someone handed me an over-poured shot of rum. We promised each other that no one would chicken out and that no one was too old for this, and clanked five sticky shot glasses together.

"Here's to the yogi!" Lauren said.

"And to Cristina's new pages!" Courtney said.

"Courtney, the freelance journalist!" I said.

"LB's fancy editor job!" Katie said.

"Katie's sweet work-from-home gig!" Courtney said.

"Min—here in spirit—who's getting *married!*" I said.

"And Al, too, the brilliant writer who needs to quit her job!" Katie said.

"We are really kicking 2011's ass—in a good way!" Cristina said.

"To us amazing j-school girls!" Lauren said.

We lifted our shot glasses higher, trickles of cheap liquor running down our knuckles. We tossed it back, making faces and groaning. The cheap rum burned the whole way down and made my head feel like fuzz. I opened the nearest can of Natty Light and gulped. I wanted Ale and Mina to be with us, to revel in how new and good and exciting everything was.

"Trading Pumps for Prana." Pleased with my subject line, I'd sent a long email to the girls the day before.

> Hi gals,
>
> I always knew if I ever quit the 9–5 (or 8–9 in most of my cases) I'd miss putting together little outfits and all the heels and belts and scarves and jewelry that goes with them … Oh well, as LB reminded me, "there is the weekend for outfits."
>
> For a few years now, in my own head, I've been contemplating what it would be like to be a yoga teacher. More recently, I've been contemplating out loud to my lovely friends. Pardon this phrase—because I hate it—but, as my Gram Mary would say, "shit or get off the pot." So … after yet another tumultuous job in the magazine world, a smidgen away from getting the ax and oh, about, eight rounds of HR negotiations I'm O.U.T.
>
> I made the jump or the dive or the catapult (pick your poison), and I'm officially signed up, accepted, and excited for April 11th and four weeks of intense morning, noon and night yoga. We're talking yoga poses, yoga books, yoga yogis, yoga history, yoga chants (eh … that singing bit …) and mats and towels and blocks and things that look like mexican blanket ponchos.

Am I scared? Hells yes. But what's the point if I'm not? Is this where I thought I'd be at 28? Nope. But, who is?

"It never seems to work out the way we had it planned," because Jimmy Buffett is a smart, smart man and most of his job is spent barefoot making people happy.

Here goes…

Muah!

J

Sending the e-mail had felt like the first real thing I'd done in years. A real decision, a choice I made. I felt like a million bucks.

I HAD NO PLACE LIVING in New York, like New York and I didn't match. We didn't get along like we used to anymore. We should probably break up—call it quits.

My friends and I were all at a bar watching the Final Four. I had started out fine: drinking, cheering in a half-assed way, and flitting about being social. Now, maybe, I was drinking too much and thinking too much. *Five years. How had we been here for five years? All of us, and still such good friends. Really amazing friends.*

I was, in fact, drinking too much.

We had all moved here, drawn by New York's opportunity and energy, the two reasons anyone has ever moved to New York. All seven of us had big dreams of being writers, changing the world, and, hell, meeting a man, if we're being honest. All of us were family people, still figuring out how to call two places home—New York and Boston, Detroit, DC, the Valley, West-by-God Virginia, the Burgh. One home, established and the other, a medley of dynamics. Yet, it seemed that for someone craving stability and certainty, I had moved to the wrong place.

New York was becoming too much on top of brain injury, which would always be too much. It (brain injury, not New York) slaps you with an acute change and then slowly tears away everything you love about a person one piece at a time. And even though brain injury had *built my character,* just like Gram Margaret had said it would the night we drove home, the night I wished on the stars between the defogger lines, it had always been *too* much. Sure, *it was all for a reason,* a reason I had yet to come up with. Years of searching, and I still end up in the backseat, ruminating on God and existence and the consequence of good and evil in humanity. I lived my parents' struggle. I was their kid. It was my birthright. I owed it to them, to their past, to my childhood, to our old happiness.

What *karma* was this? I took a sip of my beer. My friends were engaged in basketball or their boyfriends. I checked my phone and opened an e-mail from Fred, my parents' longtime friend, someone who had been there since the beginning of all of this. A few days ago I had e-mailed him to ask what my parents used to be like, and here was his reply, telling me how they fell in love among other things. He said it was "conscious and unconscious," "in love with each others' souls."

I had forgotten that my father had a soul.

"Jan, what's wrong?" Cristina was standing in front of me.

I was sobbing. Drunk in a corner with my warm beer and my irrational emotions. I felt ridiculous. It had to be the alcohol. I wiped my face with the bar napkin that was stuck to the bottom of my beer bottle.

"Jesus, look at me Cristina … crying in a fuckin' bar. I just …"

"Tell me what happened."

"Oh, nothing happened. I just want my own person, my own dramas. I want anything other than this, just to be on my own away from all this stuff at home. It's only because I'm tired, not because I don't love them. I do. I really—"

"I know you do, Jan."

"I've had this with me for as long I can remember. I've never known anything different, and now, as an adult, I want so badly to help them, to make it better, but I can't. There is just nothing I can do. I keep trying. I'm sorry. This is so stupid. I'm crying in a goddamn sports bar."

"Jan, no one—"

"I know. I'm sorry. I just … I should have been making millions and buying ReMed stays and saddles and vacations for them."

"Saddles?"

"Yeah, my mom deserves the saddles she wants."

"Okay, Jan, you'll buy her a saddle someday." She put her hand on my shoulder. "I promise."

"I get that it's not our job to fix our parents," I said, wiping black smears off my face with the soggy napkin. "Can't they just stay forty-five forever? That would be easier."

"No kidding." She laughed.

"Good God, I'm sorry for all this," I said, hopping down from the bench. "Can we go get a beer now?"

"Yes, Jan, we can."

It wasn't just me anymore. My friends had to accept their aging parents. Even parents without brain injuries didn't turn out exactly as they'd planned.

"It's on me," I said. "For the crying stuff."

MAY ARRIVED, AND I WAS a certified yoga teacher. My dad was back at home on his regimented schedule, which was jam-packed with activities to develop skills and strategies to exist in his home life and community, and he was struggling. He was still impulsive, obsessive, and compulsive. He required maximum assistance and constant reminders. His moods were unstable, and he was unable to initiate tasks, unless the task was to find pot. That would be the first thing he wanted to do when he got his license back—go buy pot. He even admitted it to the ReMed staff.

And when he was tired, everything was worse.

ReMed began to explore permanent long-term support, indefinite treatments, and indefinite babysitters. Without supervision, "he would harm himself, put his family in dire financial straits or end up in jail," according to his evaluations. ReMed also recommended regular visits with a new psychologist, Dr. Pecorelli.

Dr. Pecorelli was the kind of person my father would like—talkative, funny, knows his shit and doesn't take shit, a little like my old dad. Dr. Pecorelli specialized in traumatic brain injury—bonus! This psychologist worked to get to know my dad. During the first couple visits, they just talked, got to know one another. Dr. Pecorelli got my father to voluntarily admit that he had a very hard time "doing the right thing" and "making a good decision." He got him to admit that he really did want to get better, and so they came up with T.L.C.

"T.L.C." was written on a tiny scrap notebook paper that my father had taped onto the face of his watch, covering the 5, 6, and 7 hours. It bothered me. It was tacky.

"What is that, Dad?"

"Dr. Pecorelli said it would help me do things right."

"Okay … but what does *T.L.C.* mean?"

"What do you think it means?"

"I dunno, tender love and care? Why do you have it?"

"Think. Like. Claudia." He smiled, cartoonishly proud.

"Huh?"

"He says: Take time. Stop and *think like Claudia*. It will help me make decisions if I think about what your mother would do."

"Oh, so like what would Claudia do?"

He'd been home for a month. My mother was furious with him. He'd gained fifty pounds. Maybe his learning was over. Maybe *we* were there to learn from him—ReMed, too. He didn't have a lot of similarities to share with other TBI patients in the program. He was older. His injury was older. He walked. He talked. He got really fucking bored. And 90 percent of the time, he thought he was perfectly okay. His case was different. He was different. My mother was different. My parents were just different.

My father was, and still is, a smart man. He had not entirely lost the ability to manipulate people, a trait he had certainly passed on to me: say what you need to say to get what you want. He was constantly telling his therapists, his psychologists, his wife, and his daughter (though we were not nearly as blind to it) whatever they needed to hear to get him one step closer to what he wanted. Frankly, he was pretty damn good at faking that he was okay.

My mother is an alien. I cannot understand her. I don't where she comes from. Her strength and love must have come from other lives, built up and reserved for this one. And she never quits. Never. Not even when maybe she should.

Their marriage is an anomaly. Few marriages last after brain injury. In fact, almost none last. Magazines, blogs, newspaper articles, studies and research all suggested that more than 95 percent of couples divorce following a brain injury. This made sense. Who on earth could do this? I had met only four people that had gone through what my family had. Four—two temporal, one frontal lobe and one affecting mainly the hippocampus. All four divorced.

Not keeping us together, for whatever reason, was not an option for my mother.

"You need to have a conversation with your dad and then tell me what you think." My mom was texting now. "And that is all I'm going to say so don't ask any ???s."

Why was she being so cryptic? I was already late to meet my yoga friend Emily for class. I'd call him later. I hoped to remember. "I talked to him," I texted her back at 8:43 p.m.

Buzz. "And?" Mom.

Jesus, I know why my friends hate it when I get cryptic. "He seemed normal-er," I texted back.

"How?"

What was she getting at? I mean, he did—dare I say it—seem *normal.* And I didn't even know what normal was anymore with him. "It was easier to have a convo with him. Seemed engaged and informed."

"That's what I kind of noticed."

"And his voice was not sluggish with strained breath. Like not at all. Kinda weird."

"Right!?! I just wanted to if you noticed it, too?" Parents' excitement over text just looks weird.

"I def did :)" So do emoticons to your parents.

"I am wondering if the girl who stays with him notices. I don't want to ask because that sets it up."

"Like you set me up?"

"What?"

"Nvmind."

I called her.

"Yeah, it was kinda weird," I said, happy this conversation was now voice-to-voice. "I can't remember the last time he was not sluggish and not groggy. Like not in ten years."

"Well, I did something," she said. She sounded childishly secretive.

"You did something?"

"I cut his medication."

"Oh … The Depakote?" For as long as I could remember, my mother has hated Depakote, and it was one of the drugs he'd been on since the very beginning. Sometimes it was the real stuff, other times generic. She had always thought the dose was too high and had been asking doctors to lower it for years.

"Yes."

"Now, I'm not supposed to do that." God, I loved it when my mother broke rules.

"But I've been asking the doctors to do it for a long time, and they just won't, so I took it upon myself. I know I shouldn't have."

"What did you do?"

"What do you mean?"

"Like, what did you do to cut it?"

"I cut the pill in half, and I put it in his pill box."

"Oh, wow. Like, you cut it with a knife?"

"Yes, Janna, I made it smaller. Don't you think he seems different?"

"Yeah, he really was so much easier to talk to. It's almost scary. Did you tell anyone, like Fred or Carolyn?"

"Just you and JoAnn. I was going to tell the girl that comes and stays with him, but I might wait."

"I would wait. I don't think you need to tell anyone."

"You know, sorting out those pills in that little pill box he uses takes some concentration. He really takes a lot of medication."

"I know. I hate medication."

"Imagine how groggy you would feel."

Specifically, for the last eight days, she had cut the Depakote from 1,500 mg to 1,000 mg. Now that his Risperdal dose, another anti-seizure med, had been upped, she could not understand why they couldn't see what would happen if they cut the Depakote. He had come home too sluggish, too groggy. And now, a week later, he was having simple, intelligent phone conversations in which his breath was not labored and his speech was not slurred. I had not heard this voice in years. He had even *offered* to help last Tuesday.

Tuesday was when Rose, our cleaning lady, came. She had been coming on Tuesday for years. Last Tuesday, she called a few minutes after my mother had left for work, twenty minutes before the ReMed person arrived, and my dad picked up. She told him that she would not be able to come today, because one of her sheep (Rose raised sheep) was very sick. Could he leave a note for Claudia when she got home?

He didn't leave a note.

"Hello," he said when my mother picked up the phone. "How are you?"

"Fine."

"Rose called this morning and said she won't be coming in today. She can't. One of the lambs is sick."

"Okay," my mom said. "Thanks." There wasn't much she could say. He rarely called her at work, really only when he immediately wanted something.

"You have book club tonight, right?" he asked.

"Yes ..."

"Is there anything I can do to help? Is there anything I can clean for you before book club?"

My mother told me she almost fell out of her chair when he asked. Then she remembered that Abby, the aid my father seemed to enjoy, came on Tuesdays at 10:00 a.m. She must have told him to call, but it was only 9:42 a.m. "Is Abby there?"

"No. She doesn't come until 10:00. So is there anything I can do to help?"

"So, I told him that he could sweep the living room," she said to me.

"And did he?"

"He did, and the kitchen and he hallway and back porch, too."

"Wow."

"I know, pretty unbelievable. He certainly can have his moments. I need some more of those."

IT WAS A SMALL, SMELLY plane, and the man in front of me ate slices of ham. I swear there was no bread. I sipped ginger ale. It didn't help. I threw it up in a drab airport bathroom near baggage claim, put on lip gloss and my aviators, and toted my favorite red suitcase to the passenger pickup curb, where PIT security waved cars through at an obnoxious pace. I fished out my iPod, hopped up on the cement ledge, and watched for the Acura to come around the bend.

"Are you okay?" my mother asked, watching me curl up in the backseat from the rearview mirror.

"Tiny plane," I said. "Horrible, tiny, smelly plane."

"Are you hungry?" my dad yelled.

"Maybe. I will be if we can go to the Jimmy Buffett place."

It was nice out, so we sat outside at Bahama Breeze. My mom had a coco-melon martini, which tasted like a Jolly Rancher. I had a beer, and my dad an Arnold Palmer without the booze. They played "The Weather is Here" and "Tin Cup Chalice," one of my favorites and one of my mother's. We ordered another round of drinks with our seafood dishes. Then Key lime pie for dessert with black coffees.

"Oh ... middle of America ..." I said, stabbing at the ginormous wedge. "What happened to moderation?"

"Stop being picky," my mother said.

"Tastes fine to me," my dad said, knifing into half the crust.

Jenny, my mom mouthed to us, picking up her phone. "Hello ... Hi, yeah ... She's home ... It's ninety degrees," she said into the phone. "It's nice out, so we're sitting outside having beach drinks and listening to Jimmy Buffett. Yes ... it's good to have her home. And her dramas."

I gave her an offended look, which she waved off.

After dinner, we went to Macy's. My dad needed new sneakers, a pair that would fit his drop foot with the foot brace better. I handed him an unlaced blue Puma. He put the sneaker on his foot, bent down, and then looked at me.

"I can't," he said.

"Can't what, Dad?"

"Tie them."

"Jesus Christ, Dad," I said, leaning down in front of his chair and taking the laces. "You gotta do some yoga. I'll help you learn some, okay. You can't even tie your shoes!"

"John, you have to lose some of this weight. I don't understand."

"Mom, seriously, the yoga will help with this and so much more cognitive and behavioral stuff, too. Trust me." I pointed at his feet. "What do you think of these for him? They're blue, but I think that they're—"

"No, I actually like them. John, what do you think?"

"I like them." He kicked them off. "Now I need to use the restroom."

My mom rolled her eyes and put together the box of blue Pumas. "Can you take him? I'll buy these shoes and look for more pants. He doesn't fit in any of his pants, so now I have to buy your father pants in his new size—38/30." She looked sad.

It took my father twenty minutes to use the restroom—four minutes inside and sixteen to walk the twenty-five yards of the Macy's aisle from Shoes to Home Furnishings and then down the short bathroom hallway.

"Dad …" I said on our walk back. "You gotta get in shape. You can't even walk anymore."

He stopped in the middle of the aisle and started doing a rudimentary foot-lifting exercise. "I can't get my foot to work!"

"Yes, you can! You are using it right now!"

"No I'm not!"

"Yes, you are!"

"The other foot!"

"*Ohhh.*"

He was frustrated with me, still the same ditz, the same clueless kid I was at thirteen.

He walked ahead. I watched him a few steps—the uneasy, repeated sequence of slump, pitch, drop, and drag … slump, pitch, drop and drag … Snails did it faster.

"Well, yoga will help," I said, catching up to his side. "Honestly, Dad. Yoga will help with that. Your heel, your balance, and all kinds of things. What do you think?"

"Yoga is interesting."

My mother told me to go downstairs to the shoe department. I set my father up on a plush chair between a display of Michael Kors espadrilles and a full-length mirror. He pulled out a *USA Today* while I went on a search for flats. I found my mother holding up a pair of Clarks.

"Now that's a nice shoe," she said. It was a purple clog, covered with flowers that looked like they were made to top a cake, not a shoe.

"For you? You have eight billion like that."

"It's time for flowers."

"1998 was your time for flowers."

She held up a wooden wedge sandal, leather with a less offensive flower—Clarks. She and Vicky had a recent thing for Clarks.

"Yeah. I suppose that one is okay," I said.

"The orange is nice."

I thought of it more as tomato red, but my mother likes orange better than red. The shoe was certainly tomato, but she wanted to see the orange, and I wanted to see the red in it. I had finally learned to just let the stupid shit go. It didn't matter. They didn't have her size.

"Don't you need a suit?"

"Yes, because *all mine are missing.*"

"That is pretty hard to believe, Janna. *All* of your bathing suits?"

"Yes. *All* of them, Mom."

I had kept bathing suits around like Christmas ornaments, each one with its own significance: vacations, lakes, summers, foreign countries, impulse buys. The day after our Christmas in Paoli, my mom drove me back to New York. Lauren was in California, so she decided to stay for one night, but a blizzard blocked the streets and closed the bridges, and one night became three. We did all the Christmas-in-New-York things we could think of. We bundled up and walked around in the snow, shopped, marveled at the tree, and ate fancy sandwiches and drank spiked hot cocoa while watching the ice skaters at Rockefeller Center.

Back at my apartment, we organized my closet, because my mother loves organizing. Piles and piles of things that didn't fit (shirts, dresses), things she was sick of (the faded blue "Arabians don't saddle for less" T-shirt that used to be hers), and things I didn't need that many of (jeans, shoes). Two days later, when it had stopped snowing and my mother was back in Mercer, I called to tell her that all my bathing suits were gone.

"Why are you crying?"

"Mom, I can't find the butterfly, either. She's gone. I can't find her anywhere."

"Oh, honey ..." It was her little kid voice. "Are you sure?"

"I am sure! I've torn my room apart. She's gone. You threw her away!" *Jesus. How was I almost 30?*

"Well, I didn't do it on purpose."

"I know, but she's gone now and—"

"—You're sure? I bet she'll turn up."

"Mom, she's at, like, Salvation Army or with Children's Aid families. Or wherever you took all those bags."

"Well then she'll get to go to a new home—"

"They will throw her away in some trash bin and ..." I was sitting cross-legged on my bed, weeping, carrying on about velveteen scraps of felt that were worn and faded and hardly, if they ever were, recognizable as a butterfly.

"Janna …"

"Mom. No one will care. My friends all thought she was ugly. Ryan and Adam made fun of her."

"Oh, they loved her, too, come on. She's okay. You're okay."

"No. It's not. I've had her for twenty-six years. She's gone everywhere with me. Now, I've just abandoned her. Like I didn't even care. I really did care about her!"

"I know … I know. Janna, I'm so sorry."

I stopped crying. This had to be bigger than Priscilla. "Wow. God, Mom. I'm sorry. I'm being so ridiculous. I just … I don't know … She was my favorite, and …"

"I know. I guess it is just time for some change. She had a good life, Janna. It's okay."

Two weeks later, I got a package, a manila envelope that contained a flattened piece of black felt with shiny satin wings that stuck to the Velcro opening of her abdomen. I pulled it apart and found a note inside.

Meet Priscilla II. Be nice to her. Love her just as much.

Love Mom.

She was ugly, but I named her Henrietta, because none of it was my mother's fault. And she had felt bad. She still felt bad.

She bought my dad his pants and Pumas, herself a shirt-dress for work, and a red one-piece for me. On the way home, we stopped at the Super Walmart, the only place I could think of to buy my dad a yoga mat. My parents sat in the car, and I went in bought a mat, two cheap sports bras, a medium Coke, and a small vanilla milkshake.

"But you had fun, right?" I asked, turning off Cold War Kids so that we could talk. I could hear my dad sucking down his shake in the back seat, and I wished my mother was okay with yelling our conversation over the music, the way Krystal and I always did in the car.

"What do you mean, fun?" she said. She took the Coke from me. Her sips were big. That annoyed me. I bit the straw. I know that annoyed her.

"Like, you've had … fun? In your life …"

"Not really. I didn't have a fun first marriage. We had no money. We didn't do anything fun. It was not a good thing. Now I have your father."

"But you had a good marriage with him … with Dad? I mean you guys were happy, right? Didn't you enjoy that?"

"Well, I don't know. That was a long time ago."

"Yeah, but I mean—"

"And it really doesn't matter one way or another right now."

"But—"

"—How fast are you going?" she asked, peering over at the dashboard.

"Like, sixty-nine," I said. I lied. I knew she couldn't see that I was going seventy-eight. You couldn't see the speedometer from the angle of the passenger seat.

"Really?"

"Really. Well, I know it's hard for you to understand, but being single is getting really boring. It would be nice to have someone to share my life with. You have had that."

"Yes, but it's not all that great. Maybe I shouldn't have."

"Mom, why do you say things like that?"

She laughed. Life had become all so very matter-of-fact to her lately. Strange things were humorous.

The Coke had become nothing but ice cubes and water. We both shook it before we took sips. The stars were bright, and Interstate 80 was dark. I squeezed the leather steering wheel and willed myself not to push this point of Claudia and John happiness any further. My dad woke up as we pulled in the garage. He got the dog, and my mother and I carried the shopping bags to the house. I looped three over my shoulder, and with the other hand, I picked up my suitcase.

I borrowed a floor-length Henley of a nightgown from my mom's drawer. Lauren would have made fun of its utter un-sexiness. I washed my face with hand soap and dug for a spare toothbrush. Each time I came home, I had a list of things I needed to borrow, as if they were necessities that only my parents could provide. Pajamas, socks, toothbrushes, sweaters—I loved borrowing my mom's sweaters. In high school, it was my dad's.

"It's nice to have you home," My mom had walked into my room.

We went over the list of things to do tomorrow. She set the list under the car keys, which she had tucked to right of the mirror, hidden in the small space where my vanity extends into the wall behind the fireplace, where my father would never think to look.

fitness
clean car
mow grass
Visit Gram and Pa
(You don't need to do all of these—pick some)

"I like coming home," I said.

"ARE YOU READY FOR THIS?" I asked, my voice sounding too much like my mother's.

I pulled the plastic wrap off my dad's new yoga mat. He sat down on the steps, waiting as I pondered how it would be most feasible to do yoga in my parents' hallway. He said nothing, just sat and watched me choose a spot for the mat and stomp it flat, fighting the cheap rubber from furling into itself. I turned it over, and it bubbled up, convex. But at least it no longer looked like fat little blue logs constantly rolling toward each other.

"There?" he asked, pointing at the mat, which was framed by the fish tank, the front door, the steps, and an antique lamp.

I nodded.

He stood up, the hardwood floor creaking under his 210 pounds.

"Okay, come to the top of your mat."

My voice was now disturbingly yoga-teachery. I watched his feet as he took tiny steps toward his mat. He didn't wear bare feet well, not like he used to. His feet were mangled and stiff, and he moved them as if they were two bricks attached to the bottom of his legs rather than feet. They were swollen, his toes like sausage links, and I could tell how little he clipped his toenails. This, I'm sure, was one of things that really bothered my mother.

He stood on his mat, facing the fish.

"Not like that." I put my hands on his shoulders and turned him. "Like this. Face front, the steps. *This* is the top of your mat."

I tapped the top of the mat with my toes, perfectly manicured with red polish.

"Okay," he said.

"Now, bring your hands like this—prayer position." I brought my hands together in front of my chest, the flesh of my palms, fingers and wrists perfectly flush. "Like this, in front of your heart."

"Okay." He sounded so obedient, but he looked like the Tower of Pisa, tilted, crumbling, old.

His hands met, mismatched in front of his chest. Fingers like tangled brambles, all bent and twisted, growing from knotted and knobby knuckles. He could only straighten a few fingers on the right hand, and looking at his left hand, I was reminded of the many surgeries he'd had to keep it functioning following various unfortunate incidents with mowers, band saws, and a nerve disorder he'd developed post-accident.

His left foot jutted out to one side. His hip sunk down on the right. He had no butt, but the straighter he tried to stand, the bigger his belly grew. His thin arms, creased at the elbows, resting on the fat of his belly, looked like raw chicken wings. I couldn't find his shoulders. I palmed the flesh around where the collarbone and scapula met and concluded that the muscle was gone, nothing left to hold them up, no carriage. Wrinkles under his chin piled in folds. He was holding his head too far back, as if that would help him with his posture somehow. It was something rigid, something strong that he could do. He looked sad.

"Dad, okay. This is called Ta-da-san-a."

He fought to say the word right.

"Ta-sana."

"Ta-da-san-a."

"Tas-sad-ana."

"Ta-da-san-a."

"Ta-da-sana."

"Yes! It means Mountain Pose. And this pose will be part of all the others you'll learn."

"Okay." He stood rigid, patient, waiting for me to start. "Ta … dasana!"

I worked from his feet to the crown of his head, demonstrating the way each body part should face and feel. Slowly, deliberately, I moved each stiff appendage and shifted his torso. His body resisted. It was like trying to mold old, hardened clay.

Then I taught him how to breathe the right way, telling him to blow on his hand like he was fogging up a window. He did so perfectly. It struck me. Strange: almost no one ever got the *ujjayi* breath on the first (or even fifth) time.

"Dad, that's great!" My voice reeked of condescension. I had to temper my enthusiasm or I would lose him. "I mean, it's perfect. You're doing it right. Breathe just like that through everything we do."

As we talked about weight and balance, tension and muscles, I thought about the last time I had felt the movement in my father's body. Years, at least. A decade? My eyes welled up. I felt ashamed of the daughter I'd become. Somewhere deep below his fucked-up brain, he was an extremely loving and affectionate person. *He had a soul.* And he was a really good hugger. He filled my childhood with hugs. The hugs didn't happen anymore, and that was my fault. He'd still rub my shoulders—twenty-five seconds of a deep attack on my muscles from his warped hands. But it felt funny to hug him. I always half-assed it, wrapping one arm around his shoulder, kissing him on the cheek, like I was saying good-bye to someone on a New York City sidewalk. I felt cheap every time.

I was thankful for the yoga—a new kind of affection I could share with him—something good for us both. I chose the most elementary *asanas* to teach him, and he tried each one with me. He did them all exactly as I asked, and he let me help him and move him when he didn't understand. He even asked questions. Two full hours, taxing on both his body and his mind. Taxing on mine, too.

"What did you think?" I asked as I peeled his sticky mat from the floor.

"Nice."

"Huh?"

He pointed at the floor to where chunks of cheap PVC mat material had stuck to the wood. It looked like patches of foamy blue moss had sprouted up.

"Shit!" I said, kneeling and plucking at the bits.

"The yoga?" he asked, kneeling next to me, pulling out his pocketknife, the same pocketknife he'd had for thirty years.

"Yeah, what did you think?"

"It's good," he said, scraping at the floor. "It's very interesting."

"Interesting?" I hated that particular nondescript adjective. "Just interesting?"

"Yes, I like it."

Scrape. Scrape. Scrape. I watched him scrape at the mat pieces, leaving little pocketknife scars in the floor's waxy finish.

"And it has been around for thousands of years, and people are still doing it. I think that is *interesting*."

I suppose *that* was *interesting*. "But, Dad, how do you *feel*?"

"Oh, I feel good." He was brushing the blue bits into a neat pile. "Yes, I feel like I worked all my muscles and I stretched. I feel smooth."

"Good! That's great!" That damn over-enthusiasm again. "I mean, that is exactly how you should feel."

"Will you write it all down for me? All the poses?"

"Yes, and I'll send it to Mom, and she can print it out for you."

He picked up the fuzzy blue pile, crawled on one hand and two legs to the steps, and hoisted himself up to stand. Then he walked into the kitchen and threw the pile in trashcan. I hoped the yoga would make simple things like this easier. I felt bad. I hadn't even helped—just stood there, yapping at him, while he cleaned up our mess. Just stood there, watching him crawl around the floor, limply holding a pocked yoga mat.

"That will be nice. I like it. I can show it to Abby."

I handed him the rolled mat.

"I'll keep this behind the TV?"

I nodded.

He took the mat and sat down on the steps to put his socks and shoes back on. I went into the kitchen to make us smoothies. I felt good—not stretched-out-and-moved-around good, not good like he did. I just felt good. I felt good about us.

We had yoga. Something we could share, like waterskiing. Something that was trying, cumbersome, unfamiliar, and in time, utterly satisfying—except yoga was something *I* was teaching *him*.

"The yard looks good," my mom said as she came in through the side door with her arms full of groceries. "I see you got it all. Thank you. That was very nice."

"I, we, did," I said, screaming over a blender.

She set the groceries on the kitchen table and stood, watching me. The counter was littered with empty plastic berry containers and splashed with milk and puddles from melted ice cubes. A gob of peanut butter slid over the edge of the counter, dangerously close to plopping into the open silverware drawer below.

"It's a smoothie," I said, looking at her. "I made it for Dad. It's healthy. A healthy snack after mowing and yoga. Do you want some?" I poured two inches of speckled purple sludge into a water glass and handed it to her.

"It smells like peanut butter."

"It *is* peanut butter."

"Well, I don't really like peanut butter." She spooned out a bite. "It's good," she said, making a face and handing it back to me. "I just don't like peanut butter."

"Ugh. Sorry. I love it, so it's hard to tell if I put too much in. I can make you one with less."

"It's okay. I'm headed out to do some work in the yard. Your father will like it."

"He likes anything."

"He eats anything. He likes peanut butter."

I poured her glass into mine. "We did yoga," I said.

"All right. How was it?"

"It really is going to be good for him."

"Okay ... I'm going to do some mulch. Can you make dinner before you go to Sarah's? I bought salmon burgers."

"Sure."

THE FIRST NIGHT I SPENT in Brooklyn was hot. I was thrilled to be showered. It was 1:00 a.m. I sat on my bed and looked out the window, tracing the silhouette of unfamiliar rooftops. The sky was pink. Looking at it, you could taste the heat from the day, from earlier when the truck had read a steaming 123 degrees. My air conditioner chugged away, a curious species of beast that the Serbian adolescents we had hired to move us from West 44th to Smith Street had ripped out of my old bedroom window and shoved into my new one. My father had tried to make it fit the window better by adding pieces of cardboard.

The stemless wine glass that sat on my windowsill dripped with rivers of condensation. I sat up to swallow the last pool of liquid, cool and sweet, the ends of a once icy ginger ale, and stretched out underneath my sheets, fishing for a cool spot with my toes, which now hit the wooden spindles at the base of the bed. Lauren and I had switched beds. She had the bigger room now, bigger Jenny Lind. I wondered if switching beds meant that I would be the one having more sex. If my twenties had been all about fun and booze and late nights and lapping up everything in sight, then I'd happily trade that all in if my thirties could be about stability and acceptance and yoga and more sex.

It was only my first night in Brooklyn, but somehow, more things seemed possible. The second night in Brooklyn, I met up with Katie.

"Janna!" she said, flipping her hair over her shoulder and giving me a pouty lip. "Drink your beer! Look at mine. You're all yippin'."

"Yeah, sorry," I said, handing her my bowl-shaped glass of Duvel to taste. "It really does smell like pineapple."

She took a sip and made a face. "It smells more like pineapple than it tastes." She handed it back.

The frothy, gold liquid sloshed down to my stomach as I drank it down. I could feel my head get lighter. "Sometimes I think beer is like yoga."

She laughed at me and ordered another Amstel Light. I clicked to illuminate my phone, hoping to see a text.

"I'm driving my mother nuts. Katie, I don't know why I'm doing this or why I'm so worried. They just have a really long drive, and she was so tired after they left this morning."

"They'll be fine, Jan."

"Can you imagine what you would do if you lost the very most important thing to you?"

"Yeah …" she said. "I can."

"Like, what would you do—say you lost the very most important thing? Do you think you could go on? I mean, you have to, right?" I swallowed another mouthful of hoppy pineapple. "If, well, tonight …" And another. "Well what if my parents are driving, and they just … ya know … they—"

"—died."

"—were killed." We finished the sentence in unison.

"Well, nothing's a guarantee," she said. I liked this about Katie. She was smart, honest and never afraid to talk about things.

"I know, how fun. We can lose it all and move on."

"Hey, your phone is ringing."

They were at a gas station west of Harrisburg. Katie ordered us two shots of Jack Daniels.

the weather is here

THE HOT FLORIDA SUN HAD BAKED the bricks by the edge of the pool, their searing heat roasting the meat of my palms as I leaned back and looked up directly at the source. I stretched my legs out in front of me and tapped my toes on the surface of the pool water. Droplets landed on my hot skin and sizzled into nothing.

"That is just the John that you knew," Michelle said.

I came to, having been somewhere else, in a daydream about golden retrievers and sailboats.

"What?" I shook my head, feeling the rattle of a baby headache. It was such a tired daydream after all these years.

"He probably smoked every day," she said. "That was your dad, the one you knew."

"Oh, yeah ..." I said, scooting my butt closer to the edge, slithering waist-deep into the pool water. "I guess so."

I was staying at Wayne and Michelle's house. They were my South Florida parents, because everyone should have parents in the little latitudes if they can. Wayne saw me as all parts my father's kid, and Michelle saw my mother in me. I saw the past in them. No matter how old I got, Wayne and Michelle's was one of my favorite places to be.

Maybe it was the sleepy sun, the outdoor shower, the beer fridge covered in magnets, the garden of tropical plants surrounding the pool, the inevitable traces of an ongoing home renovation project, or the promise that happy hour was a guarantee. Or maybe it was that down here, everyone cared about happy hour. People of every age, every day of the week. I was comforted knowing that chicken wings, beer, and at least one man in a hibiscus print shirt were only hours away.

Wayne set a Miller Lite on the ledge behind me, and for the next couple of hours, the three of us swapped stories—old memories of western Pennsylvania adventures from a life that existed years before I could enjoy it, and new memories of my friends, my life, and my adventures. It was an equal kind of jealousy.

"Well, what about you, kid?" Michelle had left to take a shower, leaving Wayne telling me about a series of weddings they had attended, girls my age who had moved from a city up north in search of a man with money and a boat. "You moving south yet?"

"Damn lucky girls."

Wayne was taller, blonder, and a hell of a lot more mellow than my dad. He had a rich, deep voice, like it came from a barrel of island rum and cigarettes. Talking to him was as close to talking to my old dad as humanly possible. I'd take his advice, his criticism. It didn't matter; I'd always listen to Wayne.

"Well?"

"Me?"

"Yeah, you. You, and men? Look at you. I mean … come on … damn."

I laughed. "Yeah, yeah. I know. I guess I'm just picky, or something. Or I like the wrong ones, I don't know."

"Yeah, there is really no rush. Are ya happy?"

I dove into the deep end of the pool, getting a rush from the water that swirled and spun around me, painting every place on my hot skin cool.

"Yeah," I said, sputtering up to the surface. "I think I am. New York might be reaching its expiration date though. I hate the men there—"

"You *hate* them?"

"No. No. I don't hate them. They're just … not ma jam."

"I know what you mean, kid." He chuckled. "What about those guys you know in DC?"

"Adam and Ryan are my best friends, Wayne."

He laughed again, checked his watch, and stood up. "I'm going in to get changed. Then it's happy hour time, and we're sending pictures to your mom! You want another beer?"

"Nah, I need to shower."

"How 'bout we leave in an hour? You know we ain't done talking about this."

"I know. I know." I pulled myself out of the pool, grabbed my towel, and headed over to Wayne's outdoor shower. It was as complex as a stream of water, a bar of Dial, and some two-in-one conditioner separated from his tropical garden by four sides of wooden fence. I promised myself I'd have one someday. Its simplicity was perfection.

The hot water melted the tension in my lower back that the plane ride had found, but my left shoulder still tweaked. All the yoga in the world couldn't cure it from the time I ripped it out of socket two Fourth of Julys ago on Ryan's boat. But the yoga—I was practicing a lot, sometimes twice a day—had me more aware of my body than I had been in years. I could process my emotions, too. It was as if they were no different than the tweaks and kinks in my body. Somehow they hurt less. Missing my father even hurt a little bit less than it ever had. I wanted to stay in the shower forever, thinking through these things, but we were meeting Samina, who had now moved to Miami with her husband Raj, somewhere on A1A. Any more shower thinking, and I'd have us running late.

"You might not know how to pick the men in your life," said Wayne as we walked down the beach, giddy after a few oceanfront happy hour beers. "But you sure as hell know how to pick friends."

"I blame my father for the men." I laughed. "I'm joking … kind of."

"Oh, come on, Janna. Give him a break. Anyway, look at the two of them yapping." Michelle and Samina had fallen behind us, caught up in their own conversation.

"You need to give him a call now that he's home from ReMed for awhile. He loves hearing from you, Wayne."

"I know. I know. Shit. I've been avoiding it."

"I know the feeling."

BEACH YOGA. THE TEACHER HAD been late and perhaps a little high. It was even overcast, but I couldn't think of one thing on earth I'd rather be doing than beach yoga with Min. I could bottle that, too. Nothing in the world is like it—back-bending through the salt air and seeing the ocean meet the sand from upside down. My world felt in perspective. It had been such a long year, a year of undoing and rebuilding, a year of dealing with shit I should have dealt with ten years ago. So much had changed, it was dizzying.

An hour later, Miami on a Monday still hadn't woken up as the two of us headed south toward the Keys in a black Dodge Charger.

"You know what happened, don't you?" Samina asked.

"I can guess."

"They rented our car already, because we were a bit late."

"We're always *a bit late,* Min. This shit is hysterical."

"What are you doing, Jan?" I had been feverishly opening and closing all the compartments in the car and was now searching the glove box.

"Looking for drugs, duh. This car is a coke deal just waiting to happen. What in the world are the two of us doing in it? Driving to the Keys?"

"You're such a joker," she said, laughing. "There are no drugs, Jan."

By the time the highway narrowed to two lanes with salt water on either side, I'd set up the radio stations: a top 40, an alternative, a rap and hip-hop, "The Joint" and "Margaritaville."

Mile Marker 104 US1: Key Largo, Caribbean Club—because Wayne said the Bloody Marys were the best in the world.

The walls were plastered with the history of sailors, writers, and musicians. It was still morning, but the lone old guy saddled up to the bar was happily sauced.

"Good morning." The bartender had a crackly voice and looked like she'd been fried by the sun, bleached and leathery. "Two?"

We nodded.

"You got it, girls."

We watched her pour this and that into a tin shaker and dump its contents into two clear plastic cups. No celery, no olives. I looked at Samina, worrying that our drink experience might be lacking. The first sip was sweet and acidic, such an intriguing sensation that I took another. The second sent the vodka to a warm and cozy place in my brain.

We left the two to their conversation and wandered out to an empty deck, where we climbed up to sit on the railing. The sun was scorching. I fought my aviators from sliding down my nose. We both liked that it was this hot. There were palm trees in every direction and boats on the ocean. It couldn't have felt more like the beginning of the Caribbean if it had tried.

"This is definitely the best Bloody Mary I've ever had," Samina said.

"I could not agree more. It's unreal."

"I'm getting another," she said, hopping down from the railing. "And so are you."

After our second, we traded picture-taking with a pair of Welsh tourists—two women who wanted to make sure we didn't get their legs in the picture. It was hard to leave this place, these drinks.

Mile Marker 84 US1: Islamorada, Holiday Isle Resort—because Krystal said so.

The sun was now fighting the rain, so we ate lunch under the deck of the weathered resort with couples, friends, and sailors, all of us eating fish sandwiches and drinking Coronas.

"I see blue sky," I said, sticking my head out from under the covered portion of the deck.

But it was still drizzling when we finished lunch, so we went to a surf shop, where I bought a turquoise and gold bikini for half-price because, we reasoned, only half the ass was there. When the sun came back out, we walked around to a small beach in front of the resort. We pulled two chairs close to the water, balled up our dresses, and stuck them in our purses, which we tucked under our chairs. Three men, old enough to be our fathers, joined us, sharing their cooler of beer and stories about fishing trips, famous authors, and Ohio.

Mile Marker 40-47 US1: Pigeon to Paradise Key, the Seven Mile Bridge— because I'd been waiting my whole life to cross it.

"I have been waiting my whole life to cross this, Min!"

Mile Marker 0 US1: Key West

Duval Street was rocking, packed with tourists, locals, parrots, and dogs. We followed the crowds to the Southernmost Point. A bartender mixed some of the best mojitos, better than we'd ever had, and we walked around. Men jumped through hoops and over bicycles on fire. A dog in swim trunks busked for cash. We ate dinner at a place with whicker tables set up on a wrap-around porch. We ordered whole fishes and whole bottles of wine, feeling like part of a crowd lucky enough to have fallen back into the Hemingway era. The waiter brought over a giant slice of Key lime pie with "Happy Birthday Janna" scrawled in deep red around the edges of the plate.

After dinner, we walked down to Captain Tony's Saloon where we signed dollar bills and pinned them to the walls, walls already covered in thousands of dollar bills and bras. Then we spent the night strolling in and out of different bars, taking pictures, meeting locals, and meeting travelers. At midnight, we toasted to my birthday and to the Irish band playing reggae covers. Then next morning we had breakfast at Louie's Backyard and stopped by Hemingway's house.

It was perfect, more perfect than men or sailboats or life plans.

I LIKED MY FATHER'S NEW psychologist. I liked picking favorites, and Dr. Pecorelli was my favorite. He drew pictures—his analogies—on a yellow legal pad. And then he shoved his yellow pad with his illustrated ideas into my father's face. He wore crisp button-ups and dark khakis and a little bit resembled Harrison Ford in a way I couldn't explain. I felt like Dr. Pecorelli was in it with us, getting genuinely pissed off at my father for the same things that we got genuinely pissed off at him for. So pissed that he would grab the arms of his office chair, squeeze until his knuckles turned white. And if he got even more pissed off, he'd scoot his chair forward and get right in my dad's face.

"What the hell were you thinking, John?" he yelled, pounding the arms of his chair. "You know that really pisses me off!"

We were sitting in his office in Niles, Ohio. My father said nothing. I said nothing. At least someone else was getting pissed off.

"*John!*" he yelled again. "Answer me, will ya?"

"I don't know what I was thinking."

It had happened on June 27. I had been in Key West with Samina, and my mother had been in Harrisburg for a board meeting. My father had been home alone, getting stoned off his ass. And then he tried to cut grass—too close to the pond, of course. So he had to call Ray Gabany when he couldn't get the tractor out by himself. Ray had called my mother.

"Look at your watch, John! What are those letters?"

Thank God Dr. P didn't say, "What does it say?" I thought. Ten bucks, my dad would have said, "Quarter past three."

"T.L.C."

Silence.

"Why did you do it? What in God's name were you thinking, John? *What in—*"

"I was thinking I wanted to get high. I wanted to feel *gooooood.*"

How could my father mock this guy?

"How could you do that? After all we'd talked about—your wife, your daughter! How?"

"I don't think putting other people first is in my father's inherent nature,"

I said, interrupting. "It's not really in mine, I guess. We're a me-first kind of people ..."

"Yeah ..." Dr. Pecorelli looked directly at me. "And?"

"I don't know. It's not always a bad thing to be that way, to put yourself first, but aren't things always amplified with brain injury?" He nodded. "So maybe we have to approach his motivations differently, like quit talking about what he can do for others so much and start talking about what he can do for himself. I think before the accident, the things he wanted for himself perfectly aligned with making other people happy. But now, those things don't ... align like they used to."

"You may have a point."

"We'll get Arby's on the way home," my dad interrupted.

"See?" I said to Dr. Pecorelli. "It's not even a *question* if anybody else wants that. Sure, Dad ... we'll get Arby's."

Dr. Pecorelli smiled.

We got Arby's, two roast beef sandwiches, two Jamocha shakes, and one curly fries. When we got home, I got his mat out from behind the TV.

"Yoga?" I asked, handing the mat to him.

"I would like that."

"All right. Give me five minutes to change."

He had gotten better: less stiff, more mobile. I pushed him a little harder. He asked more questions.

The next morning, I came down to get breakfast, and my mother was asking my dad about yoga. They were standing at the counter, eating toast.

"He used to meditate," my mom said, handing me a plate.

"What?"

"Your father used to meditate. He was into that transcendental meditation. It was the 1970s, Janna."

"Dad?"

"I had a mantra," my father responded.

"What was it?" I asked.

"I'm not telling you. You are not supposed to tell what your mantra is."

"Oh, come on, Dad. I'll tell you mine."

"I don't want to know yours—"

"*—oh shreem maha lakshmeya swaha—*"

"—It's private!"

"I just told you mine."

"And I don't have to tell you mine." He left to take the dog out for her morning walk, unprompted.

"No wonder he actually likes doing yoga," I said. "He has a mantra."

"He *should* have a new one," my mother said.

"Maybe he does."

"I will stop smoking pot." I laughed. "I will get in shape."

"I wonder what it is."

"He's not going to tell you, Janna."

"I know. It was probably something with the Beatles. That Majar-whatever stuff."

"Maharishi."

"Yeah, that."

Mildly disoriented, I woke up at 6:25 a.m. and pulled on a pair of black leggings, a sports bra, and a tank. I brushed my teeth, took two swigs of orange juice, and grabbed my aviators. The sidewalks were quiet, just a mellow hum of people waking up, coffee shops propping their doors open, dogs getting walked, and a few strollers.

Yoga at my new studio was quiet this morning, a small class, a nice morning stretch.

I came back to my apartment, promising myself that this Tuesday was meant to be the very first productive day in Brooklyn. I set a fresh cup of coffee beside my new feather-light Mac on the tiger maple kitchen table and opened an e-mail. "Purse Auction."

I assumed it was in response to my question about Children's Aid's new charity.

> Found your dad smoking pot last night. What a mess. I should have figured it out. He could not hold a thought and was always mixed up. We have had very limited in-home services in July. Main Line [the new outpatient care company that had come recommended] really dropped the ball. Bad transition. So I called ReMed this am, no call back. I called Main Line and she did call back. I just told her how it is. He can't stay here without services and it's not his fault you were not organized. Said he can't stay home if he is not going to have daily services—too risky. This really has to end.

Pa wants to know if you cashed your birthday check. That's what I got when I called him to find out if John asked him to stop at Jack Appod's yesterday. Pa had taken your dad to a dentist appointment. I wanted to know if maybe he got the pot from Jack. Gram and Pa are really failing. Your dad cannot stay with them for me to go on vacation and if he goes with me there is absolutely no point in going. So that is the end of the vacation. I knew that would happen. I cannot believe how much he has deteriorated. I knew that was going to happen, too.

Now, I must work.

XO

Mom

I took my cup of coffee over to the couch and called home.
"Hel-lo?"
"Hi, Dad."
"What?" Cracking, rattling, breathing. "I can't understand you."
"Then get to a place where you can!"
"Yes, that's better. Hel-lo. Who is this?"
"Better?" I screamed. "Are you kidding me? What is wrong with you? What on earth is wrong with you?"
"What—"
"More pot! Are you fucking kidding me, Dad? Are you ..." I was screaming, sitting in my living room on the baby couch, screaming so loud that my throat scratched. I wasn't even making sense, though the words didn't matter. Nothing ever mattered to him—nothing. Nothing bad, nothing good. Nothing mattered to my father. I swallowed.
"Dad, come on. What is the matter with you? We are trying to help you. Mom and I are doing everything, *everything*, we can possibly think of! Just ..."
"I know. I wasn't thinking. I wasn't thinking of you or your mom."
I wondered if the neighbors had heard. I felt terrible for screaming, for swearing, for yelling at him, because he could barely hear me or understand what I was saying. I knew he couldn't, because I was so angry I was speaking too fast. Fat tears rolled down my cheeks, down through the crevices between the keys of the phone. I had lost my breath. I was out of shape. I forgot how sad it was, how strong you had to be, how crazy you had to be, to fight with my father.

"Dad, I'm sorry. It breaks my heart, every single day … that this has happened to you."

He said nothing. I forgot how he does that, too. You get to bare your soul while he says nothing. It was so fucking heartbreaking. I smashed my face into the couch. I had been here so many times before, right where frustration and sorrow sit side by side on this precipice, pulling at me, trying to take my entire being with them. It was about winning, and I always won.

"I know. I shouldn't have been wearing my seat belt. I should have died."

"No. No. No. No. No, Dad." I was crying. I was losing. "I wish you could know how much I love you. I love you so, so much."

"I shouldn't have worn that seat belt!" He was angry.

"You just can't keep doing this. You didn't die. I don't know why you didn't die, but here you are. There is a reason. Why are you wasting it? You can still do so many things. Mom and I are trying so hard to find things for you to do. You have to try, too. When did you quit trying? What is it you want to do?"

"I want to get a job."

"Get. Over. It."

"What?" he asked, clearly confused.

Nine times out of ten, idioms, euphemisms, expressions, were lost on him.

Silence.

"And no driving. Jobs and driving are dead to you. And no more pot— ever! That's it. *Finito. Kaput. Nada mas. Capiche?* Can you get that?" I was talking the way he would have talked to me when I was a kid. All the same goofy vocabulary.

"Yes. I can't have a job. I can't drive. I can't smoke pot."

job-drive-pot … job-drive-pot … job-drive-pot … The trifecta of my father's damaged brain, his compulsions. I wanted to drive these points through his head like nails. I wanted them to hurt, and I wanted them to last.

"I have to go," I said.

I didn't want them to hurt. I have really never wanted to hurt him or hurt his feelings. Whether that was even possible had yet to be determined.

"Okay, I love you," he said. "I hope you have a better day."

"*You* have to get better, not this damn day."

"I will."

"Dad, I really have to go. I can't do this anymore."

"I love you."

"I love you, too. I really, really do, but I have to go."

Defeated, I went to kitchen and poured myself a giant glass of grapefruit juice. It tasted cold and bitter. I waited an hour to cool down, and then I wrote my mother a long e-mail, venting my frustrations to her, telling her I wanted to scream at people. She wrote me back that night.

> I hope the yoga gets all the screams out of you. Doesn't help to get angry—but it is hard not to. But it is truly a waste of energy. XO, MOM

Four days ago, I had called Sarah when I realized the right thing to do would be go home for a week so my mother could go on vacation with my father's sisters without my father. Sometimes I don't want to do the right thing, so I have to call Sarah or Krystal. I know they will keep me in check. But where would I write? Where would I practice yoga? I felt derailed.

When my mother and I got home from the airport, we decided to get dinner at Elephant and Castle by the outlet mall—just the two of us. She had wine, and I had a beer, and after dinner, we split a giant brownie smothered in ice cream. It was the same dessert that I'd had more than a decade ago for my high school graduation dinner—same restaurant, same brownie. We ordered black coffees, hot but weak. She told me a story about how she had helped a friend who had an abortion, and I told her stories about my friends. We talked about the institution of marriage.

After dinner, we stopped at Sheetz, and while I fumbled with the nozzle in jeans and heels, I watched her in a skirt and light summer sweater, pumping gulps of diesel into two red, dirty plastic jugs. She lifted them up into the bed of the truck, one after the other, with ease. It would be hard to be my mother for a week. It would be a difficult and daunting privilege to be Claudia for a week. I would have hours and hours to practice.

I spent my hours laying in the sun or at the Side Bar with Amelia or playing with Sarah's kids. Hours typing at the kitchen table. Hours teaching Dad yoga out in the grass. Hours driving to dentist, doctor, and therapy appointments. Hours with Dad and Gram and Pa and Dr. Pecorelli.

"Do you know how your wife and your daughter feel when you do things like smoke pot?" Dr. Pecorelli asked my dad.

It was day number three of being home.

"No."

"They feel sad, John. It makes them sad. It makes them feel like you are breaking their hearts. Do you want to do that?"

"No."

"Do you know what that feels like?"

My father looked like he was thinking about this, but gave up. "No."

"It feels like when someone you love dies. Can you remember the last person that you loved dying?"

He took time for thinking again. "Sherry's brother. He was killed by a drunk driver on Christmas Eve."

I looked at Dr. Pecorelli. This was the first time I'd heard this story.

"It was sad. Sad for the family. There were all these packages that had his name on them. No one knew what to do with them. He was killed instantly."

"Can you remember that emotion?"

"Well … I think your heart beats faster. You start to sweat; you feel uncomfortable—"

"Dad?" I said, interrupting. "Can you remember the last time you cried?"

"When the dogs died."

"The dogs?" Dr. Pecorelli asked.

"The basset hounds, right?" I said.

"Natz and Mona," my dad said.

Right. He told us how he cried when the dogs died, how sad he felt, hopeless, missing. How he remembered feeling like *that.*

"*That* is how Claudia feels when you smoke pot."

"Oh. I don't want her to feel like that."

"Do you love your wife?"

"Oh, yes. Very much."

"Why do you love Claudia?"

"She is nice. She is pretty. She is smart. She is good at—"

"No, John!" he said, waving his hands around. "Why do *you* love her? That is why anyone would love her. *You,* John! Why do you?"

350

My dad stared at us, utterly confused.

"What about Mom makes you happy?" I asked.

He looked at me. And then he smiled. It wasn't a kooky smile, like the ones I'd gotten so numb to. He closed his eyes for a second, opened them, and looked up to the left.

"She is just ... Claudia." He was beaming. "That's it. Just that she is Claudia. No one is like her."

"That *is* it!" Dr. Pecorelli jumped up. "That is what you need to remember. How you feel about Claudia, how she makes you happy—how she is the person whose heart you are breaking when you do that stuff."

I rubbed the knuckle of my thumb with my index finger, feeling the skin turn red and raw as a I listened to the two of them talk it out.

"How do you feel?" Dr. Pecorelli asked when it was clear the session was ending because my father was fatigued.

"Me?" I asked.

"Yes, how do *you* feel?"

"I, *um*—"

"You were fourteen when you lost your dad—both your parents, really. That is young, and you're an only child ..."

"Yeah, I am ... Well, it's hard. I mean ... wow. You know this would be a whole other session, right?"

I laughed. He looked at me.

"But how do you feel?"

"It's hard. It's really hard, and it's really lonely. And I feel really lost sometimes. But this is what I have, my life. I am finally starting to learn how to accept that. To let go of the anger ..." I swallowed. I really did not feel like crying right now. "Sorry ... *um* ... It's just that no one has asked me how I feel about this loss in a long time. So, thank you."

"I know. But this happened to you, too, just as much, in different ways."

"I blame my awesome childhood."

"Your childhood?"

"No, yeah. I mean, it was awesome. I had a really great childhood. Sometimes I think it's what has made this so hard. I just miss my parents a lot, and I feel bad, because I can't give them everything I want to. I just can't. Not yet. They gave me such a great childhood."

"It's not your job."

"I know."

"They have *great* daughter."

"Yes, a very nice daughter," my dad said.

It had been three hours with Dr. Pecorelli. He was late to meet his wife.

"I like him a lot," my dad said when we were in the elevator.

"Me too," I said.

THE DASHBOARD, STEERING WHEEL, AND my computer were speckled in Oreo milkshake.

"What the fuck, Dad!"

He sat stolid, sitting in the passenger seat staring at the row of cars parked in front of us at the Coolsprings Fitness Center. I retraced my steps, trying to figure out where this had gone wrong.

Sometime past 10:00 a.m. We were sitting at some crossroads, familiar yet nameless, arguing.

"Go straight!" he yelled. "What are you doing?"

"I told you," I said patiently. "I want to go the back way."

"I don't want to. We always do what you want."

"Dad, come on. I just wanted to drive by Jackie's house."

"Jackie Sheehan?"

"Yes."

"You aren't friends with Jackie Sheehan anymore."

"Dad! That's not true!"

"When's the last time you talked to her?"

"Come on. It doesn't work like that."

"Go straight."

I pulled through the intersection and looked down the road to the right. I drove slowly, picturing her big house set back in the woods and what she must look like today. She lived in California, practically neighbors with Eddie.

"Are you going to drive?"

"Yes! Jesus. I'm driving. I'm driving."

"Thank you."

Then at Coolsprings, he started to tell a dirty-ish joke to the manager.

The manager knew me. I'd sit at counter, and he'd bring me free coffee. But today, I left to work on a freelance story in the truck, so I made my father promise that he'd work out the entire forty-five minutes. He came out to the truck carrying a milkshake.

"Would you like some?" he asked, offering me a slurp of soupy gray liquid.

"No," I said, rolling my eyes at how counterproductive this was. "Why did you get a milkshake after working out?"

"It was leftover, and they gave it to me. They made too much for someone else."

"Okay … whatever. I'm really sorry, but I really need to finish this," I pointed at a half-written e-mail on my computer screen. "It's only gonna take like ten more minutes."

"Okay," he said, setting the cup in the cup holder.

I smelled the Oreo. I looked at the clock, which said that he'd only been working out for thirty-five minutes. Thirteen minutes later, I finished and closed the computer. "Ready?"

"I'm ready," he said, picking up the melted shake.

I pulled the CDs out of the center console and put a new one in. The CD player blinked "Loading Error." I took it out and tried another. "Loading Error." I put the original CD back in, and it started playing "Coconut Telegraph," so I immediately took it out.

"What are you doing?" he yelled. "Let it play."

"Dad, I've listened to that CD like eight times, sorry!"

"Leave it alone!" He picked up the milkshake, put the lid on it, and threw it out the window.

"What was that?"

"I'm doing what I want. That's what you do."

"Are you five years old? Gimme a break. Get out of the truck, and pick it up."

"No!" He screamed the earthy, scary growl from his place of hate. *"I'm not going to."*

It had been a while since I'd been home long enough to hear this voice, so long that I thought it was part of the past. I stared at him, and he stared back, fumbling to buckle his seat belt, to make some kind of point.

"Pick it up! We don't litter!"

"Then you pick it up!"

"I didn't throw it. I don't litter!"

"No!"

"What the fuck, Dad!"

People coming to and from the gym were staring at us. I took the keys from the ignition, got out, and picked up the shake, still intact, its lid keeping the melty contents secure. I walked over and handed it to him through the open window. He took it. I got back in and turned the truck on. One of the broken CDs was playing, thankfully. He looked at me, held up the milkshake, and chucked it at the dashboard.

I watched, my brain slowing everything down so that I was able to see the top pop off upon impact and the wave of black-specked cream spray across the air and land in splats and specks all across the interior of the truck, the windshield, the radio, his daughter, and her laptop.

"What the fuck is your problem!" I yelled.

I licked milkshake off my hand, grabbed napkins from the door, and wiped off my computer before putting it in the backseat. I started the truck and peeled out of the parking lot, shouting intelligible obscenities. By the time we drove through the tunnel on Route 62, I was sobbing, my face covered in tears, snot, and sticky streaks of milkshake. I punched the power button on the radio.

"What is wrong?" he asked calmly.

"What is wrong? What is wrong with you? You just threw a milkshake at me!"

"I didn't throw it at you. I threw it at the truck."

"Dad … you threw a goddamn milkshake."

"Yes, I threw a goddamn milkshake!"

I could feel my heart crawling up my esophagus, where it would suffocate and die. Then, somewhere as we drove through town, I would just die. So dramatic. So not going to happen. Such normal thoughts with nowhere to go.

"You wouldn't stop changing the CD. You made me wait."

"Made you wait?"

"I had to go exercise and then sit in the car and wait for you."

"Dad, I told you that I was writing an e-mail."

"And I had just had to sit there and wait for you."

I started crying again, gasping. It was awkward. I always thought I'd get past this. Nope, so this time I'd just accept it, revel in the release.

"Why are you crying?"

"You threw a milkshake at me, Dad. I'm crying because this shit is always so messed up."

"Do you always cry like this? Maybe one of your friends from DC would like you if you quit crying all the time."

"Dad ..."

"Well, you don't have a boyfriend. I thought you would have had one by now—"

"Me too, Dad. Me too. Thanks."

"Well, why do you keep crying?"

"You, Dad. *You.* You are the one that keeps breaking my fucking heart, over and over and over again."

We said nothing until I'd parked the truck and started walking back to the Suhries.

"Where are you going?"

"To talk to Vicky, because I can't be here right now."

"I'm sorry I made you feel bad."

"Whatever."

"I'll cut the grass."

"Whatever you want, Dad."

"I am sorry."

Halfway down the driveway, I worried about the consequence of not giving my father explicit instructions on how to spend his afternoon. Three quarters down, I realized this time I didn't care.

"Oh, honey," Vicky said, giving me a hug as I walked into the Suhries' kitchen, still crying.

"I know," I said, wiping tears off my face, instantly feeling ridiculous. "I'm sorry, and I know you have to go to work."

"I still have three hours. I made us coffee, or do you want wine?"

"Both?"

She laughed. "So what happened?"

"Everything. Nothing. I don't know. He threw a milkshake at me. I don't get how my mother does it."

We sat out on the back porch and talked. We called my mom to see how vacation was going. Pat came home, and the three of us talked until she had to leave for work.

When I got home, the grass had all been cut, and my father was inside, making himself a sandwich. He asked if I wanted one, and I said no. He hugged me, and I fought back tears. Men don't like them, apparently.

This was my mother's life.

He didn't throw anything else, no more littering, and I didn't cry again. We played cards, a lot of cards. We did yoga every day. We even talked. I made dinners, and I helped him make dinners. We had lunches with Gram and Pa, and we went to Bike Night with Pat and Vicky at Quaker Steak & Lube and talked about new bikes and old cars. I woke up every morning and took care of the horses, which made me understand why the horses kept my mother sane, why she enjoyed their company so much. Even scooping poop could feel like therapy. Mornings in the barn became a routine that paved the way for clear thoughts.

Open the door, flip on the lights, talk to the cats, and give everyone their breakfast.

In the barn, I thought about my dad, or a yoga sequence, or the men I liked, the men I wanted to share a life with. I thought about how Adam thought I had the best group of New York friends, that I was lucky because they were all so smart and fun. I thought about my friends from college and from high school, how lucky I was to have them, too. I thought about my 'siblings'—Nicole, Steven, and Lisa—and how they were exactly what siblings should be like. I thought about how sad and strong my mother must be, how much love she must have. She told me before she left that week that she'd always thought my dad's intellect would get him through this. A month later, she told me it was all for shit.

it just takes awhile

T HERE WAS A POINT WHEN LIFE had begun to seem normal, just plain old normal. Oh, how normal was something I'd been waiting for, watching for. I had craved the comfort that would accompany living in the new normal—yes, the *new normal,* that grossly clichéd phrase from the TBI world—because, really, there is no other way to describe what integrating a brain injury into your life is like. It's not what was. It's certainly not what's ordinary. It's just something that we families can maybe, possibly, get used to.

I had painted the picture of what this new normal would look like. It would be exhilaratingly different than all that was and all that had passed. All the feelings and experiences in the new normal would be from the very opposite end of the spectrum: cheery, hopeful, happy, exciting, warm, soft, safe, solid.

I was so ready for it. Mentally, standing there and waiting for it, ready to embrace the new normal as soon as it got here.

"HOW MANY YEARS?" KATIE ASKED my parents.

Bacchus was a perfectly adorable French bistro on Atlantic Avenue. Bacchus was the place to have a first date, a tenth date, to intimately celebrate a birthday, a new job, a friendship. It was the place to bring your parents when they come visit and see your new and perfectly adorable—read: tiny—apartment on a whim.

"Thirty-four," my father said at the same time my mother said, "a hundred and fifty."

We laughed. Everyone thought "a hundred and fifty" was really funny. Maybe it was that our bellies were full with generous cuts of meat and French wine. Maybe it was the sleepy atmosphere, which after a long day of shopping, drinking, or doing pretty much anything, makes you loopier than you should be. Maybe "a hundred and fifty" was actually funny because it was a really normal anniversary joke.

My mom, dad, Katie and I had been discussing the boons of adulthood, marriage, independence—perfectly normal dinner fodder for parents taking out roommates. Timely, too, seeing as my friends and I were all lingering around that crag of real, honest-to-goodness adulthood where— yes—the decisions you make are now of your own volition. Get married, or don't get married. Have kids, or don't have them. Settle down, or don't ever settle down. Be happy, or just sit around and think about what life would be like if you were happy.

All through dinner, and not a hint of brain injury in sight, save the green BIA (Brain Injury Association) awareness band my father now wore on his left wrist to accompany the watch with the battery that never works and the copper bracelet I brought him back from Mexico over a decade ago.

There was talk of the Tigers winning and the Steelers forgetting how to play defense. There was talk of memoirs and movies and global warming. There was talk of my mother taking people out in her flippant *if-I-were-in-the-mob* kind of way. There was talk of sicknesses and ailments that belonged to no one at our table.

This dinner was the new normal, and it was—dare I say it—borderline boring, and goddamn it felt good. It was life, finally, as my mother puts it best, in moderation. It wasn't overly jolly, and all our problems hadn't been fixed. No one had gotten rich, and nothing bad had been in erased.

Listening to my mother tell Katie about a book about a woman who lied about being a 9/11 victim, I ran an inner dialogue, asking myself when I realized that we'd—or maybe just I—had started to feel normal.

ON THE FIRST FRIDAY OF spring, Pa had died. The day after his funeral, there was a mad scramble for his hats. Annie, Carrie, and I had raced to the hall closet and pawed through newsboy caps, ivy caps, ball caps, and wool fedoras.

"Vultures," Aunt Jeannie kept yelling. "Just vultures, you three are."

We took shirts, too. It seemed the only thing right to do, rummage through my grandparents' closet, smelling Pa's shirts and trying them on. Annie and Carrie took T-shirts, and I took a flannel. The flannel was at least three sizes too big, and when I looked in the mirror, I looked just like the Janna who stole her grandfather's flannels in junior high. I had paired them with low-slung, boot-cut Levis and clunky boots. It was my grunge look.

I also took his coin rolls for laundry, because my mother said I should. And I took his Mason ring, because somehow being the firstborn grandkid and being in a sorority convinced me that I had the rights to it.

Vultures.

MY MOTHER HAD BEEN TRYING to get a hold of me that Monday. She had left three voicemails and two texts that said nothing other than "call me about Pa." I had been participating in a Gabby Bernstein group, a spiritual healing group of sorts, the kind of place where it's respectable to disengage from your phone.

"They can't seem to stop the bleeding," she told me when I finally called her back, somewhere on a rain-slicked sidewalk as I walked between friends from the group on Avenue A. "They don't know what is going to happen, so they took him to Allegheny General tonight."

"AGH?"

"Yes."

"Oh."

"Yes, they will know more around 4:00 this morning. I'll call you, if that's okay. Do you want me to? I mean, it will be early in the morning, so—"

"Yes, yes. Please do. I'll stay up and write or ... should I come home now?"

"Well, we don't know anything right now, so let's wait."

The next day, I was on a 4:00 p.m. flight from John F. Kennedy International Airport. It had been the kind of day I'd always rehearsed but never expected to live out. Get a phone call. Stop what you are doing. Go home, and buy the fastest ticket to Pittsburgh. Throw things in the little red suitcase. Make sure somewhere in there is a black dress—wonder if people still do black—and heels.

I didn't know what else to bring with me. I couldn't get my thoughts to catch up with my actions. I drank half of a Miller Lite that had been in the fridge since New Year's and added some new bands to my iPod.

There were no seats on the E-train. I wrapped my elbow around a pole and thumbed through song after song. Pa was bleeding from the brain. My father's father was in a coma in AGH. The next day was National Brain Injury Awareness Day. The irony was un-fucking real. All the songs sounded empty. I stared at the Con Edison ads, wondering how inappropriate it was to be finding irony in this situation. Wondering if that made me heartless.

Three quarters of the way to JFK, I turned around to find myself facing a picture of firemen sitting in a row—subway art. They looked like birds on a wire. The irony passed. I held the subway pole with both hands, and tears rolled down from under my Aviators. People looked at me. I looked at my reflection in the windows, watching myself cry for the rest of the trip.

Mom, Carrie, and Colin picked me up at the airport. The plane had been late. I had sat next to a charming man wearing a wedding ring, the kind of man you'd have a crush on if you were into older married men. I told him that I thought my grandpa would be dead by the time we landed.

"We're hungry," Carrie yelled at me as I jogged across the roof of the short-term parking lot where the three of them had been waiting outside of the car for me. No one had died.

"We needed to get out of there," Colin said.

I hadn't seen Colin in years. "Hi!" I reached up and swung my arms around his six foot three frame. "Holy crap—it's been a while."

Colin was nine years older than I was, and together, we were Pa's combination of the oldest and first grandchildren. He was my step-cousin, and the moment he entered our family, I'd looked forward to looking up to him, but we had lost touch.

"Janna Marie, it *has* been a while," he said, lifting my feet off the ground.

I hoped we didn't have to go back to the hospital to see dying Pa.

"Where have you been?" Gram asked when the four of us walked into the waiting room three hours later. John, Jean, Biz, Gram, Uncle Steve, Stephen, Annie, Jami—the whole lot of us together again in the same damn hospital, waiting on a brain. Paralyzed, I said nothing.

"Oh, Janna Marie, you're here," she said. "It doesn't matter. Come here, and sit next to me, and then you need to go see your Pa."

"Yes," I said. "I'm … here …"

"There was traffic, and Janna needed to eat," my mother interrupted.

"And Carrie and I were starving," Colin said.

"Yeah, traffic," I said, sitting down next to Gram. "Sorry."

I could taste the second beer of my dinner. She took my hands. Hers were cold, and I wondered if I should have felt bad having enjoyed dinner with my mother and my cousins and all the dumb, pointless things we had talked about when the rest of the world thought we were in traffic.

"How is he, Gram?"

"Oh, Janna Marie."

I'VE NEVER BEEN BACK IN time—who has? But when you are sitting at the cement tables outside of the AGH cafeteria, eating a chicken salad sandwich on a bagel and talking to your grandmother, aunts, and mother about intubation, you really start to wonder about the linear element of time. I mean, Jesus Christ, it was weird. We'd all been exactly there before, all of us—same cafeteria, same tables, same sorrow, same hot sun, same smells, same frozen candy bar selection, same, same, same, same.

I ruminated on this as I went back to the cafeteria to pick up a frozen Snickers from the ice cream bins just before the checkout line, the same place they had been fifteen years ago. I hadn't eaten one since high school. Why did I need one now—to prove how nothing changes, ever? I could feel it melting through the wrapper as I held it, still deciding. I was ruining the Snickers for someone else. Now I had to buy it.

I smiled at the woman and handed her two dollars. I walked past the tables where my family sat, still talking about the day and the days to come, and over to an empty patch of concrete in the sun. I lay down on my back, opened the wrapper, and bit away the melting mess. The bite was too big and too cold. This was me. This was my dramatics, just shy of thirty, and no one was going to stop me from separating myself from my family to go lay on a slab of sidewalk with my aviators hiding my tears.

Pa might have stopped me. "Hey, Toots," he would say. "Come on over here with us." Or maybe he wouldn't have stopped me. Either way, he would have known what to do with me. But Pa was upstairs, dying.

After lunch, we reconvened in our waiting room chairs, and the more I sat and thought about the uncanny possibility of my family hanging out in AGH on National Brain Injury Awareness Day, waiting to hear if my dad's dad was going to live, the more ferociously my heart beat. It was distracting. It was a migraine waiting to happen. I could've thrown up—the chicken salad, the Snickers, all of it. I wanted to cry in a bathroom somewhere, but that felt as unnecessary as throwing up. I paced around the squared hallway of the ninth floor, calling Krystal and then Adam, both of whom reaffirmed how uncanny the situation was.

I went back to the waiting room to find out that they would be taking Pa off of life support within the next hour. We'd been asked to say our good-byes. We'd been told he could die in seconds, hours, or days. Nobody said much or argued. We went to his room and circled around his bed.

I stood at his feet, between Gram and my dad. I listened to the respirations, the beeping, and the sniffling. Gram grabbed my hand. I didn't tell her I didn't want anyone to touch me and didn't want to be there. My insides felt full of water, bloated with sadness. My dad put his arm around my shoulders. I wanted to squirm away.

My mother went up to him first. She nuzzled up to his cheek and cried into his collarbone. She was so brave. Brave at the sides of hospital beds, brave with death, sadness, change, and good-byes. I couldn't touch him, not this quiet Pa with his cold, bald head, slack face, and cracked hands.

"You were a dad to me," my mom sobbed into the folds of his neck. "You were. You really, really, really ..."

Like an obedient audience, we lost it, the tears of the Leyde family coming in their different forms—snorts, sniffles, bawls. I sighed, sad that nothing was coming from me. No tears. Everything stuck inside. Gram squeezed my hand harder, and with her other hand, she dabbed underneath her nose with a ratty tissue. I looked up at my dad, and he unwrapped his arm and took off his glasses to wipe away tears.

Tears. My dad was crying. Fifteen years, I'd waited for these damn tears. Fifteen years—I'd fought, cried, thrown fits in exchange for his tears. Pets died for them. Parts of Mom died for these damn tears. He put his arm back around me and squeezed. Then he kissed me on the head.

"Go over there with your mother," he said, wiping away more tears. "Go be with her. She needs you. Go over there with Pa and your mother."

I listened to him. I walked over to the bed, mouth agape, tears flooding my vision. It was the first time I did something that my father wanted me to do that I didn't want to do in fifteen years.

"Landslide," really? I'd been hearing it everywhere lately. I closed my eyes. I was not, no, no way, was *not* going to cry in Starbucks. Just get my tall Pikes Peak—yes, of course, hot—to go and go. Go before Stevie Nicks had me admitting that I was still afraid of changing, that I had still built my entire life around my father. Go before I wound up pissed and sad.

Outside, it was sunny, and the air was crisp, the kind of weather that begs for autumn to be here in Brooklyn. I decided to call my father, subject of all change.

We had an easy conversation, an organic father-daughter exchange, one surprisingly, exactly, the way pre-accident me would have envisioned our conversations to be like when I was thirty and he was sixty-two. We talked and talked for blocks: about the dog and about how she was aging, about the Steelers and the economy of Pittsburgh, about Nicole's art, about how Krystal was now a surgeon, about how I liked the guy I had just met and how the guy had the same birthday as Pa, about how we missed Pa, about good riding weather for Mom, about how he thought I should get my hair cut, about Gram, and about how I thought he should try a yoga class at the gym.

Eventually, I had to hang up, teach a yoga class, and get going. We traded "I love yous," and I dropped my iPhone into my bag and sat down on a bench. The normalness was dizzying. I pulled off my aviators and wiped away black streaks of mascara. My heart was pounding so hard I felt it loud in my ears, and a voice from somewhere inside of me was screaming: *This is a good thing, you ninny! Why are you crying?*

Change. More change. Always change. My dad was changing—again, and here I was afraid of it and all that may come with it—again. Here was the *new normal* I'd been wanting-hoping-craving-believing in-waiting for. And here I was making a big deal about it, because it wasn't as comforting as I'd expected. It wasn't a big, giant eraser to wipe clean all the shit we'd gone through. And it came with no guarantee that there would be no more shit to go through.

But the new normal isn't anything at all like that. Life just isn't like that.

epilogue

Life is good on our boat

IT WAS MONDAY, AND I forced myself out of bed, angry at the world. *Claustrophobic* was the word that kept repeating in my mind, the only word to describe the weird feeling. It was as if I was unable to get out from inside of something. I was trapped, stuck.

I sat on the edge of my bed, dangled my feet over the side, and picked up my picture of Pa. He was looking spiffy in a tweed jacket and smiling at the camera for his 1985 School Board President picture for the yearbook. I had begged Gram for the gold-framed photo that came back with me, along with his flannel, his ring, $52 worth of quarters, and his green Accord.

It had been almost a year since he'd died. Life in Brooklyn had settled into a rhythm of writing and yoga. I kissed the frame and set it back in place. I had fourteen minutes to move my car, eight of which were spent slipping into the jeans and sweater that I'd lazily hung over my bed rail from the night before and grumbling around my room in search of my aviators and wallet. The NYPD kept sending the tickets to my parents' address, and if you are thirty, your parents should not be paying your *I-forgot-to-move-my-car-for-street-cleaning* tickets, let alone even know that the car spent the night in the Brooklyn Navy yard because you parked too close to the Baptist pastor's special spot and said pastor had the car towed.

The sidewalks were covered with dead, crunchy leaves. I found the car safe and un-ticketed. I got in and turned the ignition to make sure it would start after a week of driving nowhere. I stayed inside and turned on NPR's music station. I had to wait out the seventy-six minutes that were left in the street-cleaning ticket window. I read an *Atlantic Monthly,* and then called Gram Margaret to pass the time.

Walking back to my apartment, the leaves had me thinking about my father. Decades ago, he and I used to burn leaves between our yard and the

Riegs'. He'd draw lines with dribbles of gasoline, light one match, and then we'd watch lines of fire wipe the yard clean.

I turned the key to our door, now consciously thankful for the apartment's emptiness. Katie had spent the night at her boyfriend's, and it would be just me and my bad mood this morning. I changed into a sports bra and yoga pants, moved the coffee table, rolled up the carpet, and forced myself through an hour of yoga on the shiny hardwood floor. I'd accepted that this was just going to be the kind of day where I'd have to force myself through things. It was either that or dwell in this sticky, claustrophobic feeling. I forced myself through a sink full of dishes, cleaning the coffee maker and making a fresh pot of coffee, and then a twenty-minute mediation while the coffee was brewing.

I felt better, looser, freer. The mediation had melted away the trapped feeling to reveal what was really bugging me—fear. I was tired of being trapped under the fear of what happens if I get what I want, the fear of what happens if I'm happy.

My defensive mechanism was outdated, that crash-and-burn warning signal that floods my brain when things get—dare I say it—easy. I wanted to deactivate it, bust it into a million pieces, so that I would never again hear it saying, *Don't you dare get what you want, because it sucks when it crashes and burns. Don't you forget the summer of 1996. Don't you dare get comfortable. Don't you know it all crashes and burns?*

"Christ, when am I gonna get over this?" I said out loud as I switched Katie's giant flat screen to play Pandora's "Wilco" playlist. "My mother is right—just get over it!"

I poured coffee into my "Write Like a Motherfucker" mug, the same one Courtney has. I dropped a piece of bread into the toaster and decided to give myself a break.

"I am getting over it. It's just a day, a morning. It's just a feeling. Isn't that what everyone is supposed to be doing at thirty anyways? Getting over stuff, finally."

The toast popped. I stood in my kitchen and buttered it in the palm of my hand, without a plate or paper towel. Toast makes me think of my dad, especially that slice that morning. Dark, glistening in butter, and about to be covered in cinnamon and sugar—just the way he would have made toast for me in third grade.

Toast, Rolling Rock, Dave Matthews's *Under the Table and Dreaming*, M&Ms, Pirates baseball, Click and Clack the Tappet Brothers, hot wings, slalom buoys, Robert Frost, sweaters, golden retrievers, Chucks, handwriting in all caps, hot air balloons, sandalwood incense …

He doesn't remember any of it. He told me so a few months ago.

"I DON'T REMEMBER YOUR CHILDHOOD." It was a succinct statement and rather out of the blue. It was just past 7:00 a.m., and I was not yet awake.

"What do you mean?"

My dad handed me a cup of coffee. "I can't remember things. I don't remember that period of my life. Would you like some toast?"

"Sure. You can't remember my childhood … like, what can't you remember?"

"Did you go to the prom?"

"Yeah, with Richard when I was a junior, and then with this other guy my senior year."

"I don't remember that. What color was your dress?"

"First is was cobalt blue, and then it was a taffeta and lavender two-piece my senior year. And I crimped my hair."

"That's nice."

"How about the trip to New York?"

"No."

"No, not that New York, the one with mom and the parade with the Santas and—"

"—No. When was that?"

"I think I was seven or something. You guys bought me Tabitha the cat at FAO Swartz. We saw the Macy's Day parade, and it was so cold that all the Santas were handing out plastic baggies for little kids to put on to keep their feet warm and dry—"

"I'm sorry. I don't remember that."

"It's okay. How about the night we got Marble?"

"Did she come from the barn?"

"Yes. You went and got her."

"I don't remember that."

I sat down at the kitchen table, and he set the piece of toast in front of me that I no longer wanted. I sipped my coffee, and we talked about all the things about us that he couldn't remember: skiing, my math homework, teaching me all the state capitals, sledding on the hill, building me a rope swing, playing chess, constructing paper airplanes, throwing the Frisbee to Meagan, getting Marble, riding with him on Dodger or Thunder, riding bikes with me or riding the go-cart or riding in the sparkling blue dune buggy, picking blackberries, carving pumpkins, chopping wood, burning leaves together, reading me *Animal Tales* or Shel Silverstein every night, listening to CDs or records or endless evenings of my Alto Sax scales.

Getting Marble

WE WERE EATING DINNER, AND every five minutes, I had run into the living room to check on the kitten that was stretched out on folds of towels, a bed that I had made for her under an end table. We had discussed that he and I would take her to the vet as soon as we'd finished eating.

I'd chosen her from the surprise litter that my mom had found under the chest in the laundry room. I spent almost every night of third grade down in the laundry room with our cat, Elizabeth, and her kittens—four fluff balls that she was raising in the upturned lid of a dog crate. Tabitha was the most elegant kitten, and with much convincing, my mom allowed us to keep her. We gave her brother away to a friend, and her two sisters went to Gram Mary's to live in the barn.

"Dad!" I ran back into the kitchen, hands covering my mouth. "Mom?" "John?"

He got up from the table and went into the living room. He got down on his hands and knees and crawled under the table to inspect the kitten. I ran into the living room after him.

"I'm sorry, Peanut." He scooped his arms under the towels to gently lift the kitten. I started to cry. "She's dead."

"Honey, she was very sick," my mom said, joining us. "She was very uncomfortable."

That night, my dad went to the barn to get Marble, the kitten that his horse had stepped on a few weeks ago. I sat by the heating register in the living room for over an hour, not moving until he came back with the new kitten in a cardboard box, filled with the towels.

Two weeks later, the three of us were taking Meagan for a walk, and Marble followed us down the road. My dad put her in his jacket pocket. Cars passed us, people waved, and we thought she had fallen asleep. A neighbor drove by, and honked.

"Ohhh-whoa!" my dad yelled. *"Cat!"* He lifted her up by the skin of her neck, stretching her away from his body. She squirmed and mewed with her tail curled into her fluffy stomach. "She just peed on me." His jacket pocket was a deeper shade of green in one corner. My dad handed the kitten to my mom and took off his jacket. We laughed at him.

"Oh man, Dad, that's gross!" I said. "She peed on you. She's such a wimp. It was just a car honking."

"Oh … you're a good kitten," my mom said, rubbing her tiny face with her thumb. "It's okay. You just got scared, and you peed on John. We still love you."

Chopping Wood

"Dad, it's so heavy," I said, lugging the burnt orange canvas tote across the snowy yard between the Rieg's woodpile and our own. "The stupid logs are falling out."

"Well, pick them up," he said, effortlessly carrying a stack on his shoulder—bare logs, no bag.

I dumped the bag in front of the woodpile, and logs rolled in all directions.

"Not like that, you nimrod."

"They're too heavy."

I sat on the stump and watched him reach into our neatly stacked pile and pull the ax out from a crack between logs, where he kept it. He picked up a chunk of tree and set it on the flat stump. I watched him, trying to study his movements. He was a small man, and he stood in front of the log, widened his stance, picked up the ax, and raised it over his head.

Crack. With just one strike, the log split in two clean blocks.

"You try," he said, handing me the ax and setting up another chunk of tree for me to split.

I picked up the ax, swung it over my head and behind me, and came close to hitting myself from behind. He laughed. I whined. I found my stance, and I swung and missed the log entirely three times in a row. The fourth time, I hit the log but got the tip of the ax stuck in it. He watched me pull and pry at it. I drug it through the snow and tried hitting it off a tree to get the ax free.

"Not like that, ya ninny."

"I'm too little for this."

"You're twelve."

"I don't want to learn this, Dad."

"Why not? What if you ever need to cut wood?"

I laughed at him. "I'm a girl."

"You can still learn."

I still can't split wood. I've tried and tried.

Listening to CDs

"Dad?"

"Janna Marie?"

"Where are we?"

"Where do you think we are? We're right here."

I said nothing. I wound the seat belt around my neck and pulled. I watched the signs blur past my window. "No, we're in Emlenton. Where is that? How much longer?"

"We have about an hour."

"This is sooooo long. I'm soooo bored."

It felt like we'd been driving through Pennsylvania for days. For the first couple hours, it was cool. It was just me and my dad, switching CDs and playing every song we wanted to hear until he squashed my entertainment with NPR's *All Things Considered* halfway into our drive.

"So what did you think of New York City?" he asked. "A bit different than the last trip, huh?"

We'd stayed at his cousin's house, a beautiful stone house, like someone had pulled a chunk off of a castle and set down in the middle of nature. They lived upstate on the grounds of an estate owned by Columbia University.

"It was really fun. Mom needs to come with us next time."

"Yes, she would have a good time. Maybe you can come back and look at the university, right there in the middle of New York. Something to think about."

I was fourteen. Besides, I wanted to go to Penn State, like Danny did and like Jackie wanted to.

My dad had loved our insider's tour of Columbia—old buildings, libraries, lecture halls, all organized into a campus that sat right between Harlem and the Hudson.

"How about this one?" he asked, holding up a double CD that he had bought with a few others in a shop on Bleecker Street. "We can switch from the news now."

"Thank God." I unwrapped the plastic wrap and put in Neil Young's *Harvest Moon*. I took my shoes off and pulled my feet up to the seat. They still hurt. When we weren't upstate, watching deer and watching my five-year-old cousin run around naked, avoiding his kiddie pool or touring campus, we were walking all over New York City.

"… used to work in a diner …"

I was excited to get home, see my animals, and tell my mother all about everything we did.

"… grew up in a small town … never put her roots down …"

He was going to sing every word the whole way home.

"Can we go skiing tomorrow?"

"We'll see. Let's make sure your mom doesn't need help with anything. We might have to cut some grass first."

"Really?"

"We'll see."

"You always say that—*we'll see.*"

He laughed and squeezed my knee. "Are you ready for Buffett this year?"

"I am so excited!" I said, sitting up straight in my seat. "I was afraid he'd get too old and I'd never see him live."

"I don't think he'll stop playing for a while, Peanut."

"I can't believe you and Mom are letting me go. I thought you were going to make me wait until I was sixteen, like everything else in the world."

"Well, you're fourteen. I think that's old enough."

I SIGH AND TAKE A bite of the toast I've been holding, the shimmery butter and cinnamon tasting like a piece of my past.

The list of things that make me think of my father, make me miss him, make love him, is endless. Many things I cannot let go of, because they will waste away to nothing if I do that. My knuckles will go numb before I ever let go of toast, newspapers, Frisbees, firewood, and deep-fried crappies—the myriad of feelings tethered to these inanimate things.

I stay standing in my kitchen, eating the toast one bite at time and thinking about how I can't be the only person on the planet who has a list of things that make her think of her dad. In fact, I have lists of things that make me think of my mother, too: Clinique, dressage, huaraches, white pizza, Chardonnay, NPR, Snickers, bread. I have one for Krystal: Diet Cherry Coke, Primanti Bros, jukeboxes, cinnamon gum, Ford Tempos, kale. And for Sarah: Doritos, The Clarks, rose-flavored hookahs, French braids, Sri Lanka. Lists for Adam and Ryan and Annie. Lists of stuff for the New York girls, everyone, all my friends, guys I've dated, aunts, all the Suhries.

The lists are of fun little things that pop up in life and make me think about the people in it. They keep my memory on its toes.

But my father's list is different. It's more like a responsibility than a casual gathering of fun stuff. I must remember all of it—all my dad's stuff, all of *our* stuff—because his life with me has been lost well beyond the window of the months before and after the accident. I'm in charge of our John and Janna moments, our whole life together. It's my responsibility. If I let go of any of it, and he doesn't remember anything, then will anything have ever existed?

I pour a second cup of coffee. I put in another piece of toast.

Maybe it's time I let it go. Just let it all go and see what sticks. Just let it go and be every other girl who idly remembers some of the stuff she loves most about her dad.

acknowledgements

Dear reader, I want to acknowledge you—you who ended up with this book in your hands, you who read my story. I want to acknowledge my 'orginal supporters,' the team at Pubslush, the teams at Balboa Press, the Hay House Insight Non-Fiction judges, Mark Palmer, Joanne Finegan, Paul Boucherle, Patty Gift, Emily Leonardo, Meghan McNeer, Nate Manges, and Joseph Pecorelli, for helping me see this through in so many beautiful ways. All of my incredible family, friends, neighbors and my second family, for all of your love and support. Michael Norman, for showing me the power of the re-write. The Mala Yoga ladies, for believing in all that I am. Gabrielle Bernstein, for guiding me to my authentic truth. My dearest j-school girls, may our continued adventures outlast us. Adam and Ryan, may we always keep epic alive. Natalie, may we always seek the exciting. Amelia, for listening. Annie, for not crying too much. Lauren, for keeping me honest, always. Sarah, for auditorium visions, necessary laughs, and so much more. Krystal, I'd be nowhere without you, KP. Nicole, my sister, my friend, thank you for being my first reader, DKF. Amy, for finishing this in Paris. Katie Karlson, my editor and dear friend, you're a wand on words, and I am forever grateful to you for your hours, your passion, and your brilliance in bringing this book to life with me. Pa, for always holding my hand.

Dedicated Supporters

Amelie Walker	*Jim Vicars*	*Oliver Barham*
Lauren Berger	*Alex MacMillan*	*Grant McClelland*
Krystal Renszel	*Nashira Burk*	*Jennifer Young*
Jessica Shenker	*Brittany Rieg*	*Vicki Gershon*
Genevieve Little	*Rosalie King*	*Pamela Carson*
Bobby Berger	*JoAnn Hogue*	*John Carrier*
Jodie Mount	*Kristen S. Lindeman*	*Ryan R. Knight*
Nicholas Bajis	*Nicole Masson*	*Danielle Henderson*
Cathy Thomas	*Todd Landfried*	*Joanne Jackal*
Nicole Ryan	*Josh Christy*	*Frederick S. Clark*

Julie Bauer
John Joseph Podleyon
Dan Thomas
Amy Helmick Nadolson
Tiffani Barton
Angeline Evans
Lisa Gregg
Karen Tennant
Vicky Suhrie
Jessica Harkins
Scott Kawa
Barbara Connelly
Matthew Tamagni
Margaret Lyons
Sean Berti
Michelle Robinson
Dan Rieg
Christine Muller
Patricia Rieg King
Frances Homa
Alejandra Serret
John Nepola
Jessica Dudzenski
Anne McCaffrey
Jesse Reilly
Colin and
Elizabeth McCaffrey
Bob Hallisey
Sarah Reiber
Mohsin Alikhan
Adam Berti
KB Suarez
Matthew Postage
Lauren Wilson Miller
Adriana Ennab
Walter Orwin

Kenneth J. Ferrans Jr.
Stephen Karlson
Anusha Alikhan
Azhar Khan
Nancy Albert
Jeremy Albert
Rizwan Velji
Natalie King
Valerie K. Young
Brenda McBride
Debbi Beers
Sheryl Ashford
Jean Leyde
Paul Boucherle
Emily Leonardo
Joseph Pecorelli
Dustin Buss
Jim Duffett and
Leslie Martin
Shawn Snyder
Joanne Finegan
Sarah Boal
Mark Palmer
Paul Morrison
Claudia Leyde
Allison Lloyds O'Neill
Margaret Leyde
Laurie Jalenak
Nate Manges
Katlyn O'Keefe
Patrick Stack
Kristen Davis
Heidi Reiss
Fred Gallo
Mala Yoga
Elizabeth Bagdasarian

Andrea and
Michael Berger
Caitlin Hill
Kevin Martinez
Talene Megerian
Justine Schofield
Steve and
Elizabeth McCaffrey
Kate Levin
Najmaldeen Alsnai
Gladys Frankel
Alexandra Spessot

CPSIA information can be obtained at www.ICGtesting.com
Printed in the USA
BVOW081654200313

315989BV00002B/465/P